LANGUAGE, MAN and SOCIETY
Foundations of the Behavioral Sciences

HARTLEY'S THEORY OF THE HUMAN MIND

by

DAVID HARTLEY

With a New Introduction

by

Thom Verhave

AMS PRESS, INC.
NEW YORK
1973

LANGUAGE, MAN and SOCIETY
Foundations of the Behavioral Sciences

This reprint series makes available some of the most important works upon which the modern behavioral sciences were founded. Each book has been chosen for its relevance to the general theme of communication and, more specifically, to the various relationships between language, the individual, and society. The areas of discipline covered include psychology, anthropology, sociology, linguistics, and communication disorders.

Each book in the series contains an introduction or preface written by an expert in the field, thus supplying the reader with the orientation needed to place the data in its historic context. It is our hope that the reprinting of these works, with their added critical apparatus, will encourage further research into the history of the behavioral sciences.

We would like to express our thanks to the members of our editorial advisory board for their valuable assistance in preparing this series.

          R. W. Rieber
          John Jay College, City University of New York
          General Editor

ADVISORY BOARD

David Bakan, Dept. of Psychology, York University, Toronto
John W. Black, Dept. of Speech, Ohio State University
Julian Boyd, Dept. of English, University of California, Berkeley
Noam Chomsky, Dept. of Linguistics, Massachusetts Institute of Technology
Robert Ellenbogen, Alfred Adler Institute, New York
Austin Fowler, Dept. of English, John Jay College, City University of New York
H. R. Gillis, Dept. of Speech, C. W. Post Center of Long Island University
Dell Hymes, Dept. of Anthropology, University of Pennsylvania
George A. Miller, Dept. of Psychology, Rockefeller University, New York
W. Keith Percival, Dept. of Linguistics, University of Kansas, Lawrence
Phillip Pochoda, Dept. of Sociology, University of Pennsylvania
Jules Paul Seigel, Dept. of English, University of Rhode Island, Kingston, R.I.
James H. Stam, Dept. of Philosophy, Upsala College, East Orange, N.J.
Karl D. Uitti, Dept. of Romance Languages, Princeton, New Jersey
Thom Verhave, Dept. of Psychology, Queens College, New York
Carl E. Zimmer, Dept. of Linguistics, University of California, Berkeley

HARTLEY's
THEORY OF THE
HUMAN MIND,
ON THE PRINCIPLE OF THE
ASSOCIATION of IDEAS;
WITH
ESSAYS
RELATING TO THE SUBJECT OF IT.

By JOSEPH PRIESTLEY, LL. D. F. R. S.

Æquum est ut ab hominibus impetremus, ut qui de hisce nostris aliquid statuere aut existimare velit, ne id in transitu, aut velut aliud agendo, facere se posse speret; sed, ut rem pernoscat, pravos, atque alte hærentes mentis habitus, tempestiva mora corrigat, atque tum demum judicio suo utatur.
Lord BACON.

LONDON:
PRINTED FOR J. JOHNSON, N°. 72, ST. PAUL'S CHURCH-YARD.
M.DCC.LXXV.

Library of Congress Cataloging in Publication Data

Hartley, David, 1705-1757.
  Hartley's theory of the human mind.

  (Language, man, and society: foundations of the behavioral sciences)
  Reprint of the 1775 ed. published by J. Johnson, London.
  Selections from Hartley's Observations on man.
  1. Association of ideas. I. Title.
II. Title: Theory of the human mind.
B1376.O3 2E5 1973   128'.2   74-147987
ISBN 0-404-08286-6

Reprinted from an original copy in the collections of the Princeton University Library

Language, Man and Society. General Editor, R.W. Rieber, John Jay College, New York, N.Y.

Copyright © 1973 by AMS Press, Inc.

All rights reserved. Published in the United States by AMS Press, Inc. 56 East 13th St. New York, N.Y. 10003

Manufactured in the United States of America

David Hartley: The Mind's Road to God

An Introduction to the New Edition of
HARTLEY'S THEORY OF THE HUMAN MIND

Thom Verhave
Queens College of the
City University of New York

But since with respect to the mirror of sensible things it happens that God is contemplated not only through them, as by his traces, but also in them . . . therefore a consideration of (His traces in the sensible world) holds next place as a second step in contemplation, by which we should be led to the contemplation of God in all creatures which enter into our midst through the bodily senses.

>   Saint Bonaventura (1221-1274): *Itinerarium Mentis ad Deum* (1259?) in *The Mind's Road to God*. (1953 edition, page 14)

Every living being is also a fossil. Within it, all the way down to the microscopic structure of its proteins, it bears the traces if not the stigmata of its ancestry.

>   Jacques Monod: *Chance and Necessity. An Essay on the Natural Philosophy of Modern Biology*. (1971, page 160)

Because an individual cannot contain the truth, it means that only the ignorant claim to be free. The wise understand exactly what a world weighs down upon them. And so we have a paradox: the ignorant scream that they are free of the tragedy, and in claiming to be liberated individuals can never truly be so. The wise know that the individual is not and cannot be free, and, therefore, in expressing the will of

God or the Marxist dialectics of history, they become free. He who would gain his life must lose it.

>William Irwin Thompson: *At the Edge of History. Speculations on the Transformation of Culture.* (1971, page 120)

Hartley's Theory of the Human Mind on the Principle of the Association of Ideas was first published in 1775 and reissued, with minor corrections, in 1790. It is an abridgment by Joseph Priestley (1733-1804) of David Hartley's major work: the *Observations on Man, His Frame, His Duty, and His Expectations,* first published in 1749.

What is the significance of Hartley's eighteenth-century treatise with its long and strange title, containing, it is said, a form of "Christian Materialism" which was "the most curious philosophic product of its age" (Robertson, 1929, I, page 198).

Hartley's title is actually not as "curious" as one might think. It was still quite common during that century to have such long titles, and people still had time to read such ponderous books. Hartley's heading is similar to those of quite a number of other philosophical productions. Christian Wolff (1679-1754) published an entire series of "Vernünfftige Gedanken" (Rational Considerations), one of which had the impressive title *Vernünfftige Gedanken von Gott, der Welt und der Seele der Menschen, auch allen Dingen überhaupt* (1719). It was filled with many thoughts so "clever" that it was repeatedly reprinted. The early draft of the *Ethics* (1677) of Spinoza (1632-1677) had a more succinct Latin title: "Tractatus (brevis) de Deo et Homine ejusque Felicitate" or "Short Treatise concerning God, Man and his Well-being." I will spare the tolerant reader further titles, but might mention that in the 19th-century Cardinal J. H. Newman (1801-1890) still spoke of the "knowledge of God, of his will, and of our duties towards him" (*An Essay in Aid of a Grammar of Assent*, 1870, page 378).

Certainly, Hartley's title, no matter how odd today, is part of a long and established tradition. It goes back at least as far as the time of Thomas Aquinas and his *Summa Theologica* (1267-1273). No doubt the general college-educated public of today is not likely to read a single page in any of these works. But the views of David Hartley and Joseph Priestley are still with us — although in modified form. Furthermore, they are just as controversial today as they were in 1749.

To say that an author's views are controversial implies that opinions about his work are radically divided. Praise and rejection have indeed been extravagant in Hartley's case.

"Johnson, one day, observing a friend of his packing up two volumes of 'Observations on Man', written by this good and great man, to take into the country, said, 'Sir, you do right to take Dr. Hartley with you: Priestley said of him, that he had learned more from Hartley than from any book he had ever read, except the Bible!" (James Boswell on Samuel Johnson, as quoted in Allibone, 1901)

Lant Carpenter (1780-1840), another admirer, "used to speak of Hartley as one who had the intellectual qualities of the seraphic order combined with the affections of the cherubic." (H. Martineau, 1877, volume 1, page 104) Apparently for Lant, the *Observations* was another *Summa*, and Hartley was another Aquinas, the Angelic Doctor.

Thomas Reid (1710-1796), however, accused Hartley of "building a castle in the air" and Dugald Stewart (1753-1828) called his work a "metaphysical romance" (cited by T. Mischel, 1966, page 126). "The intentions of both [Charles Bonnet (1720-1793) and Hartley] are allowed, by those who best knew them, to have been eminently pure and worthy; but it cannot be said of either that his metaphysical writings have contributed much to the instruction or to the improvement of the public. On the contrary, they have been instrumental in spreading a set of speculative tenets very nearly allied to that sentimental and fantastical modification of Spinozism which for many years past has prevailed so much and produced such mischievous effects in some parts of Germany." (Allibone, 1901)

Further indication that Hartley did not go unnoticed comes from Thomas Brown (1778-1820), another Scottish stalwart, who was not inclined to assign Hartley a place in Lant's angelic hierarchy. According to Brown, "it was chiefly in the southern part of the island, that the hypothesis of Dr. Hartley has met with followers; and his followers have generally been extravagant admirers of his philosophical genius, which, I own, seems to be to be very opposite to the genius of sound philosophy." Brown did not completely dismiss Hartley: "That there is considerable acuteness, however, displayed in his work, and that it contains some successful analysis of complex feelings, I am far from denying . . ." (1820: 1830 edition, volume 1, page 438)

Hartley's reputation, however, was not so easily snuffed out by the cynicism of a mere cabal of Scottish academicians. F. A. Carus, the German author of an early *History of Psychology* (1808) thought that "David Hartley hatte richtige Beobachtungsgabe, philosophischen und originellen Scharfsinn und war systematischer Kopf" (page 613). Germans, it seems, have always liked "systems," it gives a man something to hang on to, especially when he threatens to fall apart.

Thomas Brown's reference to Hartley's followers being "chiefly in the Southern part" of England may well have been to a number of admirers among — now forgotten — Unitarian circles around 1800. There were not only the previously mentioned Lant Carpenter (1780-1840), but also Eliezer Cogan (1762-1855), Thomas Cogan (1736-1818), William Belsham (1752-1827) and, last but not least, his older brother Thomas Belsham (1750-1829). He, according to the *London Quarterly Review*, "seems to be as deeply infected as any man with the itch for writing. Seldom a year passes without his sending forth two or three treatises." (Allibone, 1901) The reviewer strongly advised his readers not to rush to their local booksellers or libraries to obtain his works.

With so much going for and against Hartley, one can appreciate William Hazlitt's (1778-1830) comment when he wrote in 1829 that "the fame of this great metaphysician is, like that of so many others, of the subterranean class, 'hushed in the hollow mine of earth;' or you trace him, like the mole, only by the quantity of matter he has thrown up, and which Scotch professors carry off in lofty succession, to manure their dry brain and barren quartes with." (*Works*, 1934, volume 20, page 205)

So much for gossip. A more sober and scholarly approach to Hartley and his followers has been slow in developing. (Stephen, 1876; Heider, 1913; Willey, 1940; Fairchild, 1947; Marsh, 1959; Gay, 1969; D'Elia, 1970) It has been all too common to criticise or dismiss Hartley with a few snap judgments and pat labels: "sensationalist," "empiricist," "dualist," "mechanist," "near-materialist," "determinist," "associationist," "necessitarian," "utilitarian," "Christian optimist," and "mystic." All these are ". . . troublebreeding and usually thought-obscuring terms, which one sometimes wishes to see expunged from the vocabulary of the philosopher and the historian altogether . . ." (Lovejoy, 1936, page 6) Many writers have pidgeon-holed Hartley by means of one or another of these labels. In doing so they have often misunderstood Hartley himself, and have failed to see that he was a sincere eighteenth-century spokesman for the religious tradition of St. Augustine. (Marsh, 1959)

To those who would pass judgment on Hartley then, whether favorable or not, scholarship and fair-play would require that they first make the effort to understand the man whom Samuel T. Coleridge (1772-1834) once called "that great master of Christian Philosophy" (E. H. Coleridge, Ed., 1895, volume 1, page 169).

In a recent discussion of Hartley's *Observations*, R. M. Young observed that "Hartley certainly deserves a more careful study than any which I have seen." (1970, page 97) Peter Gay (1969, page 624) in a similar way noticed that "while Hartley and associationism have not been neglected, they could use deeper study."

The present essay can only indicate the scope of what remains to be done before a detailed analytical and comparative analysis of Hartley's "system" and influence can be undertaken. If, according to Gay's estimation, Hartley is ". . . perhaps the most inventive and certainly, despite intermittent periods of eclipse, the most influential psychologist of the eighteenth century" (1969, page 181), the effort to understand him and his sources will be well spent.

According to many current accounts of Hartley's work, it ". . . comprises three parts which are really unconnected. The first contains the physical doctrine of the vibrations; the second is concerned with the operations of the mind; the third treats of the Christian religion. The want of real connection is obvious from the fact that Priestley saw fit to publish the middle part without the other two; and [Hartley] himself frankly says [that] 'the Doctrine of Association may be laid down as a certain Foundation, and a clue to direct our future Inquiries, whatever becomes of that of Vibrations' "

(Peters, 1962, pages 436-437) D. B. Klein observes that Part II of the *Observations*, which "in terms of the history of psychology . . . is far less important than the first . . . in general . . . reflects Hartley's theology . . . [which] has little to do with Hartley's associationism." (Klein, 1970, pages 615-616). Such statements, which deny any unity, if not coherence, to Hartley's thought, are not statements of fact, but uninformed opinions which are a product of the polemics and forgotten controversies of the nineteenth century. They echo Coleridge (1817, chapters VI and VII), hardly an objective and scholarly source, or Stephen (1876), Robertson (1929), Lange (1866, 1925) and Albee (1901) — each with their own personal blinders.

Even if there were no logical connection between the various sections of Hartley's work, the fact remains that they were, at one time, all written by one man. There is then, at least, that obvious connection between them and it is the task of the historian to clarify how Hartley came to write them all.

It is ironic that the currently prevalent notion that only the first part of the *Observations* is of any interest and that the doctrines of vibration and association, as well as the theology are all "really unconnected," is partially due to Joseph Priestley, Hartley's best-known disciple in theology as well as psychology.

Although Priestley's editions of 1775 and 1790 largely reproduced only Part I of the *Observations*, it was not because Priestley himself thought that Part II was without merit. It is possible that Priestley hoped that if a larger public could be enticed to read Part I, some readers might go on to examine the entire work. The first page of his Preface to the abridged and simplified edition seems consistent with such an interpretation. There is no doubt that the present Priestley edition has been an influential one, which stimulated further interest in Hartley's theology and ethics as well. Five subsequent editions appeared between 1791 and 1834, which comprised Hartley's entire work.

It may be, that the unabridged editions were read mainly in the previously-mentioned Unitarian circles. Others, however, such as Jeremy Bentham and James Mill, were mainly interested in the associationism of the first volume.

The associationist "school" which presumably took Hartley, rather than Hume, as its implicit "founder," consists of such illustrious gentlemen as James Mill (1773-1836), his son John Stuart Mill (1806-1873) and Alexander Bain (1818-1903) a transition figure to the new evolutionary, experimental and physiological psychology of the last quarter of the nineteenth century. In his autobiography, J. S. Mill recounts how his father introduced him to Hartley, probably early in 1822: ". . . while, under my father's direction, my studies were carried into the higher branches of analytic psychology. I now read Locke's *Essay*, and wrote out an account of it . . . I performed the same process with Helvétious' *De L'Esprit*, which I read of my own choice. This preparation of abstracts, subject to my father's censorship, was of great service to me, by compelling precision in conceiving and expressing psychological doctrines whether accepted as truth or only regarded as the opinion of others. After Helvétius, my father made me study what he deemed the really masterproduction in the philosophy of mind, Hartley's *Observations* . . . Hartley's explanation, incomplete as in many points it is, of the more complex mental phenomena by the law of association, commended itself to me at once as a real analysis, and made me feel by contrast the insufficiency of the merely verbal generalizations of Condillac, and even of the instructive gropings and feelings about for psychological explanations, of Locke. It was at this very time that my father commenced writing his *Analysis of the Mind*, which carried Hartley's mode of explaining the mental phenomena to so much greater length and depth." (1961 edition, pages 47-48).

In 1825 John Mill and about a dozen companions formed a class to study "several of the branches of science which we wished to be masters of." (Ibid, page 76) After going through works on political economy and logic, ". . . we launched into an analytic psychology, and having chosen Hartley for our text-book, we raised Priestley's edition to an extravagant price by searching through London to furnish each of us with a copy. When we had finished Hartley, we suspended our meetings; but my father's *Analysis of the Mind* being published soon after (1829), we reassembled for the purpose of reading it. With this our exercises ended. I have always dated from these conversations my own real inauguration as an original and independent thinker." (Ibid, pages 77-78)

Current textbooks on the history of psychology and philosophy still briefly mention Hartley's doctrine of vibrations and his "near materialism," and then go on to emphasize his doctrine of association and the "mechanistic psychology," as well as his incipient "Utilitarianism" and its subsequent influence on the Benthamites. This sometimes has led to a caricature portrayal of Hartley, as some sort of latent "Philosophical Radical," "proto-behaviorist" or "crypto-materialist." Perhaps he was a "monster" like La Mettrie (1748) who bluntly dared assert that Man was a machine!

Another factor that may have contributed to the current distorted accounts of Hartley was the eminence of his contemporaries. His immediate circle of friends consisted of rather obscure figures, known, if at all, only to scholars specializing in the literary, theological, scientific or cultural history of that particular period in England.

According to "A Sketch of the Life and Character of Dr. Hartley," written by his son, David Hartley, Jr. (1732-1813),

> Dr. Law, Dr. Butler, Dr. Warburton, afterwards bishops of Carlisle, Durham, and Gloucester, and Dr. Jortin, were his intimate friends and fellow labourers in moral and religious philosophy, in metaphysics, in divinity and ecclesiastical history. He was much attached to the highly respected character of Dr. Hoadley, bishop of Winchester, for the liberality of his opinions, both in church and state, and for the freedom, of his religious sentiments. Dr. Hales, and Dr. Smith, master of Trinity College in Cambridge, with other members of the Royal Society, were his companions in the sciences of opticks, staticks, and other branches of natural philosophy. Mr. Hawkins Browne, the author of an elegant Latin poem, De Animi Immortalitate, and Dr. Young, the inventor of a scientific short-hand writing, was much respected by him for useful and accurate judgment in the branch of philology. Mr. Hooke, the Roman historian, and disciple of the Newtonian chronology, was amongst his literary intimates. (1801 edition, pages V-VI)

Now, whoever these people were (and the *Dictionary of National Biography* will tell anyone who really cares to find out), they were not gentlemen our history books rush to mention when they get to the first half of the eighteenth century. Why would anyone want to mention these minor theologians, second-rate poets, scientists, scholars, and divines, except a man with the generaous wit and stamina of Sir Leslie Stephen? (1876) Especially when in the same period during which Hartley's work appeared, that horrible "enfant terrible" La Mettrie published *L'Homme Machine* (1748), Etienne Bonnot de Condillac wrote the *Essay sur l'Origine des Connaissances Humaines* (1746, *Traité des Systèmes* (1749), and for good measure, the *Traité des Sensations* (1754). In the very same year (1749) that Hartley's *Observations* saw the light of day, Denis Diderot published the *Lettre sur les Aveugles*, and P.L.M. de Maupertuis came out with an *Essai de Philosophie Morale*, in which there was talk about a mathematical calculus of pain and pleasures.

For the sake of brevity, other — equally notable — works shall go unmentioned, except perhaps David Hume's *Treatise* (1739) and the *Enquiry Concerning Human Understanding* (1748). In competition with so many luminaries, Drs. Law, Butler, Warburton, Jortin, etc. never had a chance! Nor did Hartley himself, who was a "zealous Christian without guile" (David Hartley, Jr. Biography, 1801 edition, page VII) among such infidels. No wonder then, that if anyone mentions Hartley at all, he usually appears among his enlightened French contemporaries, and often is made out to subscribe like them to the new shaky faith in progress and the infinite perfectability of man.

Even the informed scholar John Herman Randall, Jr., in *The Career of Philosophy* (1962) discusses Hartley in a chapter (no. 15) on "The Science of Human Nature: The Associationist Psychology" together with Condillac, Helvétius and the Ideologists Destutt de Tracy and Cabanis. Hartley's "systematic attempt at a physiological psychology," his influential associationist psychology and the notion of vibrations are all duly mentioned and described. Randall ends his discussion with a remarkable quotation from the *Observations*, meant to illustrate that Hartley was explicit about "the implications of his analysis of mental life for morals and politics:"

> It is of the utmost consequence to morality and religion, that the affections should be analyzed into their simple compounding parts, by reversing the steps of the associations which concur to form them. For thus we learn how to cherish and improve good ones, check and root out such as are mischievous and immoral, and how to suit our manner of life, in some tolerable measure, to our intellectual and religious wants. And as this holds, in respect of persons of all

ages, so it is particularly true, and worthy of consideration, in respect of children and youth. If beings of the same nature, but whose affections and passions are, at present, in different proportions to each other, be exposed for an indefinite time to the same impressions and associations, all their particular differences will, at last, be overruled, and they will become perfectly similar, or even equal. They may also be made perfectly similar in a finite time, by a proper adjustment of the impressions and associations.

(Part I, ch. 1, section II, proposition XIV, corollaries 5 and 6, 1749 edition, pages 81 and 82)

This passage, as Willey points out (1940, page 144), influenced William Wordsworth when writing about someone who is the product of a faulty education. He was, in Wordsworth's phrases to "go back, as occasion will permit, to Nature and to solitude" and to "measure back the track of life he has trod."

The current relevance of the above quotes may be obvious to those forever looking for anticipation of concepts fashionable today. Freud's "royal road to the unconscious" by means of free-association comes readily to mind here.

Others, when reading the Hartley quote might cry fascist, communist, brainwasher, totalitarian, *Brave New World*, *1984*, or *Walden Two!* On the other hand, readers of Randall's chapter will see Hartley side by side with Condillac, and Helvetius, that great prophet of the idea of progress and the perfectability of man.

Yet Hartley does not belong with any of them. One need only read the reasons he himself gave for writing the entire *Observations* in his introduction to "Part the Second, containing Observations on the Duty and Expectations of Mankind." This was omitted by Priestley in his abridged editions, and concludes as follows:

Yet still there are Difficulties both in the Word of

God, and in his Works; and these Difficulties are sometimes so magnified, as to lead to Scepticism, Infidelity, or Atheism. Now the Contemplation of our own Frame and Constitution appears to me to have a peculiar Tendency to lessen these Difficulties attending Natural and REvealed Religion, and to improve their Evidences, as well as to concur with them in their Determination of Man's Duty and Expectations. With this View, I drew up the foregoing Observations on the Frame and Connexion of the Body and Mind; and, in Prosecution of the same Design, I now propose,

First, To proceed upon this Foundation, and upon the other Phaenomena of Nature to deduce the Evidences for the Being and Attributes of God, and the general Truths of Natural Religion.

Secondly, Laying down all these as a new Foundation, to deduce the Evidences for Revealed Religion.

Thirdly, To inquire into the Rule of Life, and the particular Applications of it, which result from the Frame of our Natures, the Dictates of Natural Religion, and the Precepts of the Scriptures taken together, compared with, and casting Light upon, each other. And,

Fourthly, To inquire into the genuine Doctrines of Natural and Revealed Religion thus illustrated, concerning the Expectations of Mankind, here and hereafter, in consequence of their Observance or Violation of the Rule of Life.

I do not presume to give a complete Treatise on any of these Subjects; but only to borrow from the many excellent Writings, which have been offered to the World on them, some of the principal Evidences and Deductions, and to accomodate them to the foregoing Theory of the Mind; whereby it may appear, that though the Doctrines of Association and Mechanism do make some Alterations in the Method of reasoning on Religion, yet they are far from lessening either the Evidences for it, the Comfort and Joy of religious Persons, or the Fears of irreligious ones.

Hartley must first of all be recognized as a devout — although somewhat independent — Christian, fully convinced of the omnipotence and infinite benevolence of his God. The entire *Observations* were intended to be didactic within a religious-moralistic framework. The book, in fact, is a kind of eighteenth century "Guide for the Perplexed."

Even the supposedly "quasi-materialistic" and "mechanistic" Part I was written because ". . . the contemplation of our own Frame and Constitution appears to me to have a peculiar Tendency to lessen [the] Difficulties attending Natural and Revealed Religion. . . ."

Man's "frame and constitution" are only matter: the dust of a fallen creature corrupted by sin. If only such meditations could lead one to a yearning for God, Christ and righteousness!

Once this thoroughly traditional Christian aspect of Hartley is recognized and acknowledged as the controlling framework of all his thought, one can understand why Benjamin Rush (1745-1813) believed that Hartley "had established an indissoluble union between physiology, metaphysics, and Christianity . . . [and] so disposed them that they mutually afford not only support but beauty and splendor to each other." (quoted by D'Elia, 1970, page 109)

Willey points out that "throughout [the] *Observations* there is to be found a characteristic blend — rare even in England after the eighteenth century, and by that time virtually extinct in France — of scientific ardour with religious certainty. Hartley was a man of unusual originality and penetration, and he writes with the zest of one who knows he is engaged in pioneering work, but who feels, at the same time, that he is building up morality and religion on unshakable foundations. In this respect Hartley is clearly in the apostolical succession of English physico-theologians from Bacon, through Boyle, Locke, and Newton, to Joseph Priestley." (1940, page 136)

The immediate sources behind Wordsworth's previously mentioned advice to "go back to Nature and to Solitude" and "measure back the track of life" are the romantic "worship of nature" and

Hartley. But behind Hartley and Wordsworth's advice to seek solitude stands an older tradition represented, for example by Thomas à Kempis (compare Book 1, chapter 20, "of the love of solitude and silence" in the *Imitatio Christi*) or Meister Eckhart's "On solitude and the attainment of God." (Blakney, 1941, page 7)

Hartley was writing a kind of "Natural Theology" with elements as common to the Middle Ages as a triptych: Man's Frame, His Expectations, and His Duty to God.

In the eighteenth century after Spinoza, Newton and Descartes, authors of "natural theologies" often attempted to treat their subject as a coherent system of rational propositions. These were to be tested not only by the rules of logic, but by simple, "empirical" inspection of "the mirror of sensible things" as well.

When one looks at the main tenets of Hartley's speculative theology and faith, one finds variations on classical Christian themes. The three most important assumptions are the infinite benevolence of God, His infinite power and the doctrine of original sin. Hartley, kind-hearted and generous as he was, could not resign himself to a belief in eternal punishment for confirmed sinners. In an attempt to reconcile the doctrines of divine retribution, the infinite benevolence of God as well as "association," Hartley believed in a kind of purgatory.

Most of Volume Two of the *Observations* would be tedious for the majority of readers today. Perhaps the following brief excerpt gives some of its style and flavor. In Section IV (of Chapter 4), entitled "Of the Terms of Salvation," Hartley reasons that

> It follows from the foregoing Theory of our intellectual Pleasures and Pains ... that the Bulk of Mankind are not qualified for pure unmixed Happiness ... [since they are] ... by no means so advanced in

self-annihilation, and in the love of God, and of his Creatures in and through him, as appears ... to be required for the Attainment of pure Happiness. There are few, even in Christian Countries, that so much as know what the true Religion and Purity of the Heart is.... (1749, II, pages 404-405)

Thus it follows that, according to "Proposition 92," "... the Bulk of Mankind are not qualified for the Mansions of the Blessed." How is this to be reconciled with Hartley's belief that, since God is benevolent, "all Mankind will be made happy ultimately" (Proposition 94)? He informs us that all the "Evils that befall" us in this world "have a tendency to improve" either mind or body. If they fail to be beneficient (in a moral sense) "they must, however, necessarily contribute to the Annihilation of that Self, carnal or spiritual, gross or refined, which is an insuperable Bar to our Happiness in the pure Love of God and of his Works."

There is one aspect of Hartley's religiosity that deserves further comment. Some of his language has led him to be charged with Mysticism (for an eighteenth-century rebuttal, see H. A. Pistorius, 1772). The charge was based on Hartley's use of the concept of "Self-annihilation" (1749, II, pages 280-282, 404, 419). It is closely connected with his definition of the true Christian as one whose "Will [is] broken and subjected to the Divine Will (1749, II, pages 196, 405). These are traditional metaphors of a certain kind of Christian devotional literature, such as *The Imitation of Christ*. They are also crucial to an understanding of his religious and pastoral psychology. Marsh points out that "to place Hartley accurately in the history of Western thought will require reference beyond the history of such concepts as associations, scientific mechanism, and utilitarianism and beyond the characteristic devotion of writers of the 'enlightenment' to [the] analysis of the human mind as the necessary preliminary to moral, aesthetic and metaphysical knowledge." (1959, page 272) He identifies Hartley with "... a kind of unitarian Christan 'Platonism,' with a pseudo-Calvinistic flavor," rather than with "the materialistic, sensationistic 'naturalism' and relativism" that he is often (and ironically) associated with. (1959, page 272, note 18) Marsh further indicates that many of Hartley's "individual doctrines ... suggest parallels in medieval Christian philosophy, especially in Augustine and Bonaventura ... and his system as a whole perhaps has much more in common with the dialectical tradition represented in the eighteenth century by writers like Shaftesbury, Vico, Hamann, Herder, and James Harris, than with the empirical psychologistic tradition of that period." (1959, page 272)

When Hartley traces the development of the higher out of the lower pleasures from the pleasures of sense and of self-interest, through the pleasures of sympathy and benevolence, up to the supreme pleasure of the pure love of Good and of perfect self-denial, this is not just a novel application of some associationist doctrine taken from John Locke or John Gay, but a restatement — in religious language — of concepts going back to the *Symposium* of Plato.

Yet the contemporary reader will also recognize that Hartley often is distinctly "psychological" in the modern sense. Here and there, even in the midst of endless pages of theological speculation, appear discussions of clear relevance to psychology and its history. For instance, Hartley's faith, although less severe than that found among many of his contemporaries, still involved various contradictory assumptions which took a heavy toll in "mental disorders." On the one hand, "faith in Christ" was not sufficient for Hartley to be saved — a virtuous life was equally necessary. On the other hand, there was never any guarantee that even both would be sufficient in the eyes of Hartley's God or conscience. The result of these beliefs was a peculiar "double bind," of which he himself was painfully aware. It led him to describe a psychological analysis of religious conversion, that would not be out of date today:

> ... there is great Reason to fear, both from the foregoing Theory of the human Mind, and from plain Experience, that such strong Persuasion [of one's own salvation] may be generated, whilst Men continue in many gross Corruptions ... Eager Desires are attended with Hope in the Sanguine, the Vainglorious, and the Self-conceited; and this Hope, as it increases becomes a comfortable Assurance and Persuasion, drawing to itself by degrees the inward Sentiments, that attend upon Assent. On the contrary, eager Desires in the Scrupulous, Superstitious, and Dejected, end in Fear and Dissent. But if this Dejection should pass into the opposite state, then the anxious Diffidence may at once, as it were, pass into its Opposite, a joyful Persuasion ... there is great Danger of being imposed upon here by the wonderful Subtlety of the natural Operations of the Mind. When a Man begins to fancy, that an inward Sentiment, much or long desired by him, such as the Assurance of his Salvation, has happened or will happen to him, this imposes upon his Memory by imperceptible Degrees in one Case; and begets the Sentiment itself, the Assurance, in the other. Such a factitious Assurance can therefore be no Evidence for itself. It is a mental Affection, of the same kind with the rest; and can less be depended upon, as a Test, than plain Actions. (1749, II, pages 408-409 and 415-416)

Hartley was quite concerned about the dangers of excessive "anxious Diffidence" and subsequent depreysion. The following passage shows his awareness of unconscious motives and what Ellenberger has called the "pathogenic secret" (1970, pages 44-45):

> ... though it be proper to comfort religious Persons under bodily or mental Disorders, which fill their Minds with disproportionate Fears and Scruples by informing them, that a Solicitude about our Salvation is the sure Means of obtaining it; that this Affliction is to be endured with Patience, and Confidence in God,

> as much as any other; that it is attended with the same Advantages as common Afflictions, and also with some peculiar to itself, such as putting us upon a thorough Examination of our Hearts; and that this severe Chastening in the present World is the strongest Mark, that we are loved by God, and therefore shall be saved in the World to come; yet the same Persons are to be admonished that a great Degree of Fearfulness and Scrupulosity often proceeds from some Self-deceit and Prevarication at the Bottom. There is probably some secret Sin, some Sin that circumvents them more easily and frequently than the rest, of which they may not perhaps be fully aware, and yet about which they have great Suspicions and Checks, if they would hearken to them fully and fairly. (1749, II, pages 416-417)

These passages are interesting bits of psychological analysis based on sound "psychoanalytic" insight concerning the crucial role of conflict in maintaining a proper balance between "overconfidence" and "anxiety," "dejection," or "acedia." Hartley was not the only one among his contemporaries to have such insights, partly based on self-analysis, partly on the very old tradition of pastoral psychology within the Christian church. (McNeill, 1951)

What is unique about Hartley is the fact that he merges a scientific and religious determinism. Man, perhaps is a "mechanism" of sorts, but a mechanism whose fate is ultimately determined by a just and benevolent God. By his own account

> ...it may be said that a Man may prove his wn Free-will by internal Feeling. This is true, if by Free-will be meant the Power of doing what a Man wills or desires; or of resisting the motives of Sensuality, Ambition, etc., i.e. Free-will in the popular and practical Sense. Every Person may easily recollect Instances, where he has done these several Things. But then these are entirely foreign to the present Question. To prove that Man has Free-will in the Sense opposite to Mechanism, he ought to feel, that he can do different Things, while the Motives remain precisely the same: and here I apprehend the internal Feelings

are entirely against Free-will, where the Motives are of a sufficient Magnitude to be evident; where they are not, nothing can be proved. (1749, I, page 507)

However, those philosophers, who merely asserted Man's free-will, were to a Christian like Hartley self-aggrandizing boasters. Fully aware of the inevitable conflicts of the soul, he also observed that "... the Affectors of the Doctrine of Mechanism are [not] necessarily humble. For ... the Associations of Life beget the Idea and Opinion of Self again and again, refer Actions to this Self, and connect a variety of Applauses and Complacencies with these Actions." (1749, II, 268-269) The activities of human social life are the source of hubris. A Christian must remain humble, however, and according to Hartley's own "Rule of Life," "... we ought even to rejoice when we are meanly esteemed, and despised, as having then an Opportunity offered of imitating him who was *meek* and *lowly in Heart* and of *finding* Rest *to our Souls* thereby." (1749, II, page 266)

Those, who, in ignorance of his true position, have misrepresented Hartley, may still "meanly esteem and despise" him — even after they have come to a better understanding of his *Observations on Man*. Such a rejection, at least, would be of the real Hartley — and not of a distorted caricature.

REFERENCES

Albee, E. *A History of English Utilitarianism* (1901). New York: Collier, 1962

Allibone, S. A. *A Critical Dictionary of English Literature of British and American Authors.* Philadelphia: Lippincott, 1900 (2 volumes)

Blakney, R. B. *Meister Eckhart, A Modern Translation.* New York: Harper and Row, 1941

Saint Bonaventura. *Itinerarium Mentis ad Deum* (1259?). Boas, G., translator and editor: *The Mind's Road to God.* Indianapolis: Bobbs-Merrill, 1953

Brown, T. *Lectures on The Philosophy of The Human Mind* (1820). Hallowell: Glazier, Masters, 1830. (2 volumes)

Carus, F. A. *Geschichte der Psychologie.* Leipzig: Barth und Kummer, 1808

Coleridge, E. H., ed. *The Letters of S. T. Coleridge.* Boston: Houghton Mifflin, 1895 (2 volumes)

Coleridge, S. T. *Biographia Literaria.* London: Rest Fenner, 1817

D'Elia, D. J. "Benjamin Rush, David Hartley, and the Revolutionary Uses of Psychology." *Proceedings of the American Philosophical Society*, 1970, 114, 109-118

Ellenberger, H. *The Discovery of the Unconscious.* New York: Basic Books, 1970

Fairchild, H. N. "Hartley, Pistorius, and Coleridge." *Proceedings Modern Language Association*, 1947, 62, 1010-1021

Gay, P. *The Enlightenment; An Interpretation. The Science of Freedom.* New York: A. A. Knopf, 1969

Hartley, D. *Observations on Man, His Frame, His Duty, and His Expectations.* Bath: J. Leake and Wm. Frederick, 1749

Hartley, David, Jr. *A Sketch of the Life and Character of Dr. Hartley.* Prefixed to the second

(1791), third (1791) and fourth (1801) edition of David Hartley's Observations on Man... London: J. Johnson, 1791 & 1801

Hazlitt, W. *The Complete Works of William Hazlitt.* Edited by P. P. Howe, after the edition of A. R. Waller and A. Glover. London: J. M. Dent, 1930-1934 (21 volumes)

Heider, M. *Studien über David Hartley.* Bonn: Bergish-Gladbach, 1913

Klein, D. B. *A History of Scientific Psychology.* New York: Basic Books, 1970

Lange, F. A. *The History of Materialism and Criticism of its Present Importance* (1866). (New York: Harcourt, Brace, 1925) 3rd edition.

Lovejoy, A. O. *The Great Chain of Being* (1936), (New York: Harper & Row, 1960).

McNeill, J. T. *A History of the Cure of Souls.* (New York: Harper & Row, 1951)

Marsh, R. "The Second Part of Hartley's System." *Journal of the History of Ideas,* 1959, 20, 264-273

Martineau, H. *Autobiography.* (Boston: Houghton & Mifflin, 1877) 2 volumes

Mill, J. S. *Autobiography.* In: Lerner, M. ed. *Essential Works of John Stuart Mill.* (New York: Bantam Books, 1961).

Mischel, T. " 'Emotion' and 'Motivation' in the Development of English Psychology: David Hartley, James Mill, Alexander Bain." *Journal of the History of the Behavioral Sciences,* 1966, 2, 123-144

Monod, Jacques. *Chance and Necessity, An Essay on the Natural Philosophy of Modern Biology.* (New York: A. A. Knopf, 1971).

Newman, J. H. *An Essay in Aid of a Grammar of Assent.* (London: Burns, Oates, 1870).

Peters, R. S., ed. *Brett's History of Psychology.* (New York: Macmillan, 1962) revised edition.

Pistorius, H. A. *Notes and Additions to Dr. Hartley's Observations on Man.* Translated from the German original, printed at Rostock and Leipzig in 1772. (London: J. Johnson, 1791 and 1801).

Randall, J. H., Jr. *The Career of Philosophy, From the Middle Ages to the Enlightenment.* (New York: Columbia University Press, 1961).

Robertson, J. M. *A History of Freethought in the Nineteenth Century.* (London: Watts, 1929) 2 volumes.

Stephen, L. *History of English Thought in the Eighteenth Century* (1876), (New York: Harcourt, Brace and World, 1962) 2 volumes.

Thompson, W. I. *At the Edge of History, Speculations on the Transformation of Culture,* (New York: Harper & Row, 1971).

Willey, B. *The Eighteenth Century Background. Studies on the Idea of Nature in the Thought of the Period* (1940). (Boston: Beacon, 1961).

Young, R. M. *Mind, Brain and Adaptation in the Nineteenth Century, Cerebral Localization and its Biological Context from Gall to Ferrier.* (Oxford: Clarendon, 1970).

THE
PREFACE.

IT has long been the opinion of all the admirers of Dr. Hartley among my acquaintance, as well as my own, that his *Obfervations on Man* could not have failed to have been more generally read, and his *theory of the human mind* to have prevailed, if it had been made more intelligible; and if the work had not been clogged with a whole fyftem of moral and religious knowledge; which, however excellent, is, in a great meafure, foreign to it.

Both thefe obftacles it is my object in this publication to remove; by exhibiting his theory of the human mind, as far as it relates to the doctrine of *affociation of ideas* only, omitting even what relates to the doctrine of *vibrations*, and the *anatomical difquifitions* which are connected with it. And it is on thefe two accounts only that the objection to his theory, as *difficult* and *intricate*, is founded.

As, however, I am far from being willing to fupprefs the doctrine of vibrations; thinking that Dr. Hartley has produced fufficient evidence for it, or as much as the nature of the thing will admit of at prefent (that is, till we know more of the ftructure of the body in other refpects) I have not thought it neceffary fcrupuloufly to ftrike out the word *vibrations*, or *vibratiuncles* wherever they occured. As the words themfelves are fufficiently intelligible, they can occafion no difficulty or embarraffment to the reader. Befides, he may, if he pleafes, fubftitute for them the name of any other fpecies of motion, or impreffion, to which he may think the phenomena to be explained by them more exactly correfpond; and which he may think to agree better with the general doctrine of *affociation*, which is, properly fpeaking, the only *poftulatum*, or thing *taken for granted*, in this work.

The mention of vibrations occurs the moft frequently in the fections which I have felected from the account of the feveral *fenfes*, the greateft part of which, as relating more immediately to the ftructure of the *body*, I have omitted. I was unwilling to leave out the whole of that part, becaufe feveral of the fections (as I hope the reader will agree with me) are peculiarly curious and valuable, and relate more efpecially to the theory of the *mind*, though intermixed with obfervations of a different nature.

In the firft part of this work, however, for the ufe of novices in thefe inquiries, I have generally fubftituted other expreffions for *vibrations*, &c. where I could do it conveniently. But not to injure

THE PREFACE.

injure my author, or mislead my reader, I have, in all those passages, given the very words of Dr. Hartley at the bottom of the page.

Willing also, by this publication, to introduce my reader to the study of Hartley himself, I have printed the whole of his *table of contents for the first volume* of the work, that the original *extent* of it may be seen; distinguishing by a different character the sections which I have selected here. All that I have taken from the *second volume* have been the sections relating to the *mechanism of the mind*, which I have subjoined to the *conclusion* of the first volume, as they all relate to the same subject.

It is not impossible but that, if this volume be well received, I may proceed to publish other parts of *Hartley's Observations on man*, with *dissertations*, or *notes*, illustrating them. For many excellent articles (I may say *all* the articles) in this great work, have been, in a great measure, lost to the world, in consequence of being published as parts of so very extensive a system. In the preface to the second volume of my *Institutes of natural and revealed religion* I have expressed a wish that Dr. Hartley's account of *the evidences of christianity* might be published separately, for the use of the more philosophical and thinking part of mankind. If, therefore, I do any thing more in this way, I shall probably next undertake that part of the work.

INTRODUCTORY ESSAYS.

ESSAY I.

A general view of the doctrine of Vibrations.

SINCE all sensations and ideas are conveyed to the mind by means of the external senses, or more properly by the nerves belonging to them, sensations, as they exist in the brain, must be such things as are capable of being transmitted by the nerves; and since the nerves and the brain are of the same substance, the affection of a nerve during the transmission of a sensation, and the affection of the brain during the perceived presence of it, are probably the same. What sensations, or ideas, are, as they exist in the *mind*, or *sentient principle*, we have no more knowledge of, than we have of the mind or sentient principle itself. And in this ignorance of ourselves, the business of philosophy will be abundantly satisfied, if we be able to point out such a probable affection of the brain, as will correspond to all the variety of sensations and ideas, and the affections of them, of which we are conscious. Ideas themselves, as they exist in the mind, may be as different from what they are in the brain, as that peculiar difference of texture (or rather, as that difference in the rays of light) which occasions difference of colour, is from the colours themselves, as we conceive of them.

Till the time of Sir Isaac Newton, who first, I believe, suggested the doctrine of vibrations, it was generally supposed that an impression at the extremity of a nerve was transmitted to the brain by means of a *fluid* with which the nerve was filled; the nerves, for that purpose, being supposed to be tubular. But in what manner this impression was conveyed, whether in succession, by a vibratory motion of the parts of this nervous fluid, or instantaneously, there was no distinct hypothesis formed. The former supposition, however, is more consonant to the prevailing notion of this nervous fluid, as exceedingly subtle, and elastic. Still less had any tolerable hypothesis been advanced concerning the manner in which the brain is affected by this motion of the nervous fluid.

To assist the imagination, indeed, but by no means in any consistency with the notion of a nervous fluid, it had been conceived that ideas resembled characters drawn upon a *tablet;* and the language in which we generally speak of ideas, and their affections, is borrowed from this hypothesis. But neither can any such *tablet* be found in the brain, nor any *style,* by which to make the characters upon it; and though some of the more simple phenomena of ideas, as their being more or less deeply *impressed*, their being *retained* a longer

or

ESSAYS. ix

or a shorter time, being capable of being *revived* at pleasure, &c. may be pretty well explained by the hypothesis of such a tablet, and characters upon it, it is wholly inadequate to the explanation of other, and very remarkable phenomena of ideas, especially their mutual *association*. Besides, this hypothesis suggests nothing to explain any of the *mental operations* respecting ideas.

This hypothesis, therefore, if it may be said to have been one, being rejected, I do not know that any other remains to be considered but that of *vibrations*, suggested by Sir Isaac Newton, though but barely proposed by him, at the end of his *Principia*, and in the Queries at the end of his Optics. The former is quoted by Hartley himself, and therefore I shall not insert it here, but the latter I shall subjoin.

"Do not the rays of light, in falling upon the bottom of the eye, excite vibrations in the tunica retina? Which vibrations, being propagated along the solid fibres of the optic nerves into the brain, cause the sense of seeing. For because dense bodies conserve their heat a long time, and the densest bodies conserve their heat the longest, the vibrations of their parts are of a lasting nature; and therefore may be propagated along solid fibres of uniform dense matter, to a great distance, for conveying into the brain the impressions made upon all the organs of sense. For that motion which can continue long in one and the same part of a body,

INTRODUCTORY

can be propagated a long way from one part to another, fuppofing the body homogeneal, fo that the motion may not be reflected, refracted, interrupted, or difordered, by any unevenefs of the body."

" Qu. 13. Do not feveral forts of rays make vibrations of feveral bigneffes, which, according to their bigneffes, excite fenfations of feveral colours, much after the manner that the vibrations of the air, according to their feveral bigneffes, excite fenfations of feveral founds? And particularly, do not the moft refrangible rays excite the fhorteft vibrations for making a fenfation of deep violet, the leaft refrangible the largeft, for making a fenfation of deep red, and the feveral intermediate forts of rays, vibrations of feveral intermediate bigneffes, to make fenfations of the feveral intermediate colours?"

Upon thefe hints Dr. Hartley acknowledges that he built his whole fyftem of vibrations, which appears to me to correfpond to all that we know concerning ideas and their affections, and to have been demonftrated by him as fatisfactorily as can be expected, in a fubject fo very obfcure as this neceffarily is; the evidence for it being fufficiently clear in many cafes, and being capable of being transferred by analogy to other cafes, from which feparate and independent evidence could not be derived.

This hypothefis does not require that the nerves be *tubes*, or confift of bundles of tubes, for the
purpofe

purpose of containing any *fluid*, though it is no way inconsistent with the supposition of their being of that structure. It only requires that they be of such a texture, that if their extreme parts be put into a vibratory motion, that motion may be freely propagated to the brain, and be continued there.

Now that the nerves *may* be of a constitution that will admit of this cannot be denied, though the structure which this purpose requires be ever so exquisite; especially when it is considered that all bodies whatever do actually possess this very property, in a greater or less degree, in consequence of their constituent particles not being in actual contact with each other, but kept at a certain distance from one another, by a repulsive power.

That sensations are transmitted to the brain in the form of vibrations is rendered very probable from the well-known phenomena of the more perfect senses, as those of seeing and hearing. That the retina is affected with a tremulous motion, in consequence of the action of the rays of light, is evident from the impression continuing some time, and dying away gradually, after the cause of the impression has been removed. It appears to me that no person can keep his eye fixed on a luminous object, and afterwards shut it, and observe how the impression goes off, and imagine that the retina was affected in any other manner than with a tremulous

or

INTRODUCTORY

or a vibratory motion. And is it not moſt probable, not to ſay certain, that, ſince the impreſſion is actually tranſmitted to the brain, it muſt be by means of the ſame kind of motion by which the extremity of the nerve was affected, that is, a vibratory one? And ſince the *brain* itſelf is a continuation of the ſame ſubſtance with the nerves, is it not equally evident that the affection of the brain correſponding to a ſenſation, and conſequently to an idea, is a vibratory motion of its parts?

Now ſince the texture of all the nerves is, at leaſt, nearly the ſame, it will follow by analogy, that if any one of them tranſmit ſenſations by a vibratory motion of its parts, all the reſt do ſo too. That this is the caſe with the *auditory* nerve is probable independently of any argument of analogy from the optic nerve. For what is more natural than to imagine that the tremulous motion of the particles of the air, in which ſound conſiſts, muſt, ſince it acts by ſucceſſive pulſes, communicate a tremulous motion to the particles of the auditory nerve, and that the ſame tremulous motion is propagated to the brain, and diffuſed into it? It is not neceſſary to ſuppoſe that the vibrations of the particles of the air, and thoſe of the particles of the nerves, are *iſochronous*, ſince even the vibration of a muſical ſtring will affect another, an octave above, or an octave below it.

That vibrations correſponding to all the varieties of ſenſations and ideas that ever take place in any human

human mind may take place in the fame brain at the fame time, can create no difficulty to any perfon who confiders the capacity of the *air* itfelf to tranfmit different vibrations, without limits, at the fame inftant of time. In a concert, in which ever fo many inftruments are employed, a perfon fkilled in mufic, I am told, is able to attend to which of them all he pleafes. At the fame time ever fo many perfons may be fpeaking, and founds of other kinds may be made, each of which is tranfmitted without the leaft interruption from the reft. How infinitely complex muft be the vibration of the air a little above the ftreets of fuch a city as London; and yet there can be no doubt but that each found has its proper effect, and might be attended to feparately, by an ear fufficiently exquifite. That vibrations which are nearly ifochronous affect and modify one another, fo as to become perfectly fo, fufficiently correfponds to the phenomena of ideas, and therefore makes no objection to this doctrine.

The differences of which vibrations affecting the brain are capable are fufficient to correfpond to all the differences which we obferve in our original ideas or fenfations. The difference in the *degree* of vibration, correfponding to the fame found made weaker or ftronger, is confiderable. The difference in *kind*, correfponding to the difference of tone is ftill more confiderable. And farther, one vibration in the brain may be diftinguifhed from another by its *place*, in confequence of its principally affecting a particular region of the brain, and

alfo

also in its *line of direction*, as entering by a particular nerve.

If thefe original differences in vibrations are fufficient to correfpond to all the varieties of our original or *fimple ideas*, the combinations of which they are capable muft be equal in both cafes; fo that the number of *complex ideas* creates no peculiar difficulty. In fact, however, fome mechanical affection of the nerves and brain muft neceffarily correfpond to all our fenfations and ideas; and I think it is pretty evident that no other hypothefis can account for half the variety in this refpect, that may be explained by the doctrine of vibrations: fo that, on this account, and from the moft general view of the fubject, Hartley's, or rather Newton's theory, muft have the preference of any other, at leaft of any that has yet been propofed.

Befides the four differences of vibrations abovementioned, which alone are infifted upon by Dr. Hartley, there may be a farther difference in the *conftitution of the nerves* belonging to the different fenfes, or there may be fo many circumftances that affect or modify their vibrations, that they may be as diftinguifhable from one another, as different human voices founding the fame note; and probably no two individuals of the human race can found the fame note fo much alike, as that they could not be diftinguifhed from one another.

There

ESSAYS.

There will be no great difficulty in conceiving that, in a substance not *fluid*, like the air, but *solid*, though soft, like the brain, a vibration affecting any part of it will leave that part disposed to vibrate in that particular manner rather than in any other; so that a *second impression* of the same kind may be distinguished from a *first*; which may, in some measure, explain the difference between a new sensation, and the repetition of an old one. But these are chiefly distinguishable from one another by the difference of their *associations*, both with other ideas, and with a different state of the mind, or brain, in a variety of respects.

Also, one vibration having been sufficiently impressed, it may be conceived that the region of the brain affected by it will retain a disposition to the same vibrations in preference to others: so that these vibrations may take place from other causes than the original one. But these vibrations will necessarily differ considerably in strength, and other circumstances, from original vibrations; which provides for the difference between the ideas of present objects, and the same idea excited without the presence of the object. Thus circles of colours may be excited by pressing the eye with the finger, and by other causes, which, however, are easily distinguished from a similar affection of the retina by the impression of rays of light.

If it be said that these vibrations in the brain, differing chiefly in degree, might be liable to be mistaken

xvi INTRODUCTORY

miftaken for one another; I anfwer that, in fact, mankind are fubject to fallacies and miftakes from this fource; very vivid ideas actually impofing upon the mind, fo that they are miftaken for realities, as in dreams and reveries, efpecially in cafes of madnefs.

This fuppofition of the particles of the brain retaining a difpofition to vibrate as they have formerly vibrated, will be rendered more probable, from confidering that all folid fubftances feem to retain a difpofition to continue in any ftate before impreffed. For this reafon a bow of any kind, that has been bent, does not reftore itfelf to the fame form that it had before, but leans a little to the other, in confequence of the fpheres of attraction and repulfion belonging to the feveral particles having been altered by the change of their fituation. Something fimilar to this may take place with refpect to the brain.

The phenomena of vibrations correfpond happily enough to the difference between *pleafurable* and *painful* fenfations; becaufe they feem to differ only in degree, and to pafs infenfibly into one another. Thus a moderate degree of warmth is pleafant, and the pleafure increafes with the heat to a certain degree, at which it begins to be painful; and beyond this the pain increafes with the degree of heat, juft as the pleafure had done before. Dr. Hartley conjectures, and I think probably enough, that the limit of pleafure and pain is the *folution of continuity*

in

in the particles of the nerves and brain, occafioned by the vigorous vibrations which accompany the fenfe of pain.

If it be admitted, as I think it muft be, that, for any thing that yet appears, vibrations in the brain may accompany and be the caufe of all our ideas, there remains only one property of ideas, or rather of the *mind* relating to them, to which if the doctrine of vibrations can be fuppofed to correfpond, the whole theory will be eftablifhed, and that is the *affociation of ideas*. For it will be feen that this fingle property comprehends all the other affections of our ideas, and thereby accounts for all the phenomena of the human mind, and what we ufually call its different *operations*, with refpect to fenfations and ideas of every kind.

Now if two different vibrations take place in the brain at the fame time, it cannot be but they will a little alter or modify one another, fo that the particles of the medullary fubftance will not vibrate precifely as they would have done if they had taken place feparately; but each of them will vibrate as acted upon by two impulfes at the fame time; and all the particles being acted upon in the fame manner, it neceffarily follows that, if from any caufe whatever, one of thefe vibrations fhall be excited, the other will be excited alfo, fo that the whole ftate of the brain will exactly refemble what it was before; and this feems to correfpond fufficiently to the recollection of one idea by means of another.

I do

xviii INTRODUCTORY.

I do not expect that this general view of the doctrine of vibrations will satisfy those who are accustomed to consider all matter in the most gross and general manner, as if it was subject to no laws but those of the five mechanical powers, which was a turn of thinking that prevailed very much about half a century ago; so that even physicians attempted to explain the nature of diseases, and the operation of medicines, by the mere forms and weight of the particles of the different solids and fluids, and the common laws of Hydrostatics.

But as this system has been abandoned, in consequence of our becoming acquainted with the more subtle and important laws of matter exhibited in chymical operations; so now that we see that the laws and affections of mere matter are infinitely more complex than we had imagined, we may, by this time, I should think, be prepared to admit the *possibility* of a mass of matter like the brain, having been formed by the almighty creator, with such exquisite powers, with respect to vibrations, as should be sufficient for all the purposes above-mentioned; though the particulars of its constitution, and mode of affection, may far exceed our comprehension. And it is only the bare *possibility* of the thing that I now contend for. Much light, however, has been thrown upon the *manner* of operation in a variety of particular cases by Dr. Hartley. And when the attention of philosophers shall have been sufficiently turned to the subject, in consequence of the *general scheme* appearing to deserve it, it, more light, I doubt not, will be thrown upon it, efpecially by thofe who are converfant in medical and anatomical inquiries.

It will ftagger fome perfons, that fo much of the bufinefs of thinking fhould be made to depend upon mere *matter*, as the doctrine of vibrations fuppofes. For, in fact, it leaves nothing to the province of any other principle, except the fimple power of *perception*; fo that if it were poffible that matter could be endued with this property, *immateriality*, as far as it has been fuppofed to belong to man, would be excluded altogether. But I do not know that this fuppofition need give any concern, except to thofe who maintain that a future life depends upon the immateriality of the human foul. It will not at all alarm thofe who found all their hopes of a future exiftence on the chriftian doctrine of *a refurrection from the dead.*

It has been the opinion of many philofophers, and among others of Mr. Locke; that for any thing that we know to the contrary, a capacity of thinking might be given to matter. Dr. Hartley, however, notwithftanding his hypothefis would be much helped by it, feems to think otherwife. He alfo fuppofes that there is an intermediate *elementary body* between the mind and the grofs body; which may exift, and be the inftrument of giving pleafure or pain to the fentient principle after death. But I own I fee no reafon why his fcheme fhould be burdened with fuch an incumbrance as this.

I am rather inclined to think that, though the subject is beyond our comprehension at present, man does not confift of two principles, fo effentially different from one another as *matter* and *fpirit*, which are always defcribed as having not one common property, by means of which they can affect or act upon each other; the one occupying fpace, and the other not only not occupying the leaft imaginable portion of fpace, but incapable of bearing relation to it; infomuch that, properly fpeaking, my mind is no more *in my body*, than it is in the moon. I rather think that the whole man is of fome *uniform compofition*, and that the property of *perception*, as well as the other powers that are termed *mental*, is the refult (whether neceffary or not) of fuch an organical ftructure as that of the brain. Confequently, that the whole man becomes extinct at death, and that we have no hope of furviving the grave but what is derived from the fcheme of revelation.

Our having recourfe to an *immaterial principle*, to account for perception and thought, is only faying in other words, that we do not know in what they confift; for no one will fay that he has any conception how the principle of thought can have any more relation to immateriality than to materiality.

This hypothefis is rather favourable to the notion of fuch organical fyftems as plants having fome degree of fenfation. But at this a benevolent mind will rather rejoice than repine. It alfo makes the lower

lower animals to differ from us in *degree* only, and not in *kind*, which is sufficiently agreeable to appearances; but does not necessarily draw after it the belief of their surviving death, as well as ourselves; this privilege being derived to us by a *positive constitution*, and depending upon the promise of God, communicated by express revelation to man.

ESSAY II.

A general view of the doctrine of Association *of ideas.*

PREVIOUS to the reading of the following treatise, the object of which is to deduce all the phenomena of thinking from the single principle of *Association*, it may not be unuseful to have a general view of the system; in which the principal outlines may be brought nearer together, and the whole seen at one view. This, therefore, I shall endeavour to do, and as succinctly as I can.

The mechanical association of ideas that has been frequently presented to the mind at the same time was, I believe, first noticed by Mr. Locke; but he had recourse to it only to explain those sympathies and antipathies which he calls *unnatural*, in opposition to those which, he says, are born with us; and he refers them to " trains of motion in
" the animal spirits," vol. 1, p. 367, " which once
" set a going continue in the same steps they have
" been used to, which, by after treading, are worn
" into a smooth path, and the motion in it becomes
" easy, and as it were natural. As far as we can
" comprehend thinking, thus ideas seem to be
" produced in our minds; or if they are not, this
" may serve to explain their following one another
" in an habitual train, when once they are put into
" that tract, as well as it does to explain such mo-
" tions

"tions of the body." This quotation is sufficient to show how exceedingly imperfect were Mr. Locke's notions concerning the nature, cause, and effects of this principle.

Afterwards Mr. Gay, a clergyman in the West of England, endeavoured to show the possibility of deducing all our passions and affections from association, in a dissertation prefixed to Bishop Law's translation of King's Origin of Evil. But he supposed the *love of happiness* to be an original and implanted principle, and that the passions and affections were deducible from only supposing sensible and rational creatures dependent upon each other for their happiness, p. 50. " Our appro-
" bation of morality, and all affections whatsoever,"
says he, p. 32, " are resolvable into reason, point-
" ing out private happiness, and are conversant
" only about things apprehended to be means
" tending to this end: and whenever this end is
" not perceived, they are to be accounted for from
" the association of ideas, and may properly
" enough be called habits. If this be clearly made
" out, the necessity of supposing a moral sense, or
" public affections, to be implanted in us (since
" it arises only from the insufficiency of all other
" schemes to account for human actions) will im-
" mediately vanish."

His observations, however, on this subject amount to little more than conjectures, and he saw so little into the doctrine of association, as not to be

INTRODUCTORY

aware that the doctrine of *neceffity* followed from it.

It was upon hearing of Mr. Gay's opinion, that Dr. Hartley turned his thoughts to the fubject; and at length, after giving the clofeft attention to it, in a courfe of feveral years, it appeared to him very probable, not only that all our *intellectual pleafures and pains*, but that all the phenomena of *memory, imagination, volition, reafoning*, and every other mental affection and operation, are only different modes, or cafes, of the affociation of ideas: fo that nothing is requifite to make any man whatever he is, but a fentient principle, with this fingle property (which however admits of great variety) and the influence of fuch circumftances as he has actually been expofed to.

The admirable fimplicity of this hypothefis ought certainly to recommend it to the attention of all philofophers, as, independant of other confiderations, it wears the face of that *fimplicity in caufes*, and *variety in effects*, which we difcover in every other part of nature.

> In human works, tho' laboured on with pain,
> A thoufand movements fcarce one purpofe gain;
> In God's, one fingle can its end produce;
> Yet ferves to fecond too fome other ufe.
> *Pope's Effay on Man.*

To the mere novice in philofophical inveftigations, it will appear impoffible to reduce all the variety

variety of *thinking* to fo fimple and uniform a procefs; but to the fame perfon it would alfo appear impoffible, *a priori*, that all the varieties of *language*, as fpoken by all the nations in the world, fhould be expreffed by means of a fhort alphabet. Alfo thofe phenomena in nature which depend upon gravity, electricity, &c. are no lefs various and complex; and the more we know of nature, the more particular facts, and particular laws, we are able to reduce to fimple and general laws: infomuch that now it does not appear impoffible, but that, ultimately, one great comprehenfive law fhall be found to govern both the material and intellectual world.

To fhow the poffibility of Dr. Hartley's theory of the mind, and at the fame time to give fuch an idea of it as may be ufeful to thofe who are about to enter upon the ftudy of it, I would obferve, that all the phenomena of the mind may be reduced to the faculties of *memory*, *judgment*, the *paffions*, and the *will*, to which may be added the power of *mufcular motion*.

Suppofing the human mind to have acquired a ftock of ideas, by means of the external fenfes, and that thefe ideas have been varioufly affociated together; fo that when one of them is prefent, it will introduce fuch others as it has the neareft connection with, and relation to, nothing more feems to be neceffary to explain the phenomena of *memory*.

memory. For we have no power of calling up any idea at pleasure, but only recollect such as have a connection, by means of former associations, with those that are at any time present to the mind. Thus the sight, or the idea, of any particular person, generally suggests the idea of his *name*, because they have been frequently associated together. If that fail to introduce the name, we are at a loss, and cannot recollect it at all, till some other associated circumstance help us. In naming a number of words in a sentence, or lines in a poem, the end of each preceding word being connected with the beginning of the succeeding one, we can easily repeat them in that order; but we are not able to repeat them backwards, till they have been frequently named in that contrary order. By this means, however, we acquire a facility of doing it, as may be found by the names of number from one to twenty.

In the wildest flights of *fancy*, it is probable that no single idea occurs to us but such as had a connection with some other impression or idea, previously existing in the mind; and what we call *new thoughts* are only new combinations, of old simple ideas, or decompositions of complex ones.

Judgment is nothing more than the perception of the universal concurrence, or the perfect coincidence of two ideas, or the want of that concurrence and coincidence, as *that milk is white*, that *twice two*

is

is four, or transferring the idea of *truth*, by affociation, from one propofition to another that refembles it.

When we fay that *Alexander conquered Darius*, we mean that the perfon whom we diftinguifh by the name of Alexander, is the fame with him that conquered Darius; and when we fay that *God is good*, we mean that the perfon whom we diftinguifh by the name of *God*, appears, by his works and conduct, to be poffeffed of the fame difpofition that we call *good*, or *benevolent*, in men. And having attained to the knowledge of *general truths*, the idea, or feeling, which accompanies the perception of truth, is transferred, by affociation, to all the particulars which are comprifed under it, and to other propofitions that are analogous to it; having found by experience, that when we have formed fuch conclufions we have not been deceived.

When we fay that any idea or circumftance excites a particular *paffion*, it is explained by obferving that certain feelings and emotions have been formerly connected with that particular idea or circumftance, which it has the power of recalling by affociation. Thus with refpect to the paffion of *fear* it is evident to obfervation that a child is unacquainted with any fuch thing, till it has received fome hurt; upon which the painful idea left in the mind by the remembrance of the hurt becomes affociated with the idea of the circumftances in which he
received

received the hurt, and by degrees with that circumstance only which is *essential* to it, and which he therefore considers as the proper *cause* of his hurt. If a variety of painful emotions, and disagreeable feelings, have been associated with the idea of the same circumstance, they will all be excited by it, in one general *complex emotion*, the component parts of which will not be easily distinguishable; and by their mutual associations they will, at length, entirely coalesce, so as never to be separately perceived.

A child has no fear of fire till he has been burnt by it, or of a dog till he has been bit by one, or without having had reason to think that a dog would bite him, and having some notion, from things of a similar nature, what the bite of a dog is. In like manner the passion of *love* is generated by the association of agreeable circumstances with the idea of the object that excites it. And all our other passions are only modifications of these general ones of *fear* or *love*, varying with the situation of the object of fear or love, with respect to us, as whether it be near or distant, expected or unexpected, &c.

According to this hypothesis all our passions are at first *interested*, respecting our own pleasures or pains; and this sufficiently agrees with our observation: and they become *disinterested* when these complex emotions are transferred by association to other persons or things. Thus the child loves his
nurse

nurfe or parent by connecting with the idea of them the various pleafures which he has received from them, or in their company; but having received the moft happinefs from them, or with them, when they themfelves were chearful and happy, he begins to defire their happinefs, and in time it becomes as much an object with him as his own proper happinefs.

The natural *progrefs* of a paffion may be moft diftinctly feen in that of the *love of money*, which is acquired fo late in life, that every ftep in the progrefs may be eafily traced. No perfon is born with the love of money, as fuch. A child is, indeed, pleafed with a piece of coin, as he is with other things, the form or the fplendor of which ftrikes his eye; but this is very different from that emotion which a man who has been accuftomed to the ufe of money, and has known the want of it, feels upon being prefented with a guinea, or a fhilling. This emotion is a very complex one, the component parts of which are indiftinguifhable; but which have all been feparately connected with the idea of money, and the ufes of it. For after a child has received the firft fpecies of pleafure from a piece of money, as a mere *play thing*, he receives additional pleafure from the poffeffion of it, by connecting with the idea of it, the idea of the various pleafures and advantages which it is able to procure him. And, in time, that complex idea of pleafure, which was originally formed from the

various

various pleasures which it was the means of procuring, is so intimately connected with the idea of money, that it becomes an object of a proper passion; so that men are capable of pursuing it without ever reflecting on any *use* that it may possibly be of to them.

A *volition* is a modification of the passion of *desire*, exclusive of any *tumultuous emotion* which the idea of a favourite object not possessed may excite; and it is generally followed by those actions with which that state of mind has been associated; in consequence of those actions having been found, by experience, to be instrumental in bringing the favourite object into our possession.

At first a child stretches out his hand, and performs the motion of *grasping*, without any particular intention, whenever the palm of his hand is irritated, or by any general stimulus, which puts the whole muscular system into motion. But play things, &c. being put into his hand, and it closing upon them, he learns, by degrees, to stretch forth his hand, as well as to grasp at any thing. At length the action becomes familiar, and is intimately associated with a sight of a favourite object; so that the moment it is perceived, the action of reaching and grasping immediately and mechanically succeed. Any person who has been accustomed to observe the actions of children must have frequently seen all the steps of this process;

and

and in a fimilar manner it may be conceived that we learn to procure the gratification of all our defires.

There is nothing that has more the appearance of *inflinct* than the motions of particular mufcles in certain circumftances; and yet I will venture to fay that there is hardly one of them that Dr. Hartley has not in a manner demonftrated to have been originally *automatic;* the mufcles being firft forced to contract involuntarily, and becoming afterwards affociated with the idea of the circumftance, fo that the one immediately and mechanically follows the other.

What can be more inftantaneous, and have more the appearance of inftinct, than the endeavour of all animals to recover the *equilibrium* of their bodies, when they are in danger of falling; and yet I am confident, from my own obfervations, that children have it not, but acquire it gradually, and flowly: The fame is the cafe of the action of *fucking,* and the *motion of the eye lids* when any thing approaches the eye. This affociation, however, grows fo firm in a courfe of time, that it is hardly poffible to counteract it by the moft determined refolution when we are grown up; though you may bring any thing ever fo near, and ever fo fuddenly to the eye of a young child, when it is moft perfectly awake, without exciting any motion in the eye lids.

INTRODUCTORY

Who can help admiring the admirable simplicity of nature, and the wisdom of the great author of it, in this provision for the *growth of all our passions*, and propensities, just as they are wanted, and in the degree in which they are wanted through life? All is performed by the general disposition of the mind to conform to its circumstances, and to be modified by them, without that seemingly operose and inelegant contrivance, of different original, independent instincts, adapted to a thousand different occasions, and either implanted in us at different times, or contrived to lie dormant till they are wanted. Certainly there is nothing in the general view of this system that can recommend it to a philosopher, who has been used to the contemplation of a very different kind of system in other parts of nature, which have the same author.

ESSAY

ESSAY III.

Of complex and abstract Ideas.

BESIDES the simple *ideas of sensation*, as Mr. Locke calls those impressions which are made upon the mind by external objects affecting the senses, as those of *colour, sound, taste,* &c. there are others which he calls *ideas of reflection*, as those belonging to the words *mind, thought, judgment, power, duration, space,* &c. These he supposes we get by reflecting on the operations of our own minds; and that though sensible ideas may give occasion to them, they do not properly *constitute* them. On the other hand Dr. Hartley supposes that our external senses furnish the materials of all the ideas of which we are ever possessed, and that those which Mr. Locke calls ideas of reflection, are only ideas of so very complex a nature, and borrowed from so many ideas of sense, that their origin cannot be easily traced. And indeed, on the first view of them, it is not very easy to conceive how they can be composed of sensible ideas.

To lessen this difficulty a little, let it be considered how exceedingly different, to the *eye of the mind*, as we may say, are our ideas of sensible things from any thing that could have been conjectured concerning their effect upon us; as the ideas of *sound*, from the tremulous motion of the particles of the air, and much more the ideas of the different *colours* from the impulfe of rays of light of different degrees of refrangibility; and what comes rather nearer to the cafe before us, how very different an effect has the *mixture* of feveral colours from what we could have fuppofed *a priori*. What refemblance is there between *white*, and the mixture of the feven primary colours, of which it confifts, all of which are fo different from it, and from one another? What power of intellect could analize that impreffion into its conftituent parts, by attending to the *idea* only, without making thofe *experiments* which led Sir Ifaac Newton to that capital difcovery? Nay a perfon not acquainted with optics can hardly be made to believe but that *black* is as much a pofitive colour as *red, or white*. In like manner, from the combination of ideas, and efpecially very diffimilar ones, there may refult ideas, which, to appearance, fhall be fo different from the parts of which they really confift, that they fhall no more be capable of being analized by *mental reflection* than the idea of *white*.

So exquifite is the ftructure of our minds, that a whole group of ideas fhall fo perfectly coalefce into one, as to appear but a fimple idea; and fingle words may be fo connected with fuch groups, as to excite them with the fame certainty and diftinctnefs, as if they had been originally fimple fenfations.

How complex, for inftance, are the ideas expreffed by the terms which denote the different
employ-

employments, offices, and *profeffions* among men, as thofe of *king, merchant, player, lawyer, preacher,* &c. or thofe which denote various *games,* as *cricket, whift, piquet,* &c. The ideas annexed to thefe terms muft be an epitome of the *definitions* of them; and if they be acquired without definitions, by means of a feries of *obfervations,* the ideas will be ftill more complex.

Let a child be introduced to the theatre, and fee a company of perfons from time to time in a great variety of characters, and let him be told that he muft call them *players.* That word will excite an epitome, as it were, of all that he has feen them perform; and if he attend to that complex idea, even the features, and moft ftriking geftures of the principal performers will be confpicuous in it; and by degrees, as all thefe particulars get intermixed, and completely affociated, whatever belonged to the feparate perfons will be dropped, and something will remain annexed to the term, when it is explained with due precifion, that had been obferved in them all.

This is the procefs that is called *abftraction*; and it is by means of this procefs, chiefly, that we acquire thofe ideas which have been referred to *reflection*; their deduction from fenfible ideas being too remote and obfcure to be apparent, or fo much as fufpected, at firft fight.

In the fame manner in which we get the idea which we have annexed to the word *player, mer-*

chant, *king*, &c. which are at first exceedingly complex, we get the idea that we have to the word *thought*, or *thinking*; which, in fact, is an abridgment, or coalescence, of the various external signs or marks, and also of the internal feelings, by which (exclusive of the general outward form) a man is distinguished from a brute animal.

If we only consider that short and simple process by which we get the idea of *white* or *whiteness*, namely, by leaving out what is particular in all the objects which we have seen of that colour, and restricting the meaning of the term to what is common to them all, we shall not be at a loss for the manner in which we come by such ideas as are denoted by the words *substance*, *space*, *duration*, *identity*, *reality*, *possibility*, *necessity*, *contingency*, &c. for these only express those *circumstances*, in which a great variety of particular things, all originally the objects of our senses, agree; the peculiarities in each being overlooked.

In like manner the idea of *power* seems at first sight, to be a very simple one; but it is in fact, exceedingly complex. A child pushes at an obstacle, it gives way. He wishes to walk, or run, and finds that he can do it whenever he pleases. In like manner he practises a variety of other bodily and mental exercises, in which he finds that it only *depends upon himself*, whether he performs them or not; and at length he calls that general feeling, which is the result of a thousand different impressions,

by

by the name of *power*. He sees other persons perform the same things with himself, and therefore he says that they have the same power that he has; and other persons doing different things, gives him the idea of *different powers*, or *faculties*. Even inanimate things have certain invariable *effects*, when applied in a particular manner. Thus a rope sustains a weight, a magnet attracts iron, a charged electrical jar gives a shock, &c. From these, and other similar observations, we get the idea of *power, universally and abstractedly considered*; so that, in fact, the idea of power is acquired by the very same mental process by which we acquire the idea of any other property belonging to a number of bodies, viz. by leaving out what is peculiar to each, and appropriating the term to that particular circumstance, or appearance, in which they all agree.

An excellent and truly valuable writer has pitched upon the idea of *solidity*, or *impenetrability*, as what could not be deduced from *sense*, but must have its origin in the *understanding*; because " we " have had no actual experience of real impenetra" bility; since all the observations and experiments, " which we have hitherto made on bodies, may be " accounted for without that supposition." See *Dr. Price's Review of the principal questions in morals*, p. 23.

But it is obvious to remark, that the opinion of the impenetrability of matter, and the ideas belonging to it, are generated before the discovery of any fallacy in the case is made. What a child, or rather a boy, means by *impenetrability* may easily be supposed to arise from the impression that will be left upon his mind by pressing against any body that does not give way to him, and by frequently observing bodies impinging against one another, and changing places, without ever coalescing into one; except when several bodies unite to form a larger, or without some of them being received into the supposed interstices of others. And we see, in the case of Father Boscovich, and Mr. Michell, that the very idea of the proper impenetrability of matter may be disputed.

I can see no more difficulty in the idea of the *vis inertiæ* of matter, or of its *resistance* and *inactivity*. For though "we never saw any portion of matter " void of gravity, or other active powers" p. 26, it is as easy as any other process of abstraction, to leave out the idea of those powers, in the contemplation of matter; and then, judging from universal experience, we cannot possibly have any idea of a *change* either of rest or motion, with respect to it, without something external acting upon it. The phenomena of a billiard table only cannot but impress the mind in this manner. We there see balls at rest beginning to move, or change their direction in motion, by other balls impinging upon them; but never saw an instance of a ball beginning to move of itself. As the table is level, the idea of *gravity*, or of a tendency to move downwards, is easily excluded.

To

ESSAYS.

To account for the idea of *time*, it appears to me to be sufficient to attend to a few well known facts, viz. that impressions made by external objects remain a certain space of time in the mind, that this time is different according to the strength, and other circumstances of the impression, and that traces of these impressions, i. e. *ideas*, may be recalled after the intervention of other trains of ideas, and at very different intervals. If I look upon a house, and then shut my eyes, the impression it has made upon my mind does not immediately vanish; I can contemplate the idea of the house as long as I please; and also, by the help of a variety of associated circumstances, the idea of the house may be recalled several years afterwards.

Now do not these facts, and thousands of the same kind, necessarily give the ideas of *duration* and *succession*, which are the elements of our idea of *time*. If all our sensations and ideas where wholly obliterated the moment that an external object was withdrawn, there could be no ideas of duration and succession; because there could be no opportunity of *comparing* our ideas; but upon the contrary supposition (which is well known to be the truth) the ideas of *succession, duration,* and *time,* are necessarily generated; that is, states of mind are produced, to which those names (or any others synonymous to them) may be applied. The ideas of succession, duration, and time, are no more than other *ideas of reflection,* those terms expressing actual varieties in our

our *mental feelings*, occasioned by the impression of external objects.

I have very carefully considered all the other ideas mentioned by Dr. Price, but I own I can see no reason for having recourse to any thing besides mere sensation, and the restriction of the use of terms to any part of a sensible idea, or to a circumstance relating to it, in order to account for them.

He says indeed, p. 37, that " our abstract ideas
" seem most properly to belong to the under-
" standing. They are undoubtedly essential to all
" its operations, every act of judging implying
" some abstract or universal idea. Were they for-
" med by the mind, in the manner generally repre-
" sented, it seems unavoidable to concieve that it
" has them at the very time that it is supposed to
" be employed in forming them. Thus from any
" particular idea of a *Triangle*, it is said we can
" frame the general one, but does not the very re-
" flection said to be necessary to this, on a greater
" or a lesser triangle, imply that the general idea
" is already in the mind. How else should it
" know how to go to work, or what to reflect on?"

It is true that a person whose ideas have long been formed cannot name any particular triangle, as an *equilateral*, or *isosceles triangle*, but, by distinguishing it in this manner from other triangles, he will discover that he is possessed of the abstract idea of a triangle; but this was not the case when the idea

idea was formed. Originally the mind of a child is impreſſed with the idea of ſome particular triangle, at which time the word *triangle*, if he ſhould be taught to call it by that name, would ſuggeſt nothing more than a figure of that very form and ſize which he had ſeen. Afterwards he ſees other figures, bounded as that was by *three right lines*; and being taught to call theſe *triangles*, likewiſe, he then, and not before, abſtracts from his former idea of a triangle whatever was peculiar to the firſt that he happened to ſee; and he appropriates the term to the circumſtances which they have in common. Then alſo, and not before, in talking of different kinds of triangles, he ſhews that he has an idea of what a *triangle in general* is, that is, what the ſtrict *definition* of it is: for ſtill all the ideas of triangles that he actually contemplates, are ideas of particular triangles, but variable, and indefinite. ———To proceed to the conſideration of ſome complex ideas which have the apearance of being ſimple ones.

Every perſon, I believe, feels a gleam of pleaſure the moment that light is introduced into a dark room, and diſagreeable ſenſations tending to melancholy, and ſometimes verging towards the borders of terror, upon paſſing ſuddenly from a light into a perfectly dark place. Theſe feelings are inſtantaneous and conſtant, and to appearance *ſimple*, yet they are, unqueſtionably, the offspring of aſſociation; but formed by a thouſand ſenſations and ideas, which it is impoſſible to ſeparate or analize; and

and they vary exceedingly in different perſons, eſpecially according to the circumſtances of their early lives.

The ideas annexed to the words *moral right* and *wrong* are, likewiſe, far from being ſimple in reality, though the aſſociation of their parts has become ſo intimate and perfect, in a long courſe of time, that, upon firſt naming them, they preſent that appearance. So the motion of the head, or of any particular limb, may ſeem to be a very ſimple thing, though a great number of muſcles are employed to perform it.

The firſt rudiments of the ideas of *right, wrong*, and *obligation*, ſeem to be acquired by a child when he finds himſelf checked and controuled by a ſuperior power. At firſt he feels nothing but mere *force*, and conſequently he has no idea of any kind of reſtraint but that of mere *neceſſity*. He finds he cannot have his will, and therefore he ſubmits. Afterwards he attends to many circumſtances which diſtinguiſh the authority of a *father*, or of a *maſter*, from that of other perſons. Ideas of *reverence, love, eſteem* and *dependence*, accompany thoſe commands; and by degrees he experiences the peculiar *advantages* of filial ſubjection. He ſees alſo that all his companions, who are noticed and admired by others, obey their parents, and that thoſe who are of a refractory diſpoſition are univerſally diſliked.

Theſe

ESSAYS.

These and other circumstances, now begin to alter and *modify* the idea of mere *necessity*, till by degrees he considers the commands of a parent as something that *must not* be resisted or disputed, even though he has a power of doing it; and all these ideas coalescing form the ideas of *moral right*, and *moral obligation*, which are easily transferred from the commands of a parent to those of a magistrate, of God, and of conscience. I will venture to say that any person who has attended to the ideas of children, may perceive that the ideas of moral right and moral obligation are formed very gradually and slowly, from a long train of circumstances; and that it is a considerable time before they become at all distinct and perfect.

This opinion of the gradual formation of the ideas of moral right and wrong, from a great variety of elements, easily accounts for that prodigious diversity in the sentiments of mankind respecting the objects of moral obligation; and I do not see that any other hypothesis can account for the facts. If the idea of *moral obligation* was a *simple idea*, arising from the view of certain actions, or sentiments, I do not see why it should not be as *invariable* as the perception of colours or sounds. But though the shape and colour of a flower appear the same to every human eye, one man practices as a moral duty what another looks upon with abhorrence, and reflects upon with remorse. Now a thing that varies with education and instruction as moral sentiments are known to do, certainly has the

appear-

INTRODUCTORY

appearance of being generated by a series of different impressions, in some such manner as I have endeavoured to describe.

The most shocking crimes that men can commit are those of *injustice* and *murder*, and yet it is hardly possible to define any circumstances, in which some part of mankind have not, without the least scruple or remorse, seized the property, or taken away the lives of others, so that the definition of these crimes must vary in almost every country. Now an idea, or feeling, that depends upon arbitrary definition cannot be, properly speaking, natural, but must be factitious.

A crime the least liable to variation in its definition is that of a *lie*, and yet I will venture to say that a child will, upon the slightest temptation, tell an untruth as readily as the truth; that is, as soon as he can suspect that it will be to his advantage; and the dread that he afterwards has of telling a lie is acquired principally by his being threatened, punished, and terrified by those who detect him in it; till at length, a number of painful impressions are annexed to the telling of an untruth, and he comes even to shudder at the thought of it. But where this care has not been taken, such a facility in telling lies, and such an indifference to truth are acquired, as is hardly credible to persons who have been differently educated.

I was myself educated so strictly and properly, that the hearing of the slightest oath, or irreverent use of the name of God, gives me a sensation that is more than mental. It is next to shuddering, and thousands, I doubt not, feel the same; whereas other persons, and men of strict virtue and honour in other respects, I am confident, from my own observation, feel not the least moral impropriety in the greatest possible profaneness of speech. But by a different education I might have been as profane as they, and without remorse; and (with the same sensibility to impressions in general, though equally indifferent to them all) my education would have given them my exquisite sensibility in this respect. Now no principle conceived to be *innate*, or natural, can operate more certainly, or more mechanically, than this which I know to have been acquired, with respect to myself. But without reflection and observation, and judging by my own *present feelings*, I should have concluded, without the least apprehension of being mistaken, that the *dread of an oath*, had been natural, and invariable, in mankind.

But whether the feelings which accompany the ideas of virtue and vice be instinctive, or acquired, their *operation* is the very same; so that the interests of virtue may be equally secured on this scheme as on any other. There is sufficient provision in the course of our lives to generate moral principles, sentiments, and feelings, in the degree in which they are wanted in life, and with those variations,

with

INTRODUCTORY

with refpect to modes and other circumftances, which we fee in different ages and countries; and which the different circumftances of mankind, in different ages and countries, feem to require.

THE

THE
AUTHOR's PREFACE.

THE *work here offered to the public confifts of papers written at different times, but taking their rife from the following occafion.*
About eighteen years ago I was informed, that the Rev. Mr. Gay, *then living, afferted the poffibility of deducing all our intellectual pleafures and pains from affociation. This put me upon confidering the power of affociation. Mr.* Gay *publifhed his fentiments on this matter, about the fame time, in a differtation on the fundamental principle of virtue, prefixed to Mr. Archdeacon* Law's *tranflation of Archbifhop* King's *Origin of Evil.*
From inquiring into the power of affociation I was led to examine both its confequences, in refpect of morality and religion, and its phyfical caufe. By degrees many difquifitions foreign to the doctrine of affociation, or at leaft not immediately connected with it, intermixed themfelves. I have here put together all my feparate papers on thefe fubjects, digefting them in fuch order as they feemed naturally to fuggeft; and adding fuch things as were neceffary to make the whole appear more complete and fyftematical.
I think, however, that I cannot be called a fyftem-maker, fince I did not firft form a fyftem, and then fuit the

THE PREFACE.

the facts to it, but was carried on by a train of thoughts from one thing to another, frequently without any express design, or even any previous suspicion of the consequences that might arise. And this was most remarkably the case, in respect of the doctrine of Necessity; for I was not at all aware, that it followed from that of association, for several years after I had begun my inquiries; nor did I admit it at last without the greatest reluctance.

There is one thing in these papers which requires a particular apology, viz. the imperfect state in which they are presented to the reader.

But if the reader will be so favourable to me as to expect nothing more than hints and conjectures in difficult and obscure matters, and a short detail of the principal reasons and evidences in those that are clear, I hope he will not be much disappointed. However, be this as it will, I have in one part or other of these papers alledged all that I know material, in support of my system; and therefore am now desirous to recommend it to the consideration of others.

I have tried to reconcile such inconsistencies, real or apparent, and to cut off such repetitions and redundancies, as have arisen from my writing the separate parts of this work at different times, and in different situations of mind. But I have still need of great indulgence from the reader on these and other accounts.

Some persons may perhaps think, that I ought not to have delivered my opinion so freely and openly, concerning the necessity of human actions, and the ultimate happiness of all mankind; but have left the reader to deduce these consequences or not, as should appear most reasonable to him. But this would, in my opinion, have been a disingenuous procedure. Besides, these tenets appear to me not only innocent, but even highly conducive to the promotion of piety and virtue amongst mankind. However, that no one may misapprehend me to his own hurt, I will here make two remarks by way of anticipation.

First,

THE PREFACE.

First, then, I no where deny practical free-will, or that voluntary power over our affections and actions, by which we deliberate, suspend, and choose, and which makes an essential part of our ideas of virtue and vice, reward and punishment; but, on the contrary, establish it (if so plain a thing will admit of being farther established) by shewing in what manner it results from the frame of our natures.

Secondly, I do most firmly believe, upon the authority of the scriptures, that the future punishment of the wicked will be exceedingly great both in degree and duration, i. e. infinite and eternal, in that real practical sense to which alone our conceptions extend. And were I able to urge any thing upon a profane careless world, which might convince them of the infinite hazard to which they expose themselves, I would not fail to do it, as the reader may judge even from those passages for which I have above apologized.

December, 1748.

THE CONTENTS
OF THE
FIRST PART.

INTRODUCTION.

*D*Efinitions, 1. *Distribution of the first part,*
Page 4.

CHAP. I.

Of the general laws according to which the senfations and motions are performed, and our ideas generated.

The doctrines of vibrations and affociation propofed, 5. *Their mutual connexion.*

SECT. I.

Of the doctrine of vibrations, and its ufe for explaining the fenfations.

General evidences for the dependence of fenfation and motion on the brain, 7. *General evidences for the dependence of ideas on the brain,* 8. *Inftances fhewing that*

that sensations remain in the mind for a short time after the sensible objects are removed, 9. The infinitesimal medullary particles vibrate during sensation. Of the æther. Of the uniformity, continuity, softness, and active powers of the medullary substance. Of the manner in which vibrations are communicated to the whole medullary substance. Presumptions in favour of the doctrine of vibrations. Corollaries from this doctrine. Materiality of the soul no consequence of it. Phænomena of sensible pleasure and pain agreeable to the doctrine of vibrations. Phænomena of sleep agreeable to the doctrine of vibrations.

SECT. II.

Of ideas, their generation and associations, and of the agreement of the doctrine of vibrations with the phænomena of ideas.

Of the generation of the ideas of sensation, 12. The repetition of sensory vibrations generates a disposition to corresponding vibratiuncles or miniature vibrations. *Of the power of raising ideas by association in the simplest case,* 14. Of the power of raising miniature vibrations by association in the simplest case. *Of the formation of complex ideas by association,* 17. Of the formation of complex miniature vibrations by association. *The complex vibrations last-mentioned may be so exalted in some cases, as to be no longer miniatures, but equal in strength to sensory vibrations,* 24.

SECT.

the FIRST PART.

SECT. III.

Of muscular motion, and its two kinds, automatic and voluntary; and of the use of the doctrines of vibrations and association, for explaining these respectively.

It is probable, that muscular motion is performed by the same general means as sensation, and the perception of ideas, 29. Phænomena of muscular contraction agreeable to the doctrine of vibrations. Propensity of the muscles to alternate contraction and relaxation agreeable to the doctrine of vibrations. The origin of motory vibrations. The general method of explaining the automatic motions by the doctrine of vibrations. The generation and association of motory vibratiuncles. *The general method of explaining the voluntary and semivoluntary motions,* 30. *Of the manner in which the endeavour to obtain pleasure, and remove pain, is generated,* 40.

CHAP. II.

Containing the application of the doctrines of vibrations and association to each of the sensations and motions in particular.

SECT. I.

Of the sense of feeling.

Of the several kinds of feeling, and the general causes of the different degrees of exquisiteness in this sense. An inquiry how far the sensations of heat and cold are agreeable to the doctrine of vibrations. An

inquiry

liv *The* CONTENTS *of*

inquiry how far the phænomena of wounds, burns, bruises, lacerations, inflammations, and ulcers, are agreeable to the doctrine of vibrations. An inquiry how far the phænomena of itching and titillation are agreeable to the doctrine of vibrations. An inquiry how far the senfations attending preffure, and muscular contraction, are agreeable to the doctrine of vibrations. An inquiry how far the phænomena of numbneffes, and paralytical infenfibilities, are agreeable to the doctrine of vibrations. An inquiry how far the phænomena of venomous bites and ftings are agreeable to the doctrine of vibrations. An inquiry how far the tangible qualities of bodies admit of an explanation agreeable to the doctrine of vibrations. *Of the manner in which we are enabled to judge of the feat of impreffions made on the external furface of our bodies,* 43. *Of the manner and degree in which we are enabled to judge of the feat of internal pains,* 45. *Of the manner and degree in which the pleafures and pains of feeling contribute, according to the doctrine of affociation, to the formation of our intellectual pleafures and pains,* 48. *Of the ideas generated by tangible impreffions,* 50. Of the automatic motions, which arife from tangible impreffions. Of the manner and degree in which thefe automatic motions are influenced by voluntary and femivoluntary powers.

SECT. II.

Of the fenfe of tafte

Of the extent of the organ of tafte, and the different powers lodged in the different parts of it. An inquiry how far the phænomena of taftes, and their fpecific differences, are agreable to the doctrine of vibrations. An inquiry how far the feveral fenfations which affect the ftomach and bowels, are agreeable to the doctrine of vibrations. An inquiry how far the

the phænomena of hunger are agreeable to the doctrine of vibrations. An inquiry how far the phænomena of thirst are agreeable to the doctrine of vibrations. *An inquiry how far the changes, generally made in the taste, in passing from infancy to old age, are agreeable to the doctrines of vibrations and association,* 53. An inquiry how far the longings of pregnant women are agreeable to the doctrines of vibrations and association. *Of the manner and degree in which the pleasures and pains of taste contribute, according to the doctrine of association, to the formation of our intellectual pleasures and pains,* 56. *Of the ideas generated by the several tastes,* 57. Of the automatic motions which arise from the impressions made on the organ of taste. Of the manner and degree in which these automatic motions are influenced by voluntary and semivoluntary powers.

SECT. III.
Of the sense of smell.

Of the extent and powers of the organ of smell. An inquiry how far the general phænomena of smell are agreeable to the doctrine of vibrations. An inquiry how far the specific differences of odours are agreeable to the doctrines of vibrations. *Of the manner and degree in which pleasant and unpleasant odours contribute, according to the doctrine of association, to the formation of our intellectual pleasures and pains,* 59. *Of the ideas generated by the several odours,* 60. Of the automatic motions which arise from the impressions made on the organ of smell. Of the manner and degree in which these automatic motions are influenced by voluntary and semivoluntary powers.

The CONTENTS of

SECT. IV.

Of the sense of sight.

Of the immediate organ of sight, and its powers. An inquiry how far the phænomena of colours are agreeable to the doctrine of vibrations. An inquiry how far flashes of light from strokes in the eye, dark spots, and giddiness, are agreeable to the doctrine of vibrations. An inquiry how far the judgments made by sight, concerning magnitude, distance, motion, figure, and position, are agreeable to the doctrine of association, 61. *An inquiry how far the phænomena of single and double vision are agreeable to the doctrine of association,* 66. *Of the manner and degree in which agreeable and disagreeable impressions made on the eye contribute, according to the doctrine of association, to the formation of our intellectual pleasures and pains,* 69. *Of the ideas generated by visible impressions,* 70. *Of the automatic motions which are excited by impressions made on the eye. Of the manner and degree in which these automatic motions are influenced by voluntary and semivoluntary powers.*

SECT. V.

Of the sense of hearing.

Of the immediate organ of hearing, and the general uses of the several parts of the external and internal ear. An inquiry how far the phænomena of musical and other inarticulate sounds are agreeable to the doctrine of vibrations. An inquiry how far the judgments, which we make concerning the distance and position of the sounding body, are agreeable to the doctrine of association, 77. *An inquiry how far the power of distinguishing articulate sounds depends upon association,* 78. *The doctrine of sounds illustrates and favours that of*
the

the vibrations of the small medullary particles. *Of the manner and degree in which agreeable and disagreeable sounds contribute, according to the doctrine of association, to the formation of our intellectual pleasures and pains,* 81. *Of the ideas generated by audible impressions,* 82. Of the automatic motions excited by impressions made on the ear. Of the manner and degree in which these automatic motions are influenced by voluntary and semivoluntary powers.

SECT. VI.

Of the desires of the sexes towards each other.

An inquiry how far the desires of the sexes towards each other are of a factitious nature, and agreeable to the theory of these papers, 86.

SECT. VII.

Of other motions, automatic and voluntary, not considered in the foregoing sections of this chapter.

An inquiry how far the motions of the heart, ordinary and extraordinary, are agreeable to the foregoing theory. An inquiry how far the action of respiration, with those of sighing, coughing, &c. are agreeable to the foregoing theory. An inquiry how far convulsive motions are agreeable to the foregoing theory. *An inquiry how far the actions of walking, handling, and speaking, are agreeable to the foregoing theory,* 90.

SECT.

SECT. VIII.

Of the relation which the foregoing theory bears to the art of phyfic.

The art of phyfic affords many proper tefts of the doctrines of vibrations and affociation; and may receive confiderable improvement from them, if they be true, 98.

CHAP. III.

Containing a particular application of the foregoing theory to the phænomena of Ideas, or of underftanding, affection, memory, and imagination.

SECT. I.

Of words, and the ideas affociated with them.

Words and phrafes muft excite ideas in us by affociation; and they excite ideas in us by no other means, 102. *Of the manner in which ideas are affociated with words,* 104. *Confequences of this affociation of ideas with words,* 111. *Of the nature of characters intended to reprefent objects and ideas immediately, and without the intervention of words,* 123. *Of the ufe of the foregoing theory for explaining the nature of figurative words and phrafes, and of analogy,* 125. *Of the ufe of the foregoing theory for explaining the languages and method of writing of the firft ages of the world,* 131. *Of the general nature of a philofophical language; with fhort hints*

con-

the FIRST PART, lix

concerning the methods in which one might be conſtructed, 149. *An illuſtration and confirmation of the general doctrine of aſſociation, taken from the particular aſſociations which take place in reſpect of language,* 152. *Illuſtrations from muſical ſounds, colours, and taſtes,* 155.

SECT. II.

Of propoſitions, and the nature of aſſent.

Of the nature of aſſent and diſſent, and the cauſes from which they ariſe, 158. *Rules for the aſcertainment of truth, and advancement of knowledge, drawn from the mathematical methods of conſidering quantity,* 169. *A general application of the theory of this and the foregoing ſection to the ſeveral branches of ſcience,* 187.

SECT. III.

Of the affections in general.

Of the origin and nature of the paſſions in general, 202.

SECT. IV.

Of memory.

An inquiry how far the phænomena of memory are agreeable to the foregoing theory, 208.

SECT. V.

Of imagination, reveries, and dreams.

An inquiry how far the phænomena of imagination, reveries, and dreams, are agreeable to the foregoing theory, 217.

SECT.

The CONTENTS of

SECT. VI.

Of imperfections in the rational faculty.

An inquiry how far deviations from sound reason, and alienations of the mind, are agreeable to the foregoing theory, 224.

SECT. VII.

Of the intellectual faculties of brutes.

An inquiry how far the inferiority of brutes to mankind, in intellectual capacities, is agreeable to the foregoing theory, 238.

CHAP. IV.

Of the six classes of intellectual pleasures, 250.

SECT. I.

Of the pleasures and pains of imagination.

An inquiry how far the pleasures and pains of imagination are agreeable to the foregoing theory, 252.

SECT. II.

Of the pleasures and pains of ambition.

An inquiry how far the pleasures and pains of ambition are agreeable to the foregoing theory, 277.

SECT.

The FIRST PART.　　　lxi

SECT. III.

Of the pleasures and pains of self-intereſt.

An inquiry how far the pleaſures and pains of ſelf-intereſt are agreeable to the foregoing theory, 292.

SECT. IV.

Of the pleaſures and pains of ſympathy.

An inquiry how far the pleaſures and pains of ſympathy are agreeable to the foregoing theory, 305.

SECT. V.

Of the pleaſures and pains of theopathy.

An inquiry how far the pleaſures and pains of theopathy are agreeable to the foregoing theory, 320.

SECT. VI.

Of the pleaſures and pains of the moral ſenſe.

An inquiry how far the pleaſures and pains of the moral ſenſe are agreeable to the foregoing theory, 327.

CONCLUSION.

Containing ſome remarks on the mechaniſm of the human mind, 334.

CHAP.

CHAP. V.

A view of the doctrine of philosophical necessity.

SECT. I.

General remarks on the mechanism of the human mind, 334.

SECT. II.

Religion presupposes free-will in the popular and practical sense; i. e. it presupposes a voluntary power over our affections and actions, 347.

SECT. III.

Religion does not presuppose free-will in the philosophical sense, i. e. it does not presuppose a power of doing different things, the previous circumstances remaining the same, 350.

SECT. IV.

The natural attributes of God, or his infinite power and knowledge, exclude the possibility of free-will, in the philosophical sense, 361.

SECT. V.

On the practical application of the doctrine of necessity, 365.

The Conclusion, 368.

OBSERVATIONS ON MAN, &c.

INTRODUCTION.

MAN confifts of two parts, body and mind. The firft is fubjected to our fenfes and inquiries, in the fame manner as the other parts of the external material world.

The laft is that fubftance, agent, principle, &c. to which we refer the fenfations, ideas, pleafures, pains, and voluntary motions.

Senfations are thofe internal feelings of the mind, which arife from the impreffions made by external objects upon the feveral parts of our bodies.

All our other internal feelings may be called *ideas*. Some of thefe appear to fpring up in the mind of themfelves, fome are fuggefted by words, others arife in other ways. Many writers comprehend *fenfations* under *ideas*; but I every-where ufe thefe words in the fenfes here afcribed to them.

The ideas which refemble fenfations, are called *ideas of fenfation:* All the reft may therefore be called *intellectual ideas.*

INTRODUCTION.

It will appear in the course of these observations, that the *ideas of sensation* are the elements of which all the rest are compounded. Hence *ideas of sensation* may be termed *simple*, *intellectual* ones *complex*.

The *pleasures* and *pains* are comprehended under the sensations and ideas, as these are explained above. For all our pleasures and pains are internal feelings, and, conversely, all our internal feelings seem to be attended with some degree either of *pleasure* or *pain*. However, I shall, for the most part, give the names of *pleasure* and *pain* only to such degrees as are considerable; referring all low, evanescent ones to the head of *mere sensations* and *ideas*.

The pleasures and pains may be ranged under seven general classes; viz.

1. Sensation;
2. Imagination;
3. Ambition;
4. Self-interest;
5. Sympathy;
6. Theopathy; and,
7. The moral sense; according as they arise from,

1. The impressions made on the external senses;
2. Natural or artificial beauty or deformity;
3. The opinions of others concerning us;
4. Our possession or want of the means of happiness, and security from, or subjection to, the hazards of misery;
5. The pleasures and pains of our fellow-creatures;
6. The affections excited in us by the contemplation of the deity; or,
7. Moral beauty and deformity.

The human mind may also be considered as indued with the faculties of *memory*, *imagination* or *fancy*, *understanding*, *affection*, and *will*.

Memory is that faculty, by which traces of sensations

tions and ideas recur, or are recalled, in the same order and proportion, accurately or nearly, as they were once actually prefented.

When ideas, and trains of ideas, occur, or are called up, in a vivid manner, and without regard to the order of former actual impreffions and perceptions, this is faid to be done by the power of *imagination* or *fancy*.

The *underftanding* is that faculty, by which we contemplate mere fenfations and ideas, purfue truth, and affent to, or diffent from, propofitions.

The *affections* have the pleafures and pains for their objects; as the *underftanding* has the mere fenfations and ideas. By the affections we are excited to purfue happinefs, and all its means, fly from mifery, and all its apparent caufes.

The *will* is that ftate of mind, which is immediately previous to, and caufes, thofe exprefs acts of memory, fancy, and bodily motion, which are termed *voluntary*,

The *motions* of the body are of two kinds, *automatic* and *voluntary*. The *automatic* motions are thofe which arife from the mechanifm of the body in an evident manner. They are called *automatic*, from their refemblance to the motions of *automata*, or machines, whofe principle of motion is within themfelves. Of this kind are the motion of the heart, and periftaltic motion of the bowels. The *voluntary motions* are thofe which arife from ideas and affections, and which therefore are referred to the mind; the immediately preceding ftate of the mind, or of the ideas and affections, being termed *will*, as noted in the laft article. Such are the actions of walking, handling, fpeaking, &c. when attended to, and performed with an exprefs defign.

This may ferve as a fhort account of the chief fubjects confidered in the firft part of thefe *obfervations*. Thefe fubjects are fo much involved in each other, that it is difficult, or even impossible, to begin any-where upon clear ground, or so as to proceed intirely from the *data* to the *quæsita*, from things known to such as are unknown.. I will endeavour it as much as I can, and for that purpose shall observe the following order.

First, I shall lay down the general laws, according to which the sensations and motions are performed, and our ideas generated.

Secondly, I shall consider each of the sensations and motions in particular, and inquire how far the phænomena of each illustrate, and are illustrated by, the foregoing general laws.

Thirdly, I shall proceed in like manner to the particular phænomena of ideas, or of understanding, affection, memory, and imagination; applying to them what has been before delivered.

Lastly, I shall endeavour to give a particular history and analysis of the six classes of intellectual pleasures and pains; *viz.* those of imagination, ambition, self-interest, sympathy, theopathy, and the moral sense.

Of the doctrine of association *in general.*

CHAP. I.

Of the general laws according to which the sensations and motions are performed, and our ideas generated.

MY chief design in the following chapter, is, briefly, to explain, establish, and apply the (*a*) doctrine of *association*, which is taken from what Mr. *Locke*, and other ingenious persons since his time, have delivered concerning the influence of *association* over our opinions and affections, and its use in explaining those things in an accurate and precise way, which are commonly referred to the power of habit and custom, in a general and indeterminate one.

(*a*) IN THE ORIGINAL,
The doctrines of *vibrations* and *association.* The first of these doctrines is taken from the hints concerning the performance of sensation and motion, which Sir *Isaac Newton* has given at the end of his *Principia*, and in the *questions* annexed to his *Optics*; the last is taken from what Mr. *Locke*, &c.

Of the DOCTRINE of

The proper method of philosophizing seems to be, to discover and establish the general laws of action, affecting the subject under consideration, from certain select, well-defined, and well-attested phænomena, and then to explain and predict the other phænomena by these laws. This is the method of analysis and synthesis recommended and followed by Sir *Isaac Newton*.

I shall not be able to execute, with any accuracy, what the reader might expect of this kind, in respect of (a) the doctrine of *association*, on account of the great intricacy, extensiveness, and novelty of the subject. However, I will attempt a sketch in the best manner I can, for the service of future inquirers.

(a) In the original, The doctrines of *vibrations* and *association*, and their general laws, on account, &c.

SECT.

SECT. I.

Of the SENSATIONS.

PROP. 1.

The white medullary substance of the brain, spinal marrow, and the nerves proceeding from them, is the immediate instrument of sensation and motion.

UNDER the word *brain*, in these *observations*, I comprehend all that lies within the cavity of the skull, *i. e.* the *cerebrum*, or *brain* properly so called, the *cerebellum*, and the *medulla oblongata*.

This proposition seems to be sufficiently proved in the writings of physicians and anatomists; from the structure and functions of the several organs of the human body; from experiments on living animals; from the symptoms of diseases, and from diffections of morbid bodies. Sensibility, and the power of motion, seem to be conveyed to all the parts, in their natural state, from the brain and spinal marrow, along the nerves. These arise from the medullary, not the cortical part, every-where, and are themselves of a white medullary substance. When the nerves of any part are cut, tied, or compressed in any considerable degree, the functions of that part are either intirely destroyed, or much impaired. When the spinal marrow is compressed by a dislocation of the *vertebræ* of the back, all the parts, whose nerves arise below the place of dislocation, become paralytic. When any considerable

able/injury is done to the medullary fubſtance of the brain, fenſation, voluntary motion, memory, and intellect, are either intirely loſt, or much impaired; and if the injury be very great, this extends immediately to the vital motions alſo, *viz.* to thoſe of the heart, and organs of reſpiration, ſo as to occaſion death. But this does not hold equally in reſpect of the cortical ſubſtance of the brain; perhaps not at all, unleſs as far as injuries done to it extend themſelves to the medullary ſubſtance. In diſſections after apoplexies, palſies, epilepſies, and other diſtempers affecting the ſenſations and motions, it is uſual to find ſome great diſorder in the brain, from preternatural tumors, from blood, matter, or ſerum, lying upon the brain, or in its ventricles, *&c.* This may ſuffice as general evidence for the preſent. The particular reaſons of ſome of theſe phænomena, with more definite evidences will, offer themſelves in the courſe of theſe *obſervations.*

PROP. 2.

The white medullary ſubſtance of the brain is alſo the immediate inſtrument, by which ideas are preſented to the mind: or, in other words, whatever changes are made in this ſubſtance, correſponding changes are made in our ideas; and vice verſa.

THE evidence for this propoſition is alſo to be taken from the writings of phyſicians and anatomiſts; but eſpecially from thoſe parts of theſe writings, which treat of the faculties of memory, attention, imagination, *&c.* and of mental diſorders. It is ſufficiently manifeſt from hence, that the perfection of our mental faculties depends upon the perfection of this ſubſtance; that all injuries done

ASSOCIATION *in general.*

done to it, affect the trains of ideas proportionably; and that thefe cannot be reftored to their natural courfe, till fuch injuries be repaired. Poifons, fpirituous liquors, opiates, fevers, blows upon the head, *&c.* all plainly affect the mind, by firft difordering the medullary fubftance. And evacuations, reft, medicines, time, *&c.* as plainly reftore the mind to its former ftate, by reverfing the foregoing fteps. But there will be more and more definite evidence offered in the courfe of thefe *obfervations.*

PROP. 3.

The fenfations remain in the mind for a fhort time after the fenfible objects are removed.

THIS is very evident in the fenfations impreffed on the eye. Thus, to ufe Sir *Ifaac Newton's* words, " If a burning coal be nimbly moved
" round in a circle, with gyrations continually re-
" peated, the whole circle will appear like fire;
" the reafon of which is, that the fenfation of the
" coal, in the feveral places of that circle, *remains*
" *impreffed on the fenforium,* until the coal return
" again to the fame place. And fo in a quick con-
" fecution of the colours" (*viz.* red, yellow, green, blue, and purple, mentioned in the experiment, whence this paffage is taken) " the impreffion of
" every colour *remains on the fenforium,* until a
" revolution of all the colours be completed, and
" that firft colour return again. The impreffions
" therefore of all the fucceffive colours, *are at once*
" *in the fenforium*—and beget a fenfation of white."
Opt. B. I. *p.* 2. *Experiment* 10.

Thus alfo, when a perfon has had a candle, a window, or any other lucid and well-defined object, before

before his eyes for a confiderable time, he may perceive a very clear and precife image thereof to be left in the *fenforium*, fancy, or mind (for thefe I confider as equivalent expreffions in our entrance upon thefe difquifitions) for fome time after he has clofed his eyes. At leaft this will happen frequently to perfons, who are attentive to thefe things, in a gentle way: for as this appearance efcapes the notice of thofe who are entirely inattentive, fo too earneft a defire and attention prevents it, by introducing another ftate of mind or fancy.

To thefe may be referred the appearance mentioned by Sir *Ifaac Newton*, *Opt.* qu. 16. viz. " When a man in the dark preffes either corner of " his eye with his finger, and turns his eye away " from his finger, he will fee a circle of colours " like thofe in the feather of a peacock's tail. " And this appearance continues about a fecond of " time, after the eye and finger have remained " quiet." The fenfation continues therefore in the mind about a fecond of time after its caufe ceafes to act.

The fame continuance of the fenfations is alfo evident in the ear. For the founds which we hear, are reflected by the neighbouring bodies; and therefore confift of a variety of founds, fucceeding each other at different diftances of time, according to the diftances of the feveral reflecting bodies; which yet caufes no confufion, or apparent complexity of found, unlefs the diftance of the reflecting bodies be very confiderable, as in fpacious buildings. Much lefs are we able to diftinguifh the fucceffive pulfes of the air, even in the graveft founds.

As to the fenfes of tafte and fmell, there feems to be no clear direct evidence for the continuance of their fenfations, after the proper objects are removed. But analogy would incline one to believe, that they muft refemble the fenfes of fight and
hearing

hearing in this particular, though the continuance cannot be perceived diſtinctly, on account of the ſhortneſs of it, or other circumſtances. For the ſenſations muſt be ſuppoſed to bear ſuch an analogy to each other, and ſo to depend in common upon the brain, that all evidences for the continuance of ſenſations in any one ſenſe, will extend themſelves to the reſt. Thus all the ſenſes may be conſidered as ſo many kinds of feeling; the taſte is nearly allied to the feeling, the ſmell to the taſte, and the ſight and hearing to each other. All which analogies will offer themſelves to view, when we come to examine each of the ſenſes in particular.

In the ſenſe of feeling, the continuance of heat, after the heating body is removed, and that of the ſmart of a wound, after the inſtant of infliction, ſeem to be of the ſame kind with the appearances taken notice of in the eye and ear.

But the greateſt part of the ſenſations of this ſenſe reſemble thoſe of taſte and ſmell, and vaniſh to appearance as ſoon as the objects are removed.

SECT.

SECT. II.

Of IDEAS, *their generation and associations.*

PROP. 4.

Sensations, by being often repeated, leave certain vestiges, types, or images, of themselves, which may be called, simple ideas of sensation.

I TOOK notice in the introduction, that those ideas which resemble sensations were called ideas of sensation; and also that they might be called *simple ideas,* in respect of the intellectual ones which are formed from them, and of whose very essence it is to be *complex*. But the ideas of sensation are not intirely simple, since they must consist of parts both coexistent and successive, as the generating sensations themselves do.

Now, that the simple ideas of sensation are thus generated, agreeably to the proposition, appears, because the most vivid of these ideas are those where the corresponding sensations are most vigorously impressed, or most frequently renewed; whereas, if the sensation be faint, or uncommon, the generated idea is also faint in proportion, and, in extreme cases, evanescent and imperceptible. The exact observance of the order of place in visible ideas, and of the order-of-time in audible ones, may likewise serve to shew, that these ideas are copies and offsprings of the impressions made on the eye and ear, in which the same orders were observed respectively. And though

ASSOCIATION in general.

though it happens, that trains of vifible and audible ideas are prefented in fallies of the fancy, and in dreams, in which the order of time and place is different from that of any former impreffions, yet the fmall component parts of thefe trains are copies of former impreffions; and reafons may be given for the varieties of their compofitions.

It is alfo to be obferved, that this propofition bears a great refemblance to the third; and that, by this refemblance, they fomewhat confirm and illuftrate one another. According to the third propofition, fenfations remain for a fhort time after the impreffion is removed; and thefe remaining fenfations grow feebler and feebler, till they vanifh. They are therefore, in fome part of their declenfion, of about the fame ftrength with ideas, and, in their firft ftate, are intermediate between fenfations and ideas. And it feems reafonable to expect, that, if a fingle fenfation can leave a perceptible effect, trace, or veftige, for a fhort time, a fufficient repetition of a fenfation may leave a perceptible effect of the fame kind, but of a more permanent nature, *i. e.* an idea, which fhall recur occafionally, at long diftances of time, from the impreffion of the correfponding fenfation, *& vice verfa*. As to the occafions and caufes, which make ideas recur, they will be confidered in the next propofition.

The method of reafoning ufed in the laft paragraph, is farther confirmed by the following circumftance; *viz.* That both the diminutive declining fenfations, which remain for a fhort fpace after the impreffions of the objects ceafe, and the ideas, which are the copies of fuch impreffions, are far more diftinct and vivid, in refpect of vifible and audible impreffions, than of any others, To which it may be added, that, after travelling, hearing mufic, *&c.* trains of vivid ideas are very apt to recur, which correfpond very exactly to the late impreffions, and
which

Of the DOCTRINE *of*

which are of an intermediate nature between the remaining fenfations of the third propofition, in their greateft vigour, and the ideas mentioned in this.

The fenfations of feeling, tafte, and fmell, can fcarce be faid to leave ideas, unlefs very indiftinct and obfcure ones. However, as analogy leads one to fuppofe, that thefe fenfations may leave traces of the fame kind, tho' not in the fame degree, as thofe of fight and hearing; fo the readinefs with which we reconnoitre fenfations of feeling, tafte, and fmell, that have been often impreffed, is an evidence, that they do fo; and thefe generated traces or difpofitions of mind may be called the ideas of feeling, tafte, and fmell. In fleep, when all our ideas are magnified, thofe of feeling, tafte, and fmell, are often fufficiently vivid and diftinct; and the fame thing happens in fome few cafes of vigilance.

PROP. 5.

Any fenfations A, B, C, &c. by being affociated with one another a fufficient number of times, get fuch a power over the correfponding ideas a, b, c, &c. that any one of the fenfations A, when impreffed alone, fhall be able to excite in the mind b, c, &c. the ideas of the reft.

SENSATIONS may be faid to be affociated together, when their impreffions are either made precifely at the fame inftant of time, or in the contiguous fucceffive inftants. We may therefore diftinguifh affociation into two forts, the fynchronous, and the fucceffive.

The influence of affociation over our ideas, opinions, and affections, is fo great and obvious, as fcarce to have efcaped the notice of any writer who has treated of thefe, though the word *affociation*, in

the

ASSOCIATION *in general.*

the particular senfe here affixed to it, was firft brought into ufe by Mr. *Locke.* But all that has been delivered by the antients and moderns, concerning the power of habit, cuftom, example, education, authority, party-prejudice, the manner of learning the manual and liberal arts, &c. goes upon this doctrine as its foundation, and may be confidered as the detail of it, in various circumftances. I here begin with the fimpleft cafe, and fhall proceed to more and more complex ones continually, till I have exhaufted what has occured to me upon this fubject.

This propofition, or firft and fimpleft cafe of affociation, is manifeft from innumerable common obfervations. Thus the names, fmells, taftes, and tangible qualities of natural bodies, fuggeft their vifible appearances to the fancy, *i. e.* excite their vifible ideas; and, *vice verfa,* their vifible appearances impreffed on the eye raife up thofe powers of reconnoitring their names, fmells, taftes, and tangible qualities, which may not improperly be called their ideas, as above noted; and in fome cafes raife up ideas, which may be compared with vifible ones, in refpect of vividnefs. All which is plainly owing to the affociation of the feveral fenfible qualities of bodies with their names, and with each other. It is remarkable, however, as being agreeable to the fuperior vividnefs of vifible and audible ideas before taken notice of, that the fuggeftion of the vifible appearance from the name, is the moft ready of any other; and, next to this, that of the name from the vifible appearance; in which laft cafe, the reality of the audible idea, when not evident to the fancy, may be inferred from the ready pronunciation of the name. For it will be fhewn hereafter, that the audible idea is moft commonly a previous requifite to pronunciation. Other inftances of the power of affociation may be taken from compound vifible and audible impreffions. Thus the fight of part of a large

large building, fuggefts the idea of the reft inftantaneoufly; and the found of the words which begin a familiar fentence, brings the remaining part to our memories in order, the affociation of the parts being fynchronous in the firft cafe, and fucceffive in the laft.

It is to be obferved, that, in fucceffive affociations, the power of raifing the ideas is only exerted according to the order in which the affociation is made. Thus, if the impreffions A, B, C, be always made in the order of the alphabet, B impreffed alone will not raife a, but c only. Agreeably to which, it is eafy to repeat familiar fentences in the order in which they always occur, but impoffible to do it readily in an inverted one. The reafon of this is, that the compound idea c, b, a, correfponds to the compound fenfation C, B, A; and therefore requires the impreffion of C, B, A, in the fame manner as a, b, c, does that of A, B, C.

It is alfo to be obferved, that the power of affociation grows feebler, as the number either of fynchronous or fucceffive impreffions is increafed, and does not extend, with due force, to more than a fmall one, in the firft and fimpleft cafes. But, in complex cafes, or the affociations of affociations, of which the memory, in its full extent, confifts, the powers of the mind, deducible from this fource, will be found much greater than any perfon, upon his firft entrance on thefe inquiries, could well imagine.

PROP.

PROP. 6.

Simple ideas will run into complex ones, by means of affociation.

IN order to explain and prove this propofition, it will be requifite to give fome previous account of the manner in which fimple ideas of fenfation may be affociated together.

Cafe 1. Let the fenfation *A* be often affociated with each of the fenfations *B, C, D*, &c. *i. e.* at certain times with *B*, at certain other times with *C*, &c. it is evident, from the fifth propofition, that *A*, impreffed alone, will, at laft, raife *b, c, d*, &c. all together, *i. e.* affociate them with one another, provided they belong to different regions of the medullary fubftance; for if any two, or more, belong to the fame region, fince they cannot exift together in their diftinct forms, *A* will raife fomething intermediate between them.

Cafe 2. If the fenfations *A, B, C, D*, &c. be affociated together, according to various combinations of twos, or even threes, fours, *&c.* then will *A* raife *b, c, d*, &c. alfo *B* raife *a, c, d*, &c. as in cafe the firft.

It may happen, indeed, in both cafes, that *A* may raife a particular miniature, as *b*, preferably to any of the reft, from its being more affociated with *B*, from the novelty of the impreffion of *B*, from a tendency in the medullary fubftance to favour *b*, &c. and, in like manner, that *b* may raife *c* or *d* preferably to the reft. However, all this will be overruled, at laft, by the recurrency of the affociations; fo that any one of the fenfations will excite the ideas of the reft, at the fame inftant, *i. e.* affociate them together.

Case 3. Let A, B, C, D, &c. reprefent fucceffive impreffions, it follows from the tenth and eleventh propofitions, that A will raife b, c, d, &c. B raife c, d, &c. And though the ideas do not, in this cafe, rife precifely at the fame inftant, yet they come nearer together than the fenfations themfelves did in their original impreffion; fo that thefe ideas are affociated almoft fynchronically at laft, and fucceffively from the firft. The ideas come nearer to one another than the fenfations, on account of their diminutive nature, by which all that appertains to them is contracted. And this feems to be as agreeable to obfervation as to theory.

Case 4. All compound impreffions $A+B+C+D$, &c. after fufficient repetition leave compound miniatures $a+b+c+d$, &c. which recur every now and then from flight caufes, as well fuch as depend on affociation, as fome which are different from it. Now, in thefe recurrencies of compound miniatures, the parts are farther affociated, and approach perpetually nearer to each other, agreeably to what was juft now obferved; *i. e.* the affociation becomes perpetually more clofe and intimate.

Case 5. When the ideas a, b, c, d, &c. have been fufficiently affociated in any one or more of the foregoing ways, if we fuppofe any fingle idea of thefe, a for inftance, to be raifed by the tendency of the medullary fubftance that way by the affociation of A with a foreign fenfation or idea X or x, &c. this idea a, thus raifed, will frequently bring in all the reft, b, c, d, &c. and fo affociate all of them together ftill farther.

And, upon the whole, it may appear to the reader, that the fimple ideas of fenfation muft run into clufters and combinations, by affociation; and that each of thefe will, at laft, coalefce into one complex idea, by the approach and commixture of the feveral compounding parts.

It

ASSOCIATION *in general.* 19

It appears alfo from obfervation, that many of our intellectual ideas, fuch as thofe that belong to the heads of beauty, honour, moral qualities, &c. are, in fact, thus compofed of parts, which, by degrees, coalefce into one complex idea.

And as this coalefcence of fimple ideas into complex ones is thus evinced, both by the foregoing theory, and by obfervation, fo it may be illuftrated, and farther confirmed, by the fimilar coalefcence of letters into fyllables and words, in which affociation is likewife a chief inftrument. I fhall mention fome of the moft remarkable particulars, relating to this coalefcence of fimple ideas into complex ones, in the following corollaries.

Cor. 1. If the number of fimple ideas which compofe the complex one be very great, it may happen, that the complex idea fhall not appear to bear any relation to thefe its compounding parts, nor to the external fenfes upon which the original fenfations, which gave birth to the compounding ideas, were impreffed. The reafon of this is, that each fingle idea is overpowered by the fum of all the reft, as foon as they are all intimately united together. Thus, in very compound medicines, the feveral taftes and flavours of the feparate ingredients are loft and overpowered by the complex one of the whole mafs: fo that this has a tafte and flavour of its own, which appears to be fimple and original, and like that of a natural body. Thus alfo, white is vulgarly thought to be the fimpleft and moft uncompounded of all colours, while yet it really arifes from a certain proportion of the feven primary colours, with their feveral fhades, or degrees. And, to refume the illuftration above-mentioned, taken from language, it does not at all appear to perfons ignorant of the arts of reading and writing, that the great variety of complex words of languages can be analyfed up to a few fimple founds.

C 2 Cor.

Cor. 2. One may hope, therefore, that, by pursuing and perfecting the doctrine of association, we may some time or other be enabled to analyse all that vast variety of complex ideas, which pass under the name of ideas of reflection and intellectual ideas, into their simple compounding parts, *i. e.* into the simple ideas of sensation, of which they consist. This would be greatly analogous to the arts of writing, and resolving the colours of the sun's light, or natural bodies, into their primary constituent ones. The complex ideas which I here speak of, are generally excited by words, or visible objects; but they are also connected with other external impressions, and depend upon them, as upon symbols. In whatever way we consider them, the trains of them which are presented to the mind seem to depend upon the then present state of the body, the external impressions, and the remaining influence of prior impressions and associations, taken together.

Cor. 3. It would afford great light and clearness to the art of logic, thus to determine the precise nature and composition of the ideas affixed to those words which have complex ideas, in a proper sense, *i. e.* which excite any combinations of simple ideas united intimately by association; also to explain, upon this foundation, the proper use of those words, which have no ideas. For there are many words which are mere substitutes for other words, and many which are only auxiliaries. Now it cannot be said, that either of these have ideas, properly so called. And though it may seem an infinite and impossible task, thus to analyse the significations and uses of words, yet, I suppose this would not be more difficult, with the present philological and philosophical helps to such a work, than the first making of dictionaries and grammars, in the infancy of philology. Perhaps it may not be amiss just to hint, in this place, that the four following classes comprise

all

ASSOCIATION in general.

all the possible kinds into which words can be distinguished, agreeably to the plan here proposed:
1. Words which have ideas, but no definitions.
2. Words which have both ideas and definitions.
3. Words which have definitions, but no ideas.
4. Words which have neither ideas nor definitions.

It is quite manifest, that words seen or heard, can raise no ideas in the mind, or vibrations in the brain, distinct from their visible and audible impressions, except as far as they get new powers from associations, either incidental ones, or arising from express design, as in definitions; and therefore, that all other ways of considering words, besides what is here suggested, are either false or imperfect.

COR. 4. As simple ideas run into complex ones by association, so complex ideas run into decomplex ones by the same. But here the varieties of the associations, which increase with the complexity, hinder particular ones from being so close and permanent, between the complex parts of decomplex ideas, as between the simple parts of complex ones; to which it is analogous, in languages, that the letters of words adhere closer together than the words of sentences, both in writing and speaking.

COR. 5. The simple ideas of sensation are not all equally and uniformly concerned in forming complex and decomplex ideas; *i. e.* these do not result from all the possible combinations of twos, threes, fours, &c. of all the simple ideas; but, on the contrary, some simple ideas occur in the complex and decomplex ones much oftener than others: and the same holds of particular combinations by twos, threes, &c. and innumerable combinations never occur at all in real life, and consequently are never associated into complex or decomplex ideas. All which corresponds to what happens in real languages; some letters, and combinations of letters, occur much more frequently than others, and some combinations never occur at all.

Cor. 6. As persons who speak the same language have, however, a different use and extent of words, so, tho' mankind, in all ages and nations, agree, in general in their complex and decomplex ideas, yet there are many particular differences in them; and these differences are greater or less, according to the difference, or resemblance, in age, constitution, education, profession, country, age of the world, &c. i. e. in their impressions and associations.

Cor. 7. When a variety of ideas are associated together, the visible idea, being more glaring and distinct than the rest, performs the office of a symbol to all the rest, suggests them, and connects them together. In this it somewhat resembles the first letter of a word, or first word of a sentence, which are often made use of to bring all the rest to mind.

Cor. 8. When objects and ideas, with their most common combinations, have been often presented to the mind, a train of them, of a considerable length, may, by once occuring, leave such a trace, as to recur in imagination, and in minature, in nearly the same order and proportion as in this single occurrence. For since each of the particular impressions and ideas is familiar, there will want little more for their recurrency, than a few connecting links; and even these may be, in some measure, supplied by former similar instances. These considerations, when duly unfolded, seem to me sufficient to explain the chief phænomena of memory; and it will be easily seen from them, that the memory of adults, and masters in any science, ought to be much more ready and certain than that of children and novices, as it is found to be in fact.

Cor. 9. When the pleasure or pain attending any sensations, and ideas, is great, all the associations belonging to them are much accelerated and strengthened

ened. For the violent vibrations excited in such cafes, foon over-rule the natural vibrations, and leave in the brain a ftrong tendency to themfelves, from a few impreffions. The affociations will therefore be cemented fooner and ftronger than in common cafes; which is found agreeable to the fact.

Cor. 10. As many words have complex ideas annexed to them, fo fentences, which are collections of words, have collections of complex ideas, *i. e.* have decomplex ideas. And it happens, in moft cafes, that the decomplex idea belonging to any fentence, is not compounded merely of the complex ideas belonging to the words of it; but there are alfo many variations, fome oppofitions, and numberlefs additions. Thus propofitions, in particular, excite, as foon as heard, affent or diffent; which affent and diffent confift chiefly of additional complex ideas, not included in the terms of the propofition. And it would be of the greateft ufe, both in the fciences and in common life, thoroughly to analyfe this matter, to fhew in what manner, and by what fteps, *i. e.* by what impreffions and affociations, our affent and diffent, both in fcientifical and moral fubjects, is formed.

PROP. 7.

It is reasonable to think, that some (a) ideas may be as vivid as any sensation excited by the direct action of objects.

FOR (b) complex ideas may consist of so many parts co-existent and successive, and these parts may so alter and exalt one another, as that the resulting agitations in the medullary substance (c) may be equal to those excited by objects impressed on the senses. This process may be farther favoured by a mixture of vivid real impressions among the ideas, by the irritability of the medullary substance, by a previous disposition to the (d) ideas to be excited, &c.

Cor. 1. When the complex (e) ideas are thus exalted in degree, we are to conceive (f) that they pass into intellectual affections and passions. We are therefore to deduce the origin of the intellectual pleasures and pains, which are the objects of these affections and passions, from the source here laid open.

Cor. 2. Since the present proposition unfolds the nature of the affections and will, in the same manner, and from the same principles, as the sixth does that of ideas, intellect, memory, and fancy, it fol-

In the original,

(a) *It is reasonable to think, that some of the complex vibrations attending upon complex ideas, may be as vivid as any of the sensory vibrations excited by the direct action of objects.*

(b) These complex vibrations may consist, &c.

(c) May no longer be miniature vibrations, but vivid ones, equal to those, &c.

(d) Vibrations to be excited, &c.

(e) Miniature vibrations are thus exalted in degree, &c.

(f) That the corresponding complex ideas are proportionally exalted, and so pass, &c.

ASSOCIATION in general.

lows, that all thefe are of the fame original and confideration, and differ only in degree, or fome accidental circumftances. They are all deducible from the external impreffions made upon the fenfes, the veftiges or ideas of thefe, and their mutual connexions by means of affociation, taken together, and operating on one another.

Cor. 3. It follows alfo from this propofition, that the intellectual pleafures and pains may be greater, equal, or lefs, than the fenfible ones, according as each perfon unites more or fewer, more vivid or more languid (a) ideas, in the formation of his intellectual pleafures and pains, &c.

Cor. 4. It is evident, that all the vibrations which belong to ideas, and intellectual affections, muft refide in the brain, or even in the moft internal parts of it, not in the fpinal marrow, or nerves. The brain is therefore the feat of the rational foul, i. e. of the foul, as far as it is influenced by reafons and moral motives, even tho' we fhould admit, that the fpinal marrow and nerves are, in part, the fenforium, or the feat of the fenfitive foul; which is fome argument, that this ought not to be admitted, but that the fenforium, in men at leaft, ought to be placed in the internal parts of the brain.

Cor. 5. It is of the utmoft confequence to morality and religion, that the affections and paffions fhould be analyfed into their fimple compounding parts, by reverfing the fteps of the affociations which concur to form them. For thus we may learn how to cherifh and improve good ones, check and root out fuch as are mifchievous and immoral, and how to fuit our manner of life, in fome tolerable meafure, to our intellectual and religious wants. And as this holds, in refpect of perfons of all ages, fo it is par-

In the original,
(a) Miniature vibrations, in the formation, &c.

ticularly

ticularly true, and worthy of confideration, in refpect of children and youth. The world is, indeed, fufficiently ftocked with general precepts for this purpofe, grounded on experience; and whofoever will follow thefe faithfully, may expect good general fuccefs. However, the doctrine of affociation, when traced up to the firft rudiments of underftanding and affection, unfolds fuch a fcene as cannot fail both to inftruct and alarm all fuch as have any degree of interefted concern for themfelves, or of a benevolent one for others. It ought to be added here, that the doctrine of affociation explains alfo the rife and progrefs of thofe voluntary and femivoluntary powers, which we exert over our ideas, affections, and bodily motions (as I fhall fhew hereafter, *prop.* 9.); and, by doing this, teaches us how to regulate and improve thefe powers.

Cor. 6. If beings of the fame nature, but whofe affections and paffions are, at prefent, in different proportions to each other, be expofed for an indefinite time to the fame impreffions and affociations, all their particular differences will, at laft, be overruled, and they will become perfectly fimilar, or even equal. They may alfo be made perfectly fimilar, in a finite time, by a proper adjuftment of the impreffions and affociations.

Cor. 7. Our original bodily make, and the impreffions and affociations which affect us in paffing through life, are fo much alike, and yet not the fame, that there muft be both a great general refemblance amongft mankind, in refpect of their intellectual affections, and alfo many particular differences.

Cor. 8. Some degree of fpirituality is the neceffary confequence of paffing through life. The fenfible pleafures and pains muft be transferred by affociation more and more every day, upon things that afford neither fenfible pleafure nor fenfible pain in themfelves, and fo beget the intellectual pleafures and pains.

Cor.

ASSOCIATION in general.

COR. 9. Let the letters a, b, c, d, e, &c. reprefent the fenfible pleafures; x, y, and z, the fenfible pains, fuppofed to be only three in number; and let us fuppofe all thefe, both pleafures and pains, to be equal to one another: if now the ideas of thefe fenfible pleafures and pains be affociated together, according to all the poffible varieties, in order to form intellectual pleafures and pains, it is plain, that pleafure muft prevail in all the combinations of feven or more letters; and alfo, that when the feveral parts of thefe complex pleafures are fufficiently united by affociation, the pains which enter their compofition will no longer be diftinguifhed feparately, but the refulting mixed and complex pleafures appear to be pure and fimple ones, equal in quantity to the excefs of pleafure above pain, in each combination.] Thus affociation would convert a ftate, in which pleafure and pain were both perceived by turns, into one in which pure pleafure alone would be perceived; at leaft, would caufe the beings who were under its influence to an indefinite degree, to approach to this laft ftate nearer than by any definite difference. Or, in other words, affociation, under the fuppofition of this corollary, has a tendency to reduce the ftate of thofe who have eaten of the tree of the knowledge of good and evil, back again to a paradifiacal one. Now, though the circumftances of mankind are not the fame with thofe fuppofed in this corollary, yet they bear a remarkable refemblance thereto, during that part of our exiftence which is expofed to our obfervation. For our fenfible pleafures are far more numerous than our fenfible pains; and tho' the pains be, in general, greater than the pleafures, yet the fum total of thefe feems to be greater than that of thofe; whence the remainder, after the deftruction of the pains by the oppofite and equal pleafures, will be pure pleafure.

COR.

Cor. 10. The intellectual pleasures and pains are as real as the senfible ones, being, as we have seen, nothing but the senfible ones varioufly mixed and compounded together. The intellectual pleasures and pains are alfo all equally of a factitious and acquired nature. We muft therefore eftimate all our pleafures equally, by their magnitude, permanency, and tendency to procure others; and our pains in like manner.

Cor. 11. The senfible pleasures and pains have a greater tendency to deftroy the body, than the intellectual ones; for they are of a particular local nature, and so bear hard upon the organs which convey them. But the deftruction of any one confiderable part of the body is the deftruction of the whole, from the fympathy of the parts; whereas the intellectual pleafures and pains, being collected from all quarters, do not much injure any organ particularly, but rather bring on an equable gradual decay of the whole medullary fubftance, and all the parts thereon depending.

Cor. 12. This propofition, and its corollaries, afford fome pleafing prefumptions; fuch are, that we have a power of fuiting our frame of mind to our circumftances, of correcting what is amifs, and improving what is right: that our ultimate happinefs appears to be of a fpiritual, not corporeal nature; and therefore that death, or the fhaking off the grofs body, may not flop our progrefs, but rather render us more expedite in the purfuit of our true end: that affociation tends to make us all ultimately fimilar; fo that if one be happy, all muft: and, laftly, that the fame affociation may alfo be fhewn to contribute to introduce pure ultimate fpiritual happinefs, in all, by a direct argument, as well as by the juft mentioned indirect one.

SECT.

SECT. III.

Of muscular motion, and its two kinds, automatic and voluntary; and of the use of the doctrine of association, for explaining these respectively.

PROP. 8.

It is probable, that muscular motion is performed in the same general manner as sensation, and the perception of ideas.

FOR, first, sensation, the perception of ideas, and a locomotive faculty, *i. e.* muscular motion, are the three most eminent marks of distinction between the animal and vegetable world: therefore since it is already found, that the two first are performed by the same means,(*a*) there is some presumption, that the last will not require a different one.

Secondly, Of the two sorts of motion, *viz.* automatic and voluntary, the first depends upon sensation, the last upon ideas, as I shall shew particularly hereafter, and may appear, in general, to any one, upon a slight attention; whence it follows, that sensation, and automatic motion, must be performed in the same general manner, also the perception of ideas, and voluntary motion: and therefore, since sensation and perception, the two antecedents, agree in their causes, automatic and voluntary motion, the two consequents, *i. e.* all the four must likewise.

IN THE ORIGINAL,
(*a*) *i. e.* vibrations.

Thirdly.

Thirdly, It appears from the first and second propositions, that the white medullary substance is the common instrument of sensation, ideas, and motion; and this substance is uniform and continuous everywhere. Hence it follows, that the subtle motions excited in the sensory nerves, and medullary substance of the brain, during sensation and intellectual perception, must, of whatever kind they be, pass into the motory nerves; and when they are arrived there, it is probable, that they must cause the contraction of the muscles, both because otherwise their arrival at the motory nerves would be superfluous, and because some such subtle motions are required for this purpose.

PROP. 9.

The voluntary and semivoluntary motions are deducible from association.

IN order to verify this proposition, it is necessary to inquire, what connexions each automatic motion has gained by association with other motions, with ideas, or with foreign sensations, so as to depend upon them, *i. e.* so as to be excited no longer, in the automatic manner, but merely by the previous introduction of the associated motion, idea, or sensation. If it follows that idea, or state of mind, (*a*) which we term the will, directly, and without our perceiving the intervention of any other idea, or of any sensation or motion, it may be called voluntary, in the highest sense of this word. If the intervention of other ideas, or of sensations and motions (all

---

In the original,
(*a*) State of mind (*i. e.* set of compound vibratiuncles) which we term, &c.

which

ASSOCIATION *in general.* 31

which we are to suppose to follow the will directly) be neceffary, it is imperfectly voluntary; yet ftill it will be called voluntary, in the language of mankind, if it follow certainly and readily upon the intervention of a fingle fenfation, idea, or motion, excited by the power of the will: but if more than one of thefe be required, or if the motion do not follow with certainty and facility, it is to be efteemed lefs and lefs voluntary, femivoluntary, or fcarce voluntary at all, agreeably to the circumftances. Now, if it be found, upon a careful and impartial inquiry, that the motions which occur every day in common life, and which follow the idea called the will, immediately or mediately, perfectly or imperfectly, do this, in proportion to the number and degree of ftrength in the affociations, this will be fufficient authority for afcribing all that we call voluntary in actions to affociation, agreeably to the purport of this propofition. And this, I think, may be verified from facts, as far as it is reafonable to expect, in a fubject of inquiry fo novel and intricate.

In the fame manner as any action may be rendered voluntary, the ceffation from any, or a forcible reftraint upon any, may be alfo, *viz.* by proper affociations with the feeble vibrations in which inactivity confifts, or with the ftrong action of the antagonift mufcles.

After the actions, which are moft perfectly voluntary, have been rendered fo by one fet of affociations, they may, by another, be made to depend upon the moft diminutive fenfations, ideas, and motions, fuch as the mind fcarce regards, or is confcious of; and which therefore it can fcarce recollect the moment after the action is over. Hence it follows, that affociation not only converts automatic actions into voluntary, but voluntary ones into automatic. For thefe actions, of which the mind is fcarce confcious, and which follow mechanically, as it were, fome precedent

cedent diminutive senfation, idea, or motion, and without any effort of the mind, are rather to be afcribed to the body than the mind, *i. e.* are to be referred to the head of automatic motions. I shall call them automatic motions of the secondary kind, to diftinguish them both from thofe which are originally automatic, and from the voluntary ones; and shall now give a few inftances of this double tranfmutation of motions, *viz.* of automatic into voluntary, and of voluntary into automatic.

The fingers of young children bend upon almoft every impreffion which is made upon the palm of the hand, thus performing the action of grafping, in the original automatic manner. (*a*) After a fufficient repetition of the motions which concur in this action, their ideas are affociated ftrongly with other ideas, the moft common of which, I fuppofe, are thofe excited by the fight of a favourite play-thing which the child ufes to grafp, and hold in his hand. He ought, therefore, according to the doctrine of affociation, to perform and repeat the action of grafping, upon having such a play-thing prefented to his fight. But it is a known fact, that children do this. By purfuing the fame method of reafoning, we may fee how, after a sufficient repetition of the proper affociations, the found of the words *grafp, take, hold,* &c. the fight of the nurfe's hand in a ftate of contraction, the idea of a hand, and particularly of the child's own hand, in that ftate, and innumerable other affociated circumftances, *i. e.* fenfations, ideas, and motions, will put the child upon grafping, till, at laft, that idea, or ftate of mind which we may call the will to grafp, is generated, and fufficiently affo-

IN THE ORIGINAL,
(*a*) After a fufficient repetition of the motory vibrations which concur in this action, their vibratiuncles are generated, and affociated ftrongly with other vibrations and vibratiuncles, the moft common of which, &c.

ciated

ASSOCIATION *in general.*

ciated with the action to produce it inftantaneoufly. It is therefore perfectly voluntary in this cafe; and, by the innumerable repetitions of it in this perfectly voluntary ftate, it comes, at laft, to obtain a fufficient connexion with fo many diminutive fenfations, ideas, and motions, as to follow them in the fame manner as originally automatic actions do the correfponding fenfations, and confequently to be automatic fecondarily. And, in the fame manner, may all the actions performed with the hands be explained, all thofe that are very fimilar in life paffing from the original automatic ftate through the feveral degrees of voluntarinefs till they become perfectly voluntary, and then repaffing through the fame degrees in an inverted order, till they become fecondarily automatic on many occafions, tho' ftill perfectly voluntary on fome, *viz.* whenfoever an exprefs act of the will is exerted.

I will, in the next place, give a fhort account of the manner in which we learn to fpeak, as it may be deduced from the foregoing propofition. The newborn child is not able to produce a found at all, unlefs the mufcles of the trunk and larynx be ftimulated thereto by the impreffion of pain on fome part of the body. As the child advances in age, the frequent returns of this action facilitate it; fo that it recurs from lefs and lefs pains, from pleafures, from mere fenfations, and, laftly, from flight affociated circumftances, in the manner already explained. About the fame time that this procefs is thus far advanced, the mufcles of fpeech act occafionally, in various combinations, according to the affociations of the (*a*) motions with each other. Suppofe now the mufcles of fpeech to act in thefe combinations at the fame time that found is produced from fome agreeable impreffion, a mere fenfation, or a flight

IN THE ORIGINAL,
(*a*) Motory vibratiuncles with each other, &c.

affociated

associated cause, which must be supposed to be often the case, since it is so observable, that young children, when in a state of health and pleasure, exert a variety of actions at the same time. It is evident, that an articulate sound, or one approaching thereto, will sometimes be produced by this conjoint action of the muscles of the trunk, larynx, tongue, and lips; and that both these articulate sounds, and inarticulate ones, will often recur, from the recurrence of the same accidental causes. After they have recurred a sufficient number of times, the impression which these sounds, articulate and inarticulate, make upon the ear, will become an associated circumstance (for the child always hears himself speak, at the same time that he exerts the action) sufficient to produce a repetition of them. And thus it is, that children repeat the same sounds over and over again, for many successions, the impression of the last sound upon the ear exciting a fresh one, and so on, till the organs be tired. It follows therefore, that if any of the attendants make any of the sounds familiar to the child, he will be excited from this impression, considered as an associated circumstance, to return it. But the attendants make articulate sounds chiefly; there will therefore be a considerable balance in favour of such, and that of a growing nature: so that the child's articulate sounds will be more and more frequent every day—his inarticulate ones grow into disuse. Suppose now, that he compounds these simple articulate sounds, making complex ones, which approach to familiar words at some times, at others such as are quite foreign to the words of his native language, and that the first get an ever-growing balance in their favour, from the cause just now taken notice of; also, that they are associated with visible objects, actions, &c. and it will be easily seen, that the young child ought, from the nature of association, to learn to speak much in the same manner as he is

found

ASSOCIATION in general.

found in fact to do. Speech will also become a perfectly voluntary action, i. e. the child will be able to utter any word or sentence proposed to him by others, or by himself, from a mere exertion of the will, as much as to grasp: only here the introductory circumstance, viz. the impression of the sound on the ear, the idea of this sound, or the preceding motion in pronouncing the preceding word, is evident; and therefore makes it probable, that the same thing takes place in other cases. In like manner, speech, after it has been voluntary for a due time, will become secondarily automatic, i. e. will follow associated circumstances, without any express exertion of the will.

From the account here given of the actions of handling and speaking, we may understand in what manner the first rudiments are laid of that faculty of imitation, which is so observable in young children. They see the actions of their own hands, and hear themselves pronounce. Hence the impressions made by themselves on their own eyes and ears become associated circumstances, and consequently must, in due time, excite to the repetition of the actions. Hence like impressions made on their eyes and ears by others, will have the same effect; or, in other words, they will learn to imitate the actions which they see, and the sounds which they hear.

In the same manner may be explained the evident powers which the will has over the actions of swallowing, breathing, coughing, and expelling the urine and fæces, as well as the feeble and imperfect ones over sneezing, hiccoughing, and vomiting. As to the motion of the heart, and peristaltic motion of the bowels, since they are constant, they must be equally associated with every thing, i. e. peculiarly so with nothing, a few extraordinary cases excepted. They will therefore continue to move solely in the original automatic manner, during the whole course of our lives. However, association may, perhaps, have

D 2 some

some share in keeping these motions, and that of respiration, up for a time, when the usual automatic causes are deficient in any measure; and may thus contribute to their equability and constancy. It seems certain, at least, that where unequable and irregular motions of the heart and bowels are generated, and made to recur for a sufficient number of times, from their peculiar causes, in full quantity, a less degree of the same causes, or even an associated circumstance, will suffice to introduce them afterwards. And the same thing may be observed of hysteric and epileptic fits. These recur from less and less causes perpetually, in the same manner, and for the same reasons, as original automatic motions are converted into voluntary ones.

I will add one instance more of the transition of voluntary actions into automatic ones of the secondary kind, in order to make that process clearer, by having it singly in view. Suppose a person who has a perfectly voluntary command over his fingers, to begin to learn to play upon the harpsichord: the first step is to move his fingers from key to key, with a slow motion, looking at the notes, and exerting an express act of volition in every motion. By degrees the motions cling to one another, and to the impressions of the notes, in the way of association so often mentioned, the acts of volition growing less and less express all the time, till at last they become evanescent and imperceptible. For an expert performer will play from notes, or ideas laid up in the memory, or from the connexion of the several complex parts of the decomplex motions, some or all; and, at the same time, carry on a quite different train of thoughts in his mind, or even hold a conversation with another. Whence we may conclude, that the passage (a) from the sensory, or ideal, motions

---

IN THE ORIGINAL,

(a) From the sensory, ideal, or motory vibrations which precede, to those motory ones which follow, &c.

which

ASSOCIATION in general.

which precede, to thofe which follow, is as ready and direct, as from the fenfory vibrations to the original automatic motions correfponding to them; and confequently, that there is no intervention of the idea, or ftate of mind, called will. At leaft, the doctrine of affociation favours this, and the fact fhews, that there is no perceptible intervention, none of which we are confcious.

And thus, we are enabled to account for all the motions of the human body, upon principles which, tho' they may be fictitious, are, at leaft, clear and intelligible. The doctrine of vibrations explains all the original automatic motions, that of affociation, the voluntary and fecondarily automatic ones. And, if the doctrine of affociation be founded in, and deducible from, that of vibrations, then all the fenfations, ideas, and motions, of all animals, will be conducted according to the vibrations of the fmall medullary particles. Let the reader examine this hypothefis by the facts, and judge for himfelf. There are innumerable things, which, when properly difcuffed, will be fufficient tefts of it. It will be neceffary, in examining the motions, carefully to diftinguifh the automatic ftate from the voluntary one, and to remember, that the firft is not to be found pure, except in the motions of the new-born infant, or fuch as are excited by fome violent irritation or pain.

Cor. 1. The brain, not the fpinal marrow, or nerves, is the feat of the foul, as far as it prefides over the voluntary motions. For the efficacy of the motory vibratiuncles depends chiefly on that part of them which is excited within the brain.

Cor. 2. The hypothefis here propofed is diametrically oppofite to that of *Stahl*, and his followers. They fuppofe all animal motions to be voluntary in their original ftate, whereas this hypothefis fuppofes them all to be automatic at firft, *i. e.* involuntary, and

and to become voluntary afterwards by degrees. However, the *Stahlians* agree with me concerning the near relation of these two sorts of motion to each other, as also concerning the transition (or rather return, according to my hypothesis) of voluntary motions into involuntary ones, or into those which I call secondarily automatic. As to final causes, which are the chief subject of inquiry amongst the *Stahlians*, they are, without doubt, every-where consulted, in the structure and functions of the parts; they are also of great use for discovering the efficient ones. But then they ought not to be put in the place of the efficient ones; nor should the search after the efficient be banished from the study of physic, since the power of the physician, such as it is, extends to these alone. Not to mention, that the knowledge of the efficient causes is equally useful for discovering the final, as may appear from many parts of these observations.

Cor. 3. It may afford the reader some entertainment, to compare my hypothesis with what *Des Cartes* and *Leibnitz* have advanced, concerning animal motion, and the connexion between the soul and body. My general plan bears a near relation to theirs. And it seems not improbable to me, that *Des Cartes* might have had success in the execution of his, as proposed in the beginning of his treatise on man, had he been furnished with a proper assemblage of facts from anatomy, physiology, pathology, and philosophy, in general. Both *Leibnitz*'s pre-established harmony, and *Malebranche*'s system of occasional causes, are free from that great difficulty of supposing, according to the scholastic system, that the soul, an immaterial substance, exerts and receives a real physical influence upon and from the body, a material substance. And the reader may observe, that the hypothesis here proposed stands clear also of this difficulty. If he admits the simple case of the

connexion

ASSOCIATION *in general.* 39

connexion between the foul and body, in refpect of fenfation, as it is laid down in the firft propofition; and only fuppofes, that there is a change made in the medullary fubftance, proportional and correfpondent to every change in the fenfations; the doctrine of vibrations, as here delivered, undertakes to account for all the reft, the origin of our ideas and motions, and the manner in which both the fenfations and thefe are performed.

Cor. 4. I will here add Sir *Ifaac Newton*'s words, concerning fenfation and voluntary motion, as they occur at the end of his *Principia*, both becaufe they firft led me into this hypothefis, and becaufe they flow from it as a corollary. He affirms then, " both " that all fenfation is performed, and alfo the limbs " of animals moved in a voluntary manner, by the " power and actions of a certain very fubtle fpirit, " *i. e.* by the vibrations of this fpirit, propagated " through the folid capillaments of the nerves from " the external organs of the fenfes to the brain, and " from the brain into the mufcles."

Cor. 5. It follows, from the account here given of the voluntary and femivoluntary motions, that we muft get every day voluntary and femivoluntary powers, in refpect of our ideas and affections. Now this confequence of the doctrine of affociation is alfo agreeable to the fact. Thus we have a voluntary power of attending to an idea for a fhort time, of recalling one, of recollecting a name, a fact, *&c.* a femivoluntary one of quickening or reftraining affections already in motion, and a moft perfectly voluntary one of exciting moral motives, by reading, reflection, *&c.*

D 4 PROP.

PROP. 10.

It follows, from the hypothesis here proposed, concerning the voluntary motions, that a power of obtaining pleasure, and removing pain, will be generated early in children, and increase afterwards every day.

FOR the motions which are previous and subservient to the obtaining of pleasure, and the removal of pain, will be much more frequent, from the very instant of birth, than those which occasion pain. The number also of the first will be perpetually increasing, of the last decreasing. Both which positions may be evinced by the following arguments:

First, The pleasures are much more numerous than the pains. Hence the motions which are subservient to them are much more numerous also.

Secondly, The associated circumstances of the pleasures are many more in number than the pleasures themselves. But these circumstances, after a sufficient association, will be able to excite the motions subservient to the pleasures, as well as these themselves. And this will greatly augment the methods of obtaining pleasure.

Thirdly, It favours the position here advanced, that the motions subservient to pleasure are of a moderate nature; and therefore, that they can be excited with the more ease, both in an automatic and voluntary manner.

Fourthly, The pains, and consequently the motions subservient to them, are few, and of a violent nature. These motions are also various, and therefore cannot be united to objects and ideas with constancy and steadiness; and, which is most to be regarded. they end, at last, from the very make of the body, in that species of motion which contributes

most

ASSOCIATION in general. 41

moſt to remove or aſſwage the pain. This ſpecies therefore, ſince it recurs the moſt frequently, and continues longeſt, muſt be confirmed by aſſociation, to the excluſion of the reſt.

Cor. 1. Many changes in the actions of young children, very difficult to be explained, according to the uſual methods of conſidering human actions, appear to admit of a ſolution from this propoſition. Theſe changes are ſuch as tend to the eaſe, convenience, pleaſure, of the young child; and they are ſufficiently obſervable in the tranſition of the originally automatic actions into voluntary ones, as matters of fact, whatever be determined concerning their cauſe. I ſhall therefore refer to them occaſionally, in the courſe of theſe papers, as allowed matters of fact.

Cor. 2. It ſeems alſo, that many very complex propenſities and purſuits in adults, by which they ſeek their own pleaſure and happineſs, both explicitly and implicitly, may be accounted for, upon the ſame, or ſuch-like principles.

Cor. 3. To ſimilar cauſes we muſt alſo refer that propenſity to excite and cheriſh grateful ideas and affections, and trains of theſe, which is ſo obſervable in all mankind. However, this does not hold in ſo ſtrict a manner, but that ungrateful trains will preſent themſelves, and recur on many occaſions, and particularly whenever there is a morbid, and ſomewhat painful, ſtate of the medullary ſubſtance.

Cor. 4. Since God is the ſource of all good, and conſequently muſt at laſt appear to be ſo, *i. e.* be aſſociated with all our pleaſures, it ſeems to follow, even from this propoſition, that the idea of God, and of the ways by which his goodneſs and happineſs are made manifeſt, muſt, at laſt, take place of, and abſorb all other ideas. and he himſelf become, according to the language of the ſcriptures, *all in all.*

Cor. 5. This proposition, and its corollaries, afford some very general, and perhaps new, instances of the coincidence of efficient and final causes.

Cor. 6. The agreement of the doctrines of vibrations and association, both with each other, and with so great a variety of the phænomena of the body and mind, may be reckoned a strong argument for their truth.

CHAP.

CHAP. II.

Containing the application of the doctrine of association to each of the sensations and motions, in particular.

SECT. I.

Of the sense of feeling.

PROP. 11.

To explain in what manner we are enabled to judge of the seat of impressions made on the external surface of our bodies.

WHEN we apply the parts of our bodies to each other, particularly our hands to the several parts of the surface of our bodies, we excite vibrations in both parts, *viz.* both in the hands, and in that part of the surface which we touch. Suppose the hand to pass over the surface gradually, and the first impression will remain the same, while the last alters perpetually, because the vibrations belonging to the last are excited in different nerves, and by consequence enter the brain, or spinal marrow, at different parts. And this difference in the last impression, or its vibrations, corresponding always to the part on which the impression is made, will at last enable us to determine immediately what part of our bodies we touch; *i. e.* what is the distance of the part touched from the mouth, nose, shoulder, elbow, or other remarkable part, considered as a fixed point.

For

For by paffing frequently from the mouth, nofe, &c. to the part under confideration, children learn this very early, even without attending to it at all explicitly.

Sight alfo helps us to judge of this diftance in the parts, which are frequently expofed to view, and this in proportion to that frequency.

Let us fuppofe then, that we are able to determine at once what external parts of our bodies we touch, *i. e.* to determine how it is fituated in refpect of the other parts, and to fhew the correfponding part in the body of another perfon; it will follow, that if a like impreffion be made not by our own hand, but by that of another, or by any foreign body, we fhall know at once the part on which it is made. We fhall alfo, fuppofing us arrived at a fufficient degree of voluntary power over the mufcles, be able at once to put our hand upon the part on which the impreffion is made.

By degrees we fhall learn to diftinguifh the part, not only when an impreffion like the gentle ones of our hands is made upon it, but alfo when a vivid, rude, or painful one is. For, firft, all impreffions made upon the fame part agree in this, whatever be their differences as to kind and degree, that they enter by the fame nerves, and at the fame part of the brain, and fpinal marrow. Secondly, we imprefs a great variety of fenfations ourfelves by our hands, accordingly as they are hot or cold, by friction, fcratching, &c. and moft impreffions from foreign bodies will bear fome refemblance to fome of thefe. Thirdly, we often fee upon what part impreffions from foreign bodies are made. Fourthly, when they leave permanent effects, as in wounds, burns, &c. we always examine by feeling, where the impreffion was made.

Now from all thefe things laid together it follows, that in itchings from an internal caufe, and in impreffions

Of FEELING. 45

preffions where neither our hand nor eye give us any information, we fhall, however, be able to determine at once with tolerable accuracy what external part is affected, and to put our hand upon it, fo as to confirm our prefent judgment, and render our future judgment, and voluntary power, more certain and ready. We fhall alfo do this moft readily in thofe parts which we fee and feel moft frequently, the hands for inftance, lefs fo, *cæteris paribus*, in thofe we feldom fee or feel, and leaft fo, where we never fee the part, and feldom touch it. At leaft this feems to refult from the theory. But it is to be obferved, that the fact ought to be tried chiefly in children. For in adults the feveral degrees approach more to perfection, *i. e.* to an equality among themfelves.

PROP. 12.

To explain in what manner, and to what degree, we are enabled to judge of the feat of internal pains.

HERE we may obferve, firft, that as we never fee or feel the internal parts, fuch as the lungs, heart, ftomach, inteftines, liver, kidneys, bladder, *&c.* we can have no direct information in the manner explained under the foregoing propofition.

Secondly, Since all pains diffufe an increafe of vibrations into the neighbouring parts, the increafed vibrations in the external parts, arifing from internal pains, will be a grofs general direction, fo as to determine the feat of the pain within grofs limits, in refpect of fuperior and inferior, anterior and pofterior, right and left.

Thirdly, Preffing the external parts, fo as to augment or alleviate the internal pain, muft contribute alfo.

Fourthly, Since all the internal parts in the *thorax* and

and *abdomen* receive branches from the intercostal nerve, which communicates with each vertebral pair, it follows that the internal pains will send vibrations up to the spinal marrow, which will enter in at the same parts of it, as the vibrations from external pains in the neighbourhood. At the same time it appears from the many ganglions, plexuses, and communications of nerves in the *thorax* and *abdomen*, also from the origin and distribution of the nerves of the *cauda equina*, that this can be no more than a gross general direction; and that the great number of sympathetic influences from these causes, also from the running of vibrations along membranes and from their fixing particularly in nervous parts, or extreme ones, will give occasion to many deceptions here, and in certain cases make the pain be felt, *i. e.* appear to be, in parts at a considerable distance from the seat of the disorder.

Fifthly, Suppose the patient to shew by the external parts whereabouts his pain is felt internally, then the physician may, from his knowledge of the situation of the internal parts in respect of the external, guess pretty nearly, what internal part is affected.

Sixthly, The symptoms attending the pain, its cause and consequences, compared with the natural functions of the parts, with the history of diseases, and morbid dissections, will enable the physician to determine with great precision in some cases, and help a little in most.

Seventhly, When the patient has had long experience of the same kind of internal pains, or of different ones, he describes more exactly, and also gets certain fixed points, to which he refers his pains.

Eightly, Anatomists and physicians may sometimes judge with great exactness in their own cases, having both a knowledge of the parts, and their functions, and also their own feelings, to guide them.

This subject deserves a particular and accurate examination,

amination, it being of great consequence to be able to discover the seat and *causa proxima* of the distemper, from the complaints of the patient, and from the previous, concomitant, and consequent circumstances. I hope these two propositions may cast some light upon it.

Here we may add an observation deducible from the doctrine of association; *viz.* as we learn by degrees, from impressions made on the surfaces of our bodies, to attend particularly to the sensations impressed on, or existing in each part, at pleasure, *i. e.* to magnify the vibrations which take place in it; so, after disorders in the internal parts, the associated circumstances seem often to renew the painful vibrations there, and to occasion either the return of the like disorder, or some other; at least to have a considerable share in these effects, when produced by their causes in an inferior degree. Thus disorders in the bowels, caused at first by acrid impressions, lay the foundation for a return of like disorders on less occasions. Thus women that have often miscarried, seem to irritate the muscular fibres of the *uterus* by the recollection of the associated circumstances, and so to dispose themselves to miscarry more than according to the mere bodily tendency: fear and concern having also a great influence here. All this will be farther illustrated by what follows under the next proposition.

PROP. 13.

To explain in what manner, and to what degree, the pleasures and pains of feeling contribute, according to the doctrine of association, to the formation of our intellectual pleasures and pains.

IT follows from the foregoing account of the power of leaving traces, and of association, that all the pains from intense heat and cold, wounds, inflammations, &c. will leave a disposition in the nervous system to run into miniature vibrations of the same kind, and that these miniature vibrations will be excited chiefly by the associated circumstances. That is to say, the appearance of the fire, or of a knife, especially in circumstances like to those in which the child was burnt or cut, will raise up in the child's nervous system painful vibrations of the same kind with, but less in degree than, those which the actual burn or wound occasioned.

By degrees these miniature pains will be transferred upon the words, and other symbols, which denote these and such-like objects and circumstances: however, as the diffusion is greater, the pain transferred from a single cause must become less. But then, since a great variety of particular miniatures are transferred upon each word, since also the words expressing the several pains of feeling affect each other by various associations, and each of them transfers a miniature of its own miniature upon more general words, &c. it comes to pass at last, that the various verbal and other symbols of the pains of feeling, also of other pains bodily and mental, excite a compound vibration formed from a variety of miniatures, which exceeds ordinary actual pains in strength. These compound vibrations will also have a general resemblance, and particular differences in respect of each other.

It

Of FEELING.

It follows therefore *a priori*, as one may fay, and by a fynthetic kind of demonftration, that, admitting the powers of leaving traces, and of affociation, compound or mental pains will arife from fimple bodily ones by means of words, fymbols, and affociated circumftances. And they feem to me to anfwer in kind and degree to the facts in general. If, farther, we admit the doctrine of vibrations, then thefe compound mental pains will arife from, or be attended by, violent vibrations in the nervous fyftem, and particularly in the brain.

Agreeably to this account, we may obferve, that the mere words denoting bodily pains, though not formed into propofitions or threatenings, affect children. However, fince there happen daily affociations of the mere words with freedom and fecurity, and of propofitions and threatenings with fufferings, children learn by degrees to confine their fear, forrow, &c. to thofe things which are efteemed the genuine figns, reafons, caufes, &c. of fufferings. This is the cafe in general; but there are great particular differences both in children and adults; which yet, if accurately purfued, would probably not only be confiftent with, but even confirm and illuftrate, the doctrine of affociation.

And we may conclude upon the whole, fince the pains of feeling are far more numerous and violent than thofe of all the other fenfes put together, that the greateft part of our intellectual pains are deducible from them.

In like manner the pleafures of an agreeable warmth, and refrefhing coolnefs, when we are cold or hot refpectively, of gentle friction and titillation, leave traces of themfelves, which by affociation are made to depend upon words, and other fymbols. But thefe pleafures, being faint and rare in comparifon of others, particularly of thofe of tafte, have
E but

but a small share in forming the intellectual pleasures. Titillation may perhaps be excepted. For laughter, which arises from it, is a principal pleasure in young children, and a principal source of the other pleasures, particularly of those of sociality and benevolence. Farther, since the miniatures left by the pains of feeling must in some cases be faint originally, in others decline from the diffusion, the faintness of the association, &c. these miniature pains will often fall within the limits of pleasure, and consequently become sources of intellectual pleasure; as in recollecting certain pains, in seeing battles, storms, wild beasts, or their pictures, or reading descriptions of them.

PROP. 14.

To give an account of the ideas generated by tangible impressions.

HERE it may be observed, first, that the very words, *burn, wound,* &c. seem even in adults, though not formed into propositions, or heightened by a conjunction of circumstances, to excite, for the most part, a perception of the disagreeable kind; however, so faint in degree, that it may be reckoned amongst the number of ideas, agreeably to the definitions given in the introduction.

Secondly, the words expressing the pleasures of this sense are probably attended with perceptions, though still fainter in degree. These perceptions may therefore be called the ideas belonging to those words.

Thirdly, the words *moist, dry, soft, hard, smooth, rough,* can scarce be attended with any distinguishable vibrations in the fingers, or parts of the brain corresponding thereto, on account of the faintness of the

the original impreffions, and the great varieties of them; however, analogy leads us to think, that fomething of this kind muft happen in a low degree. But when the qualities themfelves are felt, and the appropriated vibrations raifed, they lead by affociation to the words expreffing them; and thus we can diftinguifh the feveral tangible qualities from each other by the differences of their vibrations, and declare in words what each is.

Fourthly, the vibrations excited in the fenfe of feeling by motion, diftance, and figure, are fo faint, and fo various, that neither thefe words, nor any related expreffions, can be fuppofed to excite any miniature vibrations in this fenfe. Yet ftill, upon feeling motions and figures, and paffing over diftances, the differences of vibrations from preffure and mufcular contraction, *i. e.* from the *vis inertiæ* of our own bodies, or of foreign matter, fuggeft to us the words expreffing thefe, with their varieties, by affociation.

Fifthly, the great extent of the fenfe of feeling tends to make the miniatures fainter, efpecially as far as the external parts are concerned; and would probably have fo powerful an effect upon the miniatures raifed in the internal parts, as to make them, by oppofing deftroy one another, did not all the impreffions of the fame nature, *viz.* all thofe from heat, from cold, from friction, *&c.* by whatever external part they enter, produce nearly the fame effect upon the brain. Whence the feveral miniatures left by particular impreffions of the fame kind muft ftrengthen one another in the internal parts, at the fame time that they obliterate one another in the external ones. However, where a perfon has fuffered much by a particular wound, ulcer, *&c.* it feems according to the theory, that an idea of it fhould be left

Of the SENSE

left in the part affected, or correfponding region of the brain, or fpinal marrow.

Sixthly, the vifible ideas of the bodies which imprefs the feveral fenfations of feeling upon us, are, like all other vifible ones, fo vivid and definite, that they mix themfelves with, and fomewhat obfcure, the moſt vivid ideas of feeling, and quite overpower the faint ones. Sight communicates to us at once the fize, fhape, and colour of objects; feeling cannot do the laſt at all, and the two firſt only in a tedious way; and is fcarce ever employed for that purpofe by thofe who fee. Hence perfons born blind muſt have far more vivid and definite ideas of feeling than others. An inquiry into their real experiences would greatly contribute to correct, illuftrate, and improve, the theory of ideas, and their affociations.

SECT.

SECT. II.

Of the Senſe of Taſte.

PROP. 15.

To examine how far the changes generally made in the taſte, in paſſing from infancy to old age, are agreeable to the doctrines of vibrations and aſſociation.

SOME of theſe changes are,

That ſweets generally grow leſs and leſs agreeable, and ſometimes even diſagreeable, or nauſeous at laſt.

That aſtringent, acid, and ſpirituous liquids, which diſpleaſe at firſt, afterwards become highly grateful.

That even bitters and acrids firſt loſe their offenſive qualities, and after a ſufficient repetition give a reliſh to our aliment.

And that many particular foods and medicines become either extremely pleaſant or diſguſting, from aſſociations with faſhion, joy, hope of advantage, hunger, the pleaſures of chearful converſation, &c. or with ſickneſs, vomitings, gripings, fear, ſorrow, &c.

Now, in order to account for theſe changes, we may conſider the following things.

Firſt, that the organs become leſs and leſs ſenſible by age, from the growing calloſity and rigidity of all the parts of animal bodies. The pleaſant ſavours may therefore be expected to become leſs pleaſant, and the moderately diſagreeable ones to fall down within the limits of pleaſure, upon this account.

Secondly, the diſpoſition to vibrations in the organ and correſponding part of the brain muſt alſo receive some alteration by the frequent repetition of impressions. For though this returns, at a proper distance from each meal, to its former state, within an indefinite distance, as one may say, yet some difference there probably is, upon the whole, which, in a sufficient length of time, amounts to a perceptible one. However, we must also suppose on the other hand, that the make of the nervous system sets some bounds to this gradual alteration in the disposition to vibrate; else the taste would be much more variable than it is, and continue to change more after adult age, than it is found to do in fact. It may perhaps change faster in the use of a high diet than of a low one; which would be an evidence of the reality of the cause here assigned.

Thirdly, the pleasant and painful impressions which particular foods and medicines make upon the stomach, always either accompany the taste, or follow it in a short time; and by this means an association is formed, whereby the direct pleasantness or nauseousness of the taste is enhanced, if the impressions upon the tongue and stomach be of the same kind; or diminished, and perhaps overpowered, and even converted into its opposite, if they be of different kinds. For if the two impressions A and B, made upon the tongue and stomach respectively, be repeated together for a sufficient number of times, b will always attend A upon the first moment of its being made. If therefore B be of such a magnitude as to leave a trace b sufficiently great, the addition of this trace b to A, the impression made upon the tongue, may produce all the changes in it above-mentioned, according to their several natures and proportions. This follows from the doctrine of association, as it takes place in general; but here the free propagation of vibrations from the stomach to the mouth, along the surface of the membranes, adds a particular force. In like manner a disagreeable taste, by being often

Of TASTE. 55

often mixed with a pleasant one, may at last become pleasant alone, and *vice verſa:* hunger and satiety may also, by being joined with particular tastes, contribute greatly to augment or abate their relish. And I believe it is by the methods of this third kind, that the chief and most usual changes in the taste are made.

Fourthly, the changes which are made by associations with mental pleasures and pains, or bodily ones not belonging to this organ, as with fine colours, music, *&c.* receive a like explication as the last mentioned instances of associations. Here the pleasure excited in the eye or ear over-rules the taste at first: afterwards we may suppose the organ to be so altered by degrees, in respect of the disagreeable taste from its frequent impression, or other cause, as to have the solution of continuity no longer occasioned by its action. It is probable also, that evanescent pleasures of sight and hearing, at least pleasant vibrations in the parts of the brain corresponding to these two organs, accompany these tastes ever afterwards.

It may be observed here, that the desire of particular foods and liquors is much more influenced by the associated circumstances, than their tastes, it being very common for these circumstances, particularly the sight or smell of the food or liquor, to prevail against men's better judgment, directing them to forbear, and warning them of the mischiefs likely to arise from self-indulgence.

PROP. 16.

To explain in what manner, and to what degree, pleasant and unpleasant tastes contribute, according to the doctrine of association, to form our intellectual pleasures and pains.

THE pleasures of the taste, considered as extending itself from the mouth through the whole alimentary duct, are very considerable, and frequently repeated; they must therefore be one chief means, by which pleasurable states are introduced into the brain, and nervous system. These pleasurable states must, after some time, leave miniatures of themselves, sufficiently strong to be called up upon slight occasions, *viz.* from a variety of associations with the common visible and audible objects, and to illuminate these, and their ideas. When groups of these miniatures have been long and closely connected with particular objects, they coalesce into one complex idea, appearing, however, to be a simple one; and so begin to be transferred upon other objects, and even upon tastes back again, and so on without limits. And from this way of reasoning it may now appear, that a great part of our intellectual pleasures are ultimately deducible from those of taste; and that one principal final cause of the greatness and constant recurrency of these pleasures, from our first infancy to the extremity of old age, is to introduce and keep up pleasurable states in the brain, and to connect them with foreign objects.

The social pleasures seem, in a particular manner, to be derived from this source; since it has been customary in all ages and nations, and is, in a manner, necessary, that we should enjoy the pleasures of taste

Of TASTE.

in conjunction with our relatives, friends, and neighbours.

In like manner, nauseous tastes, and painful impressions upon the alimentary duct, give rise and strength to mental pains. The most common of these painful impressions is that from excess, and the consequent indigestion. This excites and supports those uneasy states, which attend upon melancholy, fear, and sorrow.

It appears also to me, that these states are introduced, in a great degree, during sleep, during the frightful dreams, agitations, and oppressions, that excess in diet occasions in the night. These dreams and disorders are often forgotten; but the uneasy states of body, which then happen, leave vestiges of themselves, which increase in number and strength every day from the continuance of the cause, till at last they are ready to be called up in crouds upon flight occasions, and the unhappy person is unexpectedly, and at once, as it were, seized with a great degree of the hypochondriac distemper, the obvious cause appearing no ways proportionable to the effect. And thus it may appear, that there ought to be a great reciprocal influence between the mind and alimentary duct, agreeably to common observation; which is farther confirmed by the very large number of nerves distributed there.

PROP. 17.

To give an account of the ideas generated by the several tastes.

AS the pleasures of taste are in general greater than those of feeling, and the pains in general less, it follows that the ideas which are affixed to the several words expressing the several pleasant and unpleasant tastes, will be of a middle nature in respect of of the ideas generated by tangible impreſſions; and lie between the ideas of the pains of feeling, and thoſe of its pleaſures.

Agreeably to this, it ſeems very difficult, or even impoſſible, to excite a genuine vivid miniature of an acid, ſweet, ſalt, or bitter taſte, by the mere force of imagination. However, the vibrations peculiar to each of theſe leave ſuch veſtiges of themſelves, ſuch an effect in the tongue, and correſponding parts of the brain, as, upon taſting the qualities themſelves, at once to bring up the names whereby they are expreſſed, with many other aſſociated circumſtances, particularly the viſible appearances of the bodies indued with theſe qualities. And theſe veſtiges may be called ideas. Analogy leads us alſo to conclude, as before obſerved under feeling, that ſome faint veſtiges or ideas muſt be raiſed in the parts of the brain correſponding to the tongue, upon the mere paſſage of each word, that expreſſes a remarkable taſte, over the ear. And, when the imagination is aſſiſted by the actual ſight or ſmell of a highly grateful food, we ſeem able to raiſe an idea of a perceptible magnitude. This is confirmed by the manifeſt effect exerted upon the mouth, and its glands, in ſuch caſes.

The ſight of what we eat or drink ſeems alſo, in ſeveral inſtances, to enable us to judge more accurately of the taſte and flavour; which ought to be effected, according to this theory, by raiſing ſmall ideas of the taſte and flavour, and magnifying the real impreſſions in conſequence thereof. For an actual impreſſion muſt excite vibrations conſiderably different, according to the difference in the previous ones; and where the previous ones are of the ſame kind with thoſe impreſſed, the laſt muſt be magnified.

SECT.

SECT. III.
Of the Senſe of Smell.

PROP. 18.

To explain in what manner, and to what degree, pleaſant and unpleaſant odours contribute, in the way of aſſociation, to form our intellectual pleaſures and pains.

IT will be evident, upon a moderate attention, that the grateful ſmells, with which natural productions abound, have a great ſhare in enlivening many of our ideas, and in the generation of our intellectual pleaſures; which holds particularly in reſpect of thoſe that ariſe from the view of rural objects and ſcenes, and from the repreſentations of them by poetry and painting. This ſource of theſe pleaſures may not indeed be eaſy to be traced up in all the particular caſes; but that it is a ſource, follows neceſſarily from the power of aſſociation.

In like manner, the mental uneaſineſs, which attends ſhame, ideas of indecency, &c. ariſes, in a conſiderable degree, from the offenſive ſmells of the excrementitious diſcharges of animal bodies. And it is remarkable in this view, that the *pudenda* are ſituated near the paſſages of the urine and *fæces*, the two moſt offenſive of our excrements.

We may ſuppoſe the intellectual pleaſures and pains, which are deducible from the flavours, grateful and ungrateful, that aſcend behind the *uvula* into the noſe during maſtication, and juſt after deglutition, to have been conſidered in the laſt ſection under the head of taſte, ſince theſe flavours are always eſteemed a part of the taſtes of aliments and medicines. And indeed

indeed the olfactory nerves seem to have as great a share in conveying to us both the original and derivative pleasures, which are referred to the taste, as the nerves of the tongue; which may help us to account for the largeness of those nerves in men, to whom smell, properly so called, is of far less consequence than any other of the senses, and taste of the greatest, while yet the nerves of taste are comparitively small.

We may add here, that the smell is a guide and guard placed before the taste, as that is before the stomach, in a great degree in men, but much more so in brutes, who have scarce any other means than that of smell, whereby to distinguish what foods are proper for them. It is likewise probable, that the smell is a guard to the lungs; and that the grateful odours of flowers, fruits, and vegetable productions, in general, are an indication of the wholsomeness of country air; as the offensiveness of putrefaction, sulphureous fumes, &c. warn us beforehand, of their mischievous effects upon the lungs. However, the rule is not universal in either case.

PROP. 19.

To give an account of the ideas generated by the several odours.

WHAT has been delivered concerning the ideas of feeling and taste, may be applied to the smell. We cannot, by the power of our will or fancy, raise up any miniatures or ideas of particular smells, so as to perceive them evidently. However, the associated circumstances seem to have some power of affecting the organ of smell, and the corresponding part of the brain, in a particular manner; whence we are prepared to receive and distinguish the several smells more readily, and more accurately, on account
of

of the previous influence of these associated circumstances. And, conversly, the actual smells of natural bodies enable us to determine them, though we do not see them, always negatively, and often positively; *i. e.* by suggesting their names, and visible appearances. And, when we are at a loss in the last respect, the name or visible appearance of the body will immediately revive the connexion.

S E C T. IV.

Of the Sense of Sight.

P R O P. 20.

To examine how far the judgments which we make by sight concerning magnitude, distance, motion, figure, and position, are agreeable to the doctrine of association.

I Have already observed, *prop.* 30. that these judgments are to be esteemed true or false, according as they agree or disagree with those made by touch.

Now the associates of greater tangible magnitude are a larger picture on the *retina*, the distance being the same; and a larger distance, the picture being the same. The associates of a less tangible magnitude are the opposites to these. And the associates of the sameness of tangible magnitude are the increase or diminution of the picture on the *retina*, while the distance is diminished or increased suitably thereto.

All

All this appears from optical confiderations. Hence it follows, that where the picture on the *retina* is of a juft fize, and alfo the previous judgment concerning the diftance juft, our eftimate of tangible magnitude by fight will be juft likewife. But if the picture on the *retina* be magnified or diminifhed by glaffes, or our previous judgment concerning the diftance be erroneous, our eftimate of tangible magnitude will be erroneous in like manner. And, whether it be juft or erroneous, it is intirely founded on affociation.

The following inftances, among many others, confirm thefe pofitions. Young children judge rightly of magnitude only in familiar places, or at fmall diftances. At great diftances they always judge the objects to be lefs than the truth, not having learnt to judge rightly of thefe diftances, and make allowance for them. The generality of adults judge far better of magnitude at great diftances on level ground, than from above, or from below, on account of their greater experience in the former cafe. The horizontal moon appears larger than the meridional, becaufe the picture on the *retina* is of nearly the fame fize, and the diftance efteemed to be greater. And yet the horizontal moon appears far lefs than the truth, becaufe we can form no conception of its vaft diftance. A tree referred to the horizon in the dufk of the evening, or a fly to the ground at a diftance, through the indiftinctnefs of vifion, appears much bigger than the truth. In looking through glaffes, which magnify or diminifh the picture on the *retina*, the objects themfelves feem to be magnified or diminifhed, becaufe our judgment concerning the diftance is not altered proportionally, &c. &c.

There are, befides thefe, fome other affociated circumftances, which occafionally impofe upon us in eftimating magnitudes. Thus a perfon of an ordinary height ftanding near a very tall one,

or

or coming in at a very high door, appears shorter than the truth; lean persons seem tall, fat persons short, &c.

The principal criterion of distance is the magnitude of the picture, which some known object makes on the *retina*. But the five following associated circumstances seem to have also some influence on our judgments concerning distance, in certain cases, and under certain limitations: The number of objects which intervene, the degree of distinctness in which the minute parts are seen, the degree of brightness, the inclination of the optic axes, and the conformation of the eye. It will appear from the 62d and 63d *prop.* that the two last are associates to each other in their proper degrees, since each depends on the distance of the object. The influence of the three first, as well as that of the magnitude of the picture on the *retina*, is evident from the methods of expressing distance in pictures.

From the principles laid down in the last paragraph, we may explain the following fallacies in vision. An object viewed through a perspective appears to be nearer than it is, because the picture on the *retina* is thereby rendered both larger, and more distinct; but if we invert the perspective, and so diminish the picture, the object will appear farther off. At sea, and on plains, where few or no objects intervene, we judge the distances to be less than than the truth; and the contrary happens in scenes diversified with a proper variety of objects. A large object, when apprehended to be one of a common size, appears nearer than the truth; and the same happens when we view objects in rural scenes, such as houses, towns, hills, &c. in a bright light, or through a very clear atmosphere. In trying to judge of small distances by one eye, it is usual to to be mistaken for want of the criterion from the inclination of the optic axes.

Since our judgment concerning the magnitude of an unknown object depends upon the distance, and our judgment concerning the distance of every object chiefly upon that concerning its magnitude, the conjectures of different persons, concerning the magnitudes and distances of unknown remote objects, both as seen through telescopes, and with the naked eye, may vary considerably from each other, according to their respective associated prejudices. If the distance be fixed previously by a known object, we may afterwards judge of the magnitude of an unknown object thereby. The number of intervening objects, and the inclination of the optic axes, seem to afford considerable assistance in determining distances, where known objects are wanting; the first in large distances, the last in small ones: but the other three inferior criterions above mentioned viz. the degree of distinctness, the degree of brightness, and the conformation of the eye, when singly taken, are of small signification.

We judge of motion by the motion of the pictures on the *retina*, or of our eyes in following the objects. After some time, we learn to make allowance for the line of direction, our own motions, &c. If we fail to make the due allowance through associated circumstances of any kind, we must in consequence of this, make a disproportionate estimate of motion, or place it in an undue object.

We judge of the figure or shape of bodies, chiefly by the variations of light and shade; and our associations taken thence are so strong, as that we are easily imposed upon by a just imitation of the light and shades belonging to each shape and figure, in their several situations with respect to the quarter from which the illumination proceeds.

It

It is from the affociations, confidered under this propofition, and particularly in the laft paragraph, that painting conveys fuch exact ideas of fhapes, figures, magnitudes, and diftances, and the *camera obfcura* of motions alfo, by means of impreffions that proceed from a plane furface.

The pofition of objects is judged of intirely by the part of the *retina* on which the rays fall, if we be in an erect pofture ourfelves. If we be not, we allow for our deviation from it, or make a reference to fomething judged to be in an erect pofture. If we fail in thefe, errors concerning the pofition of vifible objects muft happen. Our calling bodies *erect*, when the rays proceeding from their tops fall upon the lower parts of the *retina*, and *vice verfa*, is merely from an affociation of the fame kind with thofe by which the fenfes of other words are determined.

Thofe who are difpofed to examine the fubjects of this and the following propofition with accuracy, may fee a large variety of proper inftances well explained by Dr. *Smith*, and Dr. *Jurin*, in Dr. *Smith*'s optics. Thefe gentlemen infift chiefly on optical confiderations; but they every-where admit the prevalence of affociation, though it is not always to their purpofe to take exprefs notice of it.

I will juft remind the reader, that in all the cafes of magnitude, diftance, motion, figure, and pofition, the vifible idea is fo much more vivid and ready than the tangible one, as to prevail over it, notwithftanding that our information from feeling is more precife than that from fight, and the teft of its truth. However, if we could fuppofe a perfon to be endued with the fenfes of feeing and hearing, and yet to be deftitute of that of feeling, and of the power of moving himfelf, he might have all the words expreffing diftances, magnitudes, &c. fo much, and fo properly, affociated with the vifible appearances of thefe, these, as that, by passing over his ear, they would raise up all the same trains of visible ideas, as in us.

PROP. 21.

To examine how far the circumstances of single and double vision, are agreeable to the doctrine of association.

WHEN we have attained a voluntary power over the external motions of our eyes, so as to direct them to objects at pleasure, we always do it in such a manner, as that the same points of objects fall upon correspondent points of the two *retina's*. And this correspondence between the respective points of the *retina's* is permanent and invariable. Thus the central points, or those where the optic axes terminate, always correspond; a certain point on the right side of the right *retina* always corresponds, (whatever object we view) to another certain point on the right side of the left *retina*, equally distant from the centre with it, &c. Hence, if the optic axes be directed to the object *A*, the picture made by it on the right *retina* corresponds to that made on the left; whereas the impressions made by two similar objects, *A* and *B*, upon the two *retina's*, do not correspond. The impressions therefore, that are made upon portions of the *retina's*, which do or do not correspond, are the associated criterions of single and double vision. For I here suppose, that the common appearances of a single object, and two similar ones, are respectively called single and double vision.

Let us now inquire into the fallacies which these associated criterions may occasion.

First, then, when a person directs his eyes by a voluntary power to a point nearer or farther off than the object which he views, so as to make the pictures

tures of the object fall upon the points of the two *retina's*, that do not correspond, this object will appear double. The same thing happens when one eye is distorted by a spasm, when persons lose the voluntary power of directing their optic axes to objects, and in general whenever the pictures which the object imprints on the two *retina's*, fall upon points that do not correspond.

It resembles this, and illustrates it, that if we cross the fingers, and roll a pea between two sides, which are not contiguous naturally, it feels like two peas.

Secondly, after a person whose eye is distorted by a spasm, has seen double for a certain time, this ceases, and he gains the power of seeing single again provided the distortion remains fixed to a certain degree. For the association between the points of the two *retina's*, which corresponded formerly, grows weaker by degrees; a new one also between points, that now correspond, takes place, and grows stronger perpetually.

Thirdly, if two lighted candles, of equal height, be viewed at the distance of two or three feet from the eyes, so that the picture of the right-hand candle on the left *retina* shall correspond to that of the left-hand candle on the right *retina*, only one image will be produced by these two corresponding pictures. But the two pictures which do not correspond, *viz.* that of the right-hand candle on the right *retina*, and that of the left-hand candle on the left *retina*, will each produce its proper image. See *Smith's Optics*, *Rem.* 526.

But here two questions may be asked: first, why single objects appear the same to one as to both eyes, allowing for the diminution of brightness, since, in the first case, there is one picture only, in the last two. Ought not every single object to appear single to one eye and double to both?

Secondly, how can one object appear like two to both eyes, since, however the eyes be directed or distorted, it can make but two pictures, whereas two objects make four, *viz.* two in each eye?

It is evident, that the difficulty is the same in both these questions. And it seems to be a sufficient answer to allege, that impressions so much alike, and which are so constantly made together, as those upon the corresponding portions of the two *retina's*, must unite into one intirely in the brain, and produce the same effect in kind, though somewhat different in degree, as one alone. And thus, whether we see with one eye or both, hear with one ear or both, the impression on the common sensory in the brain is the same in kind; and therefore, if the first be called single, the other must also.

But it deserves particular attention here, that the optic nerves of men, and such other animals as look the same way with both eyes, unite in the *sella turcica*, in a *ganglion*, or little brain, as one may call it, peculiar to themselves; and that the associations between synchronous impressions on the two *retina's* must be made sooner, and cemented stronger, on this account; also, that they ought to have a much greater power over one another's images, than in any other part of the body. And thus an impression made on the right eye alone by a single object, may propagate itself into the left, and there raise up an image almost equal in vividness to itself: And consequently, when we see with one eye only, we may, however, have pictures in both eyes; and when we see a single object, with our eyes directed to one at a different distance, we may have four pictures, *viz.* two from direct impression in parts that do not correspond, and two others from association in parts that do. And thus both the foregoing questions may be answered, in a manner that leaves no doubt or hesitation.

PROP.

Of SIGHT.

PROP. 22.

To explain in what manner, and to what degree, agreeable and disagreeable impressions on the eye contribute, in the way of association, to form our intellectual pleasures and pains.

IT is evident, that gay colours, of all kinds, are a principal source of pleasure to young children; and they seem to strike them more particularly, when mixed together in various ways. Whether there be any thing in colours, which corresponds to the harmony between sounds, may be doubted. If there be, it must, however, admit of much greater latitude than the harmony between sounds, since all mixtures and degrees of colours, unless where the quantity of light overpowers the eye, are pleasant; however, one colour may be more so originally than another. Black appears to be originally disagreeable to the eyes of children; it becomes disagreeable also very early from associated influences. In adults, the pleasures of mere colours are very languid in comparison of their present aggregates of pleasure, formed by association. And thus the eye approaches more and more, as we advance in spirituality and perfection, to an inlet for mental pleasure, and an organ suited to the exigencies of a being, whose happiness consists in the improvement of his understanding and affections. However, the original pleasures of mere colours remain, in a small degree, to the last, and those transferred upon them by association with other pleasures (for the influence is in these things reciprocal, without limits) in a considerable one. So that our intellectual pleasures are not only at first generated, but afterwards supported and recruited, in part from the pleasures affecting the eye; which holds

holds particularly in refpect of the pleafures afforded by the beauties of nature, and by the imitations of them, which the arts of poetry and painting furnifh us with. And for the fame reafons the difagreeable impreffions on the eye, have fome fmall fhare in generating and feeding intellectual pains.

It deferves notice here, that green, which is the colour that abounds far more than any other, is the middle one among the primary colours, and the moft univerfally and permanently agreeable to the eye of any other: Alfo, that as the common juice of vegetables is in general green, fo that of animals is in general red; the firft being, perhaps, of the third order, the laft of the fecond. It appears to be extremely worth the time and pains of philofophers to inquire into the orders of the colours of natural bodies, in the manner propofed and begun by Sir *Ifaac Newton*; and particularly to compare the changes of colour, which turn up in chemical operations, with the other changes, which happen to the fubjects of the operations at the fame time. Nothing feems more likely than this to be a key to the philofophy of the fmall parts of natural bodies, and of their mutual influences.

PROP. 23.

To give an account of the ideas generated by vifible impreffions.

HERE we may make the following obfervations: Firft, that the ideas of this fenfe are far more vivid and definite than thofe of any other; agreeably to which, the word *idea* denoted thefe alone in its original and moft peculiar fenfe. Hence it is proper to make the ftricteft examination into the ideas of this fenfe, and their properties, fince it is probable, from the analogies every-where confpicuous

cuous in natural things, that thefe are patterns of all the reft. Their peculiar vividnefs and precifion may therefore be confidered as ferving like a microfcope in refpect of other ideas, *i. e.* as magnifying their properties.

Secondly, the vividnefs and precifion here fpoken of relate chiefly to diftance, magnitude, motion, figure, and pofition, *i. e.* to the things confidered in the 58th *Prop*. However, colours leave diftinct ideas of themfelves; but then they require an exertion of our voluntary powers for the moft part, whereas the ideas of diftances, magnitudes, *&c.* recur inceffantly in the trains which pafs over the fancy.

Thirdly, The peculiar vividnefs and precifion of vifible ideas may probably be owing to the following caufes, as well as to fome peculiar unknown ftructure of the optic nerve, and correfponding region of the brain; *viz*. The perpetual recurrency of vifible objects, either the fame, or fimilar ones, during the whole time that we are awake; the diftinct manner in which they are impreffed by means of the feveral proper conformations of the eye; and their being received in general upon the fame part of the *retina*, precifely or nearly. For, when we view any object with attention, we make the central point of it fall upon the central part of the *retina*. Farther, as the optic nerve fends off no branches, but is fpent wholly upon the *retina*, this may perhaps contribute in fome degree. And thefe confiderations may a little help us to conceive, how the optic nerve, and correfponding region of the brain, may be the repofitory of fuch an immenfe variety of vifible ideas, as they are in fact.

Fourthly, the idea of every familiar object has, for the moft part, fome particular magnitude, pofition, and aggregate of affociates, in its recurrences to the mind. And this fomewhat leffens the difficulty

difficulty mentioned in the laſt paragraph. The reaſon of this fourth obſervation is, that though every viſible object appears under different magnitudes, in different poſitions, and with different aſſociates, yet theſe differences deſtroy one another, ſo that the ſtrongeſt particularity only remains. However, changes are made from time to time, each ſubſiſting for a ſhort period, and then giving way to the next in ſucceſſion.

Fifthly, we have fictitious viſible ideas of places and perſons that we have never ſeen, as well as of thoſe which we have. Theſe are derived from aſſociation evidently, and they often undergo ſucceſſive changes, like thoſe ſpoken of in the laſt paragraph.

Sixthly, our viſible ideas are ſubject to the voluntary power in a high degree, and may be called up by the ſlighteſt aſſociated circumſtance, at the ſame time that they have very numerous connexions with other ideas, and with actual impreſſions. The name, or its idea in the region of the brain correſponding to the ear, are the circumſtances moſt commonly made uſe of for calling up viſible ideas. But there are many ideas, *i. e.* internal feelings, which have no names, and which yet, by attending our ſeveral viſible ideas, get this power of introducing them.

Here it is to be obſerved, that an idea cannot be ſaid to be voluntarily introduced, till it be previouſly determined by ſome of its aſſociates. If I deſire to introduce a viſible idea of any kind, an *individuum vagum*, and that of an horſe offers itſelf, it was not owing to the command of my will, that it was an horſe, and nothing elſe, but to the connexion which the idea of an horſe had with ſome other idea or impreſſion, which then happened to take place. But if I deſire to recollect the features of a perſon's face whom I ſaw yeſterday, I make uſe of his name, his dreſs, the place in which I ſaw him, or ſome other aſſociated circumſtance, for this purpoſe. And this

Of SIGHT.

this may be called a voluntary introduction of an idea. However, the introduction of the idea of an horse, in the circumstances just described, might be termed voluntary in a different sense, if any person thought fit to denominate it so, on account of the command of the will to introduce some idea. My design here is, only to suggest to the reader the processes generally made use of in these things. It is to be observed farther, that the associated circumstance, which determines what idea shall be called up voluntarily, does, for the most part, raise it. Thus, if a person desires me to call up the idea of an horse, the very sound of the word proceeding from his mouth will do it, for most part, immediately. If not, I go back, by my memory, to the trace left by the word, and thence to the idea, or to some common associate of both the word and idea, capable of raising the last.

Seventhly, when we have conversed much with the same visible objects, as after having been in a croud, travelling, *&c.* for many hours without intermission, we may find the ideas of these objects peculiarly strong, so as to intrude upon our fancies, and interfere with all our other ideas. This may serve to shew, that the permanence of the sensations impressed, mentioned in the third proposition, and which shews itself particularly in visible impressions, as there remarked, is of the nature of an idea. And it coincides remarkably with this, that the ideas should be peculiarly vivid and precise in the same sense, where the permanency of the sensation impressed is most conspicuous.

Eighthly, the ideas of sight and hearing, and the impressions from whence they proceed, have a peculiar connexion with each other. For as words pronounced call up visible ideas, so visible ideas and objects call up the ideas of words, and the actions by which they are pronounced.

Ninthly,

Ninthly, The trains of visible ideas are in a particular manner affected by the general states of the brain, as may appear from the trains which present themselves in madness, phrensies, and common deliriums. This agrees remarkably with what has been already observed concerning the ideas of this sense; and we may infer from altogether, that the regions of the brain corresponding to the optic nerve are comparatively large, or peculiarly susceptive of impressions, or both.

Tenthly, the imagery of the eye sympathizes also remarkably with the affections of the stomach. Thus the grateful impressions of opium upon the stomach raise up the ideas of gay colours, and transporting scenes, in the eye; and spasms, and indigestions have often a contrary effect. The ghastly faces which sometimes appear in idea, particularly after drinking tea, seem to be an effect of this kind, or perhaps of the last-mentioned one; for they are common to persons of irritable nervous systems. Ghastly faces may take place preferably to other disagreeable ideas, perhaps because characters, affections, passions, are principally denoted and expressed by the countenance; because faces are the most common of visible objects, and attended to with the greatest earnestness; because we criticize much upon the beauty of faces, and upon the proportion of the several features to each other; and because evil spirits (the notions of which generally take strong and early possession of our fancies) are painted with ghastly faces. This mixture of reasons hinders each particular one from being so obvious, as might otherwise be expected; however, the same thing is common in many other cases. The trains of visible ideas, which occur in dreams, are deducible partly from the sympathy here mentioned, partly from that of the last paragraph.

Eleventhly,

Eleventhly, our stock of visible ideas may be considered as a key to a great part of our knowledge, and a principal source of invention in poetry, painting, mathematics, mechanics, and almost every other branch of the arts and sciences. In mathematics and mechanics the invention of the diagram is, in effect, the solution of the problem. Our memories are also much assisted by our visible ideas in respect of past facts, and the preservation of the order of time depends in a particular manner upon our visible trains suggesting each other in due succession. Hence eye witnesses generally relate in order of time, without any express design of doing so. This recollection of visible ideas, in the order in which they were impressed, gives rise to the *loci memoriales*, in which matters principally worthy of remembrance are to be reposited, and to the artificial memory, that is borrowed from the eye; just as the facility of remembring words formed into verses does to the artificial memory borrowed from the ear. It may deserve notice here, that some persons have imaginary places for the natural numbers, as far as 100, or farther.

Twelfthly, the ideas which different persons have of the same persons faces, though they be very like one another, cannot yet be precisely the same, on account of the addition and omission of little circumstances, and a variety of associated ones, which intermix themselves here. Hence the same picture may appear much more like to one person than to another, *viz.* according as it resembles his idea more or less.

Thirteenthly, painters, statuaries, anatomists, architects, &c. see at once what is intended by a picture, draught, &c. from the perfection of their visible ideas; and carry off the scene, plan, &c. in their memories, with quickness and facility. All which is still owing to association. But it would be
endless

endless to enumerate the instances of associations, which this sense affords.

Fourteenthly, it is probable, that fables, parables, similes, allegory, &c. please, strike and instruct, chiefly on account of the visible imagery, which they raise up in the fancy. They are also much more easily remembered on the same account. We may add, that idolatry, heathenish and popish, has made a much quicker and more extensive progress in the world on account of the stability and vividness of visible impressions and ideas, and the difficulty, obscurity, and changeable nature, of abstract notions. And image-worship seems even to have been derived in great measure from this source.

Fifteenthly, it would be a matter of great curiosity and use (as far as these speculations can be of any use to inquire carefully into the progress of the mind, and particularly of the fancy, in persons born blind, and compare the result with what is advanced under this proposition, and with other parts of these papers, in order to correct and improve the theory of association thereby. It is probable, that they are considerable losers, upon the whole, in respect of knowledge; though their greater degree of attention, and the superior acuteness of the senses of feeling and hearing, and consequently, perfection of the ideas of these senses, must give them some particular advantages.

SECT.

Of HEARING.

SECT. V.
Of the Sense of Hearing.

PROP. 24.

To examine how far the judgments which we make concerning the distance and position of the sounding body, are agreeable to the doctrine of association.

SOUNDS ought to decrease in the reciprocal duplicate ratio of the distance, did they not receive some support from the reflexion of the bodies over which they pass. This makes them decrease in a less ratio; however, they do decrease in general with the distance; and this decrease, being an associate of the increase of distance, ought to suggest it to the imagination. And, agreeably to this, we may observe, that, when the wind opposes the sound of bells, they appear farther off; when a person calls through a speaking trumpet, he appears nearer, than at the true distance.

As to the position of the sounding body, we have no clear or certain criterion, unless it be very near us; so as that the pulses may strike one ear, or one part of the head, considerably stronger than another. Hence we judge of the position of the speaker, or sounding body, by the eye, or by some other method independent on the ear. And thus, if from some mistaken presumption a voice, or sound, shall be deemed to come from a quarter different from the true place of it, we shall continue in that error from the strength of that mistaken presumption.

By laying these things together, and also considering farther, that indistinctness in articulate sounds is an associated mark of distance, we may see how *ventriloqui*, or persons that speak in the throats, without moving their lips, impose upon their audience. Their voice is faint and indistinct, and therefore appears to come from a more distant quarter than the speaker. The hearers look about therefore, and, being surprised, their imagination fixes strongly upon that corner, or cavity, which appears most plausible; and afterwards they continue to impose upon themselves by the strength of this prejudice.

PROP. 25.

To examine how far the power of distinguishing articulate sounds depends upon the power of association.

ONE may suppose the external and internal ear to be so formed, as that all the differences in the vibrations of the air, which arrive at the ear, may affect the auditory nerves with corresponding differences. Let us therefore first consider in what manner different sounds impress different vibrations upon the air.

First, then, since not only the parts about the throat, but those of the mouth, cheeks, and even of the whole body, especially of the bones, vibrate in speaking, the figure of the vibrations impressed upon the air by the human voice will be different from that of the vibrations proceeding from a violin, flute, &c. provided the distance be not too great. This therefore may be considered as one help for distinguishing articulate sounds from all others.

Secondly, articulation consists in breaking out from a whisper into a sound, or closing the sound in different manners, the organs of speech being put also into different shapes, so as to join the differences mentioned

Of HEARING.

mentioned in the laſt paragraph with various eruptions and interruptions, aſcents and deſcents of ſound. And thus each letter may be diſtinguiſhed from every other by hearing.

Thirdly, it is agreeable to all this, that it is difficult at great diſtances to diſtinguiſh the tone of one muſical inſtrument from another, or of any from the tone of a human voice, *cæteris paribus*; or to diſtinguiſh articulate ſounds from one another. For at great diſtances the vibrations of the air are circular to ſenſe, and all the aſcents, deſcents, eruptions, and interruptions of ſound, which diſtinguiſh one compound ſound from another, are confounded by numberleſs reflections from the intermediate bodies.

Fourthly, we may obſerve, that as the preſerving the diſtinction of place is the chief end of the coats and humours in the organ of ſight, ſo the diſtinction of time is of the greateſt importance in hearing. It ſeems probable therefore, that the *membrana tympani*, ſmall bones, and their muſcles, are ſo contrived, as by their actions to preſerve the diſtinction of time, *i.e.* to extinguiſh ſtrong ſounds, and to keep up weak ones, ſo as that the laſt may not be too much overpowered by the continuance of the firſt; juſt as the treble notes of a harpſichord would be by the baſs ones, did not the bits of cloth affixed to the jacks check the vibrations of the ſtrings in due time.

Having now ſhewn how articulate ſounds may be diſtinguiſhed from one another, and from all other ſounds; I next obſerve, that, in fact, the ſpeakers do not pronounce ſo articulately and diſtinctly in common converſation, as to furniſh the hearers with the requiſite criterions according to the foregoing theory; but that we arrive at a facility of underſtanding one another's diſcourſe, chiefly by the power of aſſociation.

And,

And, first, it is needless to pronounce every letter so as to distinguish it from all others. For then words, which are composed of letters, would each have as many criterions as they have letters, and even more; for the order of the letters is a criterion, as well as the sound of each letter. In like manner, sentences would have as many compound criterions as they have words, besides the criterion arising from the particular order of the words.

Secondly, since words are formed from combinations, not according to any rule, which brings up all the combinations of two's, three's, &c. in order, but by particular associations, agreeably to the nature of each language, since also sentences are formed in the same way, the several component parts of words and sentences suggest each other, and also the whole words and sentences, by the power of association. Thus the beginning is commonly observed to suggest the whole, both in words and sentences; and the same is true, in a less degree, of the middles and ends.

Thirdly, the subject-matter of the discourse, the gestures used in speaking, a familiar acquaintance with the particular voice, pronunciation, gestures, &c. of the speaker, and other associated circumstances, contribute greatly also. And therefore, on the other hand, we find it difficult to distinguish proper names and the words of an unknown language, and to understand a person that is a stranger, or that uses no action.

We may see also, that it is chiefly by the means of associated circumstances, that the sounds uttered by *ventriloqui* suggest to us the words, which they are supposed to pronounce; for their articulations must be very incomplete, as they do not move their lips at all.

It is by a like set of associated circumstances that we are enabled to read with so much facility the
irregular

Of HEARING.

irregular hand-writing of various perſons, and of ſome more than others, in proportion as we are better acquainted with the ſubject, language, hand-writing, &c.

PROP. 26.

To explain in what manner, and to what degree, agreeable and diſagreeable ſounds contribute, in the way of aſſociation, to the formation of our intellectual pleaſures and pains.

AS all moderate and tolerably uniform ſounds pleaſe young children, and the original pleaſures from concords ſounded together, from the ſucceſſion of both concords and diſcords, and even from clear, muſical ſounds, conſidered ſeparately, remain with us through the whole progreſs of life, it is evident, that many of our intellectual pleaſures muſt be illuminated and augmented by them. And, on the contrary, harſh, irregular, and violently loud noiſes muſt add ſomething to the diſagreeableneſs of the objects and ideas, with which they are often aſſociated.

The pleaſures of muſic are compoſed, as has been already obſerved, partly of the original, corporeal pleaſures of ſound, and partly of aſſociated ones. When theſe pleaſures are arrived at tolerable perfection, and the ſeveral compounding parts cemented ſufficiently by aſſociation, they are transferred back again upon a great variety of objects and ideas, and diffuſe joy, good-will, anger, compaſſion, ſorrow, melancholy, &c. upon the various ſcenes and events of life; and ſo on reciprocally without perceptible limits.

The corporeal pleaſures from articulate ſounds are either evaneſcent from the firſt, or, however, become so very early in life. By this means we are much better qualified to receive information, with mental pleasure and improvement, from them; and the ear becomes like the eye, a method of perception suited to the wants of a spiritual being. And indeed when we compare the imperfections of such as have never heard, with those of persons that have never seen, it appears that the ear is of much more importance to us, considered as spiritual beings, than the eye. This is chiefly owing to the great use and necessity of words for the improvement of our knowledge, and inlargement of our affections; of which I shall have particular occasion to treat hereafter. An accurate inquiry into the mental progress of persons deprived of the advantages of language, by being born deaf, would be a still better test of the theory of these papers, than a like inquiry concerning persons born blind.

PROP. 27.

To give an account of the ideas generated by audible impressions.

THE ideas which audible impressions leave in the region of the brain, that corresponds to the auditory nerves, are, next to the ideas of sight, the most vivid and definite of any; and all the observations above made upon the ideas of sight may be applied to those of hearing, proper changes and allowances being made. Thus, after hearing music, conversing much with the same person, in general disorders of the brain, or particular ones of the nervous spasmodic kind in the stomach, after taking opium, in dreams, in madness, trains of audible ideas force themselves upon the fancy, in nearly the same manner, as trains of visible ideas do in like cases. And it may be, that in passing over words

with

Of HEARING. 83

with our eye, in viewing objects, in thinking, and particularly in writing and speaking, faint miniatures of the sounds of words pass over the ear. I even suspect, that in speaking, these miniatures are the associated circumstances which excite the action, be it voluntary or secondarily automatic. For children learn to speak chiefly by repeating the sounds which they hear, *i. e.* these sounds are the associated circumstances, which excite to action. But if the sound does this, the idea of it must get the same power by degrees. I grant indeed, that the pictures of words in the eye, and their ideas, may be like associated circumstances, exciting to speak; and since it is necessary, according to the theory of these papers, that every semivoluntary, voluntary, and secondarily automatic action, should be excited by an associated circumstance, one may reckon words seen, and their visible ideas, amongst the number of such circumstances. But words heard, and their audible ideas, have a prior claim; and, in persons that cannot read or write, almost the only one. It confirms this, that in writing one is often apt to mis-spell in conformity with the pronunciation, as in writing *hear* for *here*; for this may proceed from the audible idea, which is the same in both cases; cannot from the visible one. Where a person mis-spells suitable to a mispronunciation, which sometimes happens, it can scarce be accounted for upon other principles. However, in writing, the associated circumstance, which excites the action of the hand, is most probably the visible idea of the word, not the audible one.

If it be objected to the supposition of these audible trains, that we ought to be conscious of them, I answer, that we are in some cases; which is an argument, that they take place in all, in a less degree; that the greater vividness of the visible trains makes

G 2 us

us not attend to, or recollect them, till the confcioufnefs or memory be vanifhed; and that even vifible trains do not appear as objects of confcioufnefs and memory, till we begin to attend to them, and watch the evanefcent perceptions of our minds.

The ideas of fight and hearing together are the principal ftorehoufe of the fancy or imagination; and the imaginative arts of painting and mufic ftand in the fame relation to them refpectively. Poetry comprehends both by taking in language, which is the general reprefentative of all our ideas and affections.

As there is an artificial memory relative to the eye, by which trains of vifible ideas, laid up in the memory in a certain order, are made to fuggeft both things themfelves, and the order in which we defire to remember them; fo compendious trains of technical words formed into verfes may be made to fuggeft other words, alfo the numeral figures in a certain order; and, by this means, to bring to view, at pleafure, the principles and materials of knowledge for meditation, inquiry, and more perfect digeftion by the mind, as appears from Dr. *Grey's Memoria Technica*. The vifible *loci* make a ftronger impreffion on the fancy, and therefore excel the audible ones in that view; but the audible ones have a much more ready and definite connexion with the things to be remembered; and therefore feem moft proper, upon the whole, in moft branches of literature. And as Dr. *Grey's* method is highly ufeful in general, fo it is particularly excellent in refpect of all memorables that are reprefented by numeral figures. For, when the numeral figures are denoted by letters, collections of them, fuch as dates, and quantities of all kinds, make fhort and definite impreffions upon the ear; which are not only eafy to be remembered, but alfo preferve the order of the figures without

danger

danger of error; whereas neither the impreffions which collections of figures make upon the eye, nor thofe which their enunciations in words at length make upon the ear, can be remembered with facility or precifion; becaufe neither figures, nor their names, cohere together, fo as that the precedent fhall fuggeft the fubfequent; as the letters do in collections of them, capable of being pronounced. When the technical word coincides with, or approaches to, a familiar one, it is remembered with greater facflity. Affociation is every where confpicuous in thefe things.

SECT. VI.

Of the desires of the sexes towards each other.

PROP. 28.

To examine how far the desires of the sexes towards each other are of a factitious nature, and deducible from the theory of these papers.

HERE we are to observe, first, that when a general pleasurable state is introduced into the body, either by direct impressions, or by associated influences, the organs of generation must sympathize with this general state, for the same reasons as the other parts do. They must therefore be affected with vibrations in their nerves, which rise above indifference into the limits of pleasure from youth, health, grateful aliment, the pleasures of imagination, ambition, and sympathy, or any other cause, which diffuses grateful vibrations over the whole system.

Secondly, as these organs are endued with a greater degree of sensibility than the other parts from their make, and the peculiar structure and disposition of their nerves, whatever these be, we may expect, that they should be more affected by these general pleasurable states of the nervous system than the other parts.

Thirdly, the distention of the cells of the *vesiculæ seminales*, and of the *sinuses* of the *uterus*, which take place about the time of puberty, must make these organs more particularly irritable then. It may perhaps be, that the acrimony of the urine and *fæces*, which make vivid impressions on the neighbouring parts, have also a share in increasing the irritability of the organs of generation.

Fourthly,

Fourthly, young persons hear and read numberless things, in this degenerate and corrupt state of human life, which carry nervous influences of the pleasurable kind (be they vibrations, or any other species of motion) to the organs of generation. This will be better understood, if the reader pleases to recollect what was delivered above concerning the methods, by which we learn to distinguish the sensations of the parts external and internal from each other. For it will be easy to see, that when we are once arrived at this power, the associated circumstances of any sensations, such as the language that relates to them, will recal the ideas of these sensations.

Fifthly, the particular shame, which regards the organs of generation, may, when considered as an associated circumstance, like other pains, be so far diminished as to fall within the limits of pleasure, and add considerably to the sum total.

Sixthly, the sources here pointed out seem sufficient to account for the general desires, which are observable in young persons; and which, when not allowed and indulged, may be considered as within the confines of virtue.

Seventhly, it is usual for these desires, after some time, to fix upon a particular object, on account of the apprehended beauty of the person, or perfection of the mind, also from mutual obligations, or marks of affection, from more frequent intercourses, &c. after which these desires suggest, and are suggested by, the idea of the beloved person, and all its associates, reciprocally and indefinitely, so as in some cases to engross the whole fancy and mind. However this particular attachment, when under proper restrictions and regulations, is not only within the confines of virtue, but often the parent of the most disinterested, and pure, and exalted kinds of it.

Eighthly, when these desires are gratified, the idea of the beloved person, and its associates, must now

now be associated with the state of neutrality and indifference, that succeeds after gratification. Whence it appears, that that part of the affection towards the beloved person, which arises from gross animal causes, cannot remain long at its height, and may fall very fast. However, if the other sources of affection grow stronger, the sum total may continue the same, or even increase.

Ninthly, when impure desires are allowed, indulged, and heightened voluntarily, it is evident from the doctrine of association, that they will draw to themselves all the other pleasures of our nature, and even, by adhering to many neutral circumstances, convert them into incentives and temptations. So that all the desires, designs, and ideas of such persons are tainted with lust. However, the diseases and sufferings, bodily and mental, which this vice brings upon men, do, after some time, often check the exorbitancy of it, still in the way of association. But impure desires subsist, like vicious ones of other kinds, long after the pains outweigh the pleasures; inasmuch as they must be supposed not to begin to decline till the pains apprehended to arise from them, and thus associated with them, become equal to the pleasures.

Tenthly, it appears from the course of reasoning here used, that impure and vicious desires, indulged and heightened voluntarily, can by no means consist with a particular attachment and confinement; also that they must not only end frequently in indifference, but even in hatred and abhorrence. For the proper mental sources of affection are not only wanting in these cases, but many displeasing and odious qualities and dispositions of mind must offer themselves to view by degrees.

Eleventhly, as the desires and pleasures of this kind are thus increased by associated influences from other parts of our natures, so they are reflected back

by

by innumerable associated methods, direct and indirect, upon the various incidents and events of life, so as to affect in secondary ways even those who have never experienced the gross corporeal gratification. And, notwithstanding the great and public mischiefs, which arise from the ungovernable desires of the vicious, there is great reason, even from this theory, to apprehend, that, if this source of the benevolent affections was cut off, all other circumstances remaining the same, mankind would become much more selfish and malicious, much more wicked and miserable, upon the whole, than they now are.

Twelfthly, I have hitherto chiefly considered how far the present subject is agreeable to the doctrine of association; but, if physicians and anatomists will compare the circumstances of the sensations and motions of these organs with the general theory delivered in the first chapter, they may see considerable evidences for sensory vibrations, for their running along membranes, and affecting the neighbouring muscles in a particular manner: They may see also, that muscular contractions, which are nearly automatic at first, become afterwards subject to the influence of ideas.

Thirteenthly, the theory here proposed for explaining the nature and growth of these desires shews in every step, how watchful every person, who desires true chastity and purity of heart, ought to be over his thoughts, his discourses, his studies, and his intercourses with the world in general, and with the other sex in particular. There is no security but in flight, in turning our minds from all the associated circumstances, and begetting a new train of thoughts and desires, by an honest, virtuous, religious attention to the duty of the time and place. To which must be added great abstinence in diet, and bodily labour, if required.

SECT.

SECT. VII.

Of other motions, automatic and voluntary, not considered in the foregoing sections of this chapter.

PROP. 29.

To examine how far the motions, that are most perfectly voluntary, such as those of walking, handling, and speaking, with the voluntary power of suspending them, and their being formed according to patterns set by those with whom we converse, are agreeable to the foregoing theory.

IT was necessary to deliver many things which properly relate to this proposition under the twenty-first, in order to make the derivation of voluntary motion from automatic, by means of association, in some measure intelligible to the reader. I will now resume the subject, and add what I am able for the full explication and establishment of the theory proposed.

Walking is the most simple of the three kinds of voluntary motion here mentioned, being common to the brute creation with man, whereas handling and speaking are, in a manner, peculiar to him. His superiority in this respect, when compared with the superiority of his mental faculties, agrees well with the hypothesis here advanced concerning handling and speaking; *viz.* their dependence on ideas, and the power of association.

The new-born child is unable to walk on account of the want of strength to support his body, as well as as of complex and decomplex motory vibratiuncles, generated by affociation, and depending upon fenfations and ideas by affociation alfo. As he gets ftrength, he advances likewife in the number and variety of compound motions of the limbs, their fpecies being determined by the nature of the articulations, the pofition of the mufcles, the automatic motions excited by friction, accidental flexures and extenfions made by the nurfe, &c. When he is tolerably perfect in thefe rudiments of walking, the view of a favourite plaything will excite various motions in the limbs; and thus if he be fet upon his legs, and his body carried forward by the nurfe, an imperfect attempt to walk follows of courfe. It is made more perfect gradually by his improvement in the rudiments, by the nurfe's moving his legs alternately in the proper manner, by his defire of going up to perfons, playthings, &c. and thence repeating the procefs which has fucceeded (for he makes innumerable trials, both fuccefsful and unfuccefsful); and by his feeing others walk, and endeavouring to imitate them.

It deferves notice here, that in the limbs, where the motions are moft perfectly voluntary, all the mufcles have antagonifts, and often fuch as are of nearly equal ftrength with themfelves; alfo, that the mufcles of the limbs are not much influenced at firft by common impreffions made on the fkin, and fcarce at all when the child is fo far advanced as to get a voluntary power over them. For thefe things facilitate the generation of the voluntary power, by making the mufcles of the limbs chiefly dependent on the vibrations which defcend from the brain, and alfo difpofing them to act from a fmall balance in favour of this or that fet of antagonifts.

When the child can walk up to an object that he defires to walk up to, the action may be termed voluntary; *i. e.* the ufe of language will then juftify
this

this appellation. But it appears from the reasoning here used, that this kind and degree of voluntary power over his motions is generated by proper combinations and associations of the automatic motions, agreeably to the corollaries of the twentieth proposition. Voluntary powers may therefore result from association, as is asserted in these papers.

When he is arrived at such a perfection in walking, as to walk readily upon being desired by another person, the action is esteemed still more voluntary. One reason of which is, that the child, in some cases, does not walk when desired, whilst yet the circumstances are apparently the same as when he does. For here the unapparent cause of walking, or not walking, is *will*. However, it follows from this theory, that all this is still owing to association, or to something equally suitable to the foregoing theory; *e. g.* to the then present strength or weakness of the association of the words of the command with the action of walking, to its proceeding from this or that person, in this or that manner, to the child's being in an active or inactive state, attentive or inattentive, disposed by other circumstances to move as directed, or to move in a different way, &c. A careful observation of the fact will always shew, as far as is reasonable to be expected in so nice a matter, that when children do different things, the real circumstances, natural or associated, are proportionably different, and that the state of mind called *will* depends upon this difference. This degree of voluntary power is therefore, in like manner, of an acquired nature.

Suppose an adult to walk, in order to shew his perfectly voluntary power; still his selecting this instance is owing to one association, and his performing the action to another, *viz.* to the introduction of the audible idea of the word the visible one of the action, &c.

Walking

Walking paffes into the fecondarily automatic ftate more perfectly perhaps, than any other action; for adults feldom exert any degree of volition here, fufficient to affect the power of confcioufnefs or memory for the leaft perceptible moment of time. Now this tranfition of walking, from its voluntary to its fecondarily automatic ftate, muft be acknowledged by all to proceed merely from affociation. And it feems to follow by parity of reafon, that the tranfition of primarily automatic actions into voluntary ones may be merely from affociation alfo, fince it is evident that affociation has at leaft a very great and extenfive influence there.

The complex artificial motions of the lower limbs, ufed in the feveral kinds of dancing, bear nearly the fame relation to the common motions ufed in walking forwards, backwards, upwards, downwards, and fideways, as thefe common motions do to the fimple rudiments above-mentioned, fuch as the flexion and extenfion of the ancle or knee. Since therefore the voluntary and fecondarily automatic power of dancing are plainly the refult of affociation, why may we not fuppofe the fame of the common motions in walking, both in their voluntary and fecondarily automatic ftate? In learning to dance, the fcholar defires to look at his feet and legs, in order to judge by feeing when they are in a proper pofition. By degrees he learns to judge of this by feeling; but the vifible idea left partly by the view of his mafter's motions, partly by that of his own, feems to be the chief affociated circumftance, that introduces the proper motions. By farther degrees thefe are connected with each other, with the mufic, and with other more and more remote circumftances,

I have already fhewn, in what manner children learn the voluntary and fecondarily automatic power of grafping. How they learn the various complex motions, by which they feed and drefs themfelves, &c.

alfo

also how children and adults learn to write, to practise manual arts, &c. and in what senses and degrees all these actions are voluntary, and secondarily automatic, and yet still remain as purely mechanical, as the primarily automatic actions are, may now be understood from what has been already delivered under this proposition. The method of playing upon musical instruments has also been explained, so as to concur in establishing the same conclusions.

In like manner, the account given of the action of speaking might now be compleated, and extended to all the modes of it, vulgar and artificial ; and to singing, with its modes. I will add a few words concerning stammering, and the loss of speech by palsies.

Stammering seems generally to arise from fear, eagerness, or some violent passion, which prevents the child's articulating rightly, by the confusion which it makes in the vibrations that descend into the muscular system ; so that, finding himself wrong, he attempts again and again, till he hits upon the true sound. It does not begin therefore in general, till children are of an age to distinguish right from wrong in respect of pronunciation, and to articulate with tolerable propriety. A nervous disorder of the muscles of speech may have a like effect. When the trick of stammering has once begun to take place in a few words, it will extend itself to more and more from very slight resemblances, and particularly to all the first words of sentences, because there the organs pass in an instant from inactivity to action ; whereas the subsequent parts of words and sentences may follow the foregoing from association ; just as, in repeating *memoriter*, one is most apt to hesitate at the first word in each sentence.

A defect of memory from passion, natural weakness, &c. so that the proper word does not occur readily, occasions stammering also. And, like all other

other modes of speaking, it is caught, in some cases, by imitation.

A palsy of the organs of speech may be occasioned in the same manner as any other palsy; and yet the muscles of the lips, cheeks, tongue, and *fauces*, may still continue to perform the actions of mastication and deglutition sufficiently well, because these actions are simpler than that of speech, and are also excited by sensations which have an original influence over them.

A defect of memory may also destroy the power of speaking, in great measure, though the organs be not much affected in a paralytical way. Thus a person who plays well upon a harpsichord, may by some years disuse become unable to play at all, though the muscles of his hands be in a perfect state, merely because his memory, and the associations of the motions of his fingers, with the sight of notes, with the ideas of sounds, or with one another, are obliterated by distance of time, and disuse.

The suspension of an action may be performed two ways, as before-mentioned; *viz.* either by putting the muscles concerned in it into a languid inactive state, or by making the antagonists act with vigour. In the first case, the whole limb is put into a state of relaxation, and extreme flexibility; in the last, into a state of rigidity. The voluntary power of the first kind is obtained by associations with the languor that arises from fatigue, heat, sleepiness, *&c.* that of the last from the general tension of the muscles, which happens in pain, and violent emotions of mind. Children improve in both these kinds of voluntary power by repeated trials, as occasion requires, by imitation, desire, *&c.* But they are both difficult for some time. Thus we may observe, that children cannot let their heads or eyelids fall from their mere weight, nor stop themselves in running or striking, till a considerable time after they can

can raife the head, or bend it, open the eyes, or fhut them, run or ftrike, by a voluntary power.

Imitation is a great fource of the voluntary power, and makes all the feveral modes of walking, handling, and fpeaking, conformable to thofe of the age and nation in which a perfon lives in general, and to thofe of the perfons with whom he converfes in particular. Befides the two fources already mentioned, *prop.* 21. *viz.* the fight of the child's own actions, and the found of his own words, it has many others. Some of thefe are the refemblance which children obferve between their own bodies, with all the functions of them, and thofe of others; the pleafures which they experience in and by means of all motions, *i. e.* imitations; the directions and encouragements given to them upon this head; the high opinions which they form of the power and happinefs of adults; and their confequent defire to refemble them in thefe, and in all their affociates. Imitation begins in the feveral kinds of voluntary actions about the fame time, and increafes not only by the fources alledged, but alfo by the mutual influences of every inftance of it over every other, fo that the velocity of its growth is greatly accelerated for fome time. It is of the higheft ufe to children in their attainment of accomplifhments, bodily and mental. And thus every thing, to which mankind have a natural tendency, is learnt much fooner in fociety, than the mere natural tendency would beget it; and many things are learnt fo early, and fixed fo deeply, as to appear parts of our nature, though they may be mere derivatives and acquifitions.

It is remarkable, that apes, whofe bodies refemble the human body, more than thofe of any other brute creature, and whofe intellects alfo approach nearer to ours, which laft circumftance may, I fuppofe, have fome connexion with the firft, fhould likewife refemble us fo much in the faculty of imitation. Their

aptnefs

aptnefs in handling is plainly the refult of the fhape and make of their fore legs, and their intellects together, as in us. Their peculiar chattering may perhaps be fome attempt towards fpeech, to which they cannot attain, partly from the defect in the organs, partly, and that chiefly, from the narrownefs of their memories, apprehenfions, and affociations; for they feem not to underftand words to any confiderable degree. Or may not their chattering be an imitation of laughter?

Parrots appear to have far lefs intellect than apes, but a more diftinguifhing ear, and, like other birds, a much greater command of the mufcles of the throat. Their talk feems to be almoft devoid of all proper connexion with ideas. However, in refpect of founds, they imitate as much as children, or as apes in refpect of other actions. And indeed the talk of children, by out-running their underftandings in many things, very much refembles that of parrots.

As we exprefs our inward fentiments by words, fo we do alfo by geftures, and particularly by the mufcles of the face. Here, again, affociation and imitation difplay themfelves. This dumb fhew prevails more in the hotter climates, where the paffions are more impetuous, than in thefe northern ones. It is alfo probable, that the narrownefs and imperfection of the antient languages made it more neceffary and prevalent in antient times. Deaf perfons have an extraordinary aptnefs both in learning and decyphering this, as might well be expected. The imitation of manners and characters by dumb fhew is often more ftriking, than any verbal defcription of them.

SECT. VIII.

Of the relation which the foregoing theory bears to the art of Physic.

PROP. 30.

The art of physic affords many proper tests of the doctrines of vibrations and association; and may receive considerable improvement from them, if they be true.

THIS proposition may appear from several hints to that purpose, which have been already given. But it will be more fully manifest, if I give a short view of the *data* and *quæsita* in the art of physic.

Now the general problem, which comprehends the whole art, is,

Having the *symptoms* given, to find the *remedy*.

This problem may be solved in some cases empirically and directly by the histories of distempers, and of their cures. But then there are other cases, and those not a few, to which the learning and experience of the most able physicians either cannot find histories sufficiently similar, or none where the event was successful. Hence it is necessary to attempt the solution of the general problem rationally and indirectly, by dividing it into the two following less comprehensive and consequently more manageable problems; *viz.*

First, *having the symptoms given, to find the deviation of the body from its natural state.*

Secondly, *having this deviation given, to find the remedy.*

It is proper also to invert these two problems, and to inquire, first, *having the deviation given, what the symptoms must be.*

Secondly, *having the manner of operation of a successful remedy given, what the deviation must be.*

I here use the words *symptoms, deviation,* and *remedy,* in the most general sense possible, for the sake of brevity.

Now it is very evident, that the doctrine of vibrations, or some other better doctrine, which teaches the law of action of the nervous system, has a close connexion with all these last four problems. For the nerves enter every part, as well as the blood-vessels; and the brain has as great a share in all the natural functions of the parts, and its disorders, in all their disorders, as the heart, and its disorders, can have; and much more than any other part, besides the heart.

Farther, if the doctrine of association be the necessary consequence of the doctrine of vibrations, in any such manner as I have proposed above, *Prop.* 9. and 11. it must have a most intimate connexion with the theory of nervous distempers, and some with that of others, on account of the just-mentioned dependence of all the parts on the brain. Or, if we separate these doctrines, still, if that of association be true, of which I suppose there is no doubt, it cannot but be of great use for explaining those distempers in which the mind is affected,

And it seems to me, that, agreeably to this, the distempers of the head, spasmodic ones, the effects of poisonous bites and stings, which, as Dr. Mead justly observes, are more exerted upon the nerves than on the blood, receive much light from the doctrine of vibrations, and, in return, confirm it; and that all the disorders of the memory, fancy, and mind, do the same in respect of the doctrine of association.

I do not mean to intimate here, that the rational and indirect folution of the general problem, which comprehends the art of phyfic, is preferable to the empirical and direct one, where this is to be had; but only, fince this cannot be had always, that we ought to proceed in an explicit and fcientifical manner, rather than in a confufed and popular one. For where practice is filent, phyficians muft and will have recourfe to fome theory, good or bad. And if they do not acquaint themfelves with the real ftructure and functions of the parts, with the fenfible qualities and operations of medicines, and with the moft probable method of explaining both the fymptoms of diftempers, and the operations of medicines, they muft fancy fomething in the place of thefe, and reafon from fuch falfe imaginations, or perhaps from the mere agreements, oppofitions, and fecondary ideas, of words. The hiftory of difeafes and their cures, is the bafis of all; after this come anatomical examinations of the body, both in its natural and morbid ftates; and, laft of all, pharmacy; thefe three anfwering refpectively to the general problem, and the two fubordinate ones abovementioned. And if we reafon at all upon the functions and diforders of the parts, and the effects of medicines upon the body, fo important an organ as the brain muft not be left out intirely.

It may not be amifs to add here, that as all the natural functions tend to the welfare of the body, fo there is a remarkable tendency in all the diforders of the body to rectify themfelves. Thefe two tendencies, taken together, make what is called nature by phyficians; and the feveral inftances of them, with their limits, dangers, ill confequences, and deviations in particular cafes, deferve the higheft attention from phyficians, that fo they may neither interrupt a favourable crifis, nor concur with a fatal one. *Stahl* and his followers fuppofe, that thefe tendencies arife

from

from a rational agent prefiding over the fabric of the body, and producing effects, that are not subject to the laws of mechanifm. But this is *gratis dictum*; and the plain traces of mechanifm, which appear in fo many inftances, natural and morbid, are highly unfavourable to it. And all the evidences for the mechanical nature of the body or mind are fo many encouragements to ftudy them faithfully and diligently, fince what is mechanical *may* both be underftood and remedied.

CHAP. III.

Containing a particular application of the foregoing theory to the phænomena of ideas, or of understanding, affection, memory, and imagination.

SECT. I.

Of words, *and the* ideas *associated with them.*

PROP. 31.

Words and phrases must excite ideas in us by association, and they excite ideas in us by no other means.

WORDS may be considered in four lights. First, as impressions made upon the ear.

Secondly, as the actions of the organs of speech.

Thirdly, as impressions made upon the eye by characters.

Fourthly, as the actions of the hand in writing.

We learn the use of them in the order here set down. For children first get an imperfect knowledge of the meaning of the words of others; then learn to speak themselves; then to read, and, lastly, to write.

Now

Of Words, *and the* Ideas, *&c.*

Now it is evident, that in the first of these ways many sensible impressions, and internal feelings, are associated with particular words and phrases, so as to give these the power of raising the corresponding ideas; and that the three following ways increase and improve this power, with some additions to and variations of the ideas. The second is the reverse of the first, and the fourth of the third The first ascertains the ideas belonging to words and phrases in a gross manner, according to their usage in common life. The second fixes this, and makes it ready and accurate; having the same use here as the solution of the inverse problem has in other cases in respect of the direct one. The third has the same effect as the second; and also extends the ideas and significations of words and phrases, by new associations; and particularly by associations with other words, as in definitions, descriptions, *&c.* The advancement of the arts and sciences is chiefly carried on by the new significations given to words in this third way. The fourth, by converting the reader into a writer, helps him to be expert in distinguishing, quick in recollecting, and faithful in retaining, these new significations of words, being the inverse of the third method, as just now remarked. The reader will easily see, that the action of the hand is not an essential in this fourth method. Composition by persons born blind has nearly the same effect. I mention it as being the common attendant upon composition, as having a considerable use deducible from association, and as making the analogy between the four methods more conspicuous and complete.

This may suffice, for the present, to prove the first part of the proposition; *viz.* that words and phrases must excite ideas in us by association. The second part, or that they excite ideas in us by no other means, may appear at the same time, as it may be found

found upon reflection and examination, that all the ideas which any word does excite are deducible from some of the four sources above-mentioned, most commonly from the first or third.

It may appear also from the instances of the words of unknown languages, terms of art not yet explained, barbarous words, &c. of which we either have no ideas, or only such as some fansied resemblance, or prior association, suggests.

It is highly worthy of remark here, that articulate sounds are by their variety, number, and ready use, particularly suited to signify and suggest, by association, both our simple ideas, and the complex ones formed from them, according to the twelfth proposition.

Cor. It follows from this proposition, that the arts of logic, and rational grammar, depend intirely on the doctrine of association. For logic, considered as the art of thinking or reasoning, treats only of such ideas as are annexed to words; and, as the art of discoursing, it teaches the proper use of words in a general way, as grammar does in a more minute and particular one.

PROP. 32.

To describe the manner in which ideas are associated with words, beginning from childhood.

THIS may be done by applying the doctrine of association, as laid down in the first chapter, to words, considered in the four lights mentioned under the last proposition.

First, then, the association of the names of visible objects, with the impressions which these objects make upon the eye, seems to take place more early than any other, and to be effected in the following manner:

manner: the name of the vifible object, the nurfe, for inftance, is pronounced and repeated by the attendants to the child, more frequently when his eye is fixed upon the nurfe, than when upon other objects, and much more fo than when upon any particular one. The word *nurfe* is alfo founded in an emphatical manner, when the child's eye is directed to the nurfe with earneftnefs and defire. The affociation therefore of the found *nurfe*, with the picture of the nurfe upon the *retina*, will be far ftronger than that with any other vifible impreffion, and thus overpower all the other accidental affociations, which will alfo themfelves contribute to the fame end by oppofing one another. And when the child has gained fo much voluntary power over his motions, as to direct his head and eyes toward the nurfe upon hearing her name, this procefs will go on with an accelerated velocity. And thus, at laft, the word will excite the vifible idea readily and certainly.

The fame affociation of the picture of the nurfe in the eye with the found *nurfe* will, by degrees, overpower all the accidental affociations of this picture with other words, and be fo firmly cemented at laft, that the picture will excite the audible idea of the word. But this is not to our prefent purpofe. I mention it here as taking place at the fame time with the foregoing procefs, and contributing to illuftrate and confirm it. Both together afford a complete inftance for the tenth and eleventh propofitions; *i. e.* they fhew, that when the impreffions *A* and B are fufficiently affociated, *A* impreffed alone will excite *b*, B impreffed alone will excite *a*.

Secondly, this affociation of words with vifible appearances, being made under many particular circumftances, muft affect the vifible ideas with a like particularity. Thus the nurfe's drefs, and the fituation of the fire in the child's nurfery, make part of the child's ideas of his nurfe and fire. But then as the nurse often changes her dress, and the child often sees a fire in a different place, and surrounded by different visible objects, these opposite associations must be less strong, than the part which is common to them all; and consequently we may suppose, that while his idea of that part which is common, and which we may call essential, continues the same, that of the particularities, circumstances, and adjuncts, varies. For he cannot have any idea, but with some particularities in the non-essentials.

Thirdly, when the visible objects impress other vivid sensations besides those of sight, such as grateful or ungrateful tastes, smells, warmth or coldness, with sufficient frequency, it follows from the foregoing theory, that these sensations must leave traces, or ideas, which will be associated with the names of the objects, so as to depend upon them. Thus an idea, or nascent perception, of the sweetness of the nurse's milk will rise up in that part of the child's brain which corresponds to the nerves of taste, upon his hearing her name. And hence the whole idea belonging to the word *nurse* now begins to be complex, as consisting of a visible idea, and an idea of taste. And these two ideas will be associated together, not only because the word raises them both, but also because the original sensations are. The strongest may therefore assist in raising the weakest. Now, in common cases, the visible idea is strongest, or occurs most readily at least; but, in the present instance, it seems to be otherwise. We might proceed in like manner to shew the generation of ideas more and more complex, and the various ways by which their parts are cemented together, and all made to depend on the respective names of the visible objects. But what has been said may suffice to shew what ideas the names of visible objects, proper and appellative, raise in us.

Fourthly,

Fourthly, we muſt, however, obſerve, in reſpect of appellatives, that ſometimes the idea is the common compound reſult of all the ſenſible impreſſions received from the ſeveral objects compriſed under the general appellation; ſometimes the particular idea of ſome one of theſe, in great meaſure at leaſt, viz. when the impreſſions ariſing from ſome one or more novel, frequent, and vivid, than thoſe from the reſt.

Fifthly, the words denoting ſenſible qualities, whether ſubſtantive or adjective, ſuch as *whiteneſs*, *white*, &c. get their ideas in a manner which will be eaſily underſtood from what has been already delivered. Thus the word *white*, being aſſociated with the viſible appearances of milk, linen, paper, gets a ſtable power of exciting the idea of what is common to all, and a variable one in reſpect of the particularities, circumſtances, and adjuncts. And ſo of other ſenſible qualities.

Sixthly, the names of viſible actions, as walking, ſtriking, &c. raiſe the proper viſible ideas by a like proceſs. Other ideas may likewiſe adhere in certain caſes, as in thoſe of taſting, feeling, ſpeaking, &c. Senſible perceptions in which no viſible action is concerned, as hearing, may alſo leave ideas dependent on words. However, ſome viſible ideas generally intermix themſelves here. Theſe actions and perceptions are generally denoted by verbs, though ſometimes by ſubſtantives.

And we may now ſee in what manner ideas are aſſociated with nouns, proper and appellative, ſubſtantive and adjective, and with verbs, ſuppoſing that they denote ſenſible things only. Pronouns and particles remain to be conſidered. Now in order to know their ideas and uſes, we muſt obſerve,

Seventhly, that as children may learn to read words not only in an elementary way, viz. by learning the letters and ſyllables of which they are compoſed, but alſo in a ſummary one, viz. by aſſociating the

the found of intire words, with their pictures, in the eye; and muſt, in ſome caſes, be taught in the laſt way, *i. e.* whereſoever the found of the word deviates from that of its elements; ſo both children and adults learn the ideas belonging to whole ſentences many times in a ſummary way, and not by adding together the ideas of the ſeveral words in the ſentence. And where-ever words occur, which, ſeparately taken, have no proper ideas, their uſe can be learnt in no other way but this. Now pronouns and particles, and many other words, are of this kind. They anſwer, in ſome meaſure, to x, y, and z, or the unknown quantities in algebra, being determinable and decypherable, as one may ſay, only by means of the known words with which they are joined.

Thus *I walk* is aſſociated at different times with the ſame viſible impreſſions as *nurſe walks*, *brother walks*, &c. and therefore can ſuggeſt nothing permanently for a long time but the action of walking. However the pronoun *I*, in this and innumerable other ſhort ſentences, being always aſſociated with the perſon ſpeaking, as *thou* is with the perſon ſpoken to, and *he* with the perſon ſpoken of, the frequent recurrency of this teaches the child the uſe of the pronouns, *i. e.* teaches him what difference he is to expect in his ſenſible impreſſions according as this or that pronoun is uſed; the infinite number of inſtances, as one may ſay, making up for the infinitely ſmall quantity of information, which each, ſingly taken, conveys.

In like manner, different particles, *i. e.* adverbs, conjunctions, and prepoſitions, being uſed in ſentences, where the ſubſtantives, adjectives, and verbs, are the ſame, and the ſame particles, where theſe are different, in an endleſs recurrency, teach children the uſe of the particles in a groſs general way. For it may be obſerved, that children are much at a loſs for the true uſe of the pronouns and particles,

for

for some years, and that they often repeat the proper name of the person instead of the pronoun; which confirms the foregoing reasoning. Some of the inferior parts or particles of speech make scarce any alteration in the sense of the sentence, and therefore are called expletives. The several terminations of the *Greek* and *Latin* nouns and verbs are of the nature of pronouns and particles.

Eighthly, the attempts which children make to express their own wants, perceptions, pains, *&c.* in words, and the corrections and suggestions of the attendants, are of the greatest use in all the steps that we have hitherto considered, and especially in the last, regarding the pronouns and particles.

Ninthly, learning to read helps children much in the same respects; especially as it teaches them to separate sentences into the several words which compound them; which those who cannot read are scarce able to do, even when they arrive at adult age.

Thus we may see, how children and others are enabled to understand a continued discourse relating to sensible impressions only, and how the words in passing over the ear must raise up trains of visible and other ideas by the power of association. Our next inquiry must be concerning the words that denote either intellectual things, or collections of other words.

Tenthly, the words that relate to the several passions of love, hatred, hope, fear, anger, *&c.* being applied to the child at the times when he is under the influence of these passions, get the power of raising the miniatures or ideas of these passions, and also of the usual associated circumstances. The application of the same words to others helps also to annex the ideas of the associated circumstances to them, and even of the passions themselves, both from the infectiousness of our natures, and from the power of associated circumstances to raise the passions.

passions. However, it is to be noted, that the words denoting the passions do not, for the most part, raise up in us any degree of the passions themselves, but only the ideas of the associated circumstances. We are supposed to understand the continued discourses into which these words enter sufficiently, when we form true notions of the actions, particularly the visible ones attending them.

Eleventhly, the names of intellectual and moral qualities and operations, such as fancy, memory, wit, dulness, virtue, vice, conscience, approbation, disapprobation, &c. stand for a description of these qualities and operations; and therefore, if dwelt upon, excite such ideas as these descriptions in all their particular circumstances do. But the common sentences, which these words enter, pass over the mind too quick, for the most part, to allow of such a delay. They are acknowledged as familiar and true, and suggest certain associated visible ideas, and nascent internal feelings, taken from the descriptions of these names, or from the words, which are usually joined with them in discourses or writings.

Twelfthly, there are many terms of art in all the branches of learning, which are defined by other words, and which therefore are only compendious substitutes for them. The same holds in common life in numberless instances. Thus riches, honours, pleasures, are put for the several kinds of each. Such words sometimes suggest the words of their definitions, sometimes the ideas of these words, sometimes a particular species comprehended under the general term, &c. But, whatever they suggest, it may be easily seen, that they derive the power of doing this from association.

Thirteenthly, there are many words used in abstract sciences, which can scarce be defined or described by any other words; and yet, by their grammatical form, seem to be excluded from the class of
particles.

associated with them.

particles. Such are identity, exiftence, &c. The ufe of thefe muft therefore be learnt as that of the particles is. And indeed children learn their firft imperfect notions of all the words confidered in this and the three laft paragraphs chiefly in this way; and come to precife and explicit ones only by means of books, as they advance to adult age, or by endeavouring to ufe them properly in their own deliberate compofitions.

This is by no means a full or fatisfactory account of the ideas which adhere to words by affociation. For the author perceives himfelf to be ftill a mere novice in thefe fpeculations; and it is difficult to explain words to the bottom by words; perhaps impoffible. The reader will receive fome addition of light and evidence in the courfe of this fection; alfo in the next, in which I fhall treat of propofitions and affent. For our affent to propofitions, and the influence which they have over our affections and actions, make part of the ideas that adhere to words by affociation; which part, however, could not properly be confidered in this fection.

Cor. 1. It follows from this propofition, that words may be diftinguifhed into the four claffes mentioned under the twelfth propofition.

1. Such as have ideas only.
2. Such as have both ideas and definitions.
3. Such as have definitions only.
4. Such as have neither ideas nor definitions.

Under definition I here include defcription, or any other way of explaining a word by other words, excepting that by a mere fynonymous term; and I exclude from the number of ideas the vifible idea of the character of a word, and the audible one of its found; it being evident, that every word heard may thus excite a vifible idea, and every word feen an audible one. I exclude alfo all ideas that are either extremely faint, or extremely variable.

It

It is difficult to fix precife limits to thefe four claffes, fo as to determine accurately where each ends, and the next begins: and if we confider thefe things in the moft general way, there is perhaps no word which has not both an idea and a definition, *i. e.* which is not attended by fome one or more internal feelings occafionally, and which may not be explained, in fome imperfect manner at leaft, by other words. I will give fome inftances of words which have the faireft right to each clafs.

The names of fimple fenfible qualities are of the firft clafs. Thus *white, fweet,* &c. excite ideas; but cannot be defined. It is to be obferved here, that this clafs of words ftands only for the ftable part of the ideas refpectively, not for the feveral variable particularities, circumftances, and adjuncts, which intermix themfelves here.

The names of natural bodies, animal, vegetable, mineral, are of the fecond clafs; for they excite aggregates of fenfible ideas, and at the fame time may be defined (as appears from the writings of natural hiftorians) by an enumeration of their properties and characteriftics. Thus likewife geometrical figures have both ideas and definitions. The definitions in both cafes are fo contrived as to leave out all the variable particularities of the ideas, and to be alfo more full and precife, than the ideas generally are in the parts that are of a permanent nature.

Algebraic qualities, fuch as roots, powers, furds, *&c.* belong to the third clafs. and have definitions only. The fame may be faid of fcientifical terms of art, and of moft abftract general terms, moral, metaphyfical, vulgar: however, mental emotions are apt to attend fome of thefe even in paffing flightly over the ear; and thefe emotions may be confidered as ideas belonging to the terms refpectively. Thus the very words, *gratitude, mercy, cruelty, treachery,* &c. feparately taken, affect the mind; and yet,

yet, since all reasoning upon them is to be founded on their definitions, as will be seen hereafter, it seems best to refer them to this third class.

Lastly, the particles *the, of, to, for, but,* &c. have neither definitions nor ideas.

Cor. 2. This matter may be illustrated by comparing language to geometry and algebra, the two general methods of expounding quantity, and investigating all its varieties from previous *data*.

Words of the first class answer to propositions purely geometrical, *i. e.* to such as are too simple to admit of algebra; of which kind we may reckon that concerning the equality of the angles at the basis of an isosceles triangle.

Words of the second class answer to that part of geometry, which may be demonstrated either synthetically or analytically; either so that the learner's imagination shall go along with every step of the process painting out each line, angle, &c. according to the method of demonstration used by the antient mathematicians; or so that he shall operate intirely by algebraic quantities and methods, and only represent the conclusion to his imagination, when he is arrived at it, by examining then what geometrical quantities the ultimately resulting algebraical ones denote. The first method is in both cases the most satisfactory and affecting, the last the most expeditious and not less certain, where due care is taken. A blind mathematician must use words in the last of these methods, when he reasons upon colours.

Words of the third class answer to such problems concerning quadratures, and rectifications of cures, chances, equations of the higher orders, &c. as are too perplexed to be treated geometrically.

Lastly, words of the fourth class answer to the algebraic signs for addition, subtraction, &c. to indexes, coefficients, &c. These are not algebraic quantities themselves; but they alter the import of the

the letters that are; juſt as particles vary the ſenſe of the principal words of a ſentence, and yet ſignify nothing of themſelves.

Geometrical figures may be confidered as repreſenting all the modes of extenſion in the ſame manner, as viſible ideas do viſible objects; and conſequently the names of geometrical figures anſwer to the names of theſe ideas. Now, as all kinds of problems relating to quantity might be expounded by modes of extenſion, and ſolved thereby, were our faculties ſufficiently exalted, ſo it appears poſſible to repreſent moſt kinds of ideas by viſible ones, and to purſue them in this way through all their varieties and combinations. But as it ſeems beſt in the firſt caſe to confine geometry to problems, where extenſion, and motion, which implies extenſion, are concerned, uſing algebraic methods for inveſtigating all other kinds of quantity, ſo it ſeems beſt alſo to uſe viſible ideas only for viſible objects and qualities of which they are the natural repreſentatives, and to denote all other qualities by words confidered as arbitrary ſigns. And yet the repreſentation of other quantities by geometrical ones, and of other ideas by viſible ones, is apt to make a more vivid impreſſion upon the fancy, and a more laſting one upon the memory. In ſimiles, fables, parables, allegories, viſible ideas are uſed for this reaſon to denote general and intellectual ones.

Since words may be compared to the letters uſed in algebra, language itſelf may be termed one ſpecies of algebra; and, converſly, algebra is nothing more than the language which is peculiarly fitted to explain quantity of all kinds. As the letters, which in algebra ſtand immediately for quantities, anſwer to the words which are immediate repreſentatives of ideas and the algebraic ſigns for addition, &c. to the particles; ſo the ſingle letters, which are ſometimes uſed by algebraiſts to denote ſums or differences,

ences, powers or roots univerfal of other letters, for brevity and convenience, anfwer to fuch words as have long definitions, to terms of art, &c. which are introduced into the fciences for the fake of compendioufnefs. Now if every thing relating to language had fomething analogous to it in algebra, one might hope to explain the difficulties and perplexities attending the theory of language by the correfponding particulars in algebra, where every thing is clear, and acknowledged by all that have made it their ftudy. However, we have here no independent point whereon to ftand, fince, if a perfon be difpofed to call the rules of algebra in queftion, we have no way of demonftrating them to him, but by ufing words, the things to be explained by algebra, for that purpofe. If we fuppofe indeed the fceptical perfon to allow only that fimple language, which is neceffary for demonftrating the rules of algebra, the thing would be done; and, as I obferved juft now, it feems impoffible to become acquainted with this, and at the fame time to difallow it.

Cor. 3. It will eafily appear from the obfervations here made upon words, and the affociations which adhere to them, that the languages of different ages and nations muft bear a great general refemblance to each other, and yet have confiderable particular differences; whence any one may be tranflated into any other, fo as to convey the fame ideas in general, and yet not with perfect precifion and exactnefs. They muft refemble one another, becaufe the phænomena of nature, which they are all intended to exprefs, and the ufes and exigencies of human life, to which they minifter, have a general refemblance. But then, as the bodily make and genius of each people, the air, foil, and climate, commerce, arts, fciences, religion, &c. make confiderable differences in different ages and nations, it is natural to expect,

pect, that the languages should have proportionable differences in respect of each other.

Where languages have rules of etymology and syntax, that differ greatly, which is the case of the *Hebrew* compared with *Greek* or *Latin*, this will become a new source of difformity. For the rules of etymology and syntax determine the application and purport of words in many cases. Agreeably to which we see, that children, while yet unacquainted with that propriety of words and phrases, which custom establishes, often make new words and constructions, which, though improper according to common usage, are yet very analogous to the tenor of the language, in which they speak.

The modern languages of this western part of the world answer better to the *Latin*, than according to their original *Gothic* plans, on this account; inasmuch as not only great numbers of words are adopted by all of them from the *Latin*, but also because the reading *Latin* authors, and learning the *Latin* grammar, have disposed learned men and writers to mould their own languages in some measure after the *Latin*. And, conversly, each nation moulds the *Latin* after the idiom of its own language, the effect being reciprocal in all such cases.

In learning a new language the words of it are at first substitutes for those of our native language; *i. e.* they are associated by means of these, with the proper objects and ideas. When this association is sufficiently strong, the middle bond is dropped, and the words of the new language become substitutes for, and suggest directly and immediately objects and ideas; also clusters of other words in the same language.

In learning a new language it is much easier to translate from it into the native one, than back again; just as young children are much better able to understand the expressions of others, than to express their own conceptions. And the reason is the same in both

both cafes. Young children learn at firft to go from the words of others; and thofe who learn a new language, from the words of that language, to the things fignified. And the reverfe of this, *viz.* to go from the things fignified to the words, muft be difficult for a time, from what is delivered concerning fucceffive affociations under the tenth and eleventh propofitions. It is to be added here, that the nature and connexions of the things fignified often determine the import of fentences, though their grammatical analyfis is not underftood; and that we fuppofe the perfon who attempts to tranflate from a new language is fufficiently expert in the inverfe problem of paffing from the things fignified to the correfponding words of his own language. The power of affociation is every where confpicuous in thefe remarks.

Cor. 4. It follows alfo from the reafoning of this propofition, that perfons who fpeak the fame language cannot always mean the fame things by the fame words; but muft miftake each others meaning. This confufion and uncertainty arifes from the different affociations transferred upon the fame words by the difference in the accidents and events of our lives. It is, however, much more common in difcourfes concerning abftract matters, where the terms ftand for collections of other terms, fometimes at the pleafure of the fpeaker or writer, than in the common and neceffary affairs of life. For here frequent ufe, and the conftancy of the phænomena of nature, intended to be expreffed by words, have rendered their fenfe determinate and certain. However, it feems poffible, and even not very difficult, for two truly candid and intelligent perfons to underftand each other upon any fubject.

That we may enter more particularly into the caufes of this confufion, and confequently be the better

better enabled to prevent it, let us confider words according to the four claffes above-mentioned.

Now miftakes will happen in the words of the firft clafs, *viz.* fuch as have ideas only, where the perfons have affociated thefe words with different impreffions. And the method to rectify any miftake of this kind is for each perfon to fhew with what actual impreffions he has affociated the word in queftion. But miftakes here are not common.

In words of the fecond clafs, *viz.* fuch as have both ideas and definitions, it often happens, that one perfon's knowledge is much more full than another's, and confequently his idea and definition much more extenfive. This muft caufe a mifapprehenfion on one fide, which yet may be eafily rectified by recurring to the definition. It happens alfo fometimes in words of this clafs, that a man's ideas, *i. e.* the miniatures excited in his nervous fyftem by the word, are not always fuitable to his definition, *i. e.* are not the fame with thofe which the words of the definition would excite. If then this perfon fhould pretend, or even defign, to reafon from his definition, and yet reafon from his idea, a mifapprehenfion will arife in the hearer, who fuppofes him to reafon from his definition merely.

In words of the third clafs, which have definitions only, and no immediate ideas, miftakes generally arife through want of fixed definitions mutually acknowledged, and kept to. However, as imperfect fluctuating ideas, that have little relation to the definitions, are often apt to adhere to the words of this clafs, miftakes muft arife from this caufe alfo.

As to the words of the fourth clafs, or thofe which have neither ideas nor definitions, it is eafy to afcertain their ufe by inferting them in fentences, whofe import is known and acknowledged; this being the method in which children learn to decypher them: fo that miftakes could not arife in the words of this clafs class, did we use moderate care and candour. And indeed since children learn the uses of words most evidently without having any *data*, any fixed point at all, it is to be hoped, that philosophers, and candid persons, may learn at last to understand one another with facility and certainty; and get to the very bottom of the connexion between words and ideas.

It seems practicable to make a dictionary of any language, in which the words of that language shall all be explained with precision by words of the same language, to persons who have no more than a gross knowledge of that language. Now this also shews, that with care and candour we might come to understand one another perfectly. Thus sensible qualities might be fixed by the bodies, in which they are most eminent and distinct; the names of a sufficient number of these bodies, being very well known. After this these very bodies, and all others, might be defined by their sensible properties; and these two processes would help each other indefinitely, actions might be described from animals already defined, also from the modes of extension, abstract terms defined, and the peculiar use of particles ascertained. And such a dictionary would, in some measure, be a real as well as a nominal one, and extend to things themselves. The writer of every new and difficult work may execute that part of such a dictionary which belongs to his subject; at least in the instances where he apprehends the reader is likely to want it.

COR. 5. When words have acquired any considerable power of exciting pleasant or painful vibrations in the nervous system, by being often associated with such things as do this, they may transfer a part of these pleasures and pains upon indifferent things, by being at other times often associated with such. This is one of the principal sources of the several factitious pleasures and pains of human life. Thus, to give an instance from childhood, the words *sweet, good, pretty, fine,* &c. on the one hand, and the words, *bad, ugly, frightful,* &c. on the other, being applied by the nurse and attendants in the young child's hearing almost promiscuously, and without those restrictions that are observed in correct speaking, the one to all the pleasures, the other to all the pains of the several senses, must by association raise up general pleasant and painful vibrations, in which no one part can be distinguished above the rest; and, when applied by farther associations to objects of a neutral kind, they must transfer a general pleasure or pain upon them.

All the words associated with pleasures must also affect each other by this promiscuous application. And the same holds in respect of the words associated with pains. However, since both the original and the transferred pleasures and pains heaped upon different words are different, and in some cases widely so, every remarkable word will have a peculiar internal feeling, or sentiment, belonging to it; and there will be the same relations of affinity, disparity, and opposition, between these internal sentiments, *i. e.* ideas, belonging to words, as between the several *genera* and *species* of natural bodies, between tastes, smells, colours, &c. many of these ideas, though affording considerable pleasure at first, must sink into the limits of indifference; and some of those which afforded pain at first, into the limits of pleasure. What is here said of words, belongs to clusters of them, as well as to separate words. And the ideas of all may still retain their peculiarities, by which they are distinguished from each other, after they have fallen below the limits of pleasure into indifference, just as obscure colours, or faint tastes, do.

It is observable, that the mere transit of words expressing strong ideas over the ears of children affects them; and the same thing is true of adults, in

a

a lefs degree. However, the laft have learnt from experience and habit to regard them chiefly, as they afford a rational expectation of pleafure and pain. This cannot be difcuffed fully, till we come to confider the nature of affent; but it may give fome light and evidence to the reafoning of this corollary, juft to have mentioned the manner, in which we are at firft affected by words.

Cor. 6. Since words thus collect ideas from various quarters, unite them together, and transfer them both upon other words, and upon foreign objects, it is evident, that the ufe of words adds much to the number and complexnefs of our ideas, and is the principal means by which we make intellectual and moral improvements. This is verified abundantly by the obfervations that are made upon perfons born deaf, and continuing fo. It is probable, however, that thefe perfons make ufe of fome fymbols to affift the memory, and fix the fancy: and they muft have a great variety of pleafures and pains transferred upon vifible objects from their affociations with one another, and with fenfible pleafures of all the kinds; but they are very deficient in this, upon the whole, through the want of the affociations of vifible objects, and ftates of mind, &c. with words. Learning to read muft add greatly to their mental improvement; yet ftill their intellectual capacities cannot but remain very narrow.

Perfons blind from birth muft proceed in a manner different from that defcribed in this propofition, in the firft ideas, which they affix to words. As the vifible ones are wanting, the others, particularly the tangible and audible ones, muft compofe the aggregates which are annexed to words. However, as they are capable of learning and retaining as great a variety of words as others, or perhaps a greater, *cæteris paribus,* and can affociate with them pleafures and pains from the four remaining fenfes, alfo ufe them as algebraifts

braifts do the letters that reprefent quantities, they fall little or nothing fhort of others in intellectual accomplifhments, and may arrive even at a greater degree of fpirituality, and abftraction in their complex ideas.

Cor. 7. It follows from this propofition, that, when children or others firft learn to read, the view of the words excites ideas only by the mediation of their founds, with which alone their ideas have hitherto been affociated. And thus it is that children and illiterate perfons underftand what they read beft by reading aloud. By degrees, the intermediate link being left out, the written or printed characters fuggeft the ideas directly and inftantaneoufly; fo that learned men underftand more readily by paffing over the words with the eye only, fince this method, by being more expeditious, brings the ideas clofer together. However, all men, both learned and unlearned, are peculiarly affected by words pronounced in a manner fuitable to their fenfe and defign; which is ftill an affociated influence.

Cor. 8. As perfons, before they learn to read, muft have very imperfect notions of the diftinction of words, and can only underftand language in a grofs general way, taking whole clufters of words for one undivided found, fo much lefs can they be fuppofed to have any conceptions concerning the nature or ufe of letters. Now all mankind muft have been in this ftate before the invention of letters. Nay, they muft have been farther removed from all conceptions of letters, than the moft unlearned perfons amongft us, fince thefe have at leaft heard of letters, and know that words may be written and read by means o: them. And this makes it difficult to trace out by what fteps alphabetical writing was invented; or is even fome prefumption, that it is not a human invention. To which it is to be added, that the analyfing complex articulate founds into their fimple component parts appears to be a problem of too difficult and perplexed

a

a nature for the rude early ages, occupied in getting neceſſaries, and defending themſelves from external injuries, and not aware of the great uſe of it, even though they had known the ſolution to be poſſible and practicable. However, I ſhall mention ſome preſumptions of a contrary nature under the next propoſition.

PROP. 33.

To explain the nature of characters intended to repreſent objects and ideas immediately, and without the intervention of words.

SINCE characters made by the hand are capable of the greateſt varieties, they might be fitted by proper aſſociations to ſuggeſt objects and ideas immediately, in the ſame manner as articulate ſounds do. And there are ſome inſtances of it in common uſe, which may ſerve to verify this, and to lead us into the nature of characters ſtanding immediately for objects and ideas. Thus the numeral figures, and the letters in algebra, repreſent objects, ideas, words, and cluſters of words, directly and immediately; the pronunciation of them being of no uſe, or neceſſity, in the operations to be performed by them. Thus alſo muſical characters repreſent ſounds and combinations of ſounds, without the intervention of words, and are a much more compendious and ready repreſentation, than any words can be.

Characters ſeem to have an advantage over articulate ſounds in the repreſentation of viſible objects, inaſmuch as they might by their reſemblance, even though only a groſs one, become rather natural, than mere arbitrary repreſentatives.

They had alſo an advantage as repreſentatives in general, before the invention of alphabetical writing, since persons could by this means convey their thoughts to each other at a distance.

If we suppose characters to be improved to all that variety and multiplicity, which is necessary for representing objects, ideas, and clusters of characters, in the same manner as words represent objects, ideas, and clusters of words, still they might be resolved into simple component parts; and rendered pronunciable by affixing some simple or short sound to each of these simple component parts; just as articulate sounds are painted by being first resolved into their simple component parts, and then having each of these represented by a simple mark or character.

If we suppose the most common visible objects to be denoted both by short articulate sounds, and by short characters bearing some real, or fansied, imperfect resemblance to them, it is evident, that the sound and mark, by being both associated with the visible object, would also be associated with one another; and consequently that the sound would be the name of the mark, and the mark the picture of the sound. And this last circumstance seems to lead to the denoting all sounds by marks, and therefore perhaps to alphabetical writing.

At the same time it must be observed, that the marks would bear different relations of similarity and dissimilarity to one another from those which the corresponding sounds did.

This would happen according to whatever law the marks were made, but especially if they were resemblances of visible objects. And this, as it seems, would occasion some difficulty and perplexity in representing sounds by marks, or marks by sounds.

PROP.

PROP. 34

To explain the nature of figurative words and phrases, and of analogy, from the foregoing theory

A Figure is a word, which, firſt repreſenting the object or idea *A*, is afterwards made to repreſent *B*, on account of the relation, which theſe bear to each other.

The principal relation, which gives riſe to figures, is that of likeneſs; and this may be either a likeneſs in ſhape, and viſible appearance, or one in application, uſe, &c. Now it is very evident from the nature of aſſociation, that objects which are like to a given one in viſible appearance, will draw to themſelves the word by which this is expreſſed. And indeed this is the foundation upon which appellatives are made to ſtand for ſo great a number of particulars. Let the word *man* be applied to the particular perſons *A*, *B*, *C*, &c. till it be ſufficiently aſſociated with them, and it will follow, that the appearance of the new particular perſon *D* will ſuggeſt the word, and be denoted by it. But here there is no figure, becauſe the word *man* is aſſociated with different particular perſons from the firſt, and that equally or nearly ſo.

In like manner, the correſponding parts of different animals, *i. e.* the eyes, mouth, breaſt, belly, legs, lungs, heart, &c. have the ſame names applied in a literal ſenſe, partly from the likeneſs of ſhape, partly from that of uſe and application. And it is evident, that if we ſuppoſe a people ſo rude in language and knowledge, as to have names only for the parts of the human body, and not to have attended to the parts of the brute creatures, aſſociation would lead them to apply the ſame names to the parts of the brute creatures, as ſoon as they became

came acquainted with them. Now here this application would at first have the nature of a figure; but when by degrees any of these words, the eye for instance, became equally applied from the first to the eyes of men and brutes, it would cease to be a figure, and become an appellative name, as just now remarked.

But when the original application of the word is obvious, and remains distinct from the secondary one, as when we say the mouth or ear of a vessel, or the foot of a chair or table, the expression is figurative.

Hence it is plain, that the various resemblances which nature and art afford are the principal sources of figures. However, many figures are also derived from other relations, such as those of cause, effect, opposition, derivation, generality, particularity; and language itself, by its resemblances, oppositions, &c. becomes a new source of figures, distinct from the relations of things.

Most metaphors, i. e. figures taken from likeness, imply a likeness in more particulars than one, else they would not be sufficiently definite, nor affect the imagination in a due manner. If the likeness extend to many particulars, the figure becomes implicitly a simile, fable, parable, or allegory.

Many, or most common figures, pass so far into literal expressions by use, i. e. association, that we do not attend at all to their figurative nature. And thus by degrees figurative senses become a foundation for successive figures, in the same manner, as originally literal senses.

It is evident, that if a language be narrow, and much confined to sensible things, it will have great occasion for figures; these will naturally occur in the common intercourses of life, and will in their turn as they become literal expressions in the secondary senses, much augment and improve the language
and

and affift the invention. All this is manifeft from the growth of modern languages, in thofe parts where they were heretofore particularly defective.

We come now to the confideration of analogy. Now things are faid to be analogous to one another, in the ftrict mathematical fenfe of the word *analogy*, when the correfponding parts are all in the fame ratio to each other. Thus if the feveral parts of the body in different perfons be fuppofed exactly proportional to the whole bodies, they might be faid to be analogous in the original mathematical fenfe of that word. But as this reftrained fenfe is not applicable to things, as they really exift, another of a more enlarged and practical nature has been adopted, which may be thus defined. Analogy is that refemblance, and in fome cafes famenefs, of the parts, properties, functions, ufes, &c. any or all, of *A* to *B*, whereby our knowledge concerning *A*, and the language expreffing this knowledge, may be applied in the whole, or in part, to *B*, without any fenfible, or, at leaft, any important practical error. Now analogies, in this fenfe of the word, fome more exact and extenfive, fome lefs fo, prefent themfelves to us every where in natural and artificial things; and thus whole groups of figurative phrafes, which feem at firft only to anfwer the purpofes of convenience in affording names for new objects, and of pleafing the fancy in the way to be hereafter mentioned, pafs into analogical reafoning, and become a guide in the fearch after truth, and an evidence for it in fome degree. I will here fet down fome inftances of analogies of various degrees and kinds.

The bodies of men, women, and children, are highly analogous to each other. This holds equally in refpect of every other fpecies of animals; alfo of the feveral correfponding parts of animals of the fame fpecies, as their flefh, blood, bones, fat, &c. and their properties. Here the words applied to the
feveral

several analogous things are used in a sense equally literal in respect of all. And the analogy is in most cases so close, as rather to be esteemed a coincidence or sameness.

In comparing animals of different kinds the analogy grows perpetually less and less, as we take in a greater compass; and consequently our language more and more harsh, when considered as literal, whilst yet it cannot well be figurative in some things, and literal in others; so that new words are generally assigned to those parts which do not sufficiently resemble the corresponding ones. Thus the fore-legs of men and fowls as we might call them in a harsh literal, or a highly figurative way, are termed hands and wings respectively. However, in some cases, the same word is used, and considered as a figure; as when the cries of birds and beasts are termed their language. We may also observe, that every part in every animal may, from its resemblance in shape and use to the corresponding parts in several other animals, have a just right to a name, which shall be common to it and them.

What has been said of animals of the same and different kinds holds equally in respect of vegetables. Those of the same kind have the same names applied to the corresponding parts in a literal sense. Those of different kinds have many names common to all used in a literal sense, some new ones peculiar to certain kinds, and some that may be considered as so harsh in a literal sense, that we may rather call them figurative terms.

The same may be said of the mineral kingdom, considered also according to its *genera* and *species*.

Animals are also analogous to vegetables in many things, and vegetables to minerals: so that there seems to be a perpetual thread of analogy continued from the most perfect animal to the most imperfect mineral, even till we come to elementary bodies themselves. Suppose

associated with them.

Suppose the several particulars of the three kingdoms to be represented by the letters of an alphabet sufficiently large for that purpose. Then we are to conceive, that any two contiguous species, as A and B, M and N, are more analogous than A and C, M and O, which have one between them. However, since A and B, M and N, are not perfectly analogous, this deficiency may be supplied in some things from C and O, in others from D and P, &c. so that M can have no part, property, &c. but what shall have something quite analogous to it in some species, near or remote, above it or below it, and even in several species. And in cases where the parts, properties, &c. are not rigorously exact in resemblance, there is, however, an imperfect one, which justifies the application of the same word to both : if it approach to perfection, the word may be said to be used in a literal sense ; if it be very imperfect, in a figurative one. Thus when the names of parts, properties, &c. are taken from the animal kingdom, and applied to the vegetable, or *vice versa*, they are more frequently considered as figurative, than when transferred from one part of the animal kingdom to another.

In like manner, there seems to be a gradation of analogies respecting the earth, moon, planets, comets, sun, and fixed stars, compared with one another. Or if we descend to the several parts of individuals, animals, vegetables, or minerals, the several organs of sensation are evidently analogous to each other ; also the glands, the muscles, the parts of generation in the different sexes of the same kind, &c. &c. without limits. For the more any one looks into the external natural world, the more analogies, general or particular, perfect or imperfect, will he find every-where.

Numbers, geometrical figures, and algebraic quantities, are also mutually analogous without limits.

and here there is the exacteft uniformity, joined with an endlefs variety, fo that it is always certain and evident how far the analogy holds, and where it becomes a difparity or oppofition on one hand, or a coincidence on the other. There is no room for figures here; but the terms muft be difparate, oppofite, or the fame, in a ftrictly literal fenfe refpectively.

The feveral words of each particular language, the languages themfelves, the idioms, figures, &c. abound alfo with numerous analogies of various kinds and degrees.

Analogies are likewife introduced into artificial things, houfes, gardens, furniture, drefs, arts, &c.

The body politic, the body natural, the world natural, the univerfe;——the human mind, the minds of brutes on one hand, and of fuperior beings on the other, and even the infinite mind himfelf;—the appellations of father, governor, judge, king, architect, &c. referred to God;—the ages of man, the ages of the world, the feafons of the year, the times of the day;—the offices, profeffions, and trades, of different perfons, ftatefmen, generals, divines, lawyers, phyficians, merchants;—the terms night, fleep, death, chaos, darknefs, &c. alfo light, life, happinefs, &c. compared with each other refpectively; life and death, as applied in different fenfes to animals, vegetables, liquors, &c.—earthquakes, ftorms, battles, tumults, fermentations of liquors, law-fuits, games, &c. families, bodies politic leffer and greater, their laws, natural religion, revealed religion, &c. &c. afford endlefs inftances of analogies natural and artificial. For the mind being once initiated into the method of difcovering analogies, and expreffing them, does by affociation perfevere in this method, and even force things into its fyftem by concealing difparities, magnifying refemblances, and accommodating language thereto. It is eafy to fee, that in the inftances laft alledged

alledged the terms used are for the most part literal only in one sense, and figurative in all their other applications. They are literal in the sense which was their primary one, and figurative in many or most of the rest. Similes, fables, parables, allegories, &c. are all instances of natural analogies improved and set off by art. And they have this, in common to them all, that the properties, beauties, perfections, desires, or defects and aversions, which adhere by association to the simile, parable, or emblem of any kind, are insensibly, as it were, transferred upon the thing represented. Hence the passions are moved to good or to evil, speculation is turned into practice, and either some important truth felt and realized, or some error and vice gilded over and recommended.

PROP. 35.

To apply the foregoing account of words and characters to the languages and method of writing of the first ages of the world.

HERE there is a great difficulty through the want of sufficient *data*. I will assume a few of those that appear to me most probable, and just shew the method of applying the doctrine of association to them; leaving it to learned men, as they become possessed of more and more certain *data*, to make farther advances.

I suppose then, that *Adam* had some language, with some instinctive knowledge concerning the use of it, as well as concerning divine and natural things, imparted to him by God at his creation. It seems indeed, that God made use of the visible appearances or actions, or perhaps of the several cries of the brute creatures, as the means whereby he taught *Adam* their names. But whether this was so, also whether,

whether, if it was, any analogous method was taken in refpect of the names of other objects, or of ideas, and internal feelings. is an inquiry, in which nothing that yet appears can afford fatisfaction.

I fuppofe alfo, that the language, which *Adam* and *Eve* were poffeffed of in Paradife, was very narrow, and confined in great meafure to vifible things; God himfelf condefcending to appear in a vifible, perhaps in a human fhape, to them, in his Revelations of himfelf. It might alfo be monofyllabic in great meafure. They who fuppofe *Adam* to be capable of deep fpeculations, and to have exceeded all his pofterity in the fubtilty and extent of his intellectual faculties, and confequently in the number and variety of his words, and the ideas belonging to them, have no foundation for this opinion in fcripture; nor do they feem to confider, that innocence, and pure unmixed happinefs, may exift without any great degrees of knowledge; or that to fet a value upon knowledge confidered in itfelf, and exclufively of its tendency to carry us to God. is a moft pernicious error, derived originally from *Adam's* having eaten of the tree of knowledge.

After the fall we may fuppofe, that *Adam* and *Eve* extended their language to new objects and ideas, and efpecially to thofe which were attended with pain; and this they might do fometimes by inventing new words, fometimes by giving new fenfes to old ones. However, their language would ftill continue narrow, becaufe they had only one another to converfe with, and could not extend their knowledge to any great variety of things; alfo becaufe their foundation was narrow. For the growth and variations of a language fomewhat refemble the increafe of money at intereft upon intereft.

If to thefe reafons we add the long lives of the antediluvian patriarchs, the want of arts and fciences in the antediluvian world, and the want of leifure

through

through the great labour and fatigue neceffary to provide food, cloathing, &c. we fhall have reafon to conjecture, that the whole antediluvian world would fpeak the fame language with *Adam*, and that without any great additions or alterations. After a hundred or two hundred years, affociation would fix the language of each perfon, fo that he could not well make many alterations; but he muft fpeak the language of his forefathers till that time, becaufe thofe to the fixth or feventh generation above him were ftill living; and confequently he would continue to fpeak the fame language, *i. e.* the *Adamic*, with few variations, to the laft. The narrownefs of the languages of barbarous nations may add fome light and evidence here.

If we fuppofe fome kind of picture-writing to have been imparted to *Adam* by God, or to have been invented by him, or by any of his pofterity, this might receive more alterations and improvements than language, from the fucceffive generations of the antediluvians. For the variety of figures in vifible objects would fuggeft a fufficient variety in their characters; the hand could eafily execute this; and their permanency would both give the antediluvians diftinct ideas of all the original characters, and all their variations, and alfo fix them in their memory. We may fuppofe therefore, that though their words and marks would be fo affociated together (agreeably to what was before obferved), as that the word would be the name of the correfponding mark, and the mark the picture of the word in many cafes, yet their marks would in fome inftances extend farther than their words; and confequently, that on this account, as well as becaufe the marks would be fimilar and different, where the words were not, there would be no alphabetical writing in the antediluvian world.

K 3 They

They might, however, hand down a history of the creation, fall, and principal events, in this picture-writing, attended with a traditional explanation, which might remain uncorrupted and invariable till the deluge. And indeed, if we suppose picture-writing to be of divine original, it will be most probable, that they received a divine direction to do this, and that they would not apply their picture-writing to any other purpose for some time: just as the *Israelites* afterwards seem to have employed alphabetical writing chiefly for recording the divine dispensations and interpositions.

After the flood the great change made in the face of things, and in natural bodies, with the appearance perhaps of some intirely new ones, would make some parts of the antediluvian language superfluous, at the same time that it would be greatly defective upon the whole. Hence we may suppose, that the antediluvian language must receive much greater alterations and additions just after the flood, than at any time before. But *Noah* and his wife, having their words and ideas more firmly associated together, than *Shem, Ham,* and *Japhet,* and their wives, on account of their superior age, would be far less able to make their requisite changes in their language. Something like this must also take place in respect of their picture-writing, if we suppose there was any such thing in the antediluvian world.

Let us suppose this, and also with Mr. *Whiston* and Mr. *Shuckford,* that *Noah,* his wife, and their postdiluvian posterity, settled early in *China,* so as to be cut off from *Shem, Ham,* and *Japhet,* and their posterity. Here then we may suppose farther, that they would alter and improve their picture-writing, or character, so as to suit it to the new face of things in the postdiluvian world, and to make it grow with the growth of knowledge, more than they would their language, from the greater facility of doing

doing this: for I prefume, that the antediluvian language contained but few of the articulate founds which are now known, and that they could not invent more. Thus their character and language would both of them be the immediate reprefentatives of objects and ideas; only the ufe and application of the character would be much more extenfive than that of the language. After fome time, fome centuries, or even chiliads, fuppofe, both the character and language would begin to be fixed, to have fewer new marks and words added, and fewer alterations made in the old ones in any given interval of time. The words would alfo be fo firmly affociated with the correfponding marks, as to be the names of them, *i. e.* to reprefent them, as well as the objects or ideas, to which they were originally affixed. But then there would be many marks, to which there would be no fuch names, taken from the names of objects and ideas, on account of the poverty of the language here fuppofed. They would, however, endeavour to give them fome names; and hence a diverfity would arife in their language. We may conceive alfo, that as they feparated farther from one another in multiplying, particular clans would deviate even in the pronunciation of the monofyllabic words of the original language, as in the feveral dialects of other languages; and confequently deviate ftill more in the compound names of the marks: but the marks, being permanent things, capable of being handed down accurately to the fucceffive generations, and of being conveyed to diftant countries, would continue intelligible to all. And thus we may conceive, that the poftdiluvian pofterity of *Noah* might all write the fame characters, and yet fpeak different languages; alfo that their character would be very extenfive, and always the immediate reprefentative of objects and ideas, whereas their language would be narrow, and in fome cafes the immediate reprefentative of the character,

character, and only denote objects and ideas by means of this. And this I take to be the cafe with the people of *China*, and the neighbouring countries of *Japan, Tonquin, Siam*, &c. But I only prefume to offer conjectures, not having any knowledge of the character or languages of thefe countries.

Since the *Chinefe* marks are very numerous, and their fimple words very few, whereas our words are very numerous, and our fimple marks, or the letters of our alphabet, very few; alfo fince our words are the fole immediate reprefentatives of objects and ideas, our written and printed marks being merely artificial pictures of words; one might fufpect, that the *Chinefe* words are, in correfpondence to this, merely an artificial enunciation of their character. But I think this not fo probable, as the mixed fuppofition mentioned in the laft paragraph. For it cannot be fuppofed, that any nation fhould be fo far deftitute of language, as not to have words for common objects, and internal feelings; or, having thefe, that they fhould lay them intirely afide, and adopt the artificial names of the marks reprefenting thofe objects and ideas in their fteads. But they might eafily adopt names, fimple or compound, at firft afcribed artificially to marks, whofe objects and ideas had before this adoption no names.

That in affixing names artificially to marks a great diverfity might arife, appears from the great diverfity of alphabetical characters expreffing the fame words. Thus the *Hebrew, Samaritan,* and *Syriac* languages, agree nearly in found and fenfe, but differ intirely in characters. Thus alfo, amongft modern languages, feveral are written in different characters, as *Englifh* in the common round-hand, in various law-hands, and various fhort-hands.

Let us now return to *Shem, Ham,* and *Japhet,* and their pofterity. They muft be fuppofed to proceed in the fame manner, in general, as *Noah,* and his
immediate

associated with them.

immediate posterity, till the confusion of tongues at *Babel*; excepting that *Shem*, *Ham*, and *Japhet*, with their wives, would be more apt to alter their character and language, and suit them to their present exigencies, than *Noah* and his wife, on account of their being all young persons; also that, being all as it were equal to each other they might each of them be the authors of certain diversities in the common character and language, and establish them in their respective posterities. However, if *Noah* be supposed to have continued with them till the division of the earth by God's command, and then only to have departed with his postdiluvian posterity for *China*, the country assigned to him, whilst *Shem*, *Ham*, and *Japhet*, with their posterity, began to build the tower of *Babel* in opposition to God's command, then *Noah* and all his sons, *&c.* must be supposed to have suited their character and language to the new world in nearly the same manner.

The confusion of tongues at *Babel* appears to me to be miraculous for the following reasons.

First, this appears to be the most natural interpretation of the text.

Secondly, thus the confusion of tongues will correspond to the gift of language imparted to *Adam* at his creation, which must be supposed; also to the gift of tongues at *Pentecost*.

Thirdly, learned men seem to have shewn, that the diversity of antient languages does by no means favour the supposition of a natural derivation of them all from one original form.

Fourthly, the original plan of the *Greek* and *Latin* tongues (which I consider as sister languages derived from the same mother or original plan), appears to have been very uniform, yet with a considerable variety. Now I think this uniformity and variety could scarce be invented and established by rude multitudes, almost intirely occupied in providing

necessaries

neceffaries for themfelves, and much lefs as alphabetical writing feems to be of later date than the diverfity of languages. And in fact we do not find, that barbarous nations do by length of time improve their languages fo as in any meafure to approach to the perfection of the *Greek* or *Latin*, or of their common mother. It adds ftrength to this argument, that the original plan of the *Greek* and *Latin*, i. e. the rules of etymology and fyntax, as grammarians call them, is intirely different from that of the *Hebrew* and *Arabic* (whofe original plans agree), though the firft colonies, which came by fea into *Greece* and *Italy*, came from *Palestine* and *Egypt*, i. e. from the neighbourhood of countries where *Hebrew* and *Arabic* were fpoken.

• Fifthly, the natural deviation of languages fince hiftory has been clear and certain, does by no means correfpond to a fuppofed natural derivation of all languages from one mother tongue, efpecially in fo fhort a time as the interval between the flood and the rife of many different antient languages. Let the reader here only reflect upon the great difference of the biblical *Hebrew* from the antienteft *Greek* extant, and the fmall difference of this from modern *Greek*, or of the biblical *Hebrew* from the rabbinical.

If now the confufion of tongues was miraculous, we may conjecture from the agreements and difagreements of mother languages from each other, that it was of the following kind.

Firft, that the original monofyllabic words of the antediluvian language were incorporated into each new language.

Secondly, that as thefe words included only few of the articulate founds of which the human voice is capable, the feveral families were put upon making new articulations, fome having one fet, fome another, imparted to them.

Thirdly,

Thirdly, that each family had a new stock of words given them, consisting partly of old, partly of new articulations; and that this new stock far exceeded the old one in number and variety.

Fourthly, that a new and different etymology and syntax were also communicated to each family.

Fifthly, that there were as many new languages given as there are heads of families mentioned *Gen*. x; the confusion of tongues, by which the division of the earth was effected, not happening till *Joktan*'s sons were old enough to be heads of families, though it had been determined and declared by God before. Those families, however, which were derived from the same stock, or had contiguous countries assigned to them, might be inspired with languages, that had a proportionable affinity.

Whatever may become of these particular conjectures, I think it highly probable, that the new languages far exceeded the old common one in the number and variety of words: and that the confusion of tongues was by this means a beneficial gift and blessing to mankind, as all God's other chastisements use to be.

We may also see reasons to make us judge that a diversity of languages is suited to the other circumstances of mankind. For this must prevent the infection of vice from spreading with such rapidity, as it would otherwise have done, had mankind lived together in one large body, and had a free communication with each other by means of the same language.

Diversity of languages does also both help the invention, and correct false judgments. For we think in words as appears by the foregoing theory, and invent chiefly by means of their analogies; at the same time that a servile adherence to those of any one language, or the putting words for things, would lead us into many errors. Now diversity of languages does both enlarge the field of invention, and by oppofing analogy to analogy preferve us from the prejudices derived from mere verbal agreements. Let me add here, that the abftract terms of logicians, metaphyficians, and fchoolmen, which may be confidered as a diftinct language, have fpiritualized men's underftandings, and taught them to ufe words in reafoning, as algebraifts do fymbols.

Different languages do likewife improve one another, and help one another to grow in fome proportion to the advancement in the knowledge of things.

Let us now examine the probable confequences of fuppofing different languages, and fuch as were far more copious than the old one, to be given at once miraculoufly.

Firft, then, the character, which fuited the old language very imperfectly, would be ftill lefs fuited to the new one.

Secondly, the new language might be more copious and better adjufted to exprefs objects and ideas, than the character. And this I think can fcarce be doubted, if we fuppofe the new languages given miraculoufly.

Thirdly, the agreement between many of the marks of the character, and the words of the old language, may be fuppofed likely to put fome perfons upon denoting the words of the new language by marks. But whether this would neceffarily lead to alphabetical writing, is very doubtful. I think not. The firft attempts at leaft would not be alphabetical writing.

Fourthly, perfons of different families, who could not underftand one another's language might yet correfpond by the character. However, one may guefs from the circumftances of things in antient times, that this would feldom take place in fact.

Fifthly,

Fifthly, this and the convenience of corresponding with persons of the same family at a distance, also the desire of preserving memorials of remarkable events and transactions, might make them continue the use of the character, and improve it, considered as a method of conveying ideas, distinct from that of language. And the character thus separated from the language might give rise to hieroglyphical writing in all its varieties.

Sixthly, the patriarchs after the flood in the line of *Shem* might convey in succession the history of the creation, fall, deluge, calling of *Abraham*, &c. either in the original picture-writing improved, or in the mixed character, which, according to the third of these consequences, denoted in some imperfect gross way the words of the new language. And some of the difficulties of the book of *Genesis* may be owing to its consisting of patriarchal records of one of these kinds, translated by *Moses* into the *Hebrew* of his own times, and then written alphabetically.

I do not think it *necessary* to have recourse to any such hypothesis as this, in order to vindicate the truth and authority of the book of *Genesis*. The length of life, even after the flood, to the time of *Moses*, appears sufficient for the preservation of such important traditional histories uncorrupted in the religious line of *Shem*, by natural means. Or God might interpose miraculously, as in so many other instances in patriarchal times.

If it be objected, that we have not the least intimation of writing of any kind in *Genesis*, I answer, that this is a difficulty. However, one cannot draw any certain conclusions from an omission. The original of writing is not likely to be one of the first things, which would be committed to writing. And if it was used only for the conveyance of important facts to the succeeding generations, we have no reason to expect the incidental mention of it. It
was

Of Words, *and the* Ideas

was probably fo tedious and difficult a thing to exprefs themfelves accurately in it, and verbal meffages and contracts fo eafy and natural in thofe fimple ages, when the veracity of the meffenger or contractor was not fufpected, as that writing was never ufed after the confufion of tongues, when language became copious, unlefs in affairs of great confequence.

Picture-writing is alluded to in the fecond commandment, and muft have been in ufe for fome time before, fince a fyftem of idolatry had been founded upon it. And this may incline one to think, that it had been chiefly employed in facred affairs, and therefore perhaps communicated originally to *Adam* by God. However, if we fuppofe, that it did not take place till after the flood, this will not totally vitiate the foregoing conjectures. The main purport of them may ftand, with due alterations and allowances. But it would be tedious to ftate all the varieties in things of fo uncertain a nature.

I come now to the art of alphabetical writing. This I conjecture to have been communicated miraculoufly by God to *Mofes* at *Sinai*, for the following reafons, which, however, I do not judge to be decifive ones.

Firft, then, God is faid to have written with his own finger upon the tables of ftone. And I think it would be harfh to fuppofe this done in conformity to, and, as one may fay, imitation of, any mere imperfect human invention.

Secondly, the *Ifraelites* are the only people in the whole world that have preferved any regular account of their own original. This is eafily accounted for upon fuppofition, that alphabetical writing was firft given to them in perfection; and afterwards, fuppofe in the time of *Eli*, borrowed by other nations, and accommodated in an imperfect manner to their languages. But if we fuppofe any other nation, the *Egyptians* or *Arabians* for inftance, to have invented

writing

writing before the time of *Mofes*, it will be somewhat difficult to affign a reafon, why other perfons fhould not have borrowed this invention as well as *Mofes*, and, like him, have given fome account of their own nation, and their anceftors ; and more difficult to affign a reafon why the people who invented alphabetical writing, fhould not do this.

As to the *Egyptians* in particular, their continuing to ufe hieroglyphical writing, and excelling in it, fhews, that they could not have invented alphabetical; for this, if we fuppofe it invented fo early as before the time of *Mofes*, would have abolifhed that, juft as the ufe of the ten cyphers has all the other imperfect methods of notation of numbers. Nor does it feem very likely, that hieroglyphical writing fhould lead to alphabetical, but rather from it, fince hieroglyphical characters are the immediate reprefentatives of objects and ideas, and the mediate reprefentatives not of letters, or fimple articulate founds, but of words, and even of clufters of words. It feems probable alfo that the *Egyptians* would even be backward in receiving alphabetical writing from the *Ifraelites* at the time that the *Philiftines* or *Phœnicians* did; as being then greatly advanced in the ufe of their own hieroglyphical writing, and prejudiced in its favour. And thus we may folve that very difficult queftion, why the *Egyptians*, who feem to have erected a kingdom early (however, I judge *Nimrod*'s to have been the firft by the manner in which *Mofes* has mentioned it), and to have brought it to confiderable perfection before *Jofeph*'s time, and to very great perfection afterwards, chiefly by his means, fhould yet have left no hiftory of their affairs, not even of the great empire under *Sefac* or *Sefoftris*, and his fucceffors. For they had no public calamities fufficient in any meafure to deftroy all their records, till the time of *Cambyfes*; and the defolation under him being lefs in degree, fhorter in duration, in a kingdom of greater extent, and two generations later in time, than that of the *Jewish* ſtate under *Nebuchadnezzar*, which yet did not deſtroy the *Jewiſh* records, could not have totally deſtroyed the *Egyptian* records had they been more early, and ſuperior to the *Jews*, in the uſe of alphabetical writing. Even the *Greeks*, who had no alphabetical writing till 600 years after the time of *Moſes*, have given a better account of their affairs, than the *Egyptians*. It ought, however, to be remarked in this place, that if we ſuppoſe the *Jewiſh* hiſtory to have been recorded by the divine appointment and direction, which is highly probable, this will leſſen the force of the preſent argument, but not quite deſtroy it.

Thirdly, the late reception of writing amongſt the *Greeks* is both an argument, that it did not exiſt in any other neighbouring nation before the time of *Moſes*, and alſo is conſiſtent with its being miraculouſly communicated to *him*, to be made uſe of for ſacred purpoſes, and for the preſervation of the hiſtory of the world, and true religion, amongſt God's peculiar people the *Iſraelites*. I here ſuppoſe, that the art of writing was not known to the *Greeks*, till the time of *Cadmus*; and that he came into *Greece*, agreeably to Sir *Iſaac Newton*'s opinion, about the middle of *David*'s reign. And indeed, unleſs the principal points of his chronology be admitted, it does not appear to me, that any *rationale* can be given of antient times, the inventions that roſe up in them, the eſtabliſhment and duration of kingdoms, their mutual intercourſes, &c.

For, firſt, if alphabetical writing was known upon the continent of *Aſia* and *Africa* 600 years before *Cadmus*, how could it be kept from the *Greeks* till his arrival amongſt them, and then accommodated to the *Greek* tongue only very imperfectly? for the *Greeks* received but ſixteen letters from him. The *Greek* tongue came itſelf perhaps from *Egypt*, in ſome meaſure;

associated with them. 145

measure; and they who brought the language two generations before *Cadmus*, would have brought an exact method of writing it alphabetically, had they been possessed of any such. For it was not probable that *Inachus*, and the colonies of *Egyptians* that came with him, and after him, should change their language intirely for that of the poor wandering *Cimmerians*, whom they found in *Greece*, since we see in fact, that the colonies of *Europeans* do sometimes teach the barbarous natives, where they go, an *European* language; but never change it for theirs.

Secondly, if alphabetical writing was given to *Moses* miraculously, it is easy to be conceived, that it should not arrive at *Greece* sooner than the time of *Cadmus*. For the *Jews* were a separate people, their priests kept the writings of *Moses* in the ark, *i. e.* the only alphabetical writings in the world; and must be some time before they could be ready and expert either in reading or writing: in their attempts to copy, it is probable they would make some mistakes, so as to fall short of the purity and perfection of the art, as communicated by God; the neighbouring nations feared and hated the *Israelites*, their religion, and their God; they had probably a picture-writing, or perhaps some imperfect method of denoting words, agreeably to what has been remarked above, which answered all purposes that seemed necessary to them; and thus the art of alphabetical writing might not transpire to any of the neighbouring nations till the time of *Eli*, when the ark, with the writings of *Moses* in it, was taken by the *Philistines*. For since the writings of *Moses* were not in the ark, when it was put into the temple of *Solomon*, it may be, that the *Philistines* kept them, and learnt from them the art of writing alphabetically, being now sufficiently prepared for it by such notions concerning it, as had transpired to them previously in their former intercourses with the *Israelites*. And thus the *Phœnicians*

L or

or *Philistines*, will have appeared the inventors of letters to the *Greeks*; and *Cadmus* may well be supposed to have been able to accommodate the *Phœnician* method of writing, in an imperfect manner, to the *Greek* language, about two generations after the taking of the ark. Thus also, when *Samuel* put the writings of *Moses* together, as they had been copied by the priests, or others, in the order in which they now stand in the pentateuch, there would be some deviations from the original method of writing communicated to *Moses* by God; and these, with such as happened in after-times, particularly upon the return from the *Babylonish* captivity (when it is supposed by some, that even the original letters were changed), may have made the antient method of writing the *Hebrew*, as the *Jews* practise it in their bibles for the synagogues without points, so imperfect as not to appear to be of divine original. For the same reasons, the corruptions of the *Hebrew* language, or the language given to *Heber* or *Peleg*, at the confusion of tongues, before *Moses*'s time, may incline us to think the *Hebrew* of the pentateuch not sufficiently regular for a divine communication. Much is also to be ascribed to our own ignorance in both these cases. However, there is a wonderful simplicity and uniformity still left, both in the biblical *Hebrew*, and in the manner of writing it without points; so great, as to appear to me superior to the invention of rude antient times.

Fourthly, the order of the *Greek* and *Latin* alphabets, by being taken from that of the *Hebrew*, as we have it in the alphabetical Psalms, bears testimony to the great antiquity of the *Hebrew* alphabet. It is to be observed here, that both the *Greek* and *Latin* alphabets coincide with the *Hebrew* alphabet, as much as with each other, or more; and that there is no other antient alphabet remaining to be a competitor to the *Hebrew*.

Fifthly,

Fifthly, the refolution of the complex articulate founds of antient languages into fimple elements or letters, and then recompofing thefe complex founds in writing them down alphabetically, feems to me, as obferved above, too difficult a problem for antient times; efpecially as they neither could fee the ufe of it, nor conceive the practicability. It would have appeared to them a tafk of an infinite extent; they would never conceive that fo fmall a number of elements would be fufficient, even fuppofing they could firft hit upon the defign. It confirms this, that no barbarous nation has ever invented alphabetical writing for themfelves. They continue ignorant of it till taught. However, let it be obferved, on the other hand, that as the antient languages were fimple and narrow, the difficulty of analyfing their complex founds would be the lefs on that account.

Sixthly, fince the method of making and erecting the tabernacle was communicated by God to *Mofes*, *Bezaleel*, and *Aholiab*, in a fupernatural manner, we may more eafily fuppofe the art of writing alphabetically to be a divine gift. But then it is fome objection to this, that *Mofes* has not mentioned it as a divine gift, at leaft not exprefly.

Seventhly, the time of *Mofes* appears to be a fuitable one for fuch a gift, as human life was then, perhaps, juft brought down to the prefent degree of fhortnefs. Till *Mofes*'s time, the length of life had preferved the facred traditions uncorrupted, either with or without the helps above mentioned, at leaft in the line of *Abraham*; but then tradition began to be mixed with fables, and to lead to idolatry.

Eighthly, alphabeticl writing, by being introduced among the *Ifraelites* in the Wildernefs, would abolifh hieroglyphical, and confequently cut off one fource of idolatry. It would likewife make them fuperior to the *Egyptians*, their enemies, in the art of writing; who, perhaps, prided themfelves much upon

upon account of their perfection in hieroglyphical writing, as they might alſo in their river, the wiſdom of their policy, the comparative greatneſs of their kingdom, their magical arts, religious ceremonies, &c. For this would tend to the glory of the God of the *Iſraelites*, and the eſtabliſhment of the true religion amongſt them.

It may be objected here, that alphabetical writing was in uſe before the giving of the law at *Sinai*, ſince *Moſes* was directed before this to write an account of the battle with *Amalek* in a book; alſo to write the names of the children of *Iſrael* upon the highprieſt's breaſt-plate, like the engravings of a ſignet. I anſwer, that both theſe may refer to a picturewriting, or to ſome improvement of it, whereby intire words were denoted, without being reſolved into their ſimple ſounds. The firſt might alſo be a prophetic intimation to *Moſes*, however not underſtood by him when it was given, that he ſhould be ſoon enabled to write in a much more complete manner than he, or his enemies the *Egyptians*, could at preſent.

The *Edomites* ſeem alſo to have had ſome kind of writing early from the account which we have of their dukes in *Geneſis*. But this might be only picture or verbal writing, explained to *Samuel* by ſome *Edomite*, at the time when he put together the writings of *Moſes*: or they might learn writing from the *Iſraelites*, ſooner than any other nation, as being nearly related in blood, and contiguous to them in ſituation.

The ſimplicity and uniformity of the *Arabic* tongue would alſo incline one to think, that the inhabitants of *Arabia* had alphabetical writing early, this having a great tendency to preſerve a fixed ſtandard in a language. But the *Iſhmaelites* or *Midianites*, who were nearly related to the *Iſraelites*, or the *Kenites*, who lived amongſt them, might learn it from them, perhaps even during their abode in the Wilderneſs. We may obſerve alſo, that the *Arabic* tongue

tongue was not only fixed, but perhaps rendered more regular, foon after the time of *Mahomet,* by means of the *Alcoran,* and of the grammars that were made for this language fome time afterwards; and that, before *Mahomet's* time, the *Arabians* had little communication with their neighbours, and therefore would preferve their language more pure and fimple.

The changes which have happened to languages, and to the methods of writing them, fince the invention of letters, and which are treated of with great copioufnefs in the writings of grammarians and critics, afford innumerable atteftations to the doctrine of affociation, and may, converfly, be much illuftrated by it. But the full detail of this muft be left to thofe, who are well fkilled in the feveral antient and modern languages.

P R O P. 36.

To explain the general nature of a philofophical language, and hint fome methods, in which it might be conftructed, upon the foregoing principles.

IF we fuppofe mankind poffeffed of fuch a language, as that they could at pleafure denote all their conceptions adequately, *i. e.* without any deficiency, fuperfluity, or equivocation; if, moreover, this language depended upon a few principles affumed, not arbitrarily, but becaufe they were the fhorteft and beft poffible, and grew on from the fame principles indefinitely, fo as to correfpond to every advancement in the knowledge of things, this language might be termed a philofophical one, and would as much exceed any of the prefent languages, as a paradifiacal ftate does the mixture of happinefs and mifery, which has been our portion ever fince the fall.

fall. And it is no improbable fuppofition, that the language given by God to *Adam* and *Eve*, before the fall, was of this kind; and, though it might be narrow, anfwered all their exigencies perfectly well.

Now there are feveral methods, in which it does not feem impoffible for mankind in future ages to accomplifh fo great a defign.

Thus, firft, they may examine all the poffible fimple articulations of which their organs are capable, with all the combinations, or complex articulate founds, that refult from them, and the relations which thefe bear one to another, and affign to each refpectively fuch fimple and complex ideas, and fuch variations of the laft, as a deep infight into the nature of things, objects, ideas, the powers of the human mind, *&c.* fhall demand by a natural claim, fo as to make every expreffion the fhorteft and beft poffible. And though this, in our prefent ftate of ignorance, cannot but feem an impracticable project, yet the fame ignorance fhould teach us, that we can form no notions at all of the great increafe of knowledge, which may come in future ages, and which feems promifed to come in the latter happy times predicted by the prophecies. However, the great, and to former times inconceivable, advancement of knowledge, which has been made in the two laft centuries, may help a little to qualify our prejudices.

Secondly, if all the fimple articulate founds, with all the radical words, which are found in the prefent languages, were appropriated to objects and ideas agreeably to the prefent fenfes of words, and their fitnefs to reprefent objects and ideas, fo as to make all confiftent with itfelf; if, farther, the beft rules of etymology and fyntax were felected from the prefent languages, and applied to the radical words here fpoken of, fo as to render them capable of expreffing all the variations in objects and ideas, as far as pofsible, *i. e* fo as to grow proportionably to the growth
of

associated with them.

of knowledge, this might also be termed a philosophical language; and, though more imperfect and narrow than the last, yet seems more possible to be brought to execution and practice.

Thirdly, if such simple articulations as are now wanting in the *Hebrew* alphabet were added to it, and its radical words, composed of all the combinations of two's and three's completed, proper simple senses being assigned to them, from other languages suppose, and particularly from the *Arabic, Chaldee, Syriac,* and *Samaritan,* as in *Castellus's* lexion, and other books of a like kind; if, farther, such new rules of etymology and syntax were added to those which take place at present in the biblical *Hebrew,* as this increase of the radicals, and application of the language to the whole aggregate of objects and ideas requires; we should have a much more simple, precise and extensive language, than any now in being. It would also be easy to be understood by the *Jews* in all quarters of the world. For most of them have some knowledge of the biblical *Hebrew,* and many understand the rabbinical, which seems to be formed upon a plan not very unlike that here proposed, though without any express design; and to which, therefore, a due regard ought to be had by any one, who should attempt to execute this plan. Many eastern nations, and the *Mahometans* everywhere, would also be expert in learning this language, from the relation and resemblance which it would bear to languages already known by them; and it would be easier to be learnt by perfect novices than any other, on account of its greater simplicity and regularity. A dictionary might be made for it in itself; the biblical *Hebrew,* where its sense is determinate and known, being the basis, or thing given.

In the mean time, where the writer endeavours to express himself with plainness, sincerity, and precision, cifion, being firſt duly qualified by the knowledge of his ſubject, and the reader pays a due regard to him, as his teacher, for the then preſent time, by uſing ſufficient induſtry and candour, the ill effects of the confuſion of tongues become evaneſcent in reſpect of them. But it would be happy to take away all occaſion of miſtake from the bulk of mankind, and to give them an opportunity of learning important truths with more eaſe and certainty, and in a ſhorter time, than they can at preſent.

It may not be amiſs to add here, that Mr. *Byrom's* method of ſhort-hand affords an accurate and elegant inſtance of the poſſibility of proceeding in ſuch matters upon ſimple and philoſophical principles; his ſhort-hand being a real and adequate repreſentation of the ſounds of the *Engliſh* tongue, as far as is neceſſary for determining the ſenſe, and that in the ſhorteſt manner poſſible. If we were poſſeſſed of a philoſophical language, it ought to be denoted by this character, *mutatis mutandis*.

PROP. 37.

To illuſtrate and confirm the general doctrine of aſſociation by the particular aſſociations, that take place in reſpect of language.

THIS has been done, in great meaſure, already, in the corollaries to the twelfth propoſition. I will here inſert ſome obſervations of a like kind, which would have interrupted the reader too much in that place, but may properly follow the account of language given in this ſection.

Let *a, b, c, d*, &c. the ſeveral letters of an alphabet, ſuppoſed to be ſufficiently extenſive for the purpoſe, repreſent reſpectively the ſeveral ſimple ſenſible pleaſures and pains, to which a child becomes ſubject upon its firſt entrance into the world. Then will

associated with them. 153

will the various combinations of these letters represent the various combinations of pleasures and pains, formed by the events and incidents of human life; and, if we suppose them to be also the words of a language, this language will be an emblem or adumbration of our passage through the present life; the several particulars in this being represented by analogous ones in that.

Thus the reiterated impressions of the simple sensible pleasures and pains made upon the child, so as to leave their miniatures, or ideas, are denoted by his learning the alphabet; and his various associations of these ideas, and of the pleasures and pains themselves, by his putting letters and syllables together, in order to make words: and when association has so far cemented the component parts of any aggregate of ideas, pleasures and pains, together, as that they appear one indivisible idea, pleasure or pain, the child must be supposed by an analogous association to have learnt to read without spelling.

As the child's words become more and more polysyllabic by composition and decomposition, till at length whole clusters run together into phrases and sentences, all whose parts occur at once, as it were, to the memory, so his pleasures and pains become more and more complex by the combining of combinations; and in many cases numerous combinations concur to form one apparently simple pleasure.

The several relations of words, as derived from the same root, as having the same prepositions and terminations, &c. represent corresponding relations in the compound ideas, pleasures and pains.

When the complex pleasures and pains, formed from miniatures of the sensible ones, become the means of gaining other and greater pleasures, *viz.* by fading from frequent repetition, and so becoming mere ideas, or by any other method, we must suppose, that our

present.

154   *Of* Words, *and the* Ideas

present knowledge in language is used as a means of attaining farther knowledge in it.

As the sight and sound of words, impressed upon us on common occasions, do not at all suggest the original of these words from simple letters, this being a light in which grammarians and linguists alone consider words, so the complex pleasures and pains may pass over men's minds, and be felt daily, and yet not be considered by them as mere combinations, unless they be peculiarly attentive and inquisitive in this respect.

This comparison may serve as a method of assisting the reader's conceptions, in respect of the manner in which combinations of miniatures are formed. It is also a considerable evidence in favour of the general doctrine of association, since language is not only a type of these associated combinations, but one part of the thing typified. Was human life perfect, our happiness in it would be properly represented by that accurate knowledge of things, which a truly philosophical language would give us. And if we suppose a number of persons thus making a progress in pure unmixed happiness, and capable both of expressing their own feelings, and of understanding those of others, by means of a perfect and adequate language, they might be like new senses and powers of perception to each other, and both give to and receive from each other happiness indefinitely. But as human life is, in fact, a mixture of happiness and misery, so all our languages must, from the difference of our associations, convey falsehood as well as truth, as above noted. And yet, since our imperfect languages improve, purify, and correct themselves perpetually by themselves, and by other means, so that we may hope at last to obtain a language, which shall be an adequate representation of ideas, and a pure chanel of conveyance for truth alone,

associated with them. 155

alone, analogy seems to suggest, that the mixture of pleasures and pains, which we now experience, will gradually tend to a collection of pure pleasures only, and that association may be the means of affecting this, as remarked in the 9th corollary of the 14th proposition.

SCHOLIUM.

Musical sounds afford, like articulate ones, various instances of the power of association. It ought to be remarked here also, that the concords formed from the twelve semitones in the octave, are more in number than the discords; and that the harshness of these last passes by degrees into the limits of pleasure, partly from frequent repetition, partly from their associations with concords.

The doctrine of association may likewise be illustrated by that of colours. Thus, let the seven primary colours, with their shades represent the original sensible pleasures; then will the various associated pleasures of human life, supposing that we enjoyed a state of unmixed happiness, be represented by the compound vivid colours, which natural bodies, of regular makes, and strong powers of reflexion, exhibit to the eye. White, which is compounded of all the colours reflected copiously, and which yet, as far as the eye can discern, bears no resemblance to any of them, would represent a state of great mental happiness, ultimately deduced from all the sensible pleasures, and in which, notwithstanding, the person himself distinguishes no traces of any of these. And, agreeably to this, light, brightness, and whiteness, are often put for perfection, purity, and happiness, as obscurity, blackness, and darkness, are for imperfection and misery. Besides white, there are other compound colours, which bear little or no resemblance to any of the primary ones, as well as many in which some primary colour is evidently predominant. These represent the several kinds and degrees

grees of inferior compound pleasures, some of which are, according to common estimation, quite foreign to the senses, whilst others are manifestly tinged with pleasant sensations, and their miniatures.

If the moderate agitations which light causes in bodies, when it is by them reflected back upon, or transmitted to other bodies, be supposed to correspond to pleasant vibrations in the nervous system; and the greater agitations, which it excites in those that absorb it, to the violent vibrations in which pain consists; then the colours of natural bodies, some of which incline to light, and some to darkness, and that with all the possible varieties and mixtures of the primary colours, may be considered as the language by which they express that mixture of pleasures and pains in human life, to which their agitations are supposed to correspond. And here again we may observe, that though there are some natural bodies, which absorb and stifle within themselves almost all the light which they receive, and which accordingly are dark, black, and unpleasant to the beholders, yet the greatest part of natural bodies either reflect lively colours, or reflect some, and transmit others, or transmit all the colours freely. And this type is also, in part, the thing typified, inasmuch as agreeable and disagreeable colours make part of the original pleasures and pains of human life.

Compound tastes may likewise illustrate association; as above noted under the 12th proposition: for where the number of ingredients is very great, as in Venice-treacle, no one can be tasted distinctly; whence the compound appears to bear no relation to its component parts. It is to be observed farther, that ingredients which are separately disagreeable, often enter compounds, whose tastes are highly agreeable. Now in these cases either the opposite tastes must coalesce into one, which pleases from the prepollence of agreeable tastes upon the whole, as soon as

associated with them.

as the association is cemented sufficiently, or else the disagreeable tastes must, by frequent repetition, fall within the limits of pleasure at last; which seems rather to be the truth.

The similarity of the three instances of this scholium arises from the analogy of our senses to each other, and to our frame in general; which is the sum total of all our senses. And, conversly, they confirm this analogy.

SECT.

SECT. II.

Of Propositions, *and the Nature of* Assent.

PROP. 38.

To explain the nature of assent and dissent, and to shew from what causes they arise.

IT appears from the whole tenor of the last section, that assent and dissent, whatever their precise and particular nature may be, must come under the notion of ideas, being only those very complex internal feelings, which adhere by association to such clusters of words as are called *propositions* in general, or affirmations and negations in particular. The same thing is remarked in the 10th corollary to the 12th proposition.

But in order to penetrate farther into this difficult and important point, I will distinguish assent (and by consequence its opposite, dissent) into two kinds, rational and practical; and define each of these.

Rational assent then to any proposition may be defined a readiness to affirm it to be true, proceeding from a close association of the ideas suggested by the proposition, with the idea, or internal feeling, belonging to the word truth; or of the terms of the proposition with the word truth. Rational dissent is the opposite to this. This assent might be called verbal; but as every person supposes himself always to have sufficient reason for such readiness to affirm or deny, I rather choose to call it rational.

Practical assent is a readiness to act in such manner as the frequent vivid recurrency of the rational assent

assent disposes us to act; and practical dissent the contrary.

Practical assent is therefore the natural and necessary consequence of rational, when sufficiently impressed. There are, however, two cautions to be subjoined here; *viz.* first, that some propositions, mathematical ones for instance, admit only of a rational assent, the practical not being applied to them in common cases. Secondly, that the practical assent is sometimes generated, and arrives at a high degree of strength, without any previous rational assent, and by methods that have little or no connexion with it. Yet still it is, in general, much influenced by it, and, conversly, exerts a great influence upon it. All this will appear more clearly when we come to the instances.

Let us next inquire into the causes of rational and practical assent, beginning with that given to mathematical conclusions.

Now the cause that a person affirms the truth of the proposition, *twice two is four,* is the intire coincidence of the visible or tangible idea of twice two with that of four, as impressed upon the mind by various objects. We see every where, that twice two and four are only different names for the same impression. And it is mere association which appropriates the word truth, its definition or its internal feeling, to this coincidence.

Where the numbers are so large, that we are not able to form any distinct visible ideas of them; as when we say, that 12 times 12 is equal to 144; a coincidence of the words arising from some method of reckoning up 12 times 12, so as to conclude with 144, and resembling the coincidence of words which attends the just-mentioned coincidence of ideas in the simpler numerical propositions, is the foundation of our rational assent. For we often do, and might always verify the simplest numerical propositions by
reckon-

reckoning up the numbers. The operations of addition, fubtraction, multiplication, divifion, and extraction of roots, with all the moft complex ones relating to algebraic quantities, confidered as the exponents of numbers, are no more than methods of producing this coincidence of words, founded upon and rifing above one another. And it is mere affociation again, which appropriates the word truth to the coincidence of the words, or fymbols, that denote the numbers.

It is to be remarked, however, that this coincidence of words is, by thofe who look deeper into things, fuppofed to be a certain argument, that the vifible ideas of the numbers under confideration, as of 12 times 12, and 144, would coincide, as much as the vifible ideas of twice two and four, were they as clear and diftinct. And thus the real and abfolute truth is faid by fuch perfons to be as great in complex numerical propofitions, as in the fimpleft. All this agrees with what Mr. *Locke* has obferved concerning numbers; *viz.* that their names are neceffary in order to our obtaining diftinct ideas of them; for by diftinct ideas he muft be underftood to mean proper methods of diftinguifhing them from one another, fo as to reafon juftly upon them. He cannot mean diftinct vifible ideas.

In geometry there is a like coincidence of lines, angles, fpaces, and folid contents, in order to prove them equal in fimple cafes. Afterwards, in complex cafes, we fubftitute the terms whereby equal things are denoted for each other, alfo the coincidence of the terms, for that of the vifible ideas, except in the new ftep advanced in the propofition; and thus get a new equality, denoted by a new coincidence of terms. This refembles the addition of unity to any number, in order to make the next, as of 1 to 20, in order to make 21. We have no diftinct vifible idea, either of 20 or 21; but we have of the diffe-

rence

rence between them, by fanfying to ourfelves a confufed heap of things fuppofed or called 20 in number; and then farther fanfying 1 to be added to it. By a like procefs in geometry we arrive at the demonftration of the moft complex propofitions.

The properties of numbers are applied to geometry in many cafes, as when we demonftrate a line or fpace to be half or double of any other, or in any other rational proportion to it.

And as in arithmetic words ftand for indiftinct ideas, in order to help us to reafon upon them as accurately as if they were diftinct; alfo cyphers for words, and letters for cyphers, both for the fame purpofe; fo letters are put for geometrical quantities alfo, and the agreements of the firft for thofe of the laft. And thus we fee the foundation upon which the whole doctrine of quantity is built; for all quantity is expounded either by number or extenfion, and their common and fole exponent is algebra. The coincidence of ideas is the foundation of the rational affent in fimple cafes; and that of ideas and terms together, or of terms alone, in complex ones. This is upon fuppofition that the quantities under confideration are to be proved equal. But, if they are to be proved unequal, the want of coincidence anfwers the fame purpofe. If they are in any numeral ratio, this is only the introduction of a new coincidence. Thus, if, inftead of proving A to be equal to B, we are to prove it equal to half B; the two parts of B muft coincide with each other, either in idea or terms, and A with one.

And thus it appears, that the ufe of words is neceffary for geometrical and algebraical reafonings, as well as for arithmetical.

We may fee alfo, that affociation prevails in every part of the proceffes hitherto defcribed.

But thefe are not the only caufes of giving rational affent to mathematical propofitions, as this is defined above.

above. The memory of having once examined and affented to each ftep of a demonftration, the authority of an approved writer, &c. are fufficient to gain our affent, though we underftand no more than the import of the propofition; nay, even though we do not proceed fo far as this. Now this is mere affociation again; this memory, authority, &c. being, in innumerable inftances, affociated with the beforementioned coincidence of ideas and terms.

But here a new circumftance arifes. For memory and authority are fometimes found to miflead; and this oppofite coincidence of terms puts the mind into a ftate of doubt, fo that fometimes truth may recur, and unite itfelf with the propofition under confideration, fometimes falfhood, according as the memory, authority, &c. in all their peculiar circumftances, have been affociated with truth or falfhood. However, the foundation of affent is ftill the fame. I here defcribe the fact only. And yet, fince this fact muft always follow from the fixed immutable laws of our frame, the obligation to affent (whatever be meant by this phrafe) muft coincide with the fact.

And thus a mathematical propofition, with the rational affent or diffent arifing in the mind, as foon as it is prefented to it, is nothing more than a group of ideas, united by affociation, *i. e.* than a very complex idea, as was affirmed above of propofitions in general. And this idea is not merely the fum of the ideas belonging to the terms of the propofition, but alfo includes the ideas, or internal feelings, whatever they be, which belong to equality, coincidence, truth, and in fome cafes, thofe of utility, importance, &c.

For mathematical propofitions are, in fome cafes, attended with a practical affent, in the proper fenfe of thefe words; as when a perfon takes this or that method of executing a projected defign, in confequence of fome mathematical propofition affented to

from

the Nature of Affent.

from his own examination, or on the authority of others. Now, that which produces the train of voluntary actions, here denoting the practical affent, is the frequent recurrency of ideas of utility and importance. Thefe operate according to the method laid down in the 20th propofition, *i. e.* by affociation; and though the rational affent be a previous requifite, yet the degree of the practical affent is proportional to the vividnefs of thefe ideas; and in moft cafes they ftrengthen the rational affent by a reflex operation.

Propofitions concerning natural bodies are of two kinds, vulgar and fcientifical. Of the firft kind are, *that milk is white, gold yellow, that a dog barks,* &c. Thefe are evidently nothing but forming the prefent complex idea belonging to material objects into a propofition, or adding fome of its common affociates, fo as to make it more complex. There is fcarce room for diffent in fuch propofitions, they being all taken from common appearances. Or if any doubt fhould arife, the matter muft be confidered fcientifically. The affent given to thefe propofitions arifes from the affociations of the terms, as well as of the ideas denoted by them.

In fcientifical propofitions concerning natural bodies a definition is made, as of gold, from its properties, fuppofe its colour, and fpecific gravity, and another property or power joined to them, as a conftant or common affociate. Thus gold is faid to be ductile, fixed, or foluble in *aqua regia.* Now to perfons, who have made the proper experiments a fufficient number of times, thefe words fuggeft the ideas which occur in thofe experiments, and, converfly, are fuggefted by them, in the fame manner as the vulgar propofitions above-mentioned fuggeft and are fuggefted by common appearances. But then, if they be fcientifical perfons, their readinefs to affirm, that gold is foluble in *aqua regia* univerfally, arifes alfo from the experiments of others, and from their own and others obfervations on the conftancy and tenor of nature. They know that the colour, and fpecific gravity, or almoft any two or three remarkable qualities of any natural body, infer the reft, being never found without them. This is a general truth; and as thefe general terms are obferved to coincide, in fact, in a great variety of inftances, fo they coincide at once in the imagination, when applied to gold, or any other natural body, in particular. The coincidence of general terms is alfo obferved to infer that of the particular cafes in many inftances, befides thofe of natural bodies; and this unites the fubject and predicate of the propofition, *gold is foluble in aqua regia,* farther in thofe who penetrate ftill deeper into abftract fpeculations. And hence we may fee, as before, firft, that terms or words are abfolutely neceffary to the art of reafoning: fecondly, that our affent is here alfo, in every ftep of the procefs, deducible from affociation.

The propofitions formed concerning natural bodies are often attended with a high degree of practical affent, arifing chiefly from fome fuppofed utility and importance, and which is no ways proportional to the foregoing, or other fuch like allowed caufes of rational affent. And in fome cafes the practical affent takes place before the rational. But then, after fome time, the rational affent is generated and cemented moft firmly by the prevalence of the practical. This procefs is particularly obfervable in the regards paid to medicines, *i. e.* in the rational and practical affent to the propofitions concerning their virtues.

It is to be obferved, that children, novices, unlearned perfons, *&c.* give, in many cafes, a practical affent upon a fingle inftance; and that this arifes from the firft and fimpleft of the affociations here confidered. The influence of the practical affent over the rational arifes plainly from their being joined together

gether in so many cases. The vividness of the ideas arising from the supposed utility, importance, &c. does also unite the subject and predicate sooner and closer, agreeably to what has been observed in the general account of association.

The evidences for past facts are a man's own memory, and the authority of others. These are the usual associates of true past facts, under proper restrictions; and therefore beget the readiness to affirm a past fact to be true, i. e. the rational assent. The integrity and knowledge of the witnesses, being the principal restriction, or requisite, in the accounts of past facts, become principal associates to the assent to them; and the contrary qualities to dissent.

If it be asked, how a narration of an event, supposed to be certainly true, supposed doubtful, or supposed entirely fictitious, differs in its effect upon the mind, in the three circumstances here alledged, the words being the same in each, I answer, first, in having the terms *true*, *doubtful*, and *fictitious*, with a variety of usual associates to these, and the corresponding internal feelings of respect, anxiety, dislike, &c. connected with them respectively; whence the whole effects, exerted by each upon the mind, will differ considerably from one another. Secondly, if the event be of an interesting nature, as a great advantage accruing, the death of a near friend, the affecting related ideas will recur oftener, and, by so recurring agitate the mind more, in proportion to the supposed truth of the event. And it confirms this, that the frequent recurrency of an interesting event, supposed doubtful, or even fictitious, does, by degrees, make it appear like a real one, as in reveries, reading romances, seeing plays, &c. This affection of mind may be called the practical assent to past facts, and it frequently draws after it the rational, as in the other instances above alledged.

The evidence for future facts is of the same kind with that for the propositions concerning natural bodies, being, like it, taken from induction and analogy. This is the cause of the rational assent. The practical depends upon the recurrency of the ideas, and the degree of agitation produced by them in the mind. Hence reflection makes the practical assent grow for a long time after the rational is arisen to its height; or if the practical arises without the rational, in any considerable degree, which is often the case, it will generate the rational. Thus the sanguine are apt to believe and assert what they hope, and the timorous what they fear.

There are many speculative, abstracted propositions in logic, metaphysics, ethics, controversial divinity, &c. the evidence for which is the coincidence or analogy of the abstract terms, in certain particular applications of them, or as considered in their grammatical relations. This causes the rational assent. As to the practical assent or dissent, it arises from the ideas of importance, reverence, piety, duty, ambition, jealousy, envy, self-interest, &c. which intermix themselves in these subjects, and, by doing so, in some cases add great strength to the rational assent; in others, destroy it, and convert it into its opposite.

And thus it appears, that rational assent has different causes in propositions of different kinds, and practical likewise; that the causes of rational are also different from those of practical; that there is, however, a great affinity, and general resemblance, in all the causes; that rational and practical assent exert a perpetual reciprocal effect upon one another; and consequently, that the ideas belonging to assent and dissent, and their equivalents and relatives, are highly complex ones, unless in the cases of very simple propositions, such as mathematical ones.

For,

For, besides the coincidence of ideas and terms, they include, in other cases, ideas of utility, importance, respect, disrespect, ridicule, religious affections, hope, fear, &c. and bear some gross general proportion to the vividness of these ideas.

Cor. 1. When a person says, *Video meliora proboque, deterior a sequor;* it shews that the rational and practical assent are at variance, that they have opposite causes, and that neither of these has yet destroyed the other.

Cor. 2. The rational and practical faith in religious matters are excellent means of begetting each other.

Cor. 3. Vicious men, *i. e.* all persons who want practical faith, must be prejudiced against the historical and other rational evidences in favour of revealed religion.

Cor. 4. It is impossible any person should be so sceptical, as not to have the complex ideas denoted by assent and dissent associated with a great variety of propositions, in the same manner, as in other persons; just as he must have the same ideas in general affixed to the words of his native language, as other men have. A pretended sceptic is therefore no more than a person who varies from the common usage in his application of a certain set of words, *viz.* truth, certainty, assent, dissent, &c.

Cor. 5. As there is a foundation for unity amongst mankind in the use and application of words, so there is for a unity in the assent, or complex ideas belonging to propositions; and a philosophical language, or any other method of bringing about the first unity, would much conduce to this. A careful examination of things, of the world natural, the human mind, the scriptures, would conduce much also. But candor, simplicity, and a humble sense of our own ignorance, which may be called a religious or christian scepticism, is the principal requisite, and that

that without which this part of the confusion at *Babel* can never be remedied. When religion has equally and fully abforbed different perfons, fo that God is, in refpect of them, *all in all*, as far as the prefent condition of mortality will permit, their practical affent muft be the fame; and therefore their rational cannot differ long or widely.

The ideas and internal feelings which arife in the mind, from words and propofitions, may be compared to, and illuftrated by, thofe which the appearances of different perfons excite. Suppofe two perfons, *A* and *B*, to go together into a croud, and there each of them to fee a variety of perfons whom he knew in different degrees, as well as many utter ftrangers. *A* would not have the fame ideas and affociations raifed in him from viewing the feveral faces, dreffes, &c. of the perfons in the croud, as *B*, partly from his having a different knowledge of, and acquaintance with them; partly from different predifpofitions to approve and difapprove. But let *A* and *B* become equally acquainted with them, and acquire, by education and affociation, the fame predifpofitions of mind, and then they will at laft make the fame judgment of each of the perfons whom they fee.

Cor. 6. Religious controverfies concerning abftract propofitions arife generally from the different degrees of refpect paid to terms and phrafes, which conduce little or nothing to the generation of practical faith, or of love to God, and truft in him through Chrift.

PROP.

PROP. 39.

To deduce rules for the ascertainment of truth, and advancement of knowledge, from the mathematical methods of considering quantity.

THIS is done in the doctrine of chances, with respect to the events there considered. And though we seldom have such precise *data* in mixed sciences as are there assumed, yet there are two remarks of very general use and application, deducible from the doctrine of chances.

Thus, first, if the evidences brought for any proposition, fact, &c. be dependent on each other, so that the first is required to support the second, the second to support the third, &c. *i. e.* if a failure of any one of the evidences renders all the rest of no value, the separate probability of each evidence must be very great, in order to make the proposition credible; and this holds so much the more, as the dependent evidences are more numerous. For instance, if the value of each evidence be $\frac{1}{a}$, and the number of evidences be n, then will the resulting probability be $\frac{1}{a^n}$. I here suppose absolute certainty to be denoted by 1; and consequently, that a can never be less than 1. Now it is evident, that $\frac{1}{a^n}$ decreases with every increase both of a and n.

Secondly, if the evidences brought for any proposition, fact, &c. be independent on each other, *i. e.* if they be not necessary to support each other, but concur, and can, each of them, when established upon its own proper evidences, be applied directly to establish the proposition, fact, &c. in question, the deficiency in the probability of each must be very great, in order to render the propofition perceptibly doubtful; and this holds fo much the more, as the evidences are more numerous. For inftance, if the evidences be all equal, and the common deficiency in each be $\frac{1}{a}$, if alfo the number of evidences be n as before, the deficiency of the refulting probability will be no more than $\frac{1}{a^n}$, which is practically nothing, where a and n are confiderable. Thus if a and n be each equal to 10, $\frac{1}{a^n}$ will be $\frac{1}{10,000,000,000}$, or only 1 in ten thoufand millions; a deficiency from certainty, which is utterly imperceptible to the human mind.

It is indeed evident, without having recourfe to the doctrine of chances, that the dependency of evidences makes the refulting probability weak, their independency ftrong. Thus a report paffing from one original author through a variety of fucceffive hands lofes much of its credibility, and one attefted by a variety of original witneffes gains, in both cafes, according to the number of fucceffive reporters, and original witneffes, though by no means proportionably thereto. This is the common judgment of mankind, verified by obfervation and experience. But the mathematical method of confidering thefe things is much more precife and fatisfactory, and differs from the common one, juft as the judgment made of the degrees of heat by the thermometer does from that made by the hand.

We may thus alfo fee in a fhorter and fimpler way that the refulting probability may be fufficiently ftrong in dependent evidences, and of little value in independent ones, according as the feparate probability of each evidence is greater or lefs. Thus the principal facts of antient hiftory are not lefs probable practically now, than 10 or 15 centuries ago, nor lefs fo then,

then, than in the times immediately succeeding; because the diminution of evidence in each century is imperceptible. For, if $\frac{1}{a}$ be equal to 1, $\frac{1}{a^n}$ will be equal to 1 also; and if the deficiency of $\frac{1}{a}$ from 1 be extremely small, that of $\frac{1}{a^n}$ will be extremely small also, unless n be extremely great. And for the same reason a large number of weak arguments proves little; for $\frac{1}{a}$ the deficiency of each argument, being extremely great, $\frac{1}{a^n}$, the resulting deficiency of independent evidences, will be extremely great also.

It appears likewise, that the inequality of the separate evidences does not much affect this reasoning. In like manner, if the number of evidences, dependent or independent, be great, we may make great concessions as to the separate values of each. Again, a strong evidence in dependent ones can add nothing, but must weaken a little; and, after a point is well settled by a number of independent ones, all that come afterwards are useless, because they can do no more than remove the imperceptible remaining deficiency, &c. And it will be of great use to pursue these, and such like deductions, both mathematically, and by applying them to proper instances selected from the sciences, and from common life, in order to remove certain prejudices, which the use of general terms, and ways of speaking, with the various associations adhering to them, is apt to introduce and fix upon the mind. It cannot but assist us in the art of reasoning, thus to take to pieces, recompose, and ascertain our evidences.

If it be asked, upon what authority absolute certainty is represented by unity, and the several degrees of of probability by fractions lefs than unity, in the doctrine of chances? alfo, upon what authority the reafoning ufed in that doctrine is transferred to other fubjects, and made general, as here propofed? I anfwer, that no perfon who weighs thefe matters carefully, can avoid giving his affent; and that this precludes all objections. No fceptic would, in fact, be fo abfurd as to lay 2 to 1, where the doctrine of chances determines the probability to be equal on each fide; and therefore we may be fure, that he gives a practical affent at leaft to the doctrine of chances.

Mr. *de Moivre* has fhewn, that where the caufes of the happening of an event bear a fixed ratio to thofe of its failure, the happenings muft bear nearly the fame ratio to the failures, if the number of trials be fufficient; and that the laft ratio approaches to the firft indefinitely, as the number of trials increafes. This may be confidered as an elegant method of accounting for that order and proportion, which we every where fee in the phænomena of nature. The determinate fhapes, fizes, and mutual actions of the conftituent particles of matter, fix the ratios between the caufes for the happenings, and the failures; and therefore it is highly probable, and even neceffary, as one may fay, that the happenings and failures fhould perpetually recur in the fame ratio to each other nearly, while the circumftances are the fame. When the circumftances are altered, then new caufes take place; and confequently there muft be a new, but fixed ratio, between the happenings and the failures. Let the firft circumftances be called *A*, the new ones *B*. If now the fuppofition be made fo general, as equally to take in both *A* and *B*, the ratio of the happenings and failures will not be fuch as either *A* or *B* required. But ftill it will tend to a precifenefs, juft as they did, fince the fum of the

caufes

the Nature of Affent.

caufes of the happenings muft bear a fixed ratio to the fum of the caufes of the failures.

An ingenious friend has communicated to me a folution of the inverfe problem, in which he has fhewn what the expectation is, when an event has happened p times, and failed q times, that the original ratio of the caufes for the happening or failing of an event fhould deviate in any given degree from that of p to q. And it appears from this folution, that where the number of trials is very great, the deviation muft be inconfiderable: which fhews that we may hope to determine the proportions, and, by degrees, the whole nature, of unknown caufes, by a fufficient obfervation of their effects.

The inferences here drawn from thefe two problems are evident to attentive perfons, in a grofs general way, from common methods of reafoning.

Let us, in the next place, confider the *Newtonian* differential method, and compare it with that of arguing from experiments and obfervations, by induction and analogy. This differential method teaches, having a certain number of the ordinates of any unknown curve given with the points of the abfcifs on which they ftand, to find out fuch a general law for this curve, *i. e.* fuch an equation expreffing the relation of an ordinate and abfcifs in all magnitudes of the abfcifs, as will fuit the ordinates and points of the abfcifs given, in the unknown curve under confideration. Now here we may fuppofe the given ordinates ftanding upon given points to be analogous to effects, or the refults of various experiments in given circumftances, the abfcifs analogous to all poffible circumftances, and the equation afforded by the differential method to that law of action, which, being fuppofed to take place in the given circumftances, produces the given effects. And as the ufe of the differential method is to find the lengths of ordinates not given, ftanding upon points of the abfcifs
that

that are given, by means of the equation, so the use of attempts to make general conclusions by induction and analogy, from particular effects or phænomena, is to enable us to predict other phænomena in different given circumstances, by applying the general law conclusion to these circumstances.

This parallel is the more pertinent and instructive, inasmuch as the mathematical conclusion drawn by the differential method, though formed in a way that is strictly just, and so as to have the greatest possible probability in its favour, is, however, liable to the same uncertainties, both in kind and degree, as the general maxims of natural philosophy drawn from natural history, experiments, &c.

If many ordinates be given; if the distances of the points of the abscifs, on which they stand, be equal and small; if the ordinate required lie amongst them, or near them; and f there be reason to think, that the curve itself is formed according to some simple, though unknown law; then may we conclude, that the new ordinate, determined by the equation, does not vary far from the truth. And if the resulting equation be simple, and always the same, from whatever given ordinates it be extracted, there is the greatest reason to think this to be the real original law or equation of the curve; and consequently that all its points and properties may be determined with perfect exactness by means of it; whereas, if the given ordinates be few, their distances great or unequal, the ordinate required considerably distant from many or most of them, the unknown curve be a line drawn at hazard, and the resulting equation very different where different ordinates are given, though their number be the same, there will be little probability of determining the new ordinate with exactness; however, still the differential method affords us the greatest probability which the *data* permit in such cases.

In like manner, if the experiments or obfervations be many, their circumftances nearly related to
each other, and in a regular feries, the circumftances
of the effect to be inveftigated nearly related to them';
alfo, if the real caufe may be fuppofed to produce
thefe effects, by the varieties of fome fimple law,
the method of induction and analogy will carry great
probability with it. And if the general conclufion
or law be fimple, and always the fame, from whatever phænomena it be deduced, fuch as the three
laws of nature, the doctrines of gravitation, and of
the different refrangibility of light; or, to go ftill
higher, by taking a mathematical inftance, the law
for finding the coefficients of the integral powers of
a binomial, deduced from mere trials in various
powers; there can fcarce remain any doubt, but that
we are in poffeffion of the true law inquired after,
fo as to be able to predict with certainty, in all cafes
where we are mafters of the method of computation,
or applying it; and have no reafon to fufpect, that
other unknown laws interfere. But, if the given
phænomena be few, their circumftances very different from each other, and from thofe of the effect
to be predicted; if there be reafon to fuppofe, that
many caufes concur in the producing thefe phænomena, fo that the law of their production muft be
very complex; if a new hypothefis be required to
account for every new combination of thefe phænomena; or, at leaft, one that differs confiderably from
itfelf; the beft hypothefis which we can form, *i. e.*
the hypothefis which is moft conformable to all the
phænomena, will amount to no more than an uncertain conjecture; and yet ftill it ought to be preferred
to all others, as being the beft that we can form.

That inftantaneous and neceffary coalefcence of
ideas, which makes intuitive evidence, may be confidered as the higheft kind of induction, and as
amounting to a perfect coincidence of the effect concluded

cluded with thofe from which it is concluded. This takes place only in mathematics. Thus we infer, that 2 and 2 make 4, only from prior inftances of having actually perceived this, and from the neceffary coincidence of all thefe inftances with all other poffible ones of 2 and 2. Mathematical demonftrations are made up of a number of thefe, as was obferved above.

Where the inftances from whence the induction is made are alike, as far as we know, to that under confideration, at leaft in all things that affect the prefent inquiry, it affords the higheft probability, and may be termed induction, in the proper fenfe of the word. Thus we infer, that the bread before us is nutritive and wholfome, becaufe its fmell, tafte, ingredients, manner of compofition, &c. are the fame as thofe of other bread, which has often before been experienced to be fo.

But, if the inftance under confideration be in fome refpects like the foregoing ones, in others not, this kind of proof is generally termed one taken from analogy. Thus, if we argue from the ufe and action of the ftomach in one animal to thofe in another, fuppofed to be unknown, there will be a probable hazard of being miftaken, proportional in general to the known difference of the two animals, as well as a probable evidence for the truth of part, at leaft, of what is advanced, proportional to the general refemblance of the two animals. But if, upon examination, the ftomach, way of feeding, &c. of the fecond animal fhould be found, to fenfe, the fame as in the firft, the analogy might be confidered as an induction properly fo called, at leaft as approaching to it; for precife limits cannot be fixed here. If the fecond animal be of the fame fpecies, alfo of the fame age, fex, &c. with the firft, the induction becomes perpetually of a higher and higher order, approaching more and more to the coincidence, which

obtains

obtains in mathematical evidences, and yet never being able intirely to arrive at it. But then the difference, being only an infinitefimal fraction, as it were, becomes nothing to all practical purpofes whatfoever. And if a man confiders farther, that it would be hard to find a demonftration, that he does not miftake the plaineft truths; this leffens the difference theoretically alfo.

It is often in our power to obtain an analogy where we cannot have an induction; in which cafe reafoning from analogy ought to be admitted; however, with all that uncertainty which properly belongs to it, confidered as more or lefs diftant from induction, as built upon more or fewer dependent or independent evidences, &c. Analogy may alfo, in all cafes, be made ufe of as a guide to the invention. But coincidence in mathematical matters, and induction in others, where-ever they can be had, muft be fought for as the only certain tefts of truth. However, induction feems to be a very fufficient evidence in fome mathematical points, affording at leaft as much evidence there as in natural philofophy; and may be fafely relied on in perplexed cafes, fuch as complex feriefes, till fatisfactory demonftrations can be had.

The analogous natures of all the things about us, are a great affiftance in decyphering their properties, powers, laws, &c. inafmuch as what is minute or obfcure in one may be explained and illuftrated by the analogous particular in another, where it is large and clear. And thus all things become comments on each other in an endlefs reciprocation.

When there are various arguments for the fame thing taken from induction or analogy, they may all be confidered as fupporting one another in the fame manner as independent evidences. Thus, if it could be fhewed, that the human underftanding is intirely dependent on affociation (as is remarked in this and the laft fection), the many analogies and
con-

connexions between the underſtanding and affections, as theſe terms are commonly underſtood and contra-diſtinguiſhed by writers, would make it very probable, that aſſociation preſides in the ſame manner in the generation of the affections; and *vice verſa*. And the more analogies, and mutual connexions, between the underſtanding and affections, were produced, ſo many more independent or concurrent evidences would there be for this prevalence of aſſociation in one, admitting it in the other. But, if now it be ſhewn farther, that the underſtanding and affections are not really diſtinct things, but only different names, which we give to the ſame kind of motions in the nervous ſyſtem, on account of a difference in degree, and other differences which it would be tedious here to enumerate, but which make no difference in reſpect of the power of aſſociation, then all the arguments from analogy are transformed into one of induction; which, however, is ſtronger than the united force of them all. For now it may be ſhewed, that aſſociation muſt prevail in each motion in the brain, by which affection is expounded, from a large induction of particulars, in which it prevails in the generation of ideas, or of the motions by which they are expounded, and which we ſuppoſe to be proved to be of the ſame kind with thoſe that expound the affections. Thus alſo inductions may be taken from the ſmell and taſte of bread, to prove it wholſome; which would both be transformed into one ſimple argument ſtronger than both, could we ſee the internal conſtitution of the ſmall parts of the bread, from whence its ſmell, and taſte, and wholſomeneſs, are all derived. Thus, again, all the arguments of induction for the manner of extracting the ſquare root in numbers vaniſh into the ſingle demonſtrative proof, as ſoon as this is produced. And the great buſineſs in all branches of knowledge is thus to reduce, unite, and ſimplify our evidences; ſo as that

that the one refulting proof, by being of a higher order, fhall be more than equal in force to all the concurrent ones of the inferior orders.

Having now confidered in what manner the doctrine of chances, and the *Newtonian* differential method, may ferve to fhew in general the value of dependent and independent or concurrent evidences, and the probability of general conclufions formed by induction and analogy; let us next inquire by what means we are to form thefe general conclufions, and difcover their evidences. Now the different methods of doing this may be faid to refemble refpectively the rule of falfe in common arithmetic; the algebraic methods of bringing the unknown quantity into an equation, under a form capable of all the algebraic operations, addition, fubtraction, *&c*. the algebraic methods of finding the roots of equations of the higher orders by approximation; and the art of decyphering: all which four methods bear alfo a confiderable refemblance to each other. I will confider them in order, and endeavour to fhew how analogous methods may be introduced into the fciences in general, to advantage.

Firft, then, as, according to the rule of falfe, the arithmetician fuppofes a certain number to be that which is fought for; treats it as if it was that; and finding the deficiency or overplus in the conclufion, rectifies the error of his firft pofition by a proportional addition or fubtraction, and thus folves the problem; fo it is ufeful in inquiries of all kinds, to try all fuch fuppofitions as occur with any appearance of probability, to endeavour to deduce the real phænomena from them; and if they do not anfwer in fome tolerable meafure, to reject them at once; or if they do, to add, expunge, correct, and improve, till we have brought the hypothefis as near as we can to an agreement with nature. After this it muft be left to be farther corrected and improved, or intirely difproved, disproved, by the light and evidence reflected upon it from the contiguous, and even, in some measure, from the remote branches of other sciences.

Were this method commonly used, we might soon expect a great advancement in the sciences. It would much abate that unreasonable fondness, which those who make few or no distinct hypotheses, have for such confused ones as occur accidentally to their imaginations, and recur afterwards by association. For the ideas, words, and reasonings, belonging to the favourite hypothesis, by recurring, and being much agitated in the brain, heat it, unite with each other, and so coalesce in the same manner, as genuine truths do from induction and analogy. Verbal and grammatical analogies and coincidences are advanced into real ones; and the words which pass often over the ear, in the form of subject and predicate, are from the influence of other associations made to adhere together insensibly, like subjects and predicates, that have a natural connexion. It is in vain to bid an inquirer form no hypothesis. Every phænomenon will suggest something of this kind; and, if he does not take care to state such as occur fully and fairly, and adjust them one to another, he may entertain a confused inconsistent mixture of all, of fictitious and real, possible and impossible; and become so persuaded of it, as that counter-associations shall not be able to break the unnatural bond. But he that forms hypotheses from the first, and tries them by the facts, soon rejects the most unlikely ones; and, being freed from these, is better qualified for the examination of those that are probable. He will also confute his own positions so often as to fluctuate in equilibrio, in respect of prejudices, and so be at perfect liberty to follow the strongest evidences.

In like manner, the frequent attempts to make an hypothesis that shall suit the phænomena, must improve a man in the method of doing this; and be-

get

get in him by degrees an imperfect practical art, juft as algebraifts and decypherers, that are much verfed in practice, are poffeffed of innumerable fubordinate artifices, befides the principal general ones, that are taught by the eftablifhed rules of their arts; and thefe, though of the greateft ufe to themfelves, can fcarce be explained or communicated to others. Thefe artifices may properly be referred to the head of factitious fagacity, being the refult of experience, and of impreffions often repeated, with fmall variations from the general refemblance.

Laftly, the frequent making of hypothefes, and arguing from them fynthetically, according to the feveral variations and combinations of which they are capable, would fuggeft numerous phænomena. that otherwife efcape notice, and lead to *experimenta crucis*, not only in refpect of the hypothefis under confideration, but of many others. The variations and combinations juft mentioned fuggeft things to the invention, which the imagination unaffifted is far unequal to; juft as it would be impoffible for a man to write down all the changes upon eight bells, unlefs he had fome method to direct him.

But this method of making definite hypothefes, and trying them, is far too laborious and mortifying for us to hope that inquirers will in general purfue it. It would be of great ufe to fuch as intend to purfue it, to make hypothefes for the phænomena, whofe theories are well afcertained; fuch as thofe of the circulation of the blood, of the preffure of the air, of the different refrangibility of the rays of light, &c. and fee how they are gradually compelled into the right road, even from wrong fuppofitions fairly compared with the phænomena. This would habituate the mind to a right method, and beget the factitious fagacity above-mentioned.

The fecond of the four methods propofed is, that of bringing the unknown quantity to an equation, and putting it into a form fufceptible of all the algebraic

gebraic operations. Now to this anfwers, in philofophy, the art of giving names, expreffing nothing definite as to manner, quantity, &c. and then inferting thefe names, or indefinite terms, in all the enunciations of the phænomena, to fee whether, from a comparifon of thefe enunciations with each other, where the terms are ufed in the greateft latitude, fome reftrictions, fomething definite in manner, degree, or mutual relation, will not refult. Things that are quite unknown have often fixed relations to one another, and fometimes relations to things known, which, though not determinable with certainty and precifion, may yet be determined in fome probable manner, or within certain limits. Now, as in algebra it is impoffible to exprefs the relation of the unknown quantity to other quantities known or unknown, till it has a fymbol affigned to it, of the fame kind with thofe that denote the others; fo in philofophy we muft give names to unknown quantities, qualities, caufes, &c. not in order to reft in them, as the *Ariftotelians* did, but to have a fixed expreffion, under which to treafure up all that can be known of the unknown caufe, &c. in the imagination and memory, or in writing for future inquirers.

But then it is neceffary for the fame reafons, that thefe terms fhould have no more of fecondary ideas from prior affociations, than the terms x and y in algebra. Whence, if we ufe old terms excluding the old affociations, the reader fhould be made aware of this at firft, and incidentally reminded of it afterwards. Sir *If. Newton* has ufed the words *æther*, *attraction*, and fome others, in this way, not refting in them, but enumerating a great variety of phænomena; from the due comparifon of which with each other, and with fuch as farther obfervation and experiments fhall fuggeft, their laws of action will, perhaps, be difcovered hereafter; fo that we may be able to predict the phænomena. There is alfo an
inftance

instance of the proper manner of reasoning concerning the knowable relations of unknown things in Mr. Mede's *Clavis Apocaliptica*.

The third method is that of approximating to the roots of equations. Here a first position is obtained, which, though not accurate, approaches, however, to the truth. From this, applied to the equation, a second position is deduced, which approaches nearer to the truth than the first; from the 2d a 3d, &c. till the analyst obtains the true root, or such an approximation as is practically equivalent, every preceding discovery being made the foundation for a subsequent one, and the equation resolving itself, as it were, gradually. Now this is indeed the way, in which all advances in science are carried on; and scientific persons are in general aware, that it is and must be so. However, I thought it not improper to illustrate this general process by a parallel taken from algebra, in which there is great exactness and beauty. Besides, writers do not often dispose their arguments and approximations in this way, though for want of it they lose much of their clearness and force; and, where the writer does this, the reader is frequently apt to overlook the order of proofs and positions.

Sir *IJ. Newton*'s Optics, Chronology, and Comment on *Daniel*, abound with instances to this purpose; and it is probable, that his great abilities and practice in algebraic investigations led him to it insensibly. In his chronology, he first shews in gross, that the technical chronology of the antient *Greeks* led them to carry their authorities higher than the truth; and then, that the time of the *Sesostris* mentioned by the *Greek* historians was near that of *Sesac* mentioned in the Old Testament; whence it follows, that these two persons were the same; and consequently, that the exact time of *Sesostris*'s expedition may now be fixed by the Old Testament. And now, having

having two points abfolutely fixed, *viz.* the expeditions of *Sefoftris* and *Xerxes*, he fixes all the moft remarkable intermediate events; and thefe being alfo fixed, he goes on to the lefs remarkable ones in the *Greek* hiftory. And the chronology of the *Greeks* being rectified, he makes ufe of it to rectify the cotemporary affairs of the *Egyptians*, *Affyrians*, *Babylonians*, *Medes*, and *Perfians*, making ufe of the preceding ftep every where, for the determination of the fubfequent one. He does alfo, in many cafes, caft light and evidence back from the fubfequent ones upon the precedent. But the other is his own order of proof, and ought to be that in which thofe who call his chronology in queftion fhould proceed to inquire into it.

The fourth and laft method is that ufed by decypherers, in inveftigating words written in unknown characters, or in known ones fubftituted for one another, according to fecret and complex laws. The particular methods by which this is done are only known to thofe who ftudy and practife this art: however, it is manifeft in general, that it is an algebra of its own kind; and that it bears a great refemblance to the three foregoing methods; alfo that it may be faid with juftnefs and propriety in general, that philofophy is the art of decyphering the myfteries of nature; that criticifm bears an obvious relation to decyphering; and that every theory which can explain all the phænomena, has all the fame evidence in its favour, that it is poffible the key of a cypher can have from its explaining that cypher. And if the caufe affigned by the theory have alfo its real exiftence proved, it may be compared to the explanation of a cypher; which may be verified by the evidence of the perfon who writes in that cypher.

Thefe fpeculations may feem uncouth to thofe who are not converfant in mathematical inquiries; but to me they appear to caft light and evidence upon the methods of purfuing knowledge in other matters, to

fharpen

sharpen the natural sagacity, and to furnish *loci* for invention. It appears also not impossible, that future generations should put all kinds of evidences and inquiries into mathematical forms; and, as it were, reduce *Aristotle*'s Ten Categories, and Bishop *Wilkins*'s Forty *Summa Genera*, to the head of quantity alone, so as to make mathematics and logic, natural history, and civil history, natural philosophy, and philosophy of all other kinds, coincide *omni ex parte*.

I will add two more remarks relating to the present subject.

First, then, As in many mechanical problems, which fall strictly under the consideration of mathematicians, the quantities considered depend on several others, so as to increase in the simple or compound, direct or inverse ratio of several others, and not to be greatest or least, when one or two of these are so, but when the *factum* of the proper powers of all is so; so throughout natural philosophy, in physic, in the analysis of the mind, &c. it is necessary to inquire as carefully as we can, upon how many considerable causes each effect depends; also, whether the ratios be simple or compound, direct or inverse. For though it will seldom happen, that one can bring the practical problems, that occur in real life, to an exact estimate in this way, yet one may avoid part of that uncertainty and confusion, to which persons who take things merely in the gross, are liable. Or in other words, it is better in every thing to have probable or tolerable limits for the *data*, with a regular method of computation, or even an approximation thereto, than to have only such gross and general conceptions, as result from the more or less frequent recurrency of impressions; even though they be somewhat improved by natural or acquired sagacity, arising, in a kind of implicit indefinite way, from experience.

Secondly,

Of Propofitions, *and*

Secondly, it feems to me, that the rays of light may be confidered as a kind of fluxions in refpect of the biggeft component particles of matter; I mean thofe upon which Sir *If. Newton* fuppofes the colours of natural bodies, and the changes effected in chemical proceffes, to depend. For, as the increments of variable quantities, when diminifhed fo as to bear no finite ratio to the quantities of which they are the increments, fhew in a fimple way the velocities with which thefe quantities are increafed; and fo give rife to the determination of fluxions from fluents, and fluents from fluxions, and to all the applications of thefe determinations to real quantities, all which is intirely grounded upon the fuppofition, that the fluxions are not increments, but relative nothings; fo, fince the rays of light are fo fmall in refpect of the biggeft component particles, as to be relatively and practically nothing in refpect of them, to bear no relation to any of them, all the differences obfervable in the actions of light upon thefe particles, and of thefe particles upon light, will depend purely upon the differences of thefe particles in refpect of one another; it not being poffible, that any part of them fhould arife from the comparative magnitude of light, which is equally nothing in refpect of them all. And thus it feems, that optics and chemiftry will, at laft, become a mafter-key for unlocking the myfteries in the conftitution of natural bodies, according to the method recommended by Sir *If. Newton.*

Let A, B, C, be three particles, whofe magnitudes are 3, 2, and 1, refpectively. It is evident, that the mutual influences between A and C, B and C, cannot correfpond intirely to the ratio which A and B bear to each other, becaufe C bears a different ratio to A from that which it bears to B; and this difference of ratios muft have its fhare in the effects of A and B upon

the Nature of Assent. 187

upon C: whereas had C been a particle of light, it would have been equally nothing in respect both of A and B; and so the mutual influences between A and C, B and C, would intirely correspond to the difference between A and B, and decypher it. Thus the particles of light, by being infinitely smaller than the biggest component ones of natural bodies, may become a kind of *communis norma*, whereby to measure their active powers.

PROP. 40.

To make a general application of the theory of this and the foregoing section, to the several branches of science.

ALL the sciences, knowledge of all kinds, may be reduced to the seven general heads following, when they are understood in the latitude here expressed.

First, philology, or the knowledge of words, and their significations. It comprehends under it the arts of grammar and criticism. Rhetoric and poetry may be referred to it.

Secondly, mathematics, or the doctrine of quantity. It may be divided into three branches, *viz.* arithmetic, which makes use of numbers as the exponents of quantity; geometry, which uses figures for the same purpose; and algebra, which comprehends both these, and whose symbols are accordingly so general, as to represent the symbols of the two foregoing parts.

Thirdly, logic, or the art of using words, considered as symbols, for making discoveries in all the branches of knowledge. It presupposes philology to a certain degree; and must evidently, in the view here given of it, receive great illustration from mathematics,

thematics, which is the art of making discoveries in the single category of quantity, by means of the simplest kind of symbols.

Fourthly, natural history, or regular and well-digested accounts of the phænomena of the natural world. It may be distributed into six parts, *i. e.* into the natural histories of animals, plants, minerals, the earth considered as a terraqueous globe, the atmosphere, and the heavenly bodies.

Fifthly, civil history, or regular accounts of the transactions of the world politic. To this head must be referred that part of geography which treats of the present manners, customs, laws, religion, &c. of the several nations of the world.

Sixthly, natural philosophy, or the application of the arts of mathematics and logic to the phænomena of natural and civil history, communicated to us by means of our previous skill in philology, in order to decypher the laws by which the external world is governed, and thereby to predict or produce such phænomena, as we are interested in. Its parts, or mechanics, hydrostatics, pneumatics, optics, astronomy, chemistry, the theories of the several manual arts and trades, medicine and psychology, or the theory of the human mind, with that of the intellectual principles of brute animals.

Seventhly, religion, which might also be called divine philosophy. This requires the application of all the foregoing branches of knowledge to each other in an endless reciprocation, in order to discover the nature of the invisible world, of God, of good and evil spirits, and of the future state, which commences at death, with all the duties that result from these considerations. The arts of ethics and politics are to be referred to this head. For, though these arts are supposed to teach individuals, and bodies politic, how to arrive at their *summum bonum* in the present world, yet, since the rules given for this purpose

either

the Nature of Assent.

etiher are or ought to be the same with those which teach mankind how to secure a happy futurity, it is plain that these arts are included within the precepts of religion.

All these branches of knowledge are very much involved in each other; so that it is impossible to make any considerable progress in any one, without the assistance of most or all the rest. However, each has also an independent part, which being laid down as a foundation, we may proceed to improve it by the light afforded from the independent parts of the other branches. I will here subjoin a few hints concerning the proper manner of proceeding in each branch.

Of Philology.

The rudiments of the native language are learnt in infancy, by the repeated impressions of the sounds at the same time that the things signified are presented to the senses, as has been already explained. Words standing for intellectual things, particles, &c. are decyphered by their connexion with other words, by their making parts of sentences, whose whole import is known. Grammatical analogy and derivation do also, in many cases, discover the import of words. And many words may be explained by definitions. Where these several ways concur, the sense is soon learnt, and steadily fixed; where they oppose each other, confusion arises for a time, but the strongest authority prevails at last. Translations and dictionaries explain the words of unknown languages by those of known ones. Afterwards we decypher by the context, deduce the sense from analogy, &c. These last methods reflect authority upon the translations and dictionaries, where they agree with them. In living languages the import of the principal words may be ascertained with ease and certainty; and these being fixed, the rest become determinable and

and decypherable by proper care and caution, so that no practical errors can remain. In dead languages the difficulty is greater; but the certainty that ultimately results, is not less practically in respect of the bulk of the language, on account of the number of coincidences. But much remains undone yet, particularly in respect of the *Hebrew* language. Logic, natural and civil history, phylosophical and religious knowledge, may all, in their several ways, contribute to fix the true sense of words. And the fixing the senses of words, by all the methods here enumerated, may be called the art of making dictionaries. It receives great assistance from the art of grammar; and is at the same time a main foundation of it. This last art has also the same connexions with the other branches of knowledge; as that of fixing the senses of words. The same may be said of criticism; which may be defined the art of restoring the corrupted passages of authors, and ascertaining their genuine sense, and method of reasoning.

In all these things there seems to be a sufficient foundation for unity of opinion amongst those that are truly learned and candid; at least in all important points. And, in fact, the differences here amongst the *literati* are plainly owing, in great measure, to ambition, envy, affectation of singularity and novelty, &c. All these things magnify the ideas and coalescences, which a man calls his own, those of his party, &c. associate ideas of truth, excellence, genius, &c. to them, and opposite ones to all that the supposed adversary delivers.

No sceptic can proceed so far as to disclaim the sense of the words of his native tongue, or of a foreign one, which he understands. The things signified thereby must and will be suggested by, and coalesce with, the sounds; so that he cannot but understand what he hears and reads. And this is all the
truth

truth that belongs to philology as fuch. The truth of the things expreffed in words is a confideration belonging to the feveral other branches of knowledge refpectively.

As the plain didactic ftyle is intended merely to inform the underftanding, fo the rhetorical and poetical ftyles are intended to excite the paffions by the affociations, which figurative terms and forms of expreffion, flowing periods, numbers, rhymes, fimiles, fables, fictions, &c. draw after them.

Painting and mufic produce a like effect upon the paffions as rhetoric and poetry, and by means that are not very unlike. But I fhall have occafion hereafter to fay fomething more concerning all thefe imaginative arts.

Of Mathematics.

Mathematics are that branch of knowledge which is the moft independent of any, and the leaft liable to uncertainty, difference of opinion, and fceptical doubts. However, uncertainties, differences, and doubts, have arifen here; but then they have been chiefly about fuch parts of mathematics as fall under the confideration of the logician. For, it feems impoffible that a man who has qualified himfelf duly, fhould doubt about the juftnefs of an arithmetical, algebraical, or fluxional operation, or the conclufivenefs of a geometrical demonftration.

The words point, line, furface, infinitely great, infinitely little, are all capable of definitions, at leaft of being explained by other words. But then thefe words cannot fuggeft any vifible ideas to the imagination, but what are inconfiftent with the very words themfelves. However, this inconfiftency has no effect upon the reafoning. It is evident, that all that can be meant by the three angles of a triangle being equal to two right ones, or the parabolic area to two thirds of the circumfcribing parallelogram, or deduced from these positions, must always hold in future fact; and this, as observed above, is all the truth that any thing can have. In fluxional conclusions it is demonstratively evident, that the quantity under consideration cannot be greater or less by any thing assignable, than according to the fluxional conclusion; and this seems to me intirely the same thing as proving it to be equal.

I cannot presume to suggest any particular methods by which farther discoveries may be made in mathematical matters, which are so far advanced, that few persons are able to comprehend even what is discovered and unfolded already. However, it may not be amiss to observe, that all the operations of arithmetic, geometry, and algebra, should be applied to each other in every possible way, so as to find out in each something analogous to what is already known and established in the other two. The application of the arithmetical operations of division and extraction of roots to algebraic quantities, and of the method of obtaining the roots of numeral equations by approximation to specious ones, as taught by Sir *Is. Newton*, have been the sources of the greatest fluxional discoveries.

Of Logic.

It is the purport of this and the foregoing section, to give imperfect rudiments of such an art of logic as is defined above, *i. e.* as should make use of words in the way of mathematical symbols, and proceed by mathematical methods of investigation and computation in inquiries of all sorts. Not that the *data* in the sciences are as yet, in general, ripe for such methods; but they seem to tend to this more and more perpetually, in particular branches, so that it cannot be amiss to prepare ourselves, in some measure, previously.

Logic,

the Nature of Affent.

Logic, and metaphyfics, which are nearly allied to logic, feem more involved in obfcurity and perplexity, than any other part of fcience. This has probably been the chief fource of fcepticifm, fince it appears neceffary, that that part of knowledge, which is the bafis of all others, which is to fhew wherein certainty, probability, poffibility, improbability, and impoffibility, confift, fhould itfelf be free from all doubt and uncertainty.

It feems alfo, that as logic is required for the bafis of the other fciences, fo a logic of a fecond order is required for a bafis to that of the firft, of a third for that of the fecond, and fo on *fine limite:* which, if it were true, would, from the nature of dependent evidences, prove that logic is either abfolutely certain, or abfolutely void of all probability. For, if the evidence for it be ever fo little inferior to unity, it will, by the continual infinite multiplication required in dependent evidences infinitely continued, bring itfelf down to nothing. Therefore, *e converfo,* fince no one can fay, that the rules of logic are void of all probability, the *fummum genus* of them muft be certain. This *fummum genus* is the neceffary coalefcence of the fubject with the predicate. But the argument here alledged is merely one *ad hominem*, and not the natural way of treating the fubject. The neceffary coalefcence juft fpoken of carries its own evidence with it. It is neceffary from the nature of the brain, and that in the moft confirmed fceptic, as well as in any other perfon. And we need only inquire into the hiftory of the brain, and the phyfiological influences of words and fymbols upon it by affociation, in order to fee this. I am alfo inclined to believe, that the method here propofed of confidering words and fentences as impreffions, whofe influence upon the mind is intirely to be determined by the affociations heaped upon them in the intercourfes of life, and endeavouring to determine

thefe

thefe affociations, both analytically and fynthetically, will caft much light upon logical fubjects, and cut off the fources of many doubts and differences.

As the theories of all other arts and fciences muft be extracted from them, fo logic, which contains the theory of all thefe theories muft be extracted from thefe theories; and yet this is not to reafon in a circle in either cafe, fince the theory is firft extracted from felf-evident or allowed particulars, and then applied to particulars not yet known, in order to difcover and prove them.

It may not be amifs here to take notice how far the theory of thefe papers has led me to differ, in refpect of logic, from Mr. *Locke*'s excellent *Effay on Human Underftanding*, to which the world are fo much indebted for removing prejudices and incumbrances, and advancing real and ufeful knowledge.

Firft, then, it appears to me, that all the moft complex ideas arife from fenfation; and that reflection is not a diftinct fource, as Mr. *Locke* makes it.

Secondly, Mr. *Locke* afcribes ideas to many words, which, as I have defined idea, cannot be faid to have any immediate and precife ones; but only to admit of definitions. However, let definition be fubftituted inftead of idea, in thefe cafes, and then all Mr. *Locke*'s excellent rules concerning words, delivered in his third book, will fuit the theory of thefe papers.

As to the firft difference, which I think may be called an error in Mr. *Locke*, it is, however, of little confequence. We may conceive, that he called fuch ideas as he could analyfe up to fenfation, ideas of fenfation; the reft ideas of reflection, ufing reflection as a term of art, denoting an unknown quantity. Befides which it may be remarked, that the words which, according to him, ftand for ideas of reflection, are, in general, words, that, according to the theory of thefe papers, have no ideas, but

defi-

definitions only. And thus the first difference is as it were, taken away by the second; for, if these words have no immediate ideas there will be no occasion to have recourse to reflection as a source of ideas; and, upon the whole, there is no material repugnancy between the consequences of this theory, and any thing advanced by Mr. Locke

The ingenious bishop *Berkeley* has justly observed against Mr. *Locke*, that there can be no such thing as abstract ideas, in the proper sense of the word idea. However, this does not seem to vitiate any considerable part of Mr. *Locke*'s reasoning. Substitute definition for idea in the proper places, and his conclusions will hold good in general.

Of Natural History.

Natural History is a branch of knowledge, which, at the first view, appears to have a boundless extent, and to be capable of the utmost practical precision and certainty, if sufficient care and industry be employed. And, in fact, the doubts and differences here are not very considerable; they do also grow less and less every day, by the great quantity of knowledge of this kind, which is poured in from all quarters, as learning and inquisitiveness diffuse themselves more and more amongst all nations, and all orders of men.

The materials for natural history, which any single person can collect from his own observation, being very inconsiderable, in respect of those which he wants, he is obliged to have recourse to others; and therefore must depend upon their testimony, just as in civil history. And our assent in each case, being excited by a variety of concurrent proofs, and of coincident circumstances, transfers part of its authority upon the other. We believe testimony in natural history, because

because we do in civil, and *vice verfa*; and have a variety of concurrent confirmations in both cafes.

However, as the general facts are thus practically certain, fo the fubordinate ones are, in many cafes, liable to doubts. And it is evident, that for the refolution of thefe doubts in natural hiftory, we muft borrow the affiftance of all the other branches of fcience; and that fome fkill in philology muft be attained, before we can hope to arrive at any tolerable perfection in natural or civil hiftory. Natural hiftory is the only fure bafis of natural philofophy, and has fome influence upon all the other fciences.

Of Civil Hiftory.

The general evidences upon which civil hiftory is grounded, have been juft hinted at. It is manifeft, that the difcoveries of natural hiftorians, aftronomers, linguifts, antiquaries, and philofophers of all kinds, have brought great light and evidence upon this branch of knowledge within the laft two centuries; and are likely to do fo more and more.

The antient hiftory of the kingdoms of *Afia Minor*, *Egypt*, and *Greece*, will probably be much better underftood, when the inhabitants of thofe countries become learned.

He that would fearch into the firft ages of the world muft take the fcriptures for his guide, lay down the truth of thefe as unqueftionable, and force all other evidences into that pofition. This feems to have been the method taken by Sir *If. Newton* in his chronology, and which at laft unfolded to him the proper method of detecting and correcting the miftakes in the antient technical chronology of the *Greeks* by itfelf.

The concurrent independent evidences in the grand points of hiftory are fo much more numerous than the

the Nature of Assent. 197

the dependent ones, and most of them so strong, singly taken, that the deficiency from certainty in these grand points cannot be distinguished by the human mind. And therefore it is a practical error of great importance to suppose, that such kind of historical evidences are inferior to mathematical ones. They are equal, as far as we have any thing to do with them; *i. e.* can judge of them, or be influenced by them. All future facts depending on them have as good a basis as those depending on mathematical evidences. I speak here of principal matters, such as the conquests of *Alexander* and *Julius Cæsar*, and the main history, common and miraculous, of the Old and New Testaments. Till our knowledge be applied to the predicting or producing future facts, no sort of it is of use or importance to us; and the application of mathematical knowledge is just as much exposed to the several kinds and degrees of uncertainty, as that of any other. That the evidence for principal historical facts is not, in general, considered as equal to mathematical certainty, arises partly from the just-mentioned ill-grounded affirmations of learned men; partly from the complexness of the historical proofs, which require time and consideration to digest them; and partly because the uncertainty attending subordinate facts has diluted the evidence of the principal and unquestionable ones, since the same general forms of expression are, and must be, used in both cases.

Of Natural Philosophy.

It may be observed of natural philosophy, that in the parts where the ideas are simple, clear, and of the visible kind, or adequately expounded by such, and the method of investigation and computation mathematical, as in mechanics, hydrostatics, pneumatics, optics, and astronomy, the doubts and diversities

O 3 of

of opinion which arise, are inconsiderable. But in the theories of chemistry, of manual arts and trades, of medicine, and, in general, of the powers and mutual actions of the small parts of matter, the uncertainties and perplexities are as great, as in any part of science. For the small parts of matter, with their actions, are too minute to be the objects of sight; and we are as yet neither possessed of a detail of the phænomena sufficiently copious and regular, whereon to ground an investigation; nor of a method of investigation subtle enough to arrive at the subtlety of nature, even in the biggest component particles, much less in the particles of the smaller orders; and how far the number of orders may go, is impossible to say. I see no contradiction in supposing it infinite, and a great difficulty in stopping at any particular size.

Suppose the number of orders of particles infinite, or at least very great; and that particles of all orders are perpetually flying off from all bodies with great velocity. First, this may occasion the gravitation of the great bodies of the universe to each other, by the impulse of the smaller corpuscles upon particles of sizes equal to each other in the greater bodies, the impulses of the larger corpuscles, and upon particles of unequal size, being evanescent in respect of the foregoing impulses. But where particles approach near to one another, and the corpuscles bear some finite ratio to the particles, so as not to pervade them freely, before they come to particles of equal size to each other, but affect them in proportion to their surfaces, not solid content, and I suppose from many other causes, attractions of other kinds may arise: and if one or both of the contiguous particles send out many corpuscles with great force; also, if these corpuscles effervesce together in the intermediate space, and gain new forces thence, &c.; repulsive powers may rise. If it be reasonable to suppose many orders

orders of particles, it is also reasonable to suppose, that their powers and properties are somewhat analogous to one another; and that those of the larger particles arise from, and are compounded of, those of the next less in size, and so on; just as the whole gravity of the moon is compounded of the gravity of all its parts. But these are all very gross and uncertain conjectures.

In the mean time, it seems proper to use the words magnetism, electricity, attraction of cohesion, *spiritus rector*, acrimony of the animal juices, &c. as terms of art, as unknown causes of known effects. But then they ought always to be defined, the definitions rigorously kept to, and all secondary ideas from prior associations excluded. Were this done in chemistry and medicine, it would produce a great reformation, and at once cut off many incumbrances, perplexities, and obscurities. The *vis inertiæ* of bodies, and the equivalent terms, were once terms of this kind, standing for the unknown cause of known phænomena. By degrees these phænomena were digested into order, the terms contributing thereto, and the three several kinds of them, classed respectively under the three laws of nature, which have been applied synthetically since, and given rise to the greatest mechanical discoveries. The same may be observed of gravity. And if the laws of magnetism, electricity, and the attraction of cohesion, could be ascertained in the same manner as the laws of the *vis inertiæ* and gravity, we should be enabled to predict and produce many effects of great importance to us.

It is of the highest use to us in practical matters, that the properties of bodies are so closely connected with each other. Thus the colour and specific gravity of a metal, the visible idea of a plant, also its taste or smell, give us a practical certainty in respect of all the other properties. This close connexion of the properties follows undoubtedly from the powers and mutual actions of the small parts; so that, if we could arrive at the knowledge of these last, we should immediately see not only the reason of all the properties of bodies which are known at present, but be able to discover innumerable other relative ones. In the mean time we must endeavour to discover, digest, and register, the various properties of natural bodies, as they rise to view from suitable experiments; and thus prepare the way for those who shall hereafter decypher their internal constitution.

Of Religion.

All the foregoing branches of knowledge ought to be considered as mere preparitories and preliminaries to the knowledge of religion, natural and revealed. They all, in their several orders and degrees, concur to establish the principal doctrines and duties of it; and these, when established, become the best means for attaining knowledge. The benevolence of the deity, and the doctrine of final causes, are the best clue for guiding us through the labyrinths of natural phænomena, and particularly of those which relate to animals. The scriptures are the only book which can give us any just idea of antient times, of the original of mankind, their dispersion, *&c.* or of what will befal them in future generations. As to future things, predicted in the scriptures, we can as yet collect nothing more than general intimations; but there is reason to believe, that succeeding generations may arrive at a far more precise interpretation of prophecy. It may also be, that much philosophical knowledge is concealed in the scriptures; and that it will be revealed in its due time. The analogy between the word and works of God, which is a consideration of the religious kind, seems to comprehend the most important truths. To all this it must be added, that the temper of mind prescribed by religion, *viz.* modesty,

modesty, impartiality, sobriety, and diligence, are the best qualifications for succeeding in all inquiries. Thus religion comprehends, as it were, all other knowledge, advances, and is advanced by all; at the same time that where there is a morally good disposition, a very small portion of other knowledge is sufficient for the attainment of all that is necessary for virtue and comfort here, and eternal happiness hereafter.

The great differences of opinion, and contentions which happen in religious matters, are plainly owing to the violence of men's passions, more than to any other cause. Where religion has its due effect in restraining these, and begetting true candour, we may expect an unity of opinion, both in religious and other matters, as far as is necessary for useful practical purposes.

SECT.

SECT. III.

Of the Affections in general.

PROP. 41.

*To explain the origin and nature of the paſ-
ſions in general.*

HERE we may obſerve,
First, that our paſſions or affections can be no more than aggregates of ſimple ideas united by aſſociation. For they are excited by objects, and by the incidents of life. But theſe, if we except the impreſſed ſenſations, can have no power of affecting us, but what they derive from aſſociation; juſt as was obſerved above of words and ſentences.

Secondly, ſince therefore the paſſions are ſtates of conſiderable pleaſure or pain, they muſt be aggregates of the ideas, or traces of the ſenſible pleaſures and pains, which ideas make up by their number, and mutual influence upon one another, for the faintneſs and tranſitory nature of each ſingly taken. This may be called a proof *a priori*. The proof *a poſteriori* will be given, when I come to analyſe the ſix claſſes of intellectual affections; *viz.* imagination, ambition, ſelf-intereſt, ſympathy, theopathy, and the moral ſenſe.

Thirdly, as ſenſation is the common foundation of all theſe, ſo each in its turn, when ſufficiently generated, contributes to generate and model all the reſt. We may conceive this to be done in the following manner. Let ſenſation generate imagination; then will ſenſation and imagination together generate ambition; ſenſation, imagination, and ambition, self-interest; sensation, imagination, ambition, and self-interest, sympathy; sensation, imagination, ambition, self-interest, and sympathy, theopathy; sensation, imagination, ambition, self-interest, sympathy, and theopathy, the moral sense: and, in an inverted order, imagination will new model sensation; ambition, sensation, and imagination; self-interest, sensation, imagination, and ambition; sympathy, sensation, imagination, ambition, and self-interest; theopathy, sensation, imagination, ambition, self-interest, and sympathy; and the moral sense, sensation, imagination, ambition, self-interest, sympathy, and theopathy: till at last, by the numerous reciprocal influences of all these upon each other, the passions arrive at that degree of complexness, which is observed in fact, and which makes them so difficult to be analysed.

Fourthly, as all the passions arise thus from pleasure and pain, their first and most general distribution may be into the two classes of love and hatred; *i. e.* we may term all those affections of the pleasurable kind, which objects and incidents raise in us, love; all those of the painful kind, hatred. Thus we are said to love not only intelligent agents of morally good dispositions, but also sensual pleasures, riches, and honours; and to hate poverty, disgrace, and pain, bodily and mental.

Fifthly, when our love and hatred are excited to a certain degree, they put us upon a variety of actions, and may be termed desire and aversion; by which last word I understand an active hatred. Now the actions which flow from desire and aversion, are intirely the result of associated powers and circumstances, agreeably to the 20th, 21st, and 22d propositions, with their corollaries. The young child learns to grasp, and go up to the plaything that pleases him, and to withdraw his hand from the fire that burns him, at first from the mechanism of his nature, and

and without any deliberate purpose of obtaining pleasure, and avoiding pain, or any explicit reasoning about them. By degrees he learns, partly from the recurrency of these mechanical tendencies, inspired by God, as one may say, by means of the nature which he has given us; and partly from the instruction and imitation of others; to pursue every thing which he loves and desires; fly from every thing which he hates; and to reason about the method of doing this, just as he does upon other matters. And, because mankind are for the most part pursuing or avoiding something or other, the desire of happiness, and the aversion to misery, are supposed to be inseparable from, and essential to, all intelligent natures. But this does not seem to be an exact or correct way of speaking. The most general of our desires and aversions are factitious; *i. e.* generated by association; and therefore admit of intervals, augmentations, and diminutions. And, whoever will be sufficiently attentive to the workings of his own mind, and the actions resulting therefrom, or to the actions of others, and the affections which may be supposed to occasion them, will find such differences and singularities in different persons, and in the same person at different times, as no way agree to the notion of an essential, original, perpetual desire of happiness, and endeavour to attain it; but much rather to the factitious associated desires and endeavours here asserted. And a due regard to this will, as it seems to me, solve many difficulties and perplexities found in treatises upon the passions. The writers upon this subject have begun in the synthetical method prematurely, and without having premised the analytical one. For it is very true, that, after general desires and endeavours are generated, they give rise in their turn to a variety of particular ones. But the original source is in the particular ones, and the general ones never alter and new-model the particular ones so much,

Of the Affections in general.

much, as that there are not many traces and vestiges of their original mechanical nature and proportions remaining.

Sixthly, the will appears to be nothing but a desire or aversion sufficiently strong to produce an action that is not automatic primarily or secondarily. At least it appears to me, that the substitution of these words for the word *will* may be justified by the common usage of language. The will is therefore that desire or aversion, which is strongest for the then present time. For if any other desire was stronger, the muscular motion connected with it by association would take place, and not that which proceeds from the will, or the voluntary one, which is contrary to the supposition. Since therefore all love and hatred, all desire and aversion, are factitious and generated by association; *i. e.* mechanically; it follows that the will is mechanical also.

Seventhly, since the things which we pursue do, when obtained, generally afford pleasure, and those which we fly from affect us with pain, if they overtake us, it follows that the gratification of the will is generally attended or associated with pleasure, the disappointment of it with pain. Hence a mere associated pleasure is transferred upon the gratification of the will; a mere associated pain upon the disappointment of it. And if the will was always gratified, this mere associated pleasure would, according to the present frame of our natures, absorb, as it were, all our other pleasures; and thus by drying up the source from whence it sprung, be itself dried up at last: and the first disappointments, after a long course of gratification, would be intolerable. Both which things are sufficiently observable, in an inferior degree, in children that are much indulged, and in adults, after a series of successful events. Gratifications of the will without the consequent expected pleasure, and disappointments of it without the consequent expected pain,

pain, are particularly useful to us here. And it is by this, amongst other means, that the human will is brought to a conformity with the divine; which is the only radical cure for all our evils and disappointments, and the only earnest and medium for obtaining lasting happiness.

Eighthly, we often desire and pursue things which give pain rather than pleasure. Here it is to be supposed, that at first they afforded pleasure, and that they now give pain on account of a change in our nature and circumstances. Now, as the continuance to desire and pursue such objects, notwithstanding the pain arising from them, is the effect of the power of association, so the same power will at last reverse its own steps, and free us from such hurtful desires and pursuits. The recurrency of pain will at last render the object undesirable and hateful. And the experience of this painful process, in a few particular instances, will at last, as in other cases of the same kind, beget a habit of ceasing to pursue things, which we perceive by a few trials, or by rational arguments, to be hurtful to us upon the whole.

Ninthly, a state of desire ought to be pleasant at first from the near relation of desire to love, and of love to pleasure and happiness. But in the course of a long pursuit, so many fears and disappointments, apparent or real, in respect of the subordinate means, and so many strong agitations of mind passing the limits of pleasure, intervene, as greatly to chequer a state of desire with misery. For the same reasons states of aversion are chequered with hope and comfort.

Tenthly, hope and fear are, as just now observed, the attendants upon desire and aversion. These affect us more or less, according to the more or less frequent recurrency of the pleasing and painful ideas, according to the greater or less probability of the expected event, according to the greater or less distance
of

of time, &c.; the power of affociation difplaying itfelf every where in the agitations of mind excited by thefe paffions. It is particularly remarkable here, that our hopes and fears rife and fall with certain bodily difpofitions, according as thefe favour or oppofe them.

Eleventhly, joy and grief take place when the defire and averfion, hope and fear, are at an end; and are love and hatred, exerted towards an object which is prefent, either in a fenfible manner, or in a rational one; *i. e.* fo as to occupy the whole powers of the mind, as fenfible objects, when prefent, and attended to, do the external fenfes. It is very evident, that the objects of the intellectual pleafures and pains derive their power of thus affecting the mind from affociation.

Twelfthly, after the actual joy and grief are over, and the object withdrawn, there generally remains a pleafing or difpleafing recollection or refentment, which recurs with every recurrency of the idea of the object, or of the affociated ones. This recollection keeps up the love or hatred. In like manner the five grateful paffions, love, defire, hope, joy, and pleafing recollection, all enhance one another; as do the five ungrateful ones, hatred, averfion, fear, grief, and difpleafing recollection. And the whole ten, taken together, comprehend, as appears to me, all the general paffions of human nature.

SECT.

SECT. IV.

Of Memory.

PROP. 42.

To examine how far the phænomena of memory are agreeable to the foregoing theory.

MEMORY was defined in the introduction to be that faculty by which traces of fenfations and ideas recur, or are recalled, in the fame order and proportion, accurately or nearly, as they were once prefented.

Now here we may obferve,

Firft, that memory depends intirely or chiefly on the ftate of the brain. For difeafes, concuffions of the brain, fpirituous liquors, and fome poifons, impair or deftroy it; and it generally returns again with the return of health, from the ufe of proper medicines and methods. And all this is peculiarly fuitable to the notion of vibrations. If fenfations and ideas arife from peculiar vibrations, and difpofitions to vibrate, in the medullary fubftance of the brain, it is eafy to conceive, that the caufes above alledged may fo confound the fenfations and ideas, as that the ufual order and proportion of the ideas fhall be deftroyed.

Secondly, the rudiments of memory are laid in the perpetual recurrency of the fame impreffions, and clufters of impreffions. How thefe leave traces, in which the order is preferved, may be underftood from the 8th, 9th, 10th, and 11th propofitions. The traces which letters, and words, *i. e.* clufters of letters, leave, afford an inftance and example of this. And, as in languages the letters are fewer than the fyllables, the fyllables than the words, and the words

than

Of Memory.

than the sentences, so the single sensible impressions, and the small clusters of them, are comparitively few in respect of the large clusters; and, being so, they must recur more frequently, so as the sooner to beget those traces which I call the rudiments or elements of memory. When these traces or ideas begin to recur frequently, this also contributes to fix them, and their order, in the memory, in the same manner as the frequent impression of the objects themselves.

Thirdly. suppose now a person so far advanced in life, as that he has learnt all these rudiments, *i. e.* that he has ideas of the common appearances and occurrences of life, under a considerable variety of subordinate circumstances, which recur to his imagination from the slightest causes, and with the most perfect facility; and let us ask, how he can be able to remember or recollect a past fact, consisting of 1000 single particulars, or of 100 such clusters as are called the rudiments of memory; 10 single particulars being supposed to constitute a rudiment?—First, then, we may observe, that there are only 100 links wanting in the chain; for he has already learnt considerable exactness in the subordinate circumstances of the 100 clusters; and perfect exactness is not to be supposed or required.—Secondly, the 100 clusters recur again and again to the imagination for some time after the fact, in a quick and transient manner, as those who attend sufficiently to what passes in their own minds may perceive; and this both makes the impression a little deeper, and also serves to preserve the order. If the person attempts to recollect soon after the impression, the effect remaining in the brain is sufficient to enable him to do this with the accuracy required and experienced; if a longer time intervenes, before he attempts to recollect, still the number of involuntary recurrencies makes up in some measure for the want of this voluntary recollection. However, the power of recollection declines in general, and is

P intirely

intirely loft by degrees. It confirms this reafoning, that a new fet of ftrong impreffions deftroys this power of recollection. For this muft both obliterate the effects of the foregoing impreffions, and prevent the recurrency of the ideas.—Thirdly, as the fingle impreffions, which make the fmall clufters, are not combined together at hazard, but according to a general tenor in nature, fo the clufters which make facts fucceed each other according to fome general tenor likewife. Now this both leffens the number of varieties, and fhews that the affociation between many of the clufters, or rudiments, or 100 links fuppofed to be wanting, is cemented already. This may be both illuftrated and exemplified by the obfervation, that it is difficult to remember even well-known words that have no connexion with each other, and more fo to remember collections of barbarous terms; whereas adepts in any fcience remember the things of that fcience with a furprifing exactnefs and facility.—Fourthly, fome clufters are excluded from fucceeding others, by ideas of inconfiftency, impoffibility, and by the methods of reafoning, of which we become mafters as we advance in life.—Fifthly, the vifible impreffions which concur in the paft fact, by being vivid, and preferving the order of place, often contribute greatly to preferve the order of time, and to fuggeft the clufters which may be wanting.— Sixthly. it is to be obferved, that we think in words both the impreffions and the recurrencies of ideas will be attended with words; and thefe words, from the great ufe and familiarity of language, will fix themfelves ftrongly in the fancy, and by fo doing bring up the affociated trains of ideas in the proper order. accurately or nearly. And thus, when a perfon relates a paft fact, the ideas do in fome cafes fuggeft the words, whilft in others the words fuggeft the ideas. Hence illiterate perfons do not remember nearly fo well as others, *cæteris paribus*. And I fup-

I suppose the same is true of deaf persons in a still greater degree. But it arises hence also, that many mistakes in the subordinate circumstances are committed in the relations of past facts, if the relater descends to minute particulars. For the same reasons these mistakes will be so associated with the true facts after a few relations, that the relater himself shall believe, that he remembers them distinctly.—Seventhly, the mistakes which are committed both on the foregoing account and others, make considerable abatements in the difficulty here to be solved.

Fourthly, let it now be asked, in what the recollection of a past fact, consisting of 100 clusters, as above, differs from the transit of the same 100 clusters over the fancy, in the way of a reverie? I answer, partly in the vividness of the clusters, partly and principally in the readiness and strength of the associations, by which they are cemented together. This follows from what has been already delivered; but it may be confirmed also by many other observations.—Thus, first, many persons are known by relating the same false story over and over again, *i. e.* by magnifying the ideas, and their associations, at last to believe, that they remember it. It makes as vivid an impression upon them, and hangs as closely together, as an assemblage of past facts recollected by memory.— Secondly, all men are sometimes at a loss to know whether clusters of ideas that strike the fancy strongly, and succeed each other readily and immediately, be recollections, or mere reveries. And the more they agitate the matter in the mind, the more does the reverie appear like a recollection. It resembles this, that if in endeavouring to recollect a verse, a wrong word, suiting the place, first occurs, and afterwards the right one, it is difficult during the then present agitation to distinguish the right one. But afterwards, when this agitation is subsided, the right word easily regains its place. Persons of irritable

table nervous fyftems are more fubject to fuch fallacies than others. And madmen often impofe upon themfelves in this way; *viz.* from the vividnefs of their ideas and affociations, produced by bodily caufes. The fame thing often happens in dreams. The vividnefs of the new fcene often makes it appear like one that we remember, and are well acquainted with. Thirdly, if the fpecific nature of memory confift in the great vigour of the ideas, and their affociations, then, as this vigour abates, it ought to fuggeft to us a length of time elapfed; and *vice verfa*, if it be kept up, the diftance of time ought to appear contracted. Now this laft is the cafe: for the death of a friend, or any interefting event, often recollected and related, appears to have happened but yefterday as we term it; *viz.* on account of the vividnefs of the clufters, and their affociations, correfponding to the nature of a recent event.---Fourthly, it is not, however, to be here fuppofed, that we have not many other ways of diftinguifhing real recollections from mere reveries. For the firft are fupported by their connexion with known and allowed facts, by various methods of reafoning, and having been related as real recollections, *&c.*

Fifthly, in like manner we diftinguifh a new place, book, perfon, *&c.* from one which we remember, fuppofing both to be prefented in like circumftances. The parts, affociates, *&c.* of that which we remember, ftrike us more ftrongly, are fuggefted by each other, and hang together, which does not hold of the new. The old does alfo fuggeft many affociates, which a new one in like circumftances would not. And if from the then ftate of fancy, the diftance of time, *&c.* there be any doubt of thefe things, either with refpect to the old or new, a like doubt arifes in refpect of the memory. An attentive perfon may obferve, that he determines of fuch things, whether they be old or new, by the vividnefs of the ideas, and their

Of Memory.

their power of suggesting each other, and foreign associates.

Some persons seem to suppose, that the soul surveys one object, the old for instance, and comparing it with the impressions which a similar new one would excite, calls the old one an object remembred. But this is like supposing an eye within the eye to view the pictures made by the objects upon the *retina*. Not to mention that the soul cannot in the same instant, during the same τὸ νῦν, survey both the old and new, and compare them together; nor is there any evidence that this is done in fact. A person who inquires into the nature of memory, may indeed endeavour to state the difference between the impressions of old and new, as I have done here; but this is a speculation that few persons concern themselves with, whereas all remember and apply the words relative to memory, just as they do other words. We may conclude therefore, that the difference of vividness and connexion in the ideas, with the other associates of recollections, are a sufficient foundation for the proper use of the words relative to the memory, just as in other like cases.

Sixthly, the peculiar imperfection of the memory in children tallies with the foregoing account of this faculty; and indeed this account may be considered as a gross general history of the successive growth of the memory, in passing from childhood to adult age. Children must learn by degrees the ideas of single impressions, the clusters which I call rudiments, and the most usual connexions and combinations of these. They have also the use of words, and of objects and incidents, as signs and symbols, with the proper method of reasoning upon them, to learn; and during their novitiate in these things their memories must labour under great imperfections. It appears also, that the imperfections peculiar to children correspond in kind as well as degree to the reasons here assigned for them. Their not being able to digest past facts in order of time is, in great measure, owing to their not having the proper use of the symbols, whereby time is denoted.

Seventhly, the peculiar imperfection of the memory in aged persons tallies also with the foregoing account. The vibrations, and dispositions to vibrate, in the small medullary particles, and their associations, are all so fixed by the callosity of the medullary substance, and by repeated impressions and recurrencies, that new impressions can scarce enter, that they recur seldom, and that the parts which do recur bring in old trains from established associations, instead of continuing those which were lately impressed. Hence one may almost predict what very old persons will say or do upon common occurrences. Which is also the case frequently with persons of strong passions, for reasons that are not very unlike. When old persons relate the incidents of their youth with great precision, it is rather owing to the memory of many preceding memories, recollections, and relations, than to the memory of the thing itself.

Eighthly, in recovering from concussions, and other disorders of the brain, it is usual for the patient to recover the power of remembring the then present common incidents for minutes, hours, and days, by degrees; also the power of recalling the events of his life preceding his illness. At length he recovers this last power perfectly, and at the same time forgets almost all that past in his illness, even those things which he remembred, at first, for a day or two. Now the reason of this I take to be, that upon a perfect recovery the brain recovers its natural state, *i. e.* all its former dispositions to vibrate: but that such as took place during the preternatural state of the brain, *i. e.* during his illness, are all obliterated by the return of the natural state. In like manner dreams which happen in a peculiar state of the brain, *i. e.* in sleep,

Of Memory. 215

sleep, vanish, as soon as vigilance, a different state, takes place. But if they be recollected immediately upon waking, and thus connected with the state of vigilance, they may be remembred. But I shall have occasion to be more explicit on this head in the next section.

Ninthly, it is very difficult to make any plausible conjectures why some persons of very weak judgments, not much above ideots, are endued with a peculiar extraordinary memory. This memory is generally the power of recollecting a large groupe of words suppose, as those of a sermon, in a short time after they are heard, with wonderful exactness and readiness; but then the whole is obliterated, after a long time, much more completely than in persons of common memories and judgments. One may perhaps conjecture, that the brain receives all dispositions to vibrate sooner in these persons, and lets them go sooner, than in others. And the last may contribute to the first: for new impressions may take place more deeply and precisely, if there be few old ones to oppose them. The most perfect memory is that which can both receive most readily, and retain most durably. But we may suppose, that there are limits, beyond which these two different powers cannot consist with each other.

Tenthly, when a person desires to recollect a thing that has escaped him, suppose the name of a person, or visible object, he recals the visible idea, or some other associate, again and again, by a voluntary power, the desire generally magnifying all the ideas and associations; and thus bringing in the association and idea wanted, at last. However, if the desire be great, it changes the state of the brain, and has an opposite effect; so that the desired idea does not recur till all has subsided; perhaps not even then.

Eleventhly, all our voluntary powers are of the nature of memory; as may be easily seen from the foregoing account of it, compared with the account of the voluntary powers given in the firſt chapter. And it agrees remarkably with this, that, in morbid affections of the memory, the voluntary actions ſuffer a like change and imperfection.

Twelfthly, for the ſame reaſons the whole powers of the ſoul may be referred to the memory, when taken in a large ſenſe. Hence, though ſome perſons may have ſtrong memories with weak judgments, yet no man can have a ſtrong judgment with a weak original power of retaining and remembring.

SECT.

SECT. V.

Of imagination, reveries, and dreams.

PROP. 43.

To examine how far the phænomena of imagination, reveries, and dreams, are agreeable to the foregoing theory.

THE recurrence of ideas, especially visible and audible ones, in a vivid manner, but without any regard to the order observed in past facts, is ascribed to the power of imagination or fancy. Now here we may observe, that every succeeding thought is the result either of some new impression, or of an association with the preceding. And this is the common opinion. It is impossible indeed to attend so minutely to the succession of our ideas, as to distinguish and remember for a sufficient time the very impression or association which gave birth to each thought; but we can do this as far as it can be expected to be done, and in so great a variety of instances. that our argument for the prevalence of the foregoing principle of association in all instances, except those of new impressions, may be esteemed a complete induction.

A reverie differs from imagination only in that the person being more attentive to his own thoughts, and less disturbed by foreign objects, more of his ideas are deducible from association, and fewer from new impressions.

It is to be observed, however, that in all the cases of imagination and reverie the thoughts depend, in part, upon the then state of body or mind. A pleasurable or painful state of the stomach or brain, joy or grief, will make all the thoughts warp their own way, little or much But this exception is as agreeable to the foregoing theory, as the general prevalence of affociation juft laid down.

We come next to dreams. I fay then that dreams are nothing but the imaginations, fancies, or reveries of a fleeping man; and that they are deducible from the three following caufes; viz. firft, the impreffions and ideas lately received, and particularly thofe of the preceding day. Secondly, the ftate of the body, particularly of the ftomach and brain. And, thirdly, affociation.

That dreams are, in part, deducible from the impreffions and ideas of the preceding day, appears from the frequent recurrence of thefe in greater or leffer clufters, and efpecially of the vifible ones, in our dreams. We fometimes take in ideas of longer date, in part, on account of their recency: however, in general, ideas that have not affected the mind for fome days, recur in dreams only from the 2d or 3d caufe here affigned.

That the ftate of the body affects our dreams, is evident from the dreams of fick perfons, and of thofe who labour under indigeftions, fpafms, and flatulencies.

Laftly, we may perceive ourfelves to be carried on from one thing to another in our dreams partly by affociation.

It is alfo highly agreeable to the foregoing theory to expect that each of the three foregoing caufes fhould have an influence upon the trains of ideas, that are prefented in dreams.

Let us now fee how we can folve the moft ufual phænomena of dreams upon thefe principles.

Firft, then, the fcenes which prefent themfelves are taken to be real. We do not confider them as the work of the fancy; but fuppofe ourfelves prefent, and actually feeing and hearing what paffes. Now this

Of Dreams. 219

this happens, first, because we have no other reality to oppose to the ideas which offer themselves, whereas in the common fictions of the fancy, while we are awake, there is always a set of real external objects striking some of our senses, and precluding a like mistake there: or if we become quite inattentive to external objects, the reverie does so far put on the nature of a dream, as to appear a reality. —Secondly, the trains of visible ideas, which occur in dreams, are far more vivid than common visible ideas; and therefore may the more easily be taken for actual impressions. For what reasons these ideas should be so much more vivid, I cannot presume to say. I guess, that the exclusion of real impressions has some share, and the increased heat of the brain may have some likewise. The fact is most observable in the first approaches of sleep; all the visible ideas beginning then to be more than usually glaring.

Secondly, there is a great wildness and inconsistency in our dreams. For the brain, during sleep, is in a state so different from that in which the usual associations were formed, that they can by no means take place as they do during vigilance. On the contrary, the state of the body suggests such ideas, amongst those that have been lately impressed, as are most suitable to the various kinds and degrees of pleasant and painful vibrations excited in the stomach, brain, or some other part. Thus a person who has taken opium, sees either gay scenes, or ghastly ones, according as the opium excites pleasant or painful vibrations in the stomach. Hence it will follow, that ideas will rise successively in dreams, which have no such connexion as takes place in nature, in actual impressions, nor any such as is deducible from association. And yet, if they rise up quick and vividly one after another, as subjects, predicates, and other associates, use to do, they will be affirmed of each other, and appear to hang together. Thus the same

person

person appears in two places at the same time; two persons appearing successively in the same place coalesce into one; a brute is supposed to speak (when the idea of a voice comes from that quarter) or to handle; any idea, qualification, office, &c. coinciding in the instant of time with the idea of one's self, or of another person, adheres immediately, &c. &c.

Thirdly, we do not take notice of, or are offended at, these inconsistencies; but pass on from one to another. For the associations, which should lead us thus to take notice, and be offended, are, as it were, asleep; the bodily causes also hurrying us on to new and new trains successively. But if the bodily state be such as favours ideas of anxiety and perplexity, then the inconsistency, and apparent impossibility, occurring in dreams, are apt to give great disturbance and uneasiness. It is to be observed likewise, that we forget the several parts of our dreams very fast in passing from one to another; and that this lessens the apparent inconsistencies, and their influences.

Fourthly, it is common in dreams for persons to appear to themselves to be transferred from one place to another, by a kind of sailing or flying motion. This arises from the change of the apparent magnitude and positions of images excited in the brain, this change being such as a change of distance and position in ourselves would have occasioned. Whatever the reasons be, for which visible images are excited in sleep, like to the objects with which we converse when awake, the same reasons will hold for changes of apparent magnitude and position also; and these changes in fixed objects, being constantly associated with motions in ourselves when awake, will infer these motions when asleep. But then we cannot have the idea of the *vis inertiæ* of our own bodies, answering to the impressions in walking; because the nerves of the muscles either do not admit of such miniature vibrations in sleep; or do not transmit ideas

to

to the mind in confequence thereof; whence we appear to fail, fly, or ride. Yet fometimes a perfon feems to walk, and even to ftrike, juft as in other cafes he feems to feel the impreffion of a foreign body on his fkin.

Thofe who walk and talk in their fleep, have evidently the nerves of the mufcles concerned fo free, as that vibrations can defcend from the internal parts of the brain, the peculiar refidence of ideas into them. At the fame time the brain itfelf is fo oppreffed, that they have fcarce any memory. Perfons who read inattentively, *i. e.* fee and fpeak almoft without remembring, alfo thofe who labour under fuch a morbid lofs of memory, as that though they fee, hear, fpeak, and act, *pro re nata*, from moment to moment, yet they forget all immediately, fomewhat refemble the perfons who walk and talk in fleep.

Fifthly, dreams confift chiefly of vifible imagery. This agrees remarkably with the perpetual impreffions made upon the optic nerves and correfponding parts of the brain during vigilance, and with the diftinctnefs and vividnefs of the images impreffed.

We may obferve alfo, that the vifible imagery in dreams is compofed, in a confiderable degree, of fragments of vifible appearances lately impreffed. For the difpofition to thefe vibrations muft be greater than to others, *cæteris paribus*, at the fame time that by the imperfection and interruption of the affociations, only fragments, not whole images, will generally appear. The fragments are fo fmall, and fo intermixed with other fragments and appearances, that it is difficult to trace them up to the preceding day; the fhortnefs of our memory contributing alfo not a little thereto.

It happens in dreams, that the fame fictitious places are prefented again and again at the diftance of weeks and months, perhaps during the whole courfe of life. Thefe places are, I fuppofe, compounded at firft, first, probably early in youth, of fragments of real places, which we have seen. They afterwards recur in dreams, because the same state of brain recurs; and when this has happened for some successions, they may be expected to recur at intervals during life. But they may also admit of variations, especially before frequent recurrency has established and fixed them.

Sixthly, it has been observed already, that many of the things which are presented in dreams, appear to be remembered by us, or, at least, as familiar to us; and that this may be solved by the readiness with which they start up, and succeed one another, in the fancy.

Seventhly, it has also been remarked, that dreams ought to be soon forgotten, as they are in fact; because the state of the brain suffers great changes in passing from sleep to vigilance. The wildness and inconsistency of our dreams render them still more liable to be forgotten. It is said, that a man may remember his dreams best by continuing in the same posture in which he dreamt; which, if true, would be a remarkable confirmation of the doctrine of vibrations; since those which take place in the medullary substance of the brain would be least disturbed and obliterated by this means.

Eighthly, the dreams which are presented in the first part of the night are, for the most part, much more confused, irregular, and difficult to be remembered, than those which we dream towards the morning; and these last are often rational to a considerable degree, and regulated according to the usual course of our associations. For the brain begins then to approach to the state of vigilance, or that in which the usual associations were formed and cemented. However, association has some power even in wild and inconsistent dreams.

Cor.

Of Dreams.

Cor. 1. As the prophecies were, many of them communicated in the way of divine visions, trances, or dreams, so they bear many of the foregoing marks of dreams. Thus they deal chiefly in visible imagery; they abound with apparent impossibilities, and deviations from common life, of which yet the prophets take not the least notice: they speak of new things as of familiar ones; they are carried in the spirit from place to place; things requiring a long series of time in real life, are transacted in the prophetical visions, as soon as seen; they ascribe to themselves and others new names, offices, &c.; every thing has a real existence conferred upon it; there are singular combinations of fragments of visible appearances; and God himself is represented in a visible shape, which of all other things must be most offensive to a pious *Jew*. And it seems to me, that these, and such-like criterions might establish the genuineness of the prophecies, exclusively of all other evidences.

Cor. 2. The wildness of our dreams seems to be of singular use to us, by interrupting and breaking the course of our associations. For, if we were always awake, some accidental associations would be so much cemented by continuance, as that nothing could afterwards disjoin them; which would be madness.

Cor. 3. A person may form a judgment of the state of his bodily health, and of his temperance, by the general pleasantness or unpleasantness of his dreams. There are also many useful hints relating to the strength of our passions deducible from them.

SECT.

SECT. VI.

Of imperfections in the rational Faculty.

PROP. 44.

To examine how far deviations from sound reason, and alienations of mind, are agreeable to the foregoing theory.

MAD persons differ from others in that they judge wrong of past or future facts of a common nature; that their affections and actions are violent and different from, or even opposite to, those of others upon the like occasions, and such as are contrary to their true happiness; that their memory is fallacious, and their discourse incoherent; and that they lose, in great measure, that consciousness which accompanies our thoughts and actions, and by which we connect ourselves with ourselves from time to time. These circumstances are variously combined in the various kinds and degrees of madness; and some of them take place in persons of sound minds, in certain degrees, and for certain spaces of time; so that here, as in other cases, it is impossible to fix precise limits, and to determine where soundness of mind ends, and madness begins. I will make some short remarks, deduced from the theory of these papers, upon the following states of mind, which all bear some relation to one another, and all differ from the perfection of reasoning natural to adults, according to the ordinary course of things; viz.

1. The erroneousness of the judgment in children and ideots.
2. The dotage of old persons.
3. Drunkenness.

4. The

4. The deliriums attending acute or other diftempers.

5. The frequent recurrency of the fame ideas in a courfe of ftudy, or otherwife.

6. Violent paffions.

7. Melancholy.

8. Madnefs.

Of the erroneoufnefs of the judgment in children and idiots.

Children often mifreprefent paft and future facts; their memories are fallacious; their difcourfe incoherent; their affections and actions difproportionate to the value of the things defired and purfued; and the connecting confcioufnefs is in them as yet imperfect. But all this follows naturally from the obfervations made above concerning the methods in which we learn to remember and relate paft facts, to judge of future ones, to reafon, and to exprefs ourfelves fuitably to each occafion; alfo in which our hopes and fears are made to depend upon fymbols. No particular account is therefore required for thefe phænomena; they are ftrictly natural; and many of the chief reafons for the imperfection of the memory and judgment in children occurring perpetually, and being very obvious, it is not ufually fuppofed, that any particular account is required. However, if an adult fhould become fubject to a like erroneoufnefs, it would evidently be one fpecies of madnefs; as fatuity or idiotifm is. Here the brain labours under fuch an original diforder, as either not to receive a difpofition to the miniature vibrations in which ideas confift, and whence voluntary motions are derived, but with great difficulty; or if it receives fuch difpofitions readily, they have not the ufual permanency; in both which cafes it is evident that the memory, with all the faculties thereon depending, muft con-

continue in an imperfect state, such as is observed in idiots. The want of the connecting consciousness in children and ideots, and indeed in maniacs of various kinds, excites our pity in a peculiar manner, this connecting consciousness being esteemed a principal source and requisite of happiness. Their helplessness, and the dangers to which they are exposed without foreseeing them, contribute also to enhance our compassion.

Of Dotage.

The dotage of old persons is oftentimes something more than a mere decay of memory. For they mistake things present for others, and their discourse is often foreign to the objects that are presented to them. However, the imperfection of their memories in respect of impressions but just made, or at short intervals of past time, is one principal source of their mistakes. One may suppose here, that the parts of the brain, in which the miniature vibrations belonging to ideas have taken place, are decayed in a peculiar manner, perhaps from too great use, while the parts appropriated to the natural, vital, and animal motions, remain tolerably perfect. The sinuses of the brain are probably considerably distended in these cases, and the brain itself in a languishing state; for there seems to be a considerable resemblance between the inconsistencies of some kinds of dotage, and those of dreams. Besides which it may be observed, that in dotage the person is often sluggish and lethargic; and that as a defect of the nutritive faculty in the brain will permit the sinuses to be more easily distended, so a distention of the sinuses, from this or any other cause, may impede the due nutrition of the brain. We see that, in old persons, all the parts, even the bones themselves, waste and grow less. Why may not this happen to the brain, the origin of all, and

and arise from an obstruction of the infinitesimal vessels of the nervous system, this obstruction causing such a degree of opacity, as greatly to abate, or even to destroy the powers of association and memory? at the same time vibrations, foreign to the present objects, may be excited from causes residing in the brain, stomach, &c. just as in sleep.

Of Drunkenness.

The common and immediate effect of wine is to dispose to joy, *i.e.* to introduce such kinds and degrees of vibrations into the whole nervous system, or into the separate parts thereof, as are attended with a moderate continued pleasure. This it seems to do chiefly by impressing agreeable sensations upon the stomach and bowels, which are thence propagated into the brain, continue there, and also call up the several associated pleasures that have been formed from pleasant impressions made upon the alimentary duct, or even upon any of the external senses. But wine has also probably a considerable effect of the same kind after it is absorbed by the veins and lacteals; *viz.* by the impressions which it makes on the solids, considered as productions of the nerves, while it circulates with the fluids in an unassimilated state, in the same manner as has been already observed of opium; which resembles wine in this respect also, that it produces one species of temporary madness. And we may suppose, that analogous observations hold with regard to all the medicinal and poisonous bodies, which are found to produce considerable disorders in the mind; their greatest and most immediate effect arises from the impressions made on the stomach, and the disorderly vibrations propagated thence into the brain; and yet it seems probable, that such particles as are absorbed, produce a similiar effect in circulating with the blood.

Wine, after it is abforbed, muft rarefy the blood, and confequently diftend the veins and finufes, fo as to make them comprefs the medullary fubftance, and the nerves themfelves, both in their origin and progrefs; it muft therefore difpofe to fome degree of a palfy of the fenfations and motions; to which there will be a farther difpofition from the great exhauftion of the nervous capillaments, and medullary fubftance, which a continued ftate of gaiety and mirth, with the various expreffions of it, has occafioned.

It is moreover to be noted, that the pleafant vibrations producing this gaiety, by rifing higher and higher perpetually, as more wine is taken into the ftomach and blood-veffels, come at laft to border upon, and even to pafs into, the difagreeable vibrations belonging to the paffions of anger, jealoufy, envy, &c. more efpecially if any of the mental caufes of thefe be prefented at the fame time.

Now it feems, that, from a comparifon of thefe and fuch-like things with each other, and with what is delivered in other parts of thefe papers, the peculiar temporary madnefs of drunken perfons might receive a general explanation, Particularly it feems natural to expect, that they fhall at firft be much difpofed to mirth and laughter, with a mixture of fmall inconfiftencies and abfurdities; that thefe laft fhould increafe from the vivid trains which force themfelves upon the brain, in oppofition to the prefent reality; that they fhould lofe the command and ftability of the voluntary motions from the prevalence of confufed vibrations in the brain, fo that thofe appropriated to voluntary motion cannot defcend regularly as ufual; but that they fhould ftagger and fee double; that quarrels and contentions fhould arife after fome time; and all end at laft in a temporary apoplexy. And it is very obfervable, that the free ufe of fermented liquors difpofes to paffionatenefs, to diftempers

pers of the head, to melancholy, and to downright madnefs; all which things have alfo great connexions with each other.

The ficknefs and head-ach which drunkennefs occafions the fucceeding morning, feem to arife, the firft from the immediate impreffions made on the nerves of the ftomach; the fecond from the peculiar fympathy which the parts of the head, external as well as internal, have with the brain, the part principally affected in drunkennefs, by deriving their nerves immediately from it.

Of Deliriums.

I come next to confider the deliriums which fome times attend diftempers. efpecially acute ones. In thefe a difagreeable ftate is introduced into the nervous fyftem by the bodily diforder, which checks the rife of pleafant affociations, and gives force and quicknefs to difguftful ones; and which confequently would of itfelf alone, if fufficient in degree, vitiate and diftort all the reafonings of the fick perfon. But, befides this, it feems, that, in the deliriums attending diftempers, a vivid train of vifible images forces itfelf upon the patient's eye; and that either from a diforder in the nerves and blood-veffels of the eye itfelf, or from one in the brain, or one in the alimentary duct, or. which is moft probable, from a concurrence of all thefe. It feems alfo. that the wild difcourfe of delirious perfons is accommodated to this train in fome imperfect manner; and that it becomes fo wild partly from the incoherence of the parts of this train, partly from its not expreffing even this incoherent train adequately, but deviating into fuch phrafes as the vibrations excited by the diftemper in the parts of the brain correfponding to the auditory nerves, or in parts ftill more internal, and confequently the feats of ideas purely intellectual, produce by their affociated influence over the organs of fpeech.

That delirious perfons have fuch trains forced upon the eye from internal caufes, appears probable from hence, that when they firſt begin to be delirious, and talk wildly, it is generally at fuch times only as they are in the dark, fo as to have all vifible objects excluded; for, upon bringing a candle to them, and prefenting common objects, they recover themfelves, and talk rationally, till the candle be removed again. For hence we may conclude, that the real objects overpower the vifible train from internal caufes, while the delirium is in its infancy; and that the patient relapfes, as foon as he is fhut up in the dark, becaufe the vifible train from internal caufes overpowers that which would rife up, was the perfon's nervous fyftem in a natural ftate, according to the ufual courfe of affociation, and the recurrent recollection of the place and circumftances in which he is fituated. By degrees the vifible train, from internal caufes, grows fo vivid, by the increafe of the diftemper, as even to overpower the impreffions from real objects, at leaft frequently, and in a great degree, and fo as to intermix itfelf with them, and to make an inconfiftency in the words and actions; and thus the patient becomes quite delirious.

Perfons inclining to be delirious in diftempers are moft apt to be fo in going to fleep, and in waking from fleep; in which circumftances the vifible trains are more vivid, than when we are quite awake, as has been obferved above.

It cafts alfo fome light upon this fubject, that tea and coffee will fometimes occafion fuch trains; and that they arife in our firft attempts to fleep after thefe liquors.

As death approaches, the deliriums attending diftempers abound with far more incoherencies and inconfiftencies, than any other fpecies of alienations of

the

the mind; which may easily be conceived to be the natural result of the intire confusion and disorder which then take place in the nervous system. However, there are some cases of death, where the nervous system continues free from this confusion to the last, as far as the by-standers can judge.

Of the frequent recurrency of the same ideas.

When a person applies himself to any particular study, so as to fix his attention deeply on the ideas and terms belonging to it, and to be very little conversant in those of other branches of knowledge, it is commonly observed, that he becomes narrow-minded, strongly persuaded of the truth and value of many things in his own particular study, which others think doubtful or false, or of little importance, and after some time subject to low spirits, and the hypochondriacal distemper. Now all this follows from observations already made. The perpetual recurrency of particular ideas and terms makes the vibrations belonging thereto become more than ordinarily vivid, converts feeble associations into strong ones, and enhances the secondary ideas of dignity and esteem, which adhere to them, at the same time that all these things are diminished in respect of other ideas and terms, that are kept out of view; and which, if they were to recur in due proportion, would oppose and correct many associations in the particular study, which are made not according to the reality of things, and keep down our exorbitant opinions of its importance. The same perpetual recurrency of vibrations, affecting one and the same part of the brain, in nearly one and the same manner, must irritate it at last, so as to enter the limits of pain, and approach to the states peculiar to fear, anxiety, despondency, peevishness, jealousy, and the rest of the tribe of hypochondriacal passions.

Sleep, which presents ideas at hazard, as one may say, and with little regard to prior associations, seems to be of the greatest use in keeping off the hypochondriacal distemper in such persons: however, without a change of studies, this, with great narrow-mindedness, will probably come at last.

It follows from the same method of reasoning, that since the concerns of religion are infinite, so that we can never over-rate them, we ought to make the ideas, motives, and affections, of this kind, recur as often as possible. And if this be done in a truly catholic spirit, with all that variety of actions which our duty to God, our neighbour, and ourselves, requires, there will be no danger of introducing either narrow-mindedness or hypochondriacism. And it ought to be esteemed the same kind and degree of alienation of mind to undervalue a thing of great importance, as to over-value one of small.

Of violent passions.

Persons that are under the influence of strong passions, such as anger, fear, ambition, disappointment, have the vibrations attending the principal ideas so much increased, that these ideas cling together, *i. e.* are associated in an unnatural manner; at the same time that the eagerness and violence of the passion prevent the formation of such associations, or obscure them, if already formed, as are requisite for the right apprehension of the past and future facts, which are the objects of this passion. Violent passions must therefore disorder the understanding and judgment, while they last; and if the same passion returns frequently, it may have so great an effect upon the associations, as that the intervention of foreign ideas shall not be able to set things to rights, and break the unnatural bond. The same increase of vibrations makes all the principal ideas appear to affect *self*, with

with the peculiar interesting concern supposed to flow from personal identity; so that these vibrations exert a reflected influence upon themselves by this means. And thus it appears, that all violent passions must be temporary madnesses, and all habits of them permanent ones, agreeably to the judgment of the wise and good in these things. It appears also, that violent fits of passion, and frequent recurrencies of them, must, from the nature of the body, often transport persons, so that they shall not be able to recover themselves, but fall within the limits of the distemper called madness emphatically.

Of Melancholy.

The next species of alienations of the mind is melancholy. Vapours, hypochondriacal, and hysterical disorders, are comprehended under this class. The causes of it are self-indulgence in eating and drinking, and particularly in fermented liquors, want of due bodily labour, injuries done to the brain by fevers, concussions, &c. too much application of the mind, especially to the same objects and ideas, violent and long-continued passions, profuse evacuations, and an hereditary disposition; which last we may suppose to consist chiefly in an undue make of the brain.

In women the uneasy states of the *uterus* are propagated to the brain, both immediately and mediately, *i. e.* by first affecting the stomach, and thence the brain. In men the original disorder often begins and continues for a long time, chiefly in the organs of digestion.

The *causa proxima* of melancholy is an irritability of the medullary substance of the brain disposing it upon slight occasions to such vibrations as enter the limits of pain; and particularly to such kinds and degrees, as belong to the uneasy passions of fear, sorrow, anger, jealousy, &c. And as these vibrations, when

when the paffions are not in great excefs, do not much tranfgrefs the limits of pleafure, it will often happen that hypochondriac and hyiteric perfons fhall be apt to be tranfported with joy from trifling caufes, and be, at times, difpofed to mirth and laughter. They are alfo very fickle and changeable, as having their defires, hopes, and fears, increafed far beyond their natural magnitude, when they happen to fall in with fuch a ftate of brain as favours them.

It often happens to thefe perfons to have very abfurd defires, hopes, and fears; and yet, at the fame time, to know them to be abfurd; and, in confequence thereof, to refift them. While they do this, we may reckon the diftemper within the bounds of melancholy; but when they endeavour to gratify very abfurd defires, or are permanently perfuaded of the reality of very groundlefs hopes and fears, and efpecially if they lofe the connecting confcioufnefs in any great degree, and violate the rules of decency and virtue (the affociations of this kind being overpowered, as it were, in the fame manner as they are fometimes in dreams), we may reckon the diftemper to have paffed into madnefs, ftrictly fo called; of which I now come to fpeak in a general brief way.

Of Madnefs.

The caufes of madnefs are of two kinds, bodily and mental. That which arifes from bodily caufes is nearly related to drunkennefs, and to the deliriums attending diftempers. That from mental caufes is of the fame kind with temporary alienations of the mind during violent paffions, and with the prejudices and opinionativenefs, which much application to one fet of ideas only occafions.

We may thus diftinguifh the caufes for the more eafy conception and analyfis of the fubject; but, in fact, they are both united for the moft part. The bodily

bodily cause lays hold of that paffion or affection, which is moft difproportionate; and the mental caufe, when that is primary, generally waits till fome bodily diftemper gives it full fcope to exert itfelf. Agreeably to this, the prevention and cure of all kinds of madnefs require an attention both to the body and mind; which coincides in a particular manner with the general doctrine of thefe papers.

It is obferved, that mad perfons often fpeak rationally and confiftently upon the fubjects that occur, provided that fingle one which moft affects them, be kept out of view. And the reafon of this may be, that whether they firft become mad, becaufe a particular, original, mental uneafinefs falls in with an accidental, bodily diforder; or becaufe an original, bodily diforder falls in with an accidental mental one; it muft follow, that a particular fet of ideas fhall be extremely magnified, and, confequently, an unnatural affociation of famenefs or repugnancy between them generated, all other ideas and affociations remaining nearly the fame. Thus, fuppofe a perfon, whofe nervous fyftem is difordered, to turn his thoughts accidentally to fome barely poffible good or evil. If the nervous diforder falls in with this, it increafes the vibrations belonging to its idea fo much, as to give it a reality, a connexion with *felf*. For we diftinguifh the recollection and anticipation of things relating to ourfelves, from thofe of things relating to other perfons, chiefly by the difference of ftrength in the vibrations, and in their coalefcences with each other. When one falfe pofition of this kind is admitted, it begets more of courfe, the fame bodily and mental caufes alfo continuing; but then this procefs ftops after a certain number of falfe pofitions are adopted from their mutual inconfiftency (unlefs the whole nervous fyftem be deranged); and it is often confined to a certain kind, as the irafcible, the terrifying, &c.

The memory is often much impaired in madnefs, which is both a fign of the greatnefs of the bodily diforder, and a hindrance to mental rectification; and therefore a bad prognoftic. If an oppofite ftate of body and mind can be introduced early, before the unnatural affociations are too much cemented, the madnefs is cured; if otherwife, it will remain, tho both the bodily and mental caufe fhould be at laft removed.

Inquiries after the philofophers ftone, the longitude, &c. to which men are prompted by ftrong, ambitious, or covetous defires, are often both caufe and effect, in refpect of madnefs. Exceffive fits of anger and fear are alfo found often to hurry perfons into madnefs.

In diffections after madnefs the brain is often found dry, and the blood-veffels much diftended; which are arguments, that violent vibrations took place in the internal parts of the brain, the peculiar refidence of ideas and paffions; and that it was much compreffed, fo as to obftruct the natural courfe of affociation.

As in mad perfons the vibrations in the internal parts of the brain are preternaturally increafed, fo they are defective in the external organs, in the glands, &c. Hence, maniacs eat little, are coftive, make little water, and take fcarce any notice of external impreffions. The violence of the ideas and paffions may give them great mufcular ftrength upon particular occafions, when the violent vibrations defcend from the internal parts of the brain into the mufcles, according to former affociations of thefe with the voluntary motions (the fame increafe of vibrations in the internal parts of the brain, which hinders the afcending vibrations of fenfation, augmenting the defcending ones of motion). But maniacs are often very fluggifh, as well as infenfible, from the great prevalence of the ideal vibrations; juft as perfons in a ftate of deep attention are. An accurate hiftory of the feveral kinds

kinds of madnefs from thofe phyficians, who are much converfant with this diftemper, is greatly wanted, and it would probably receive confiderable light from this theory.

Religious confiderations are the beft prefervative in hereditary or other tendencies to madnefs; as being the only fure means of reftraining violent paffions, at the fame time that they afford a conftant indefinite hope, mixed with a filial awe and fear; which things are eminently qualified to keep up a fteadinefs and fobriety of mind, and to incite us to fuch a courfe of action, as adds inceffantly to the hope, and diminifhes the fear. However, bodily labour, with a variety of mental occupations. and a confiderable abftemioufnefs in the quantity and quality of diet, ought always to be joined.

SECT.

SECT. VII.

Of the Intellectual Faculties *of Brutes.*

PROP. 45.

To examine how far the inferiority of Brutes to mankind in intellectual capacities is agreeable to the foregoing theory.

IF the doctrines of vibrations and association be found sufficient to solve the phænomena of sensation, motion, ideas, and affections, in men, it will be reasonable to suppose, that they will also be sufficient to solve the analogous phænomena in brutes. And, conversly, it seems probable, that an endeavour to apply and adapt these doctrines to brutes will cast some light and evidence upon them, as they take place in men. And thus the laws of vibrations and association may be as universal in respect of the nervous systems of animals of all kinds, as the law of circulation is with respect to the system of the heart and blood-vessels; and their powers of sensation and motion be the result of these three laws, *viz.* circulation, vibrations, and association, taken together. These three laws may also be most closely united in their ultimate cause and source, and flow in all their varieties from very simple principles. At least this is the tenor of nature in many similar cases.

As the whole brute creation differs much from, and is far inferior to man, in intellectual capacities; so the several kinds of animals differ much from each other in the same respect. But I shall in this section, confine myself chiefly to the consideration of of the firſt difference, *viz.* of that between mankind and the brute creation in general; and endeavour to aſſign ſuch reaſons for it, as flow from, or are agreeable to, the theory of theſe papers. We may ſuppoſe then, that brutes in general differ from, and are inferior to man, in intellectual capacities, on the following accounts:

Firſt, the ſmall proportional ſize of their brains.

Secondly, the imperfection of the matter of their brains, whereby it is leſs fitted for retaining a large number of miniatures, and combining them by aſſociation, than man's.

Thirdly, their want of words, and ſuch-like ſymbols.

Fourthly, the inſtinctive powers which they bring into the world with them, or which riſe up from internal cauſes, as they advance towards adult age.

Fifthly, the difference betwen the external impreſſions made on the brute creation, and on mankind.

Firſt, then, as the brains of brutes are leſs in proportion to the bulk of the other parts, than thoſe of men; and as the internal parts of the brain appear from theſe papers to be the peculiar ſeat of ideas, and intellectual affections; it ſeems very natural to expect, that brutes ſhould have a far leſs variety of theſe than men. The parts which intervene between the optic and auditory nerves, being proportionably leſs, for inſtance, in brutes, will not admit of ſo great a variety of aſſociations between the ſeveral ideas of theſe ſenſes, becauſe the optic and auditory nerves cannot have ſo great a variety of connexions and communications with each other.

To this it is to be added, that the internal parts belonging to the olfactory nerves, and, perhaps, thoſe belonging to the nerves of taſte, take up, probably, a greater proportional part of the medullary ſubſtance of the brain than in us, ſince moſt brutes have

Of the Intellectual

have the fenfe of fmell, and perhaps that of tafte in greater perfection than we have. There will therefore be ftill lefs room left for the variety of intercourfes between the optic and auditory nerves in the medullary fubftance of the brain. And yet it is evident, from obvious obfervations, as well as from the whole tenor of thefe papers, that the eye and ear, with their affociations, are the chief fources of intellect; and that the greateft part of the pleafures and pains of human life arife from vifible and audible impreffions, which in themfelves afford neither pleafure nor pain.

Thus it is natural to expect, that the happinefs and mifery of brutes fhould depend principally, and in a direct manner, on the impreffions made upon their grofs fenfes, whilft that of mankind arifes, in great meafure, from long trains of affociated ideas and emotions, which enter chiefly by the eye and ear. And it feems to me a very ftriking coincidence, that mankind fhould at the fame time exceed the brute creation in the variety of their ideas, and in the proportional largenefs of that part of the body which is the peculiar feat of thefe.

The fame proportional largenefs may, as it were, detain the vibrations which afcend from external impreffions up to the brain, and fo prevent that freedom of defcent into the mufcular fyftem which takes place in brutes; and which difpofes them to move more early, and more readily, in confequence of direct impreffions, than men, at the fame time that they have a far lefs command in refpect of voluntary motion. But this difference depends, in great meafure, upon the confiderations that follow, as will be feen.

Secondly, that the very conftitution and texture of the nervous fyftem, in its infinitefimal veffels, fhould differ in brutes from that of men, appears highly reafonable to be expected. And fince the lives of brutes fall, in general, far fhort of that of man,

man, alfo fince the quadrupeds (which refemble man more than other animals) are far more hairy, and fowls have feathers, it appears probable, that the texture of the nervous fyftem in brutes fhould tend more to callofity, and fixednefs in its difpofitions to vibrate, than in men. The brains of young brute animals will therefore be fooner able to retain miniatures than thofe of children, as tending more to firmnefs and fixednefs in their ultimate texture and conftitution; at the fame time that this texture will unfit them for receiving a variety. To which, if we add the fhortnefs of their lives, and confequently of their afcent to the fummit of adult age; which afcent is the proper time for receiving inftruction; it is eafy to fee, that on this double account, as well as that mentioned under the foregoing head, they muft fall far fhort of mankind in the number of their intellectual ideas, pleafures, and pains.

It follows from the fame method of reafoning, that the few difpofitions to miniature vibrations, which are generated in brutes, may be as perfect in their kinds; and confequently the memory, and fhort, direct ratiocination depending thereon, as perfect alfo, as the analogous things in man. Nay, they may be more fo, if the particular animal under confideration excel man in the acutenefs and precifion of thofe fenfes, whofe ideas make a principal part of this ratiocination. Now it appears, that moft quadrupeds exceed us in the acutenefs of the fmell, and in the power of diftinguifhing a variety of fmells. And many birds feem to be able to fee diftinctly at much greater diftances. However, our auditory nerves, and the regions of the brain corresponding thereto, appear far better fitted for retaining a variety of miniatures of articulate founds; and our optic nerves, and the regions of the brain corresponding thereto, for retaining a variety of miniatures of fhapes and colours. And, next to man, quadrupeds, and particularly monkeys, dogs, and horſes, ſeem to have theſe regions of the brain in the greateſt perfection.

If the texture of the brains of animals here conſidered be alſo, in part, the cauſe of their being covered with hair, wool, briſtles, feathers, &c. it may, from this its effect, diſpoſe them to greater ſtrength and expertneſs in their motions, and that more early, than happens to men. For all theſe are *electrics per ſe*, and conſequently may firſt have a conſiderable degree of this power communicated to them by the heat of the circulating blood; and then, not being able to tranſmit it to the air, which is alſo an *electric per ſe*, may reflect it upon the muſcles, and thereby diſpoſe them to ſomewhat greater activity. It is well known, that the mains of horſes, and backs of cats, are made electric by their vital powers. It may farther be obſerved, that the hoofs of animals are *electrics per ſe*, and that the feathers of waterfowl repel the water; whence the electric virtue may be kept from running off to the earth and water reſpectively. However, we ought not to lay much ſtreſs upon this electric virtue in the muſcular fibres of brutes (if there be any ſuch virtue) in order to account for the ſuperior and more early power of animals, in reſpect of ordinary motions. The texture of the fibres of the muſcles, and that of the brain, muſt have the principal ſhare in this effect.

It is alſo to be conſidered, that as they have far fewer voluntary motions, on account of having far fewer ideas, ſo they may arrive at a greater perfection in the automatic ones, and the ſmall number of voluntary ones which they do perform, on this account. Man is diſtracted, as it were, by the endleſs variety of his ideas, and voluntary motions: and it is notorious, that none beſides extraordinary geniuſes arrive at perfection in any conſiderable variety; whereas a perſon of ſmall natural capacity, by ſelecting ſome one

Faculties *of Brutes.* 243

one branch of science, or manual art, and applying himself to this alone, may perform wonders. Nay, there have been instances of persons not much removed from idiotism, who could perform the arithmetical operations by memory, far better than men of good understandings, well versed in those operations; which is a thing somewhat analogous to the extraordinary sagacity in investigating and concluding, which brutes discover, in respect of some particular things.

Thirdly, the next circumstance, which renders brutes far inferior to man in intellectual acquisitions, is their want of symbols, such as words, whereby to denote objects, sensations, ideas, and combinations of ideas. This may appear from several considerations. Those men who happen to be born in a country where the mother-tongue is copious and precise, who apply themselves to the study of their mother-tongue, who, besides this, learn one or more foreign tongues, *&c.* get, by these means, a considerable share of the knowledge of things themselves, learn to remark, prove, disprove, and invent, and, *cæteris paribus,* make a quicker progress in mental accomplishments, than others. On the contrary, the mental improvement of persons born deaf is extremely retarded by their incapacity of having things suggested by articulate sounds, or the pictures of these, and also by their not being able to solve the inverse problem, and denote their own trains of thought by adequate symbols. Words are the same kind of helps in the investigation of qualities, as algebraical symbols and methods are in respect of quantity, as has been already remarked. Persons born deaf cannot therefore make any great progress in the knowledge of causes and effects, in abstracted and philosophical matters; but must approach, as it were, to the state of the brute creation. On the contrary, brute creatures, that have much intercourse with mankind, such as dogs and horses, by learning the ufe of words and fymbols of other kinds, become more fagacious than they would otherwife be. And if particular pains be taken with them, their docility and fagacity, by means of fymbols, fometimes arife to a very furprifing degree.

Parrots might be thought, according to this view of the prefent fubject, to have fome particular advantages over quadrupeds, by their being able to pronounce words ; fince, as has been obferved before, the attempts which children make to apply words to things, affift them very much in underftanding the applications made by others. But parrots do not feem to fpeak from any particular acutenefs and precifion in the auditory nerves, and parts of the brain correfponding thereto, having no cochlea, but from the perfection and pliablenefs of their vocal organs, in which they exceed other birds; as birds in general do beafts. And it is reafonable to think, that quadrupeds, which refemble man fo nearly in the make of the organ of hearing, as well as in other parts, and which alfo have naturally much more intercourfe with man (being fellow-inhabitants of the earth) than birds (which inhabit the air), fhould likewife have a greater faculty of diftinguifhing the articulate founds of man's voice, retaining their miniatures, and applying them to the things fignified, than birds; which feems evidently to be the cafe. Sagacious quadrupeds may therefore be faid to refemble dumb perfons arrived at adult age, who are poffeffed of much knowledge, which yet they cannot exprefs, except by geftures, by dumb fhew : whereas parrots, as before remarked, refemble children; thefe having many words with very little knowledge annexed to them.

Apes and monkeys, of the feveral kinds, feem to approach neareft to man, in the general faculty of reafoning, and drawing conclufions ; but in particular things, efpecially where inftinct prevails, fome
other

Faculties of Brutes. 245

other brutes far exceed them; as indeed such brutes do man himself in a few, on account of the peculiar acuteness of the sense of smell, and the same instinct.

I reckon the want of articulate sounds to be one of the reasons why brutes are so much inferior to men in intellectual capacities; becaufe it appears, from the foregoing and other considerations of the same kind, that it is so. But this is no imperfection upon the whole. The proportional smallness of their brains, the texture of these, their instincts, and their external circumstances, are such, that they do not want language much; that they could make no great use of it, had they proper organs for speaking; and that they would probably be losers, upon the whole, by having it. The efficient and final causes are here suited to each other, as in all other cases; so that no circumstance can be changed for the better, *cæteris manentibus*.

Fourthly, let us come to the instinctive powers of animals. These are a point of a very difficult consideration. They are evidently not the result of external impressions, by means of the miniatures of these, their associations and combinations, in the manner according to which I have endeavoured to shew, that the rational faculties of mankind are formed and improved; and yet, in the instances to which they extend, they very much resemble the rational faculties of mankind. Animals, in preparing and providing for themselves and their young, in future exigencies, proceed in the same manner as a person of good understanding, who foresaw the event, would do; and this, even though they be a little put out of their way. And in this they much resemble persons of narrow capacities and acquisitions, who yet excel greatly in some particular art or science; of which there are many instances. Such persons shew great ingenuity in the things to which they are accustomed, and

and in some others that border upon them within certain limits, so as to shew great ingenuity still, though put a little out of their way; but if they be put much out of their way, or questioned about things that are entirely foreign to the art or science in which they excel, they are quite lost and confounded.

Let us suppose this to be the case, and then the inquiry concerning instinct in brutes will be reduced to this; viz. by what means the nervous systems of brutes are made to put on dispositions to miniature vibrations, analogous to those which take place in the persons here considered; and which are in them the result of foregoing impressions, if we admit the theory of these papers. Now, to me, there seems no difficulty in ascribing this to the mere bodily make in brutes, so that miniature vibrations, such as answer in us to ideas, and voluntary motions, shall spring up in them at certain ages and seasons of the year, and mix themselves with impressions, and acquired ideas, so as to be, in general, suitable to them; and. in general, to direct the brute creatures in what manner to provide for, and preserve, themselves and their young.

This would be a kind of inspiration to brutes, mixing itself with, and helping out, that part of their faculties which corresponds to reason in us, and which is extremely imperfect in them. Only this inspiration might be called natural, as proceeding from the same stated laws of matter and motion as the other phænomena of nature; whereas the inspiration of the sacred writers appears to be of a much higher source, so as to be termed supernatural properly, in contradistinction to all knowledge resulting from the common laws of nature. And yet it may result from some higher laws of nature. For sacred inspiration would lose nothing of its authority, though it should appear to be within such laws, as by their fixedness might be termed nature; and indeed all

dif-

differences in these things, after the facts are once settled, will be found, upon due inquiry, to be merely verbal.

Fifthly, the last cause here assigned for the great difference and inferiority of brutes, in respect of intellectual capacities, is the difference in the events and incidents of their lives. They converse with far fewer objects than men, and both the objects and pleasures of feeling, taste, and smell, have a far greater proportional share in the sum total, than in us. Now, as in men, the common events and incidents of life give a turn to the whole frame of mind, and either inlarge the intellectual capacities, if they be various, or narrow them, if the same occurrences return again and again perpetually; so, independently of all the foregoing considerations, the sameness, paucity, and relation to mere sense, of the impressions made on brutes, must infer a great narrowness of understanding.

From all these things put together, it appears very conceivable, how the mental faculties of brutes should, consistently with the doctrines of vibrations and association, be what they are, in fact, found to be. And though I suppose, with *Descartes*, that all their motions are conducted by mere mechanism; yet I do not suppose them to be destitute of perception, but that they have this in a manner analogous to that which takes place in us; and that it is subjected to the same mechanical laws as the motions. Whether the ideal vibrations, which take place in the medullary substances of their brains, be the result of former impressions, or the mere offspring of their vital and natural powers, agreeably to the foregoing hypothesis concerning instinct, or the compound effect of both, which we may presume to be generally the case, I always suppose, that corresponding feelings, and affections of mind, attend upon them, just as in us. And the brute creatures prove their near relation to us, not only by the general resemblance of the body, but by that of the mind also; inasmuch as many of them have most of the eminent passions in some imperfect degree, and as there is, perhaps, no passion belonging to human nature, which may not be found in some brute creature in a considerable degree.

The brutes seem scarce ever able to arrive at any proper self-interest of the abstract and refined kind, at consciousness, so as to compare and connect themselves with themselves in different situations, or at any idea and adoration of God; and this from the narrowness of their capacities and opportunities in general, but particularly from their want of symbols.

The same want of symbols must make all their reasonings and affections, which resemble ours in the general, be, however, considerably different in particulars, and far less complex; but it is sufficient to intitle them to the names of sagacity, cunning, fear, love, &c. by which ours are denoted, that the trains of ideal vibrations in their brains bear a general resemblance to the corresponding ones in ours, spring from like causes, and produce like effects.

The power of association over brutes is very evident in all the tricks which they are taught; and the whole nature of each brute, which has been brought up amongst others of the same species, is a compound of instinct, his own observation and experience, and imitation of those of his own species. Instinct seems to have exerted its whole influence when the creature is arrived at maturity, and has brought up young; so that nothing new can be expected from it afterwards. But their intellectual acquisitions from observation and imitation continue; whence old brutes are far more cunning, and can act far better, *pro re nata*, than young ones.

It ought always to be remembred in speaking on this subject, that brutes have more reason than they can

can shew, from their want of words, from our inattention, and from our ignorace of the import of those symbols, which they do use in giving intimations to one another, and to us.

We seem to be in the place of God to them, to be his vicegerents, and impowered to receive homage from them in his name. And we are obliged by the same tenure to be their guardians and benefactors.

CHAP.

CHAP. IV.

Of the Six Classes of intellectual Pleasures and Pains.

I HAVE now dispatched the history and analysis of the sensations, motions, and ideas; and endeavoured to suit them, as well as I could, to the principles laid down in the first chapter. My next business, is to inquire particularly into the rise and gradual increase of the pleasures and pains of imagination, ambition, self-interest, sympathy, theopathy, and the moral sense; and to see how far these can be deduced, in the particular forms and degrees that are found to prevail, in fact, from the sensible pleasures and pains, by means of the general law of association. As to that of vibrations, it seems of little importance in this part of the work, whether it be adopted or not. If any other law can be made the foundation of association, or consistent with it, it may also be made consistent with the analysis of the intellectual pleasures and pains, which I shall here give. I do not think there is any other law that can; on the contrary, there seems to be so peculiar an aptness in the doctrine of vibrations, for explaining many of the phænomena of the passions, as almost excludes all others.

Now it will be a sufficient proof, that all the intellectual pleasures and pains are deducible ultimately from the sensible ones, if we can shew of each intellectual pleasure and pain in particular that it takes its rise from other pleasures and pains, either sensible or intel-

intellectual. For thus none of the intellectual pleasures and pains can be original. But the sensible pleasures and pains are evidently originals. They are therefore the only ones; *i. e.* they are the common source from whence all the intellectual pleasures and pains are ultimately derived.

When I say, that the intellectual pleasures A and B are deducible from one another, I do not mean, that A receives back again from B that lustre which it had conferred upon it; for this would be to argue in a circle; but that whereas both A and B borrow from a variety of sources, as well as from each other, they may and indeed must, transfer by association part of the lustre borrowed from foreign sources upon each other.

If we admit the power of association, and can also shew, that associations, sufficient in kind and degree, concur, in fact, in the several instances of our intellectual pleasures and pains, this will, of itself, exclude all other causes for these pleasures and pains. such as instinct for instance. If we cannot trace out associations sufficient in kind and degree, still it will not be necessary to have recourse to other causes. because great allowances are to be made for the novelty, complexness, and intricacy of the subject. However, on the other hand, analogy may perhaps lead us to conclude, that as instinct prevails much, and reason a little in brutes, so instinct ought to prevail a little in us. Let the facts speak for themselves.

SECT.

SECT. I.

Of the Pleasures and Pains of Imagination.

I Begin with the pleasures and pains of imagination; and shall endeavour to derive each species of them by association, either from those of sensation, ambition, self-interest, sympathy, theopathy, and the moral sense, or from foreign ones of imagination. They may be distinguished into the seven kinds that follow.

First, the pleasures arising from the beauty of the natural world.

Secondly, those from the works of art.

Thirdly, from the liberal arts of music, painting, and poetry.

Fourthly, from the sciences.

Fifthly, from the beauty of the person.

Sixthly, from wit and humour.

Seventhly, the pains which arise from gross absurdity, inconsistency, or deformity.

PROP. 46.

To examine how far the just mentioned pleasures and pains of imagination are agreeable to the doctrine of association.

Of the pleasures arising from the beauty of the natural world.

THE pleasures arising from the contemplation of the beauties of the natural world seem to admit of the following analysis.

Pains of Imagination.

The pleafant taftes, and fmells, and the fine colours of fruits and flowers, the melody of birds, and the grateful warmth or coolnefs of the air, in the proper feafons, transfer miniatures of thefe pleafures upon rural fcenes, which ftart up inftantaneoufly fo mixed with each other, and with fuch as will be immediately enumerated, as to be feparately indifcernible.

If there be a precipice, a cataract, a mountain of fnow, &c. in one part of the fcene, the nafcent ideas of fear and horror magnify and enliven all the other ideas, and by degrees pafs into pleafures, by fuggefting the fecurity from pain.

In like manner the grandeur of fome fcenes, and the novelty of others, by exciting furprife and wonder, *i. e.* by making a great difference in the preceding and fubfequent ftates of mind, fo as to border upon, or even enter the limits of pain, may greatly enhance the pleafure.

Uniformity and variety in conjunction are alfo principal fources of the pleafures of beauty, being made fo partly by their affociation with the beauties of nature; partly by that with the works of art; and with the many conveniences which we receive from the uniformity and variety of the works of nature and art. They muft therefore transfer part of the luftre borrowed from the works of art, and from the head of convenience, upon the works of nature.

Poetry and painting are much employed in fetting forth the beauties of the natural world, at the fame time that they afford us a high degree of pleafure from many other fources. Hence the beauties of nature delight poets and painters, and fuch as are addicted to the ftudy of their works, more than others. Part of this effect is indeed owing to the greater attention of fuch perfons to the other fources; but this comes to the fame thing, as far as the general theory

theory of the factitious, affociated nature of thefe pleafures is concerned

The many fports and paftimes, which are peculiar to the country, and whofe ideas and pleafures are revived by the view of rural fcenes, in an evanefcent ftate, and fo mixed together as to be feparately indifcernible, do farther augment the pleafure fuggefted by the beauties of nature.

To thefe we may add, the oppofition between the offenfivenefs, dangers, and corruption of populous cities, and the health, tranquillity, and innocence, which the actual view, or the mental contemplation, of rural fcenes introduces; alfo the pleafures of fociality and mirth, which are often found in the greateft perfection in country retirements, the amorous pleafures, which have many connexions with rural fcenes, and thofe which the opinions and encomiums of others beget in us. in this, as in other cafes, by means of the contagioufnefs obfervable in mental difpofitions, as well as bodily ones.

Thofe perfons who have already formed high ideas of the power, knowledge, and goodnefs, of the author of nature, with fuitable affections, generally feel the exalted pleafures of devotion upon every view and contemplation of his works, either in an explicit and diftinct manner, or in a more fecret and implicit one. Hence, part of the general indeterminate pleafures, here confidered, is deducible from the pleafures of theopathy.

We muft not omit in this place to remind the reader of a remark made above; *viz.* that green, which is the middle colour of the feven primary ones, and confequently the moft agreeable to the organ of fight, is alfo the general colour of the vegetable kingdom; *i. e.* of external nature.

Thefe may be confidered as fome of the principal fources of the beauties of nature to mankind in general.

Pains of Imagination.

neral. Inquifitive and philofophical perfons have fome others, arifing from their peculiar knowledge and ftudy of natural hiftory, aftronomy, and philofophy, in general. For the profufion of beauties, ufes, fitneffes, elegance in minute things, and magnificence in great ones, exceed all bounds of conception, furprize, and aftonifhment; new fcenes, and thofe of unbounded extent, feparately confidered, ever prefenting themfelves to view, the more any one ftudies and contemplates the works of God.

And upon the whole, the reader may fee, that there are fufficient fources for all thofe pleafures of imagination, which the beauties of nature excite in different perfons; and that the differences which are found in different perfons in this refpect, are fufficiently analogous to the differences of their fituations in life, and of the confequent affociations formed in them.

An attentive perfon may alfo, in viewing or contemplating the beauties of nature, lay hold, as it were, of the remainders and miniatures of many of the particular pleafures here enumerated, while they recur in a feparate ftate, and before they coalefce with the general indeterminate aggregate, and thus verify the hiftory now propofed.

It is a confirmation of this hiftory, that an attentive perfon may alfo obferve great differences in the kind and degree of the relifh which he has for the beauties of nature in different periods of his life; efpecially as the kind and degree may be found to agree in the main with this hiftory.

To the fame purpofe we may remark, that thefe pleafures do not cloy very foon, but are of a lafting nature, if compared with the fenfible ones; fince this follows naturally from the great variety of their fources, and the evanefcent nature of their conftituent parts.

When

Of the Pleafures and

When a beautiful fcene is firft prefented; there is generally great pleafure from furprife, from being ftruck with objects and circumftances which we did not expect. This prefently declines; but is abundantly compenfated afterwards by the gradual alternate exaltation of the feveral conftituent parts of the complex pleafures, which alfo do probably enhance one another. And thus we may take feveral reviews of the fame fcene, before the pleafure, which it affords, comes to its *maximum*. After this the pleafure muft decline, if we review it often: but if at confiderable intervals, fo as that many foreign ftates of mind intervene, alfo fo as that new fources of the pleafures of this kind be broken up, the pleafure may recur for many fucceffions of nearly the fame magnitude.

The fame obfervations hold in refpect of the pleafures from the beauties of nature in general, and indeed from all the other fources, works of art, liberal arts. fciences, &c. Thefe all ftrike and furprife the young mind at firft, but require a confiderable time before they come to their *maximum*; after which fome or other will always be at its *maximum* for a confiderable time. However the pleafures of imagination in general, as well as each particular fet and individual, muft decline at laft from the nature of our frame. In what manner they ought to decline, fo as to be confiftent with our *fummum bonum*, by yielding, in due time, to more exalted and pure pleafures, whofe compofition they enter, I will endeavour to fhew hereafter.

Thefe pleafures are a principal fource of thofe which are annexed to the view of uniformity with variety, as above noted, *i. e.* of analogies of various orders; and confequently are a principal incitement to our tracing out real analogies, and forming artificial ones.

The

Pains of Imagination.

The novel, the grand, and the marvellous, are also moft confpicuous in the works of nature; and the laft ftrikes us particularly in many of the phænomena of nature, by feeming to exceed all bounds of credibility, at the fame time that we are certified by irrefragable evidences of the truth of the facts. The fatiety which every pleafure begets in us, after fome continuance, makes us thirft perpetually after the grand and novel; and, as it were, grafp at infinity in number and extent; there being a kind of tacit expectation, that the pleafure will be in proportion to the magnitude and variety of the caufes, in the fame manner as we obferve, in other cafes, the effects to be in fome degree proportional to their caufes.

The pleafures of novelty decline not only in this clafs, but alfo in all the others fenfible and intellectual, partly from our bodily frame, partly from the intermixture, and confequent affociation of neutral circumftances (*i. e.* fuch as afford neither pleafure nor pain) in their fucceffive recurrencies.

A difpofition to a pleafurable ftate is a general attendant upon health, and the integrity of our bodily faculties; and that in fuch a degree, as that actual pleafure will fpring up from moderate incitements, from the tranfient introduction of the affociated circumftances of former pleafurable ftates. If the body be indifpofed in fome degree, it is, however, poffible to force it into a ftate of pleafure by the vivid introduction of various and powerful circumftances; but this unnatural ftate cannot laft long; and, if the indifpofition to pleafure be great, it cannot be introduced at all. On the contrary. where the difpofition to pleafure is preternaturally prevalent, as after wine and opium, and in certain morbid cafes, the leaft hint will excite profufe joy, leaning chiefly to the pleafures of imagination, ambition. fympathy, or devotion, according to the circumftances.

It is eafy to fee how the doctrine of vibrations, which appears to be the only one that admits of permanent ftates of motion, and difpofition to motion, in the brain, fuits thefe laft remarks in a peculiar manner.

Of the beauties of the works of art.

The works of art, which afford us the pleafures of beauty, are chiefly buildings, public and private, religious, civil, and military, with their appendages and ornaments, and machines of the feveral kinds, from the great ones employed in war, commerce, and public affairs, fuch as fhips, military engines, machines for manufacturing metals, &c. down to clocks, watches, and domeftic furniture. The furvey of thefe things, when perfect in their kinds, affords great pleafures to the curious; and thefe pleafures increafe for a certain time, by being cultivated and gratified, till at laft they come to their height, decline, and give way to others, as has been already obferved of the pleafures arifing from the beauties of nature.

The chief fources of the pleafures, which the forementioned works of art afford, appear to be the following: the beautiful illuminations from gay colours; the refemblance which the playthings, that pleafed us when we were children, bear to them; the great regularity and variety obfervable in them; the grandeur and magnificence of fome, and the neatnefs and elegance of others, and that efpecially if they be fmall; the fitnefs to anfwer ufeful ends; their anfwering a multiplicity of thefe by fimple means, or by analogous complex ones, not exceeding certain limits in complexnefs; the knowledge conveyed in many cafes; the ftrong affociations with religion, death, war, juftice, power, riches, titles, highbirth, entertainments, mirth, &c.; fafhion, with the opinions and encomiums of perfons fuppofed to be judges;

judges; the vein defire of having a tafte, and of being thought connoiffeurs and judges, &c. &c.

In architecture there are certain proportions of breadths, lengths, depths, and intire magnitudes, to each other, which are by fome fuppofed to be naturally beautiful, juft as the fimple ratio's of 1 to 2, 2 to 3, 3 to 4, &c. in mufic, yield founds which are naturally pleafant to the ear. But it rather feems to me, that œconomical convenience firft determined the ratio's of doors, windows, pillars, &c. in a grofs way; and then that the convenience of the artifts fixed this determination to fome few exact ratio's, as in the proportion between the lengths and breadths of the pillars of the feveral orders. Afterwards thefe proportions became affociated fo often with a variety of beauties in coftly buildings, that they could not but be thought naturally beautiful at laft. In merely ornamental parts the beauty of the proportions feems to arife intirely either from fafhion, or from a fuppofed refemblance to fomething already fixed as a beautiful proportion. It is eafy from thefe principles to account for the prevalency of different proportions, and general taftes, in different ages and countries.

Of the pleafures arifing from mufic, painting, and poetry.

Let us next confider the three liberal and fifter arts of mufic, painting, and poetry.

Of Mufic.

Now in refpect of mufic, it is to be obferved, that the fimple founds of all uniform fonorous bodies, and particularly the fingle notes of the feveral mufical inftruments, alfo all the concords, or notes, whofe vibrations bear to each other the fimple ratio's of 1 to 2, 2 to 3, 3 to 4, &c. founded together, or near to each other, may, be confidered as originally pleafant to the ear. Difcords are originally unpleafant, and therefore, as in other like cafes, may be made ufe of to heighten our pleafures, by being properly and fparingly introduced, fo as to make a ftrong contraft. To which if we add the uniformity and variety obfervable in all good mufic, we fhall have the chief pleafures affecting children, and young perfons, upon their being firft accuftomed to hear mufic.

By degrees the difcords become lefs and lefs harfh to the ear, and at laft even pleafant, at leaft by their affociations with the concords, that go before, or follow them; fo that more, and alfo more harfh difcords, are perpetually required to give a relifh, and keep the fweetnefs of the concords from cloying. Particular kinds of air and harmony are affociated with particular words, affections, and paffions, and fo are made to exprefs thefe; befides which there is often a natural aptitude in the mufic to reprefent the affection, as in quick mufic, and concords, to reprefent mirth. Mufic in general is connected with gaiety, public rejoicings, the amorous pleafures, riches, high-rank, &c. or with battles, forrow, death, and religious contemplations. There is an ambition to excel in tafte, in performance, and in compofition, and a difficulty which enhances the pleafure, &c. &c.; till, by thefe and fuch-like ways, the judgments and taftes of different perfons, in refpect of mufic, become as different, as we find them to be in fact.

Of Painting.

Our pleafures from pictures are very nearly related to thofe of imitation, which, as was obferved above, take up a confiderable part of our childhood; and the feveral playthings reprefenting men, houfes, horfes, &c. with which children are fo much delighted, are

are to be confidered, both as augmenting and gratifying this tafte in them.

To this it is to be added, that as the ideas of fight are the moft vivid of all our ideas, and thofe which are chiefly laid up in the memory as keys and repofitories to the reft, pictures, which are fomething intermediate between the real object and the idea, and therefore in cafes of fufficient likenefs more vivid than the idea, cannot but pleafe us by thus gratifying our defire of raifing up a complete idea of an abfent object. This an attentive perfon may obferve in himfelf in viewing pictures.

The furprife and contraft which arife in children, upon their feeing perfons and objects prefent in their pictures, which yet they know to be abfent, by ftriking the mind with the impoffible conception of the fame thing in two places, are probably the fources of confiderable pleafure to *them*.

To thefe caufes let us add the gay colours, and fine ornaments, which generally go along with pictures; and we fhall have the chief fources of the pleafures which painting affords to young perfons, and to thofe who have not yet been much affected with the various incidents of life, and their reprefentations, or acquired a tafte and fkill in thefe things.

For, after this, the pleafures arifing from pictures are quite of another kind, being derived from the fame fources as thofe that belong to the fcenes, affections, and paffions reprefented, from the poetical defcriptions of thefe, from the precife juftnefs of the imitation, from ambition, fafhion, the extravagant prices of the works of certain mafters, from affociation with the villas and cabinets of the noble, the rich, and the curious, *&c. &c.*

The nature of the caricatura, burlefque, grotefque, picturefque, *&c.* may be underftood from what is delivered in other parts of this fection, concerning laughter, wit, humour, the marvellous, abfurd, &c. to which they correfpond.

Painting has a great advantage over verbal defcription, in refpect of the vividnefs and number of ideas to be at once excited in the fancy; but its compafs is, upon the whole, much narrower, and it is alfo confined to one point of time.

The reprefentations of battles, ftorms, wild beafts, and other objects of horror, in pictures, pleafe us peculiarly, partly from the near alliance which the ideas fuggefted bear to pain, partly from the fecret confcioufnefs of our own fecurity, and partly becaufe they awaken and agitate the mind fufficiently to be ftrongly affected with the other pleafures, which may then be offered to it.

Of Poetry.

The beauties and excellencies of good poetry are deducible from three fources. Firft, the harmony, regularity, and variety of the numbers or metre, and of the rhyme. Secondly, the fitnefs and ftrength of the words and phrafes. Thirdly, the fubject-matter of the poem, and the invention and judgment exerted by the poet, in regard to his fubject. And the beauties arifing from each of thefe are much transferred upon the other two by affociation.

That the verfification has of itfelf a confiderable influence, may be feen by putting good poetical paffages into the order of profe. And it may be accounted for from what has been already obferved of uniformity and variety, from the fmoothnefs and facility with which verfes run over the tongue, from the frequent coincidence of the end of the fentence, and that of the verfe, at the fame time that this rule is violated at proper intervals in all varieties, left the

ear

ear should be tired with too much sameness, from the assistance which versification affords to the memory, from some faint resemblance which it bears to music, and its frequent associations with it, &c &c.

The beauties of the diction arise chiefly from the figures; and therefore it will be necessary here to inquire into the sources of their beauties.

Now figurative words seem to strike and please us chiefly from that impropriety which appears at first sight, upon their application to the things denoted by them, and from the consequent heightening of the propriety, as soon as it is duly perceived. For when figurative words have recurred so often as to excite the secondary idea instantaneously, and without any previous harshness to the imagination, they lose their peculiar beauty and force; and, in order to recover this, and make ourselves sensible of it, we are obliged to recal the literal sense, and to place the literal and figurative senses close together, that so we may first be sensible of the inconsistency, and then be more affected with the union and coalescence.

Besides this, figurative expressions illuminate our discourses and writings by transferring the properties, associations, and emotions, belonging to one thing upon another, by augmenting, diminishing, &c.; and thus, according as the subject is ludicrous or grave, they either increase our mirth and laughter, or excite in us love, tenderness, compassion, admiration, indignation, terror, devotion, &c.

When figures are too distant, or too obscure, when they augment or diminish too much, we are displeased; and the principal art in the use of figures is, to heighten, as far as the imagination will permit, the greatest beauty lying upon the confines of what disgusts by being too remote or bombast. And this extreme limit for figurative expressions shews evidently, that the pleasure arising from them is nearly allied

allied to pain; and their beauty owing to a certain kind and degree of inconfiftency.

However, as the various figures ufed in fpeaking and writing have great influences over each other, alter, and are much altered, as to their relative energy, by our paffions, cuftoms, opinions, conftitutions, educations, &c. there can be no fixed ftandard for determining what is beauty here, or what is the degree of it. Every perfon may find, that his tafte in thefe things receives confiderable changes in his progrefs through life; and may, by careful obfervation, trace up thefe changes to the affociations that have caufed them. And yet fince mankind have a general refemblance to each other, both in their internal make, and external circumftances, there will be fome general agreements about thefe things common to all mankind. The agreements will alfo become perpetually greater, as the perfons under confideration are fuppofed to agree more in their genius, ftudies, external circumftances, &c. Hence may be feen in part, the foundation of the general agreements obfervable in critics, concerning the beauties of poetry, as well as that of their particular difputes and differences.

It may alfo be proper to remark here, that the cuftom of introducing figures in a copious manner into poetry, together with the tranfpofitions, ellipfes, fuperfluities, and high-ftrained expreffions, which the laws of the verfification have forced the beft poets upon, in fome cafes, have given a fanction to certain otherwife unallowable liberties of expreffion, and to a moderate degree of obfcurity, and even converted them into beauties. To which it may be added, that a momentary obfcurity is like a difcord in mufic properly introduced.

The pleafure which we receive from the matter of the poem, and the invention and judgment of the poet,

Pains of Imagination. 265

poet, in this refpect, arifes from the things themfelves defcribed or reprefented. It is neceffary therefore that the poet fhould choofe fuch fcenes as are beautiful, terrible, or otherwife ftrongly affecting, and fuch characters as excite love, pity, juft indignation, &c.; or rather, that he fhould prefent us with a proper mixture of all thefe. For as they will all pleafe fingly, fo a well-ordered fucceffion of them will much enhance thefe feparate pleafures, by the contrafts, analogies, and coincidences, which this may be made to introduce. In all thefe things the chief art is to copy nature fo well, and to be fo exact in all the principal circumftances relating to actions, paffions, &c. i. e. to real life, that the reader may be infenfibly betrayed into a half belief of the truth and reality of the fcene.

Verfes well pronounced affect us much more than when they merely pafs over the eye from the imitation of the affections and paffions reprefented by the human voice; and ftill much more when acted well, and heightened by the proper conjunction of realizing circumftances.

Since poetry makes ufe of words, which are the principal channel of mutual communication for our thoughts and affections, and has by this means an unlimited compafs in refpect of time, place, &c. it muft, upon the whole, have great advantages over painting.

As the pleafures of imagination are very prevalent and much cultivated, during youth; fo, if we confider mankind as one great individual, advancing in age perpetually, it feems natural to expect that in the infancy of knowledge, in the early ages of the world, the tafte of mankind would turn much upon the pleafures of this clafs. And agreeably to this it may be obferved, that mufic, painting, and poetry, were much admired in antient times; and the two laft brought to great perfection. What was the real perfection

fection of the antient *Grecian* mufic, alfo how far the modern very artificial compofitions ought to be allowed to excel them, muft be left to thofe who are judges of thefe matters.

The beauties of oratory are very nearly allied to thofe of poetry, arifing partly from an harmonious flow and cadence of the periods, fo that uniformity and variety may be properly mixed, partly from the juftnefs and nervoufnefs of the expreffions, and partly from the force of the arguments and motives brought together by the invention of the orator, and fo difpofed as to convince the judgment, excite and gain the affections. In both cafes it is very neceffary, that the reader or hearer fhould conceive favourably of the defign and author, in a moral light, poetry has the advantage of oratory, in refpect of the fweetnefs of the numbers, and boldnefs of the figures; but oratory, being a real thing, and one which has great influence in many the moft important tranfactions, does, by this reality, affect fome perfons more than poetry; I mean perfons that are mere readers or hearers; for, as to thofe that are interefted in the debate, to whom it is a reality, there can be no doubt.

The beauties of hiftory will eafily be underftood from what is faid of poetry and oratory.

It is to be obferved, that poetry, and all fictitious hiftory, borrow one chief part of their influence from their being imitations of real hiftory, as this again does from the ftrong affections and paffions excited by the events of life, and from the contagioufnefs of our tempers and difpofitions.

The fame kind of contrafts and coincidences, which, in low and comic things, would be wit or humour, become the brilliant paffages that affect and ftrike us moft eminently in grave poetry, in oratory, and hiftory.

Of

Of the pleasures arising from the study of the sciences.

The study of the sciences has a great connexion with the natural and artificial beauties already considered, and receives great luftre from them in consequence thereof.

But besides this, there are many original sources of pleasure in the study of the sciences: as, first, from the many instances of uniformity with variety: secondly, from the marvellous and seemingly impossible, which occur in all parts of knowledge: thirdly, from the great advantages respecting human life, which accrue to mankind in general from the pursuit of knowledge, also from the honours, riches, &c. which are the rewards conferred upon particular persons that are eminent: lastly, from the numerous connexions of truth of all kinds with those most amiable and important doctrines, which religion, natural and revealed, teaches us. And when these pleasures, in their several subordinate kinds and degrees, have been sufficiently associated with the favourite study, they render it at last pleasant in itself as we usually term it; *i. e.* these several particular pleasures coalesce into a single general one, in which the compounding parts cannot be discerned separately from each other, and which consequently appears to have no relation to its several compounding parts; unless when by a particular attention to, and examination of, what passes in our minds, we lay hold of the last compounding parts, before their intire coalescence, or reason upon the causes of these pleasures, by comparing their growth, and the changes made in them, with the concomitant circumstances. Thus, if it be observed as a general fact, that persons grow fond of particular studies remarkably after having received some great present advantage, or hope of a future one from them, we may reasonably presume

that

that the pleasure which they take in these studies is in part derived from this source, even though it cannot be felt to arise from it explicitly.

Of Invention.

The copiousness and quickness of the invention being principal requisites for the cultivation of the arts and sciences with success, I will say something concerning invention here, my subject being now sufficiently opened for that purpose.

Invention then may be defined the art of producing new beauties in works of imagination, and new truths in matters of science. And it seems to depend, in both cases, chiefly upon these three things. First, a strong and quick memory: secondly, an extensive knowledge in the arts and sciences; and particularly in those that are contiguous to, or not far distant from, that under consideration: and, thirdly, the habit of forming and pursuing analogies, the deviations from these, and the subordinate analogies visible in many of these first deviations, &c. &c.

First, a strong and quick memory is necessary, that so the ideas of the poet or philosopher may depend upon, and be readily suggested by, each other.

Secondly, he must have a large stock of ideas for the purposes of figures, illustrations, comparisons, arguments, motives, criterions, &c. And it is evident, that the ideas taken from such parts of knowledge, as are pretty nearly allied to his particular study, will be of most use to him in it.

Thirdly, analogy will lead him by degrees, in works of fancy, from the beauties of celebrated masters to others less and less resembling these, till at last he arrives at such as bear no visible resemblance. Deviations, and the subordinate analogies contained within them, will do this in a much greater degree; and all analogies will instruct him how to model properly

Pains of Imagination.

perly fuch intirely new thoughts, as his memory and acquaintance with things have fuggefted to him. In fcience analogy leads on perpetually to new propofitions; and being itfelf fome prefumption of truth, is a guide much preferable to mere imagination.

It may be obferved, that the trains of vifible ideas, which accompany our thoughts, are the principal fund for invention, both in matters of fancy, and in fcience.

As invention requires the three things here fpoken of, fo, converfly, no perfon who is poffeffed of them, and who applies himfelf to any particular ftudy either of the imaginative or abftract kind, with fufficient affiduity, can fail for want of invention. And the nature of this faculty feems as reconcileable with, and deducible from, the power of affociation, and the mechanifm of the mind here explained, as that of any other.

Of the beauty of the perfon.

The word *beauty* is applied to the perfon, particularly in the female fex, in an eminent manner; and the defires and pleafures arifing from beauty, in this fenfe, may be confidered as an intermediate ftep between the grofs fenfual ones, and thofe of pure efteem and benevolence; for they are, in part, deduced from both thefe extremes; they moderate, fpiritualize, and improve the firft, and, in the virtuous, are ultimately converted into the laft.

But they arife alfo from many other fources in their intermediate ftate, particularly from affociations with the feveral beauties of nature and art already mentioned, as of gay colours, rural fcenes, mufic, painting, and poetry; from affociations with fafhion, the opinions and encomiums of others, riches, honours, high-birth, &c.; from vanity and ambition,

bition, &c. Besides which, the pleasure of gratifying a strong desire, and the pain of disappointment, are to be considered here, as being evidently distinguishable from all the rest in some cases.

That part of beauty which arises from symmetry, may perhaps be said to consist in such proportions of the features of the face, and of the head, trunk, and limbs, to each other, as are intermediate in respect of all other proportions, *i. e.* such proportions as would result from an estimation by an average one may say at least, that these proportions would not differ much from perfect symmetry.

The desires excited by the beauty of the person increase for some time, especially if the sensible ones are not gratified, and there be also a mixture of hope and fear, in relation to the attainment of the affections of the beloved person. But they sometimes decrease, like other desires, from mere want of novelty, after the affections are gained; and must always do so after gratification. Nevertheless, if there be the proper foundation for esteem and religious affection in each party, mutual love, with the pleasures arising from it, may increase upon the whole, the real circumstances of life affording more than sufficient opportunity for gaining in one respect, what is lost in another.

The beauty of the air, gesture, motions, and dress, has a great connexion with the beauty of the person, or rather makes a considerable part of it, contributing much to the sum total; and when considered separately, receiving much from the other part of the beauties of the person. The separate beauty of these things arises from some imitation of a natural or artificial beauty already established, from fashion, high-birth, riches, &c.; or from their being expressive of some agreeable or amiable quality of mind. The reciprocal influences of our ideas upon each other, and the endless variety of their combinations,

tions, are eminently confpicuous in this article; the ftrength of defire here rendering the affociations, with the feveral fteps previous to the perfect coalefcence of the ideas affociated, more vifible than in moft other cafes.

Of Wit and Humour.

I come now to examine the pleafures of mirth, wit, and humour.

But, firft, it will be neceffary to confider the caufes of laughter and particularly the mental ones.

Now it may be obferved, that young children do not laugh aloud for fome months. The firft occafion of doing this feems to be a furprife, which brings on a momentary fear firft, and then a momentary joy in confequence of the removal of that fear, agreeably to what may be obferved of the pleafures that follow the removal of pain. This may appear probable, inafmuch as laughter is a nafcent cry, ftopped of a fudden; alfo becaufe if the fame furprife, which makes young children laugh, be a very little increafed, they will cry. It is ufual, by way of diverting young children, and exciting them to laughter, to repeat the furprife, as by clapping the hands frequently, reiterating a fudden motion, &c.

This is the original of laughter in children, in general; but the progrefs of each particular is much accelerated, and the occafions multiplied by imitation. They learn to laugh, as they learn to talk and walk; and are moft apt to laugh profufely, when they fee others laugh; the common caufe contributing alfo in a great degree to produce this effect. The fame thing is evident even in adults; and fhews us one of the fources of the fympathetic affections.

To thefe things it is to be added, that the alternate motions of the cheft follow the fame degrees of mental emotion with more and more facility perpetually, fo that at laft children (who are likewife more exquifitely

fitely fenfible and irritable than adults) laugh upon every trifling occafion.

By degrees they learn the power of fufpending the actions both of laughing and crying, and affociate this power with a variety of ideas, fuch as thofe of decency, refpect, fear, and fhame: the incidents and objects, which before occafioned emotion fufficient to produce laughter, now occafion little or none, from the trafmutation of their affociations: their new affociated pleafures and pains are of a more fedate kind, and do not affect them fo much by furprife; and, which is a principal caufe in refpect of individuals, their equals laugh lefs, and, by forming them to the fame model with themfelves, make the difpofition to laughter decreafe ftill fafter. For whatever can be fhewn to take place at all in human nature, muft take place in a much higher degree, than according to the original caufes, from our great difpofition to imitate one another, which has been already explained.

It confirms this account of laughter, that it follows tickling, as noted above; *i. e.* a momentary pain and apprehenfion of pain, with an immediately fucceeding removal of thefe, and their alternate recurrency; alfo that the fofter fex, and all nervous perfons, are much difpofed both to laugh and cry profufely, and to pafs quickly from one ftate to the other. And it may deferve to be inquired, how far the profufe, continued laughter and mirth on one hand, forrow, hanging the lip, and crying on the other, which occur in madnefs, agree with it.

As children learn the ufe of language, they learn alfo to laugh at fentences or ftories, by which fudden alarming emotions and expectations are raifed in them, and again diffipated inftantaneoufly. And as they learnt before by degrees to laugh at fudden unexpected noifes, or motions, where there was no fear, or no diftinguifhable one, fo it is after fome time

time in refpect of words. Children, and young perfons, are diverted by every little jingle, pun, contraft, or coincidence; which is leval to their capacities, even though the harfhnefs and inconfiftency, with which it firft ftrikes the fancy, be fo minute as fcarce to be perceived. And this is the origin of that laughter, which is excited by wit, humour, buffoonery, &c.

But this fpecies of laughter abates alfo by degrees, as the other before-confidered did, and, in general, for the fame caufes; fo that adults, and efpecially thofe that are judges of politenefs and propriety, laugh only at fuch ftrokes of wit and humour, as furprife by fome more than ordinary degree of contraft or coindence; and have at the fame time a due connexion with pleafure and pain, and their feveral affociations of fitnefs, decency, inconfiftency, abfurdity, honour, fhame, virtue, and vice; fo as neither to be too glaring on the one hand, nor too faint on the other. In the firft cafe, the reprefentation raifes diflike and abhorrence; in the laft, it becomes infipid.

From hence may be feen, that in different perfons the occafions of laughter muft be as different as their opinions and difpofitions; that low fimilitudes, allufions, contrafts, and coincidences, applied to grave and ferious fubjects, muft occafion the moft profufe laughter in perfons of light minds; and, converfly, increafe this levity of mind, and waken the regard due to things facred; that the vices of gluttony, lewdnefs, vain-glory, felf-conceit, and covetoufnefs, with the concomitant pleafures and pains, hopes, fears, dangers, &c. when reprefented by indirect circumftances, and the reprefentation heightened by contrafts and coincidences, muft be the moft frequent fubject of mirth, wit, and humour, in this mixed degenerate ftate, where they are cenfured upon the whole; and yet not looked upon with a due degree of feverity, diftance, and abhorrence; that company,

pany, feasting, and wine, by putting the body into a pleasurable state, must dispose to laughter upon small occasions; and that persons who give themselves much to mirth, wit, and humour, must thereby greatly disqualify their understandings for the search after truth; inasmuch as by the perpetual hunting after apparent and partial agreements and disagreements, as in words, and indirect accidental circumstances, whilst the true natures of the things themselves afford real agreements and disagreements, that are very different, or quite opposite, a man must by degrees pervert all his notions of things themselves, and become unable to see them as they really are, and as they appear to considerate sober-minded inquirers. He must lose all his associations of the visible ideas of things, their names, symbols, &c. with their useful practical relations and properties; and get, in their stead, accidental, indirect, and unnatural conjunctions of circumstances, that are really foreign to each other, or oppositions of those that are united; and, after some time, habit and custom will fix these upon him.

The most natural occasions of mirth and laughter in adults seem to be the little mistakes and follies of children, and the smaller inconsistencies and improprieties, which happen in conversation, and the daily occurrences of life; inasmuch as these pleasures are, in great measure, occasioned, or at least supported, by the general pleasurable state, which our love and affection to our friends in general, and to children in particular, put the body and mind into. For this kind of mirth is always checked where we have a dislike; also where the mistake or inconsistency rises beyond a certain limit; for then it produces concern, confusion, and uneasiness. And it is useful not only in respect of the good effects which it has upon the body, and the present amusement and relaxation that it affords to the mind; but also, because it puts

puts us upon rectifying what is so amiss, or any other similar error, in one another, or in children; and has a tendency to remove many prejudices from custom and education. Thus we often laugh at children, rustics, and foreigners, when yet they act right, according to the truly-natural, simple, and uncorrupted dictates of reason and propriety, and are guilty of no other inconsistency, than what arises from the usurpations of custom over nature; and we often take notice of this, and correct ourselves, in consequence of being diverted by it.

Of inconsistency, deformity, and absurdity

Having now considered, in a short and general way, all the pleasures that seem properly to belong to the head of imagination, I will say something concerning the pains of this class, *viz.* those which arise from the view of gross inconsistency, absurdity, and deformity. Here we may observe,

First, that these pains are the root and source of many of the fore-mentioned pleasures, particularly those arising from figurative expressions, and of wit and humour, as has been shewn in treating of these things.

Secondly, that the disgust and uneasiness here considered never rise to any very great height, unless some of the pains of sympathy, or of the moral sense, mix themselves with them. From whence it seems to follow, that the mere *pleasures* of imagination and beauty are also of a kind much inferior to those of sympathy, and the moral sense.

The perplexity, confusion, and uneasiness, which we labour under in abstruse inquiries, philosophical, moral, and religious, ought, perhaps, to be referred to this head. Also the secondary perplexity which arises from our being subject to this perplexity, confusion, and uneasiness. However, all this is to be accounted for as any other evil. and does not seem to be attended either with greater or lefs difficulties. No perplexity can give us more than a limited degree of pain ; and all our perplexities have probably both the fame general good effects as our other pains; and alfo, like each of thefe, fome good effects peculiar to themfelves.

We may now obferve upon the whole, that according to the foregoing hiftory of the pleafures of imagination, there muft be great differencies in the taftes and judgments of different perfons, and that no age, nation, clafs of men, *&c.* ought to be made the teft of what is moft excellent in artificial beauty ; nor confequently of what is abfurd. The only things that can be fet up as natural criterions here feem to be uniformity with variety, ufefulnefs in general, and the particular fubfurviency of this or that artificial beauty to improve the mind, fo as to make it fuit beft with our prefent circumftances, and future expectations. How all thefe criterions confift with each other, and unite in the fingle criterion of religion, or the love of god, and of our neighbour, underftood in the comprehenfive fenfe of thefe words, I fhall endeavour to fhew hereafter.

SECT.

SECT. II.

Of the Pleasures and Pains of Ambition.

PROP. 47.

To examine how far the pleasures and pains of ambition are agreeable to the foregoing theory.

THE opinions of others concerning us, when expressed by corresponding words or actions, are principal sources of happiness or misery. The pleasures of this kind are usually referred to the head of honour; the pains to that of shame; but as it is most convenient to have a single word, to which to refer both the pleasures and pains of this class, I have made choice of ambition for that purpose. It will therefore be our business, under this proposition, to inquire, by what associations it is brought about, that men are so solicitous to have certain particulars concerning themselves made known to the circle of their friends and acquaintance, or to the world in general; and certain others concealed from them; also, why all marks and evidences, that these two several kinds of particulars are made known, so as to beget approbation, esteem, praise, high-opinion, &c. or dislike, censure, contempt, &c. occasion such exquisite pleasures and pains, as those of honour and shame; *i. e.* of ambition.

The particulars which we desire to have made known to, or concealed from, others, in order to obtain praise, or avoid dispraise, may be classed under the four following heads.

First,

First, external advantages or disadvantages.
Secondly, bodily perfections and imperfections.
Thirdly, intellectual accomplishments or defects.
Fourthly, moral ones; *i. e.* virtue or vice.

I will now endeavour to shew what pleasures and pains, bodily and intellectual, are associated with the opinions which others form of us, in these four respects; *i. e.* either with the several methods by which they receive their information; or with those by which they signify their having received it, and their consequent approbation or disapprobation, respect or contempt.

Of external advantages and disadvantages.

I begin with the consideration of external advantages or disadvantages. The principal of these are fine cloaths, riches, titles, and high-birth, with their opposites, rags, poverty, obscurity, and low-birth.

Now it is evident, that these external advantages and disadvantages become such by being made known to others; that the first gain men certain privileges and pleasures; and the last subject them to inconveniencies and evils only, or chiefly, when they are discovered to the world. It follows therefore that every discovery of this kind to others, also every mark and associate of such discovery, will, by association, raise up the miniatures of the privileges and pleasures, inconveniencies, and evils, respectively; and thus afford, in each instance, a peculiar compound pleasure or pain, which, by the use of language, has the word *honour* or *shame* respectively annexed to it.

This is the gross account of the generation of these pleasures and pains; but the subordinate particulars contain many things worthy of observation.

Thus fine cloaths please both children and adults, by their natural or artificial beauty; they enhance the

the beauty of the perſon; they excite the compliments and careſſes of the attendants in a peculiarly vivid manner; they are the common aſſociates of riches, titles, and high-birth; they have vaſt encomiums beſtowed upon them; and are ſometimes the rewards of mental accompliſhments and virtue. Rags, on the contrary, are often attended with the moſt loathſome and offenſive ideas, with bodily infirmity, poverty, contempt, and vice. It is eaſy therefore to ſee, that in our progreſs through life, a compound aſſociated deſire of fine cloaths, and abhorrence of rags, will ſpring up ſo early as to be deemed a natural one. And if a perſon paſſes of a ſudden from rags to fine cloaths, or *vice verſa*, the pleaſure or pain will be enhanced accordingly, by the juxtapoſition of the oppoſites.

Now theſe pleaſures and pains, which thus attend a perſon's being actually dreſſed in fine cloaths, or in rags, will, by farther aſſociations, be transferred upon all the concomitant circumſtances, the poſſeſſion of fine cloaths, the hopes of them, or the fear of rags, and particularly upon all narrations and ſymbols, whereby others are firſt informed of the perſon's dreſs, or diſcover their prior knowledge of it; ſo that the perſon ſhall have his vanity gratified, or his ſhame excited, by all ſuch narrations, and by all the concomitant circumſtances and ſymbols.

Riches, titles, and high-birth, are attended with aſſociates of the ſame kind as fine cloaths; with this difference, however, that it requires a farther progreſs in life to be ſufficiently affected with the compound pleaſure reſulting from the aſſociates of theſe, and conſequently for acquiring a taſte for thoſe pleaſures of honour, which riches, titles, and high-birth afford. Agreeably to which it may be obſerved, that the firſt inſtance of pride and vanity in children is that which ariſes from fine cloaths.

In the progress through life, especially in the virtuous, it often happens, that opposite associations are generated, *i. e.* such as break the connexion between the ideas of happiness and fine cloaths, riches, titles, high-birth; also between misery and rags, poverty, obscurity, and low-birth; nay, there are some instances in which these last are connected with some kinds and degrees of happiness. Now in all these cases the pride and vanity, or shame, by which we hope or fear to have our circumstances, in these respects, known to the world, lessen, cease intirely, or even turn about to the opposite quarter accordingly; so that when a person has lost his desire of being rich, or high-born, he also loses his desire of being thought so; and when he gains an opposite desire of becoming poor, on a religious account, for instance, or a complacence in being low-born, on account of his present high station, &c. he desires also to have this known to the world. And yet there may, in most cases, be perceived some distance in time between the desire of *being*, and the subsequent associated desire of *being thought; viz.* such a distance of time as may suffice for the associations to produce their effect in.

Riches are attended with many conveniencies, whether a person be known to possess them, or no; and there are inconveniencies, as well as conveniencies, attending the reputation of being rich; but titles and high-birth are then only productive of privileges and pleasures, when made known to the world; whence it is easy to see that pride and vanity may shew themselves much more commonly in respect of titles and high-birth, than in respect of riches, which is agreeable to the fact.

The shamefacedness of rustics, poor persons, and inferiors in general, in the presence of their superiors, with the great confusion and uneasiness that often attend it, arises from the sources of honour and shame

shame here laid open, and particularly from the strong contrast between their own circumstances and those of their superiors.

Of bodily perfections and imperfections.

The chief bodily circumstances, which are the sources of the pleasures of honour, or of the pains of shame, are beauty, strength, and health, on the one hand; and their opposites, deformity, imbecillity, unfitting a person for the functions of life, and disease, on the other. I will make some short remarks upon each.

Beauty has an intimate connexion with one of the most violent of our desires; affords a great pleasure, even where this desire is not felt explicitly; has the highest encomiums bestowed upon it in books, especially in such as are too much in the hands of young persons, and the highest compliments paid to it in discourse; and is often the occasion of success in life; all which holds more particularly in respect of women, than of men. No wonder therefore, that both sexes, but especially women, should desire both to *be* and *be thought* beautiful, and be pleased with all the associated circumstances of these things; and that the fear of *being* or *being thought* deformed, should be a thing to which the imagination has the greatest reluctance. And the reputation of beauty, with the scandal of deformity, influences so much the more, as beauty and deformity are not attended with their respective pleasing or displeasing associates, except when they are made apparent to, and taken notice of by the world. So that here the original desire is rather to *be thought* beautiful than to *be* so; and this last is chiefly a consequential one arising in our minds, from the close connection of *being* with *being thought*.

In

In strength it is otherwise. This is the source of many conveniencies, and imbecillity, its opposite, of many inconveniencies, whether they be taken notice of or no; as well as some which depend upon their being thus taken notice of. It is reasonable therefore here to suppose, that our first and greatest desire should be after the thing itself; and so it is in fact. However, since several advantages arise from shewing our strength; since also the ostentation of happiness of any kind belonging to ourselves, or the notice which others take of it, bring in the pleasing idea with great vigour; it is evident that there must be eager desires of *being thought* strong, agile, *&c.* as well as of *being* so. And by parity of reason, men will be much ashamed of *being thought* weak and feeble, as well as afraid of being so. And as women glory chiefly in beauty, so men do in strength; this being chiefly a source of advantages and pleasures to men, as that is to women. Nay, one may even observe, that any great degree of beauty in men, or strength in women, by being opposite to that perfection, which is peculiar to each sex, is thought rather undesirable than desirable.

Health and sickness have many connexions with beauty and strength, deformity and imbecillity, respectively; and therefore may easily be conceived to become respectively the sources of the pleasures of honour, or of the pains of shame, agreeably to the fact. But, in diseases, so many greater pains and evils, fears, anxieties, *&c.* with some pleasures, such as those of friendship, occur likewise, that there is, in most cases, little room for shame to exert itself: however, if the disease be the consequence either of a virtuous, or a vicious course of action, the honour or shame, belonging to virtue or vice respectively, will be transferred upon it.

There is an high degree of shame, which attends the natural evacuations, particularly those of the fæces and

and urine, which is in part deduced from the offenfiveness of the excrements of the body, and is nearly related to the shame attending bodily infirmities and diseases. But this shame, as it respects the fæces and urine, has also a particular connexion with that which relates to the pudenda, arising from the vicinity of the organs; and thus they give and receive mutually. They are also both of them much increased by education, custom, and the precepts and epithets of parents and governors. The original sources of the shame relating to the pudenda are probably the privacy requisite (which is both cause and effect), the greatness of the pleasure, and the sense of guilt which often attends; and there may be perhaps something of instinct, which operates here quite independently of association.

Of intellectual accomplishments and defects.

The intellectual accomplishments and defects which occasion honour and shame, are sagacity, memory, invention, wit, learning; and their oppofites, folly, dulness, and ignorance. Here we may deduce a considerable part from the many advantages arising from the accomplishments, disadvantages from the defects, in the same manner as has been done already in the two foregoing articles. But a great part, perhaps the greatest, is deduced from the high-strained encomiums, applauses, and flatteries, paid to parts and learning, and the outrageous ridicule and contempt thrown upon folly and ignorance, in all the discourses and writings of men of genius and learning; these persons being extremely partial to their own excellencies, and carrying the world with them by the force of their parts and eloquence. It is also to be observed, that in the education of young persons, and especially of boys and young men, great rewards are conferred in consequence of intellectual attainments and parts; and great punishments follow negligence and ignorance; which rewards and punishments. being respectively associated with the words expressing praise and censure, and with all their other circumstances, transfer upon praise and censure compound vivid miniatures, pleasant and painful.

In like manner all the kinds of honour and shame, by being expressed in words and symbols, that are nearly related to each other, enhance each other: thus, for instance, the caresses given to a child when he his dressed in fine cloaths prepare him to be much more affected with the caresses and encomiums bestowed upon him when he has been diligent in getting his lesson. And indeed it ought to be remarked, that the words and phrases of the parents, governors, superiors, and attendants, have so great an influence over children, when they first come to the use of language, as instantly to generate an implicit belief, a strong desire, or a high degree of pleasure. They have no suspicions, jealousies, memories, or expectations of being deceived or disappointed; and therefore a set of words expressing pleasures of any kind, which they have experienced, put together in almost any manner, will raise up in them a pleasurable state, and opposite words a painful one. Whence it is easy to see, that the fine language expressing praise, and the harsh one expressing dispraise, must instantly, from the mere associations heaped upon the separate words, put them into a state of hope and joy, fear and sorrow, respectively. And when the foundation is thus laid, praise and dispraise will keep their influences from the advantages and disadvantages attending them, though the separate words should lose their particular influences, as they manifestly do in our progress through life.

The honour and shame arising from intellectual accomplishments do often, in learned men, after some time, destroy, in great measure, their sensibility, in respect

respect of every other kind of honour and shame; which seems chiefly to arise from their conversing much with books, and learned men, so as to have a great part of the pleasures which they receive from this their conversation, closely connected with the encomiums upon parts and learning; also to have all terms of honour applied to them, and the keenest reproach, and most insolent contempt, cast upon the contrary defects. And, as the pleasures which raillery, ridicule, and satire, afford to the by-standers, are very considerable, so the person who is the object of them, and who begins to be in pain upon the first slight marks of contempt, has this pain much enhanced by the contrast, the exquisiteness of his uneasiness and confusion rising in proportion to the degree of mirth, and insolent laughter, in the by-standers: whence it comes to pass, that extremely few persons have courage to stand the force of ridicule; but rather subject themselves to considerable bodily pains, to losses, and to the anxiety of a guilty mind, than appear foolish, absurd, singular, or contemptible to the world, or even to persons of whose judgment and abilities they have a low opinion.

All this is, in general, more applicable to men than to women, just as the honour and shame belonging to beauty and deformity is more applicable to women than men; both which observations are easily deducible from the different talents and situations in life of the two sexes.

Of virtue and vice.

We come, in the last place, to consider moral accomplishments and defects, or virtue and vice. Now it is very evident, that the many advantages, public and private, which arise from the first, will engage the world to bestow upon it much honour and applause, in the same manner as the evil consequences, of vice muſt make *it* the objeƈt of cenſure and reproach. Since therefore the child is affeƈted with the words expreſſing honour and cenſure, both from the ſeparate influences of theſe words, and from the application of phraſes of this kind to other ſubjeƈts of praiſe and diſpraiſe, he muſt be affeƈted by the commendations beſtowed upon him when he has done well, and by the cenſures paſt on him when he has done ill.

Theſe commendations and cenſures are alſo attended with great immediate rewards and puniſhments, likewiſe with the hopes and fears relating to another world; and when the moral ſenſe is ſufficiently generated, with great ſecret indeterminate pleaſure or pain of this kind; and theſe aſſociations add a particular force to the honour and ſhame belonging reſpeƈtively to virtue and vice. At the ſame time it is eaſy to ſee, that ſome conſiderable progreſs in life is ordinarily required before men come to be deeply and laſtingly affeƈted by theſe things; alſo that this kind of honour and ſhame may, at laſt, from the ſuperior force of the aſſociated pleaſures and pains, abſorb, as it were, all the other kinds. A religious man becomes at laſt inſenſible, in great meaſure, to every encomium and reproach, excepting ſuch as he apprehends will reſt upon him at the laſt day, from Him whoſe judgment cannot err.

This is the general account of the honour and ſhame paid to virtue and vice reſpeƈtively. I will now make a few ſhort ſtriƈtures upon ſome of the principal virtues and vices.

Firſt, then, piety is not in general, and amongſt the bulk of mankind, had in great honour. This proceeds from ſeveral cauſes; as that in the order of our progreſs it is the laſt of the virtues, and therefore, having few votaries, it muſt have few advocates; that in the firſt attempts to attain it, men often fall into great degrees of enthuſiaſm and ſuperſtition, and ſo expoſe

expose themselves to the charges of folly, madness, and self-conceit; and that pretences to it are often made use of by hypocrites to cover the worst designs. Now from these and such-like causes it happens, that men are much ashamed to be thought devout, fearing that exquisite uneasiness, which being ridiculed and contemned as fools, madmen, and hypocrites, occasions. At the same time it appears, that amongst those who have made considerable advances in religion, piety will be had in the greatest honour: these see evidently how it may be distinguished from enthusiasm, superstition, and hypocrisy; and are very little solicitous concerning the opinions of the profane world, who are apt to confound them; and therefore as far as their piety will permit any foreign desire to arise, they have an exquisite relish for the honour and esteem proceeding from the reputation of piety.

Benevolence springs up more early in life than piety, and has at first view a more immediate good influence upon society. There are also greater numbers who arrive at some imperfect degrees of it, than who arrive at like degrees of piety; neither are the degenerations and counterfeits of benevolence so common as those of piety. On these accounts much greater and more frequent encomiums are bestowed upon it by the bulk of mankind, than upon piety; and these with the many advantages resulting from the reputation of being benevolent, make most persons eagerly desire this reputation; so that they perform many actions from mere ambition, or from a mixture of this with benevolence, which they desire the world should think to proceed from mere benevolence.

Military glory, and the high applauses bestowed upon personal courage, seem, in a considerable degree, deducible from this source, from the benevolent design of protecting the innocent, the helpless, one's friends and country, from invasions, robberies, wild beasts.

beasts, &c. The connexion of these with bodily strength, and the characteristical perfections of men as distinguished from women and children, the rarity and difficulty of them, the vast encomiums bestowed upon them by poets, orators, and historians, especially in antient times, *i. e.* by those authors which are read in schools, and lay hold of our pliant imaginations when young, the ridicule cast upon timorousness by boys and men, as not being a common imperfection amongst them, and the connexion of the fear of death with the sense of guilt, all concur likewise, and have carried mankind so far as make them confer the highest honours upon the most cruel, lawless, and abominable actions, and consequently incite one another to perform such actions from ambitious views. However, this false glare seems to fade in theory, amongst writers; and one may hope that the practice of mankind will be, in some measure, agreeable to the corrections made in their theory.

Temperance and chastity have considerable honours bestowed upon them; but the shame and scandal attending the opposite vices, and which arise from the loathsome diseases, and the many miseries, which men bring upon themselves and others by these vices, are much more remarkable. The detail of these things might easily be delivered from parallel observations already made. It happens sometimes, that some degrees of these vices are looked upon by young and ignorant persons, as honourable, from certain connexions with manliness, fashion, high-life: However, this is still in conformity with the doctrine of association, and the derivation of all the pleasures of honour from happiness under some form or other; and, when the same persons become better instructed in the real consequences and connexions of things, their opinions change accordingly.

Nega-

Pains of Ambition.

Negative humility, or the not thinking better, or more highly, of ourfelves than we ought, in refpect of external advantages, bodily, intellectual, or moral accomplifhments, and being content with fuch regards as are our due, which is the firft ftep; and then pofitive humility, or a deep fenfe of our own mifery and imperfections of all kinds, and an acquiefcence in the treatment which we receive from others, whatever it be; being virtues which are moft commodious to ourfelves and others, and highly amiable in the fight of all thofe who have made a due proficiency in religion, and the moral fenfe, come at laft to be honoured and efteemed in an eminent manner, and confequently to incite men from mere vanity and ambition to feek the praife of humility. And the ridicule and fhame which attend vanity, pride, and felf-conceit, concur to the fame purpofe; which is a remarkable inftance of the inconfiftency of one part of our frame with itfelf, as the cafe now ftands, and of the tendency and vice to check and deftroy itfelf.

From the whole of what has been delivered upon this clafs of pleafures and pains, one may draw the following corollaries.

Cor. 1. All the things in which men pride themfelves, and for which they defire to be taken notice of by others, are either means of happinefs, or have fome near relation to it. And indeed it is not at all uncommon to fee perfons take pains to make others believe, that they are happy, by affirming it in exprefs terms. Now this, confidered as a mere matter of fact, occurring to attentive obfervation, might lead one to conclude, that the pleafures of honour and ambition are not of an original, inftinctive, implanted nature, but derived from the other pleafures of human life, by the affociation of thefe into various parcels, where the feveral ingredients are fo mixed amongft one another, as hardly to be difcernible feparately.

The young, the gay, and the polite, are ambitious of being thought beautiful, rich, high-born, witty, &c. The grave, the learned, the afflicted, the religious, &c. seek the praise of wisdom and knowledge, or to be esteemed for piety and charity; every one according to his opinions of these things, as the sources, marks, or offsprings of happiness. And when men boast of their poverty, low-birth, ignorance, or vice, it is always in such circumstances, with such additions or contrasts, or under such restrictions, as that the balance, upon the whole, may, some way or other, be the more in their favour on that account.

Cor. 2. Praise and shame are made use of by parents and governors, as chief motives and springs of action; and it becomes matter of praise to a child, to be influenced by praise, and deterred by shame; and matter of reproach, to be insensible in these respects. And thus it comes to pass, that praise and shame have a strong reflected influence upon themselves; and that praise begets the love of praise, and shame increases the fear of shame. Now, though the original praise, commendation, blame, censure, &c. of good parents and preceptors, extend only, for the most part, to acquired accomplishments and defects, and particularly to virtue and vice; yet the secondary influence will affect men in respect of all sorts of encomiums and censures, of every thing that comes under the same denomination, that is associated with, or tied up by, the same words. Though the preceptor direct his pupil only to regard the judgment of the wise and good, still there are so many like circumstances attending the judgment of others, that it will be regarded something the more from the lessons received, in respect of the wise and good, exclusively of others.

Cor.

Cor. 3. In confidering the fources of honour and fhame it will appear, that they are by no means confiftent with one another; and by a farther inquiry, that the *maximum* of the pleafures of this clafs ultimately coincides, *omni ex parte*, with moral rectitude.

SECT. III.

Of the Pleasures and Pains of Self-interest.

PROP. 48.

To examine how far the pleasures and pains of self-interest are agreeable to the foregoing theory.

Self-interest may be distinguished into three kinds; viz.

First, gross self-interest, or the cool pursuit of the means whereby the pleasures of sensation, imagination, and ambition, are to be obtained, and their pains avoided.

Secondly, refined self-interest, or a like pursuit of the means that relate to the pleasures and pains of sympathy, theopathy, and the moral sense.

And, thirdly, rational self-interest, or the pursuit of a man's greatest possible happiness, without any partiality to this or that kind of happiness, means of happiness, means of a means, &c.

Of gross Self-interest.

The love of money may be considered as the chief species of gross self-interest, and will help us, in an eminent manner, to unfold the mutual influences of our pleasures and pains, with the factitious nature of the intellectal ones, and the doctrine of association in general, as well as the particular progress, windings, and endless redoublings of self-love. For it is evident at first sight, that money cannot
naturally

Pains of Self-intereft.

naturally and originally be the object of our faculties; no child can be fuppofed born with the love of it. Yet we fee, that fome fmall degrees of this love rife early in infancy; that it generally increafes during youth and manhood; and that at laft, in fome old perfons, it fo engroffes and abforbs all their paffions and purfuits, as that from being confidered as the reprefentative, ftandard, common meafure and means of obtaining the commodities which occur in common life, it fhall be efteemed the adequate exponent and means of happinefs in general, and the thing itfelf, the fum total of all that is defireable in life. Now the monftrous and gigantic fize of this paffion in fuch cafes, fupported evidently by affociation alone, will render its progrefs and growth more confpicuous and ftriking; and confequently greatly contribute to explain the correfponding particulars in other paffions, where they are lefs obvious.

Let us inquire therefore, for what reafons it is that children firft begin to love money. Now they obferve, that money procures for them the pleafures of fenfation, with fuch of imagination as they have acquired a relifh for. They fee that it is highly valued by others; that thofe who poffefs it are much regarded and careffed; that the poffeffion of it is generally attended by fine cloaths, titles, magnificent buildings, &c.;' imitation, and the common contagion of human life, having great power here, as in other cafes. Since therefore ideas exciting defire are thus heaped upon money by fucceffive affociations perpetually recurring, the defire of it in certain fums and manners, *viz.* fuch as have often recurred with the concomitant pleafures, muft at laft grow ftronger than the fainter fenfible and intellectual pleafures; fo that a child fhall prefer a piece of money to many actual gratifications to be enjoyed immediately.

And as all the fore-mentioned affociations, or fuch as are analogous to them, continue during life, it seems probable, that the love of money would at last devour all the particular desires, upon which it is grounded, was it not restrained by counter-associations; just as it was observed above, that the pleasure of gratifying the will would devour all the particular pleasures, to which it is a constant associate, did not repeated disappointments preserve us from this enormous increase of wilfulness.

Let us next examine how the love of money is checked.

First, then, it is checked by the strong desires of young persons, and others, after particular gratifications; for these desires, by overpowering their acquired aversion to part with money, weaken it gradually, and consequently weaken the pleasure of keeping, and the desire of obtaining, all which are closely linked together in this view; notwithstanding that the last, *viz.* the desire of obtaining, and by consequence (in an inverted order) the pleasure of keeping, and the aversion to part with, are strengthened by the desires of particular pleasures to be purchased by money, in another view. And this contrariety of our associations is not only the means of limiting certain passions, but is a mark set upon them by the author of nature, to shew that they ought to be limited, even in our progress through this life; and that they must ultimately be annihilated, every one in its proper order.

Secondly, the insignificancy of riches in warding off death and diseases, also shame and contempt in many cases, and in obtaining the pleasures of religion, and the moral sense, and even those of sympathy, ambition, imagination, and sensation, first lessen their value in the eyes of those who make just observations upon things in their progress through life, and afterwards fix a positive nothingness and worthlessness upon them.

Thirdly,

Thirdly, the eager pursuit of any particular end, as fame, learning, the pleasures of the imagination, &c. leaves little room in the mind either for avarice, or any other foreign end.

Now by these and such-like considerations we may account not only for the limitation put to the love of money, but also for certain mixtures of tempers and dispositions, which are often found in fact, and yet seem at first sight inconsistent ones. Thus profuseness, in respect of sensual and selfish pleasures, is often joined with avarice. Covetous persons are often rigidly just in paying, as well as exacting; and sometimes generous, where money is not immediately and apparently concerned. They have also moderate passions in other respects; for the most part, are suspicious, timorous, and complaisant. And the most truly generous, charitable, and pious persons, are highly frugal, so as to put on the appearance of covetousness, and even sometimes, and in some things, to border upon it.

We may see also, why the love of money must, in general, grow stronger with age; and especially if the particular gratifications, to which the person was most inclined, become insipid or unattainable — Why frequent reflections upon money in possession, and the actual viewing large sums, strengthen the associations by which covetousness is generated — Why children, persons in private and low life, and indeed most others, are differently affected towards the same sum of money, in different forms, gold, silver, notes, &c.

Let us next inquire, for what reasons it is that the love of money has the idea of selfishness attached to it in a peculiar manner, much more so than the pursuit of the pleasures of honour, imagination, or sympathy; whereas all are equally generated by association, from sensible and selfish pleasures, all in their several degrees promote private happiness, and are all purfued, in fome cafes, coolly and deliberately, from the profpect of obtaining private happinefs thereby. Now the reafons of this feem to be;

First, that whatever riches one man obtains, another muft lofe; fo that the circulation of money by trades, profeffions, offices, &c. is a kind of gaming; and has moft of the fame difguftful ideas annexed to it, when confidered with fome attention, and exclufively of private felfifh feelings; whereas the pleafures of fympathy confift in doing good to others; thofe of ambition are fcarce attainable in any great degree without this, or at leaft the appearance of it; and the pleafures of imagination are both capable of a very extenfive communication, and moft perfect when enjoyed in company.

Secondly, a regard to *felf* frequently recurring muft denote a pleafurable *felfifh;* fo that if any of the moft generous pleafures, and fuch as at firft view have no immediate relation to felf-intereft, be purfued in a cool, deliberate way, not from the influence of a prefent inclination, but the preconceived opinion, that it will afford pleafure, this is referred to felf-intereft. Now money has fcarce any other relation to pleafure than that of an evident means; fo that even after it has gained the power of pleafing inftantaneoufly, the intermediate deliberate fteps and affociations muft, however, frequently appear. It procures the other pleafures for us every day, after it has become pleafant in itfelf; and therefore muft always be confidered as a principal means. The other pleafures have, in general, a far greater fhare of indirect affociations with previous pleafures, and acquire the power of gratifying, not fo much from being manifeft caufes of other gratifications, as their moft common adjuncts; whereas money is generally the moft vifible of all the caufes. But honour, power, learning, and many other things are purfued, in part, after the fame manner, and for the fame reafons

as

as riches; *viz.* from a tacit suppofition, that the acquifition of every degree of thefe is treafuring up a proportional degree of happinefs, to be produced and enjoyed at pleafure. And the defires of each of thefe would in like manner increafe perpetually during life, did they not curb one another by many mutual inconfiftencies, or were not all damped by the frequent experience and recollection, that all the means of happinefs ceafe to be fo, when the body or mind ceafe to be difpofed in a manner proper for the reception of happinefs.

It is alfo worthy of obfervation, that riches, honours, power, learning, and all other things that are confidered as means of happinefs, become means and ends to each other in a great variety of ways, thus transferring upon each other all the affociated pleafures which they collect from different quarters, and approaching nearer and nearer perpetually to a perfect fimilarity and famenefs with each other, in the inftantaneous pleafures which they afford when purfued and obtained as ends.

It appears likewife that all aggregates of pleafure, thus collected by them all, muft, from the mechanifm and neceffity of our natures, and of the world which furrounds us, be made at laft to centre and reft upon Him who is the inexhauftible fountain of all power, knowledge, goodnefs, majefty, glory, property, *&c.* So that even avarice and ambition are, in their refpective ways, carrying on the benevolent defigns of Him who is *All in All.* And the fame thing may be hoped of every other paffion and purfuit. One may hope, that they all agree and unite in leading to ultimate happinefs and perfection. However they differ greatly in their prefent confequences, and in their future ones, reaching to certain intervals of time indefinite and unknown to us, thus becoming good or evil, both naturally and morally, in refpect of us, and our limited apprehenfions, judgments, and anticipations,

ticipations. And yet one may humbly hope, as was said above, that every thing muſt be ultimately good, both naturally and morally.

Of refined Self-intereſt.

The ſecond ſpecies of ſelf-intereſt is that which I call refined ſelf-intereſt. As the foregoing ſpecies is generated by an attention to, and frequent reflection upon, the things which procure us the pleaſures of ſenſation, imagination, and ambition; and therefore cannot prevail in any great degree, till theſe pleaſures have been generated, and prevailed for ſome time; ſo this ſpecies, or refined ſelf-intereſt, which is a cool, deliberate ſeeking for ourſelves the pleaſures of ſympathy, religion, and the moral ſenſe, preſuppoſes the generation of theſe pleaſures, and the enjoyment of them for a ſufficient time. And as ſome degree of groſs ſelf-intereſt is the natural and neceſſary conſequence of the three firſt claſſes of pleaſures, ſo is ſome degree of refined ſelf-intereſt of the three laſt. A perſon who has had a ſufficient experience of the pleaſures of friendſhip, generoſity, devotion, and ſelf-approbation, cannot but deſire to have a return of them, when he is not under the particular influence of any one of them, but merely on account of the pleaſure which they have afforded; and will ſeek to excite theſe pleaſures by the uſual means, to treaſure up to himſelf ſuch means, keep himſelf always in a diſpoſition to uſe them, &c. not at all from any particular vivid love of his neighbour, or of God, or from a ſenſe of duty to him, but intirely from the view of private happineſs. At leaſt, there will be a great mixture of this refined ſelf-intereſt in all the pleaſures and duties of benevolence, piety, and the moral ſenſe.

But then this refined ſelf-intereſt is neither ſo common, nor ſo conſpicuous in real life, as the groſs one,

one, since it rises late, is never of any great magnitude in the bulk of mankind, through their want of the previous pleasures of sympathy, religion, and the moral sense, in a sufficient degree, and in some it scarce prevails at all; whereas gross self-interest rises early in infancy, and arrives at a considerable magnitude before adult age. The detail of this second species of self-interest may be seen in books of practical religion.

Of rational Self-interest.

The third species of self-interest is the rational. This is the same thing with the abstract desire of happiness, and aversion to misery, which is supposed to attend every intelligent being during the whole course of his existence. I have already endeavoured to shew, that this supposition is not true in the proper sense of the words; and yet that very general desires do frequently recur to the mind, and may be excited by words and symbols of general import.

The hopes and fears relating to a future state, or to death, which is our entrance into it, are of this kind, and may be considered as proceeding from rational self-interest, in the highest and most abstracted sense that the terms admit of practically, since we have no definite knowledge of the nature and kind of the happiness or misery of another world. These hopes and fears are also the strongest of our selfish affections, and yet at the same time the chief foundation of the pure disinterested love of God, and of our neighbour, and the principal means of transferring our associations, so as that we may love and hate, pursue and fly, in the manner the best suited to our attainment of our greatest possible happiness. For hope, being itself a pleasure, may, by association, render indifferent, and even disagreeable, objects

jects and actions, pleasant; and fear may make agreeable ones painful: hence we can either increase desires and aversions, that are suitable to our state, or obliterate and convert them into their contraries, if they be unsuitable, by means of their connexion with the hopes and fears of death, and a future state. I will therefore briefly state the rise and progress of these hopes and fears.

All our first associations with the idea of death are of the disgustful and alarming kind; and they are collected from all quarters. From the sensible pains of every sort, from the imperfection, weakness, loathsomeness, corruption, and disorder, where disease, old age, death animal or vegetable, prevail, in opposition to the beauty, order, and lustre of life, youth, and health; from the shame and contempt attending the first in many instances; whereas the last are honourable, as being sources of power and happiness, the reward of virtue, &c.; and from the sympathetic passions, in general. And it is necessary, that the heedlessness and inexperience of infancy and youth should be guarded by such terrors, and their headstrong appetites and passions curbed, that they may not be hurried into danger and destruction before they are aware. It is proper also, that they should form some expectations with respect to, and set some value upon, their future life in this world, that so they may be better qualified to act their parts in it, and make the quicker progress to perfection during their passage through it.

When children begin to have a sense of religion and duty formed in them, these do still farther heighten and increase the fear of death for the most part. For though there are rewards on the one hand, as well as punishments on the other; yet fear has got the start from the natural causes of it before-mentioned: and as pain is in general greater than pleasure, as was shewn above, from its consisting in stronger vibra-

vibrations; fo fear is in general more vivid than hope, especially in children.

Moreover, the senfual and selfish appetites are the original of all the rest; yet these are sinful, and inconsistent with our own and others happiness; they must therefore be restrained, and at last eradicated. But parents and governors, are, in this case, more apt to have recourse to fear, than to hope (in general, I suppose with reason, because hope is too feeble to withstand the violence of the natural appetites and passions). And it is to be added to all, that adults, by discovering, in general, much more of fear and sorrow in the apprehensions or prospect of death, than of hope and comfort, from the continuance of the causes just mentioned, propagate and increase the fear still farther in one another, and in children, infecting all around them, as is usual in other cases of the like kind. And by this means it comes to pass, that the fear of death does in some circumstances, particularly where the nervous system is, through a bodily disorder, reduced to an aptness to receive uneasy and disgustful vibrations, only or chiefly, being in a state of irritability approaching to pain, grow to a most enormous size, collecting and uniting every disagreeable idea and impression under the associations belonging to death; so that such persons live in perpetual anxiety and slavery to the fear of death. And where there is the consciousness of past guilt, or the want of an upright intention for the future, it rages with still greater fierceness, till these be removed intirely, or in part, by repentance and amendment.

It is farther to be observed, that the fear of death is much increased by the exquisiteness of the punishments threatened in a future state, and by the variety of the emblems, representations, analogies, and evidences, of natural and revealed religion, whereby all the terrors of all other things are transferred upon thefe punifhments; alfo by that peculiar circumftance of the eternity of them, which feems to have been a general tradition previous to the appearance of chriftianity, amongft both *Jews* and *Pagans*, and which has been the doctrine and opinion of the chriftian world ever fince, fome very few perfons excepted. The confideration of any thing that is infinite, fpace, time, power, knowledge, goodnefs, perfection, &c. quite overpowers the faculties of the foul with wonder and aftonifhment: and when the peculiar feeling and concern belonging to *felf* are applied here, and excited by the word *infinite*, by meditation, reading, &c. we muft, and we ought to be alarmed to the full extent of our capacities. And the fame conclufion follows, though we fhould fuppofe the punifhments of a future ftate not to be abfolutely and metaphyfically infinite. For their great exquifitenefs, and long duration, which are moft clearly and plainly declared in the fcriptures, make them practically fo.

This is a brief fketch of the origin and progrefs of the fears attending the confideration of death, and a future ftate. We now come to inquire, how the hopes are generated.

Firft, then, we are to obferve, that repentance, amendment, the confcioufnefs of paft virtue, and of good intentions for the future, give a title to the hopes and rewards of a future ftate; and that though while there are perpetual alterations of oppofite confcioufneffes, *i. e.* recollections and judgments on our own actions, the fear may prevail in general, both from the additional weight of the natural fear, and from the previous poffeffion which the religious fear has obtained; yet by degrees the agreeable confcioufnefs muft prevail in thofe who are fincere (and fometimes it is to be feared a delufive one of the fame kind in others), moderate the religious fear by little and little, and, in great meafure, overcome the natural one;

one; for which the way has been prepared from the superior strength of the religious fear, which has already obscured it in serious persons. And thus by degrees hope will begin to take place, as the general state of the mind, and the consideration of death, and a future state, become, for the most part, matter of joy and comfort.

Secondly, the deliverance from the fear of death adds greatly to this joy, in the same way as the removal of other pains is made the source of pleasure. And the returns of the fear of death at certain intervals, according to the state of our bodies or minds, and the moral qualities of our actions, will, if they be not too frequent, keep up this source of pleasure in the hope of futurity.

Thirdly, when the slavish fear of God is thus removed by faith and hope, all the pleasing sympathetic affections, such as love, gratitude, confidence, begin to exert themselves with respect to God, in a manner analogous, but a degree far superior to that in which they are exerted towards men. And it is easy to see how these, and such-like causes concurring, may, in many cases, quite overcome the natural and religious fears of death and pain, and even make them acceptable.

Cor. From hence we may pass to the fervors of devotion; these being chiefly the hopes, and pleasing affections just spoken of, coalescing together so intimately by repeated associations, as that the separate parts there mentioned cannot be distinguished from each other in the compound. And as these fervors are themselves often esteemed a sign of holiness, and consequently a foundation of farther hope, they perpetuate and increase themselves for a certain time, *i. e.* till the new convert finds the reiterated appearance of the same ideas give less and less emotion and pleasure, just as in the other pleasures, sensible and intellectual; looks upon this as a mark of spiritual

ritual defertion; finds numberlefs, unexpected, unthought-of, fins and imperfections, not yet fubdued; falls into bodily diforders, from unfeafonable feverities, or fpiritual intemperance, &c.; and thus becomes dejected, fcrupulous, and fearful.

By degrees the fears taken from death, and a future ftate, are confined to the mere apprehenfion of tranfgreffion, without any regard had to thofe, and even where they, when confidered and expected, raife no fears.

However, all thefe things mortify pride, and the refined felf-intereft; lead, or even compel, men to refign all to God; and fo advance them to a more pure, difinterefted, and permanent love of God, and of their neighbour, than they could have arrived at (all other things remaining the fame), had they not undergone thefe anxieties; and therefore are to be efteemed the kind corrections of an infinitely merciful father.

SECT. IV.

Of the Pleasures and Pains of Sympathy.

PROP. 49.

To examine how far the pleasures and pains of sympathy are agreeable to the foregoing theory.

THE sympathetic affections may be distinguished into four classes, *viz.*

First, those by which we rejoice at the happiness of others.

Secondly, those by which we grieve for their misery.

Thirdly, those by which we rejoice at their misery.

And, fourthly, those by which we grieve for their appiness.

Of the first kind are sociality, good-will, generosity, and gratitude. Of the second, compassion and mercy. Of the third, moroseness, anger, revenge jealousy, cruelty, and malice. And of the fourth, emulation and envy.

It is easy to be conceived that association should produce affections of all these four kinds, since in the intercourses of life the pleasures and pains of one are, in various ways, intermixed with, and dependent upon, those of others, so as to have clusters of their miniatures excited, in all the possible ways in which the happiness or misery of one can be combined with the happiness or misery of another; *i. e.* in the four above-mentioned. I will now enter upon the detail of the rise and progress of each of them.

Of the affections by which we rejoice at the happiness of others.

The firſt of theſe is ſociality, or the pleaſure which we take in the mere company and converſation of others, particularly of our friends and acquaintance, and which is attended with mutual affability, complaiſance and candour. Now moſt of the pleaſures which children receive are conferred upon them by others, their parents, attendants, or play-fellows. And the number of the pleaſures which they receive in this way, is far greater than that of the pains brought upon them by others. Indeed the hurts, and bodily injuries, which they meet with, are chiefly from themſelves; and the denials of gratifications are either very few in number, or, if they be more frequent, give little uneaſineſs. It appears therefore, that, according to the doctrine of aſſociation, children ought to be pleaſed, in general, with the ſight and company of all their acquaintance. And the ſame things, with ſome alterations, hold in reſpect of adults, through the whole courſe, and general tenor, of human life.

Beſides the pleaſures for which we are indebted to others, there are many which we enjoy in common with others, and in their company and converſation, and which therefore both enhance, and are enhanced by, the gaiety and happineſs that appear in the countenances, geſtures, words, and actions, of the whole company. Of this kind are the pleaſures of feaſting, ſports and paſtimes, rural ſcenes, polite arts, mirth, raillery, and ridicule, public ſhews, public rejoicings, &c. And in general it may be obſerved, that the cauſes of joy and grief are common to great numbers, affecting mankind according to the ſeveral diviſions and ſubdiviſions thereof into nations, ranks, offices, ages, ſexes, families, &c.

And

And by all these things it comes to pass, that the face of an old acquaintance brings to view, as it were, the indistinct mixed recollection, the remaining vestiges of all the good and evil which we have felt, while his idea has been present with us.

The same observation may be made upon places; and particularly upon those where a man has spent his infancy and youth.

To all this it is to be added, that the rules of prudence, good manners, and religion, by restraining all rusticity, morofeness, and insolence, and obliging us to actions of a contrary nature, even though we have not the proper internal feelings, do by degrees contribute to beget these in us, *i. e.* to beget sociality and complaisance; just in the same manner, as a person in a passion becomes much more inflamed from his own angry expressions, gestures, and actions.

Good-will, or benevolence, when understood in a limited sense, may be termed that pleasing affection which engages us to promote the welfare of others to the best of our power. If it carry us so far as to forego great pleasures, or endure great pains, it is called generosity. But good-will and benevolence, in a general sense, are put for all the sympathetic affections of the first and second class, *viz.* those by which we either rejoice in, and promote, the happiness of others, or grieve for, and endeavour to remove, their misery; as ill-will and malevolence, understood in a general sense also, are put for the contrary affections, *viz.* those of the third and fourth class.

Benevolence, in the limited sense, is nearly connected with sociality, and has the same sources. It has also a high degree of honour and esteem annexed to it. procures us many advantages, and returns of kindness, both from the person obliged and others; and is most closely connected with the hope of reward in a future ſtate, and with the pleaſures of religion. and of ſelf-approbation, or the moral ſenſe. And the ſame things hold with reſpect to generoſity in a much higher degree. It is eaſy therefore to ſee, how ſuch aſſociations may be formed in us, as to engage us to forego great pleaſure, or endure great pain, for the ſake of others; how theſe aſſociations may be attended with ſo great a degree of pleaſure as to over-rule the poſitive pain endured, or the negative one from the foregoing of a pleaſure; and yet how there may be no direct, explicit expectation of reward, either from God or man, by natural conſequence, or expreſs appointment, not even of the concomitant pleaſure which engages the agent to undertake the benevolent or generous action. And this I take to be a proof from the doctrine of aſſociation, that there is, and muſt be, ſuch a thing as pure diſintereſted benevolence; alſo a juſt account of the origin and nature of it.

Gratitude includes benevolence, and therefore has the ſame ſources with ſome additional ones; theſe laſt are the explicit or implicit recollection of the benefits and pleaſures received, the hope of future ones, the approbation of the moral character of the benefactor, and the pleaſures from the honour and eſteem attending gratitude, much enhanced by the peculiar baſeneſs and ſhamefulneſs of ingratitude.

Of the affections by which we grieve for the miſery of others.

Compaſſion is the uneaſineſs which a man feels at the miſery of another. Now this in children ſeems to be grounded upon ſuch aſſociations as theſe that follow: the very appearance and idea of any kind of miſery which they have experienced, or of any ſigns of diſtreſs which they underſtand, raiſe up in their nervous ſyſtems a ſtate of miſery from mere memory,

Pains *of* Sympathy.

mory, on account of the ftrength of their imaginations; and becaufe the connexion between the adjuncts of pain, and the actual infliction of it, has not yet been fufficiently broken by experience, as in adults. —When feveral children are educated together, the pains, the denials of pleafures, and the forrows, which affect one, generally extend to all in fome degree, often in an equal one.—When their parents, attendants, &c. are fick or afflicted, it is ufual to raife in their minds the nafcent ideas of pains and miferies, by fuch words and figns as are fuited to their capacities; they alfo find themfelves laid under many reftraints on this account.—And when thefe and fuch-like circumftances have raifed the defires and endeavours to remove the caufes of thefe their own internal uneafy feelings, or, which is the fame thing, of thefe miferies of others (in all which they are much influenced as in other like cafes, by the great difpofition to imitate, before fpoken of); and a variety of internal feelings and defires of this kind are fo blended and affociated together, as that no part can be diftinguifhed feparately from the reft; the child may properly be faid to have compaffion.

The fame fources of compaffion remain, though with fome alterations, during our whole progrefs through life; and an attentive perfon may plainly difcern the conftituent parts of his compaffion, while they are yet the mere internal, and, as one may fay, felfifh feelings above-mentioned; and before they have put on the nature of compaffion by coalefcence with the reft.

Agreeably to this method of reafoning, it may be obferved, that perfons whofe nerves are eafily irritable, and thofe who have experienced great trials and afflictions, are, in general, more difpofed to compaffion than others; and that we are moft apt to pity in thofe difeafes and calamities, which we either have felt

felt already, or apprehend ourselves in danger of feeling hereafter.

But adults have also many other sources of compassion, besides those already mentioned, and which differ according to their educations and situations in life. When love, natural affection, and friendship, have taught men to take a peculiar delight in certain objects, in mutual endearments, and familiar intercourses, those miseries affecting the beloved objects, which either totally destroy, or greatly interrupt, these intercourses, must give an exquisite uneasiness; and this uneasiness, by mixing itself with the other parts of our compassionate affections, will greatly increase the sum total in respect of these beloved objects.—A compassionate temper being great matter of praise to those who are endued with it, and the actions which flow from it being a duty incumbent on all, men are led to practise these actions, and to inculcate upon themselves the motives of compassion, by attending to distress actually present, or described in history, real or fictitious.—The peculiar love and esteem which we bear to morally good characters, make us more sensibly touched with their miseries; which is farther augmented by our indignation, and want of compassion for morally ill characters, suffering the just punishment of their crimes. In like manner, the simplicity, the ignorance, the helplessness, and the many innocent diverting follies of young children, and of some brutes, lead men to pity them in a peculiar manner.

Mercy has the same general nature and sources as compassion, and seems to differ from it only in this, that the object of it has forfeited his title to happiness, or the removal of misery, by some demerit, particularly against ourselves. Here, therefore, resentment for an injury done to ourselves, or what is called a just indignation against vice in general, interferes, and checks the otherwise natural course of

our

our compassion, so as, in the unmerciful, intirely to put a stop to it. But, in the merciful, the sources of compassion prevail over those of resentment and indignation; whence it appears, that the compassion required in acts of mercy, is greater than that in common acts of mere compassion: agreeably to which it is observable, that mercy is held in higher esteem, than mere compassion.

Of the affections by which we rejoice at the misery of others.

We come now to the affections of the third class; viz. morofeness, anger, revenge, jealousy, cruelty, and malice. Now morofeness, peevishness, severity, &c. are most apt to raise in those persons who have some real or imaginary superiority over others, from their rank, years, office, accomplishments, &c. which either magnifies the failures of duty in inferiors with respect to them, or engages them to be very attentive to these.—Bodily infirmities, and frequent disappointments, by making the common intercourses of life insipid, and enhancing small injuries; delicacy and effeminacy, by increasing the sensibility both of body and mind, with respect to pain and uneasiness; luxury, by begetting unnatural cravings, which clash not only with the like cravings of others, but also with the common course and conveniences of human life; and, in short, all kinds of selfishness; have the same ill effect upon the temper.—The severe scrutiny which earnest penitents make into their own lives, during their noviciate, and the rigid censures which they pass upon their own actions, are often found, in proud and passionate tempers, to raise such indignation against vice, as breaks out into an undue severity of language and behaviour, in respect of others; and this especially, if they seem to themselves to have overcome all great vices,

vices, and are not yet arrived at a juſt ſenſe of the many latent corruptions ſtill remaining in them. And this is much increaſed by all opinions which repreſent the deity as implacable towards a part of mankind and this part as reprobate towards him. By all which we may ſee, that every thing which makes diſagreeable impreſſions upon our minds at the ſame time that our fellow-creatures, or their ideas, are preſent with us; and eſpecially if theſe be linked together in the way of cauſe and effect, or by any ſuch relation; will, in fact, beget in us moroſeneſs and peeviſhneſs. This follows from the doctrine of aſſociation; and is alſo an evident fact. It is likewiſe a ſtrong argument for chearfulneſs, and the pleaſures of innocent moderate mirth.

Anger and cruelty are the oppoſites to mercy and compaſſion; the firſt, as a ſudden ſtart of paſſion, by which men wiſh and endeavour harm to others, and rejoice in it when done; which is revenge: the latter, as a more ſettled habit of mind, diſpoſing men to take a delight in inflicting miſery and puniſhment, and in ſatiating their thirſt after theſe, by beholding the tortures and anguiſh of the ſufferers.

Anger and revenge may be analyſed as follows. The appearance, idea, approach, actual attack, &c. of any thing from which a child has received harm, muſt raiſe in his mind, by the law of aſſociation, a miniature trace of that harm. The ſame harm often ariſes from different cauſes, and different harms from the ſame cauſe; theſe harms and cauſes have an affinity with each other: and thus they are variouſly mixed and connected together; ſo as that a general confuſed idea of harm, with the uneaſy ſtate of the nervous ſyſtem, and the conſequent activity of the parts, are raiſed up in young children upon certain appearances and circumſtances. By degrees the denial of gratifications, and many intellectual aggregates,

Pains of Sympathy.

gates, with all the figns and tokens of thefe, raife up a like uneafinefs, in the manner before explained. And thus it happens, that when any harm has been received, any gratification denied, or other mental uneafinefs occafioned, a long train of affociated remainders of painful impreffions enhance the difpleafure, and continue it much beyond its natural period. This is the nafcent ftate of the paffion of anger, in which it is nearly allied to fear, being the continuance of the fame internal feelings, quickened, on one hand, by the actual, painful, or uneafy impreffion, but moderated on the other by the abfence of the apprehenfion of future danger.

By degrees the child learns, from obfervation and imitation, to ufe various mufcular exertions, words, geftures, &c. in order to ward off or remove the caufes of uneafinefs or pain, fo as to ftrike, talk loud, threaten, &c. and fo goes on multiplying perpetually, by farther and farther affociations, both the occafions of anger, and the expreffions of it; and particularly affociates a defire of hurting another with the apprehenfion, or the actual receiving, of harm from that other.

As men grow up to adult age, and diftinguifh living creatures from things inanimate, rational and moral agents from irrational ones, they learn to refer effects to their ultimate caufes; and to confider all the intermediate ones as being themfelves effects, depending on the ultimate caufe. And thus their refentment paffes from the inanimate inftrument to the living agent; and more efpecially if the living agent be a rational and moral one. For, firft, living rational agents are alone capable of being reftrained by threatenings and punifhments from committing the injurious action. All our expreffions of anger muft therefore be directed againft them.—Secondly, inanimate things are incapable of feeling the harms which anger wifhes: the defire of revenge muft there-

therefore be intirely confined to animals. And thefe two things have great influence on each other. Our threatening harm merely from a motive of fecurity, leads us to wifh it really; wifhing it leads us to threaten and inflict it, where it can afford no fecurity or advantage to us. —Thirdly, as we improve in obfervation and experience, and in the faculty of analyfing the actions of animals, we perceive that brutes and children, and even adults in certain circumftances, have little or no fhare in the actions referred to them; but are themfelves under the influence of other caufes, which therefore are to be deemed the ultimate ones. Hence, our refentment againft them muft be much abated in thefe cafes, and tranfferred to the ultimate living caufe, ufually called the free agent, if fo be that we are able to difcover him.— Laftly, when the moral ideas of juft and unjuft, right and wrong, merit and demerit, have been acquired, and applied to the actions and circumftances of human life in the manner to be hereafter defcribed the internal feelings of this clafs, *i. e.* the complacency and approbation attending the firft, the difguft, difapprobation, and even abhorrence, attending the laft, have great influence in moderating or increafing our refentment. The affociations of the firft kind are at utter varience with thofe fuggefted by the fenfe of pain ; of the laft, coincide with and ftrengthen it. And as the rectitude of the moral fenfe is the higheft matter of encomium, men are afhamed not to be thought to fubmit all their private feelings to its fuperior authority, and acquiefce in its determinations. And thus, by degrees, all anger and refentment in theory, all that even ill men will attempt to juftify, is confined to injury, to fufferings which are not deferved, or which are inflicted by a perfon who has no right to do it. And this at laft makes it fo in fact, to a great degree, amongft thofe who are much influenced by their own moral fenfe,

or

or by that of others. Yet still, as a confirmation of the foregoing doctrine, it is easy to observe, that many persons are apt to be offended even with stocks and stones, with brutes, with hurts merely accidental and undesigned, and with punishments acknowledged to be justly inflicted; and this in various degrees, according to the various natural and acquired dispositions of their minds.

Cruelty and malice are considered, not as passions of the mind, but as habits, as the deliberate wishing of misery to others, delighting in the view and actual infliction of it, and this without the consideration of injury received or intended. However, it will easily appear that they are the genuine and necessary offspring of anger indulged and gratified. They are most apt to arise in proud, selfish, and timorous persons, those who conceive highly of their own merits, and of the consequent injustice of all offences against them; and who have an exquisite feeling and apprehension, in respect of private gratifications and uneasinesses. The low and unhappy condition of those around a man gives a dignity to his own; and the infliction of punishment, or mere suffering, strikes a terror, and so affords security and authority. Add to these, the pleasures arising from gratifying the will before explained, and perhaps some from mere curiosity, and the rousing an obdurate callous mind to a state of sensibility. Thus we may perceive how nearly one ill passion is related to another; and that it is possible for men to arrive at last at some degree of pure disinterested cruelty and malice.

The jealousy against a rival in the affections of a beloved person of the other sex; also that peculiar resentment against this beloved person, when suspected to be unfaithful, which goes by the same name; are easily deducible from their sources, in the manner so often repeated. And it is owing to the extraordinary magnitude of the passions and pleasures between the

the sexes, and the singular contempt and ridicule thrown upon the person despised and deceived (the last of which springs from the first), that these two sorts of jealousy rise to such an height. This is more peculiarly remarkable in the southern climates, where the passions between the sexes are more violent than amongst us. The nature and origin of jealousies and suspicions of other kinds, with the affections attending them, may easily be understood from what has been already advanced.

Of the affections by which we grieve for the happiness of others.

Emulation and envy make the fourth class of the sympathetic affections. These are founded in the desire of pleasures, honours, riches, power, &c.; and the consequent engrossing what others desire, losing what they obtain, in a comparison of our own acquisitions with those of others, &c.; by which the happiness of others is connected with our misery; so that at last we become uneasy at their happiness, even where there is no such connexion; *i. e.* emulate and envy where our own interest is no-ways concerned.

Having now seen, in some measure, the nature and origin of the principal sympathetic affections, pleasing and tormenting, moral and immoral, let us consider the several objects upon which these various and contrary affections are exerted.

I begin with the most intimate of all the relations of life; that of husband and wife. Where this union is cemented by the several pleasures of sensation and imagination before-mentioned, also by those of the moral and religious kinds hereafter to be described, love, generosity, gratitude, compassion, and all the affections of the first and second class, prevail in the highest degree possible, to the exclusion of all those of the 3d and 4th class; so that the marriage-state, in these cases, affords the most perfect earnest

Pains of Sympathy.

earneft and pattern, of which our imperfect condition here admits, of the future happinefs of the good in another world. And it is remarkable, that this ftate is in fcripture made the emblem of future happinefs, and of the union of Chrift with the church.

Where the ties of affection are weaker, and particularly where there is a great deficiency in the moral or religious difpofitions of either or both the parties, the paffions of the 3d clafs intermix themfelves with thofe of the 1ft and 2d; and, in many cafes, the oppofite affections prevail in great degrees alternately, and even at fhort and frequent intervals. And indeed each kind often becomes more violent from fucceeding its oppofite.

In very immoral and wicked perfons the paffions of the 3d clafs prevail almoft intirely, and that efpecially where the peculiar affection, called love by young perfons, and which fprings from the pleafures of fenfation, imagination, and ambition, in the manner above explained, was originally weak.

The affection of parents towards children feems to begin from the pain which the mother feels in bringing them into the world, and the fympathetic fears and cares of the father in confequence thereof, and in fome degree from childrens being fuppofed to belong to their parents in a very peculiar fenfe, and being parts of their own bodies. It is increafed efpecially in mothers, by all the figns of life, fenfe, and diftrefs, which the helplefs tender infant fhews; many religious and moral confiderations, with the language in which thefe are expreffed, adding alfo great force thereto. The giving fuck in the mother, with all the fears and cares in both parents, increafes it ftill farther; and as the child advances in age and underftanding, diverts by his little follies, pleafes by his natural beauty, draws on the encomiums of others, furprifes by his agility or wit, &c. the affections continue to rife. When the time comes for the cultivation

vation of the moral and religious powers of the mind, thefe either increafe the affection by their proper appearance and growth, or check it by being deficient, and by giving occafion to cenfures and corrections. Yet even thefe laft, when juftly proportioned, and followed by mental improvement, add greatly to the warmth of affection by raifing compaffion. And thus the remainders of former affections, and the acceffions of new ones, feem to make a fum total, which grows perpetually greater in tender and religious parents.

The little affection commonly fhewn to baftards agrees very well with the foregoing hiftory of parental affection.

The affection towards grandchildren is, in general, the fame as that towards children, differing chiefly in this, that it is more fond and tender, and lefs mixed with feverity, and the neceffary corrections. This may be, perhaps, becaufe the appearance of the helplefs infant, after fo long an interval, raifes up all the old traces of parental affection with new vigour, from their not having been exerted for fome years, and by recalling many of the moft moving fcenes of the foregoing life; fo that thefe old traces increafed by the addition of new fimilar ones, make together a greater fum total than before: or, perhaps, becaufe old perfons have more experience of pain, forrow, and infirmity; and fo are more difpofed to compaffion, in the fame manner as they are more apt to weep; and becaufe they excufe themfelves from the uneafy tafk of cenfuring and reproving.

The affections of children towards their parents are founded in the many pleafures which they receive from them, or in their company. Thefe affections are afterwards increafed by their improvement in morality and religion, and by the feveral common caufes of good-will, gratitude, compaffion, &c. prevailing

vailing here with peculiar force. It seems, however, that the sources of this affection are fewer and weaker than the sources of that towards children; and it is observed in fact, that the affection of children is in general weaker than that of parents. For which also an evident final cause may be assigned, It is to be added farther, that the many engagements and distractions, which lay hold of the opening faculties of young persons, upon their entrance into life, have a principal share in this effect.

Friendship, with the bitter enmities that sometimes succeed the breaches of it, and the emulation and envy that are apt to arise in friends from the equality and similarity of their circumstances, may be easily understood from what has been delivered already.

In like manner we may explain the affections between persons of the same family, brothers, cousins, &c. of the same age, sex, district, education, temper, profession, &c.

By all these artificial ties our good-will and compassion are perpetually extended more and more, growing also perpetually weaker and weaker, in proportion to their diffusion. Yet still the common blessings and calamities, which fall upon whole nations and communities; the general resemblance of the circumstances of all mankind to each other, in their passage through life; their common relation to God, as their creator, governor, and father; their common concern in a future life, and in the religion of Christ, &c.; are capable of raising strong sympathetic affections towards all mankind, and the several larger divisions of it in persons of religious dispositions, who duly attend to these things. In like manner the opinions of savageness, barbarity, and cruelty, which ignorant and unexperienced persons are apt to entertain, concerning some distant nations, raise up in their minds some degrees of general dislike, aversion, and hatred.

SECT.

SECT. V.

Of the Pleasures and Pains of Theopathy.

PROP. 50.

To examine how far the pleasures and pains of theopathy are agreeable to the foregoing theory.

UNDER this class I comprehend all those pleasures and pains, which the contemplation of God and his attributes, and of our relation to him, raises up in the minds of different persons, or in that of the same person at different times. And in order to speak with more precision concerning this class of affections, and to deduce them more readily from the theory of these papers, it will be proper first to inquire into the idea of God, as it is found in fact amongst men, particularly amongst *Jews* and *Christians*; *i. e.* to inquire what associations may be observed in fact to be heaped upon and concur in this word, and the equivalent and related terms and phrases.

First, then, it is probable, that, since many actions and attributes belonging to men are, and indeed must be, in common language applied to God, children, in their first attempts to decypher the word God, will suppose it to stand for a man, whom they have never seen, and of whom consequently they form a compound fictitious idea, consisting of parts before generated by men, whom they have seen.

Secondly, when they hear or read, that God resides in heaven *(i. e.* according to their conceptions,

Pains of Theopathy.

in the fky, amongft the ftars), that he made all things, that he fees, hears, and knows all things, can do all things, &c. with the many particular modes of expreffion that are comprehended under thefe general ones, vivid ideas, which furprife and agitate the mind (lying upon the confines of pain), are raifed in it; and if they be fo far advanced in underftanding, as to be affected with apparent inconfiftencies and impoffibilities in their ideas, they muft feel great perplexity of imagination, when they endeavour to conceive and form definite ideas agreeable to the language of this kind, which they hear and read. Now this perplexity will add to the vividnefs of the ideas, and all together will transfer upon the word God, and its equivalents, fuch fecondary ideas, as may be referred to the heads of magnificence, aftonifhment, and reverence.

Thirdly, when children hear that God cannot be feen, having no vifible fhape, no parts; but that he is a fpiritual infinite being; this adds much to their perplexity and aftonifhment, and by degrees deftroys the affociation of the fictitious vifible idea beforementioned with the word God. However, it is probable, that fome vifible ideas, fuch as thofe of the heavens, a fictitious throne placed there, a multitude of angels, &c. ftill continue to be excited by the word God, and its equivalents, when dwelt upon in the mind.

Fourthly, when the child hears that God is the rewarder of good actions, and the punifher of evil ones, and that the moft exquifite future happinefs or mifery (defcribed by a great variety of particulars and emblems) are prepared by him for the good and bad refpectively; he feels ftrong hopes and fears rife alternately in his mind, according to the judgment which he paffes upon his own actions, founded partly upon the previous judgment of others, partly
upon

upon an imperfect moral sense begun to be generated in him.

And laying all these things together it will appear, that amongst *Jews* and *Christians*, children begin probably with a definite visible idea of God; but that by degrees this is quite obliterated, without any thing of a stable precise nature succeeding in its room; and that by farther degrees, a great variety of strong secondary ideas, *i. e.* mental affections (attended indeed by visible ideas, to which proper words are affixed, as of angels, the general judgment, &c.), recur in their turns, when they think upon God, *i. e.* when this word, or any of its equivalents, or any equivalent phrase or symbol, strike the mind strongly, so that it dwells upon them for a sufficient time, and is affected by them in a sufficient degree.

Amongst heathen nations, where idolatry and polytheism prevail, the case is different; but this difference may easily be understood by applying the foregoing method of reasoning to the circumstances of the heathen world.

I will now inquire more particularly into the nature and origin of the affections exerted towards God. They may be ranked under two general heads, love and fear; agreeably to the general division of the sympathetic affections into benevolence and malevolence. However, the analogy here is not a complete one, as will be seen presently.

To the love of God may be referred gratitude, confidence and resignation; also enthusiasm, which may be considered as a degeneration of it. To the fear, reverence (which is a mixture of love and fear); also superstition and atheism, which are degenerations of the fear of God.

Of the Love of God.

The love of God, with its affociates, gratitude, confidence, and refignation, is generated by the contemplation of his bounty and benignity to us, and to all his creatures, as thefe appear from the view of the natural world, the declarations of the fcriptures, or a man's own obfervation and experience in refpect of the events of life. It is fupported, and much increafed, by the confcioufnefs of upright intentions, and fincere endeavours, with the confequent hope of a future reward, and by prayer vocal and mental, public and private, inafmuch as this gives a reality and force to all the fecondary ideas before fpoken of. Frequent converfation with devout perfons, and frequent reading of devout books, have great efficacy alfo, from the infectioufnefs of our tempers and difpofitions, and from the perpetual recurrency of the proper words, and of their fecondary ideas; firft in a faint ftate, afterwards in a ftronger and ftronger perpetually. The contemplation of the reft of the divine attributes, his omnipotence, omnifcience, eternity, ubiquity, &c. have alfo a tendency to fupport and augment the love of God, when this is fo far advanced, as to be fuperior to the fear; till that time thefe wonderful attributes enhance the fear fo much, as to check the rife and growth of the love for a time. Even the fear itfelf contributes to the generation and augmentation of the love in an eminent degree, and in a manner greatly analogous to the production of other pleafures from pains. And indeed it feems, that, notwithftanding the variety of ways above-mentioned, in which the love of God is generated, and the confequent variety of the intellectual aggregates, and fecondary ideas, there muft be fo great a refemblance amongft them, that they cannot but languifh by frequent recurrency, till fuch time

time as ideas of an oppofite nature, by intervening at certain feafons, give them new life.

The love of God is, according to this theory, evidently deduced in part from interefted motives directly; *viz.* from the hopes of a future reward; and thofe motives to it, or fources of it, in which direct explicit felf-intereft does not appear, may yet be analyfed up to it ultimately. However, after all the feveral fources of the love of God have coalefced together, this affection becomes as difinterefted as any other; as the pleafure we take in any natural or artificial beauty, in the efteem of others, or even in fenfual gratifications.

It appears alfo, that this pure difinterefted love of God may, by the concurrence of a fufficient number of fufficiently ftrong affociations. arife to fuch an height, as to prevail over any of the other defires interefted or difinterefted; for all, except the fenfual ones, are of a factitious nature, as well as the love of God; and the fenfual ones are, in our progrefs through life, overpowered by them all in their refpective turns.

Enthufiafm may be defined a miftaken perfuafion in any perfon, that he is a peculiar favourite with God; and that he receives fupernatural marks thereof. The vividnefs of the ideas of this clafs eafily generates this falfe perfuafion in perfons of ftrong fancies, little experience in divine things, and narrow underftandings, (and efpecially where the moral fenfe, and the fcrupulofity attending its growth and improvement, are but imperfectly formed), by giving a reality and certainty to all the reveries of a man's own mind, and cementing the affociations in a preternatural manner. It may alfo be eafily contracted by contagion, as daily experience fhews; and indeed more eafily than moft other difpofitions from the glaring language ufed by enthufiafts, and from the

the great flattery and support, which enthusiasm affords to pride and self-conceit.

Of the fear of God.

The fear of God arises from a view of the evils of life, from the threatenings of the scriptures, from the sense of guilt, from the infinity of all God's attributes, from prayer, meditation, reading, and conversation upon these and such-like subjects, in a manner analogous to the love of God. When confined within certain limits, and especially when tempered with love, so as become awe, veneration and reverence, it remains in a natural state, *i. e.* suits our other circumstances; and, as before observed, has a considerable share in generating the love of God. When excessive, or not duly regarded, it degenerates either into superstition or atheism.

Superstition may be defined a mistaken opinion concerning the severity and punishments of God, magnifying these in respect of ourselves or others. It may arise from a sense of guilt, from bodily indisposition, from erroneous reasoning, *&c.* That which arises from the first cause, has a tendency to remove itself by regulating the person's behaviour, and consequently lessening his sense of guilt. The other kinds often increase for a time, come to their height at last, and then decline again. They do also, in some cases, increase without limits during life. All kinds of superstition have been productive of great absurdities in divine worship, both amongst *Pagans*, and amongst *Jews* and *Christians*; and they have all a great tendency to sour the mind, to check natural benevolence and compassion, and to generate a bitter persecuting spirit. All which is much augmented where superstition and enthusiasm pass alternately into each other at intervals; which is no uncommon case.

Under atheism I here comprehend not only the speculative kind, but the practical, or that neglect of God, where the person thinks of him seldom, and with reluctance, and pays little or no regard to him in his actions, though he does not deny him in words. Both kinds seem in christian countries, (where reasonable satisfaction in religious matters is easy to be had by all well-disposed minds, and gross ignorance uncommon except in ill-disposed ones,) to proceed from an explicit or implicit sense of guilt, and a consequent fear of God, sufficient to generate an aversion to the thoughts of him, and to the methods by which the love might be generated, and yet too feeble to restrain from guilt; so that they may properly be considered as degenerations of the fear of God. What has been delivered already in these papers, concerning the connexion of fear, aversion, and the other uneasy passions, with each other; and also of the tendency of all pain to prevent the recurrency of the circumstances, by which it is introduced, may afford some light here.

It appears upon the whole, that the theopathetic affections are, in some things, analogous to the sympathetic ones, as well as different in others; and that this difference arises chiefly from the infinity and absolute perfection of the divine nature.

Affections of an intermediate kind are generated in respect of good and evil beings of an invisible nature, and of an order superior to us (such as angels and devils); whose origin and growth will easily be understood from what is here delivered.

SECT.

SECT. VI.

Of the Pleasures and Pains of the Moral Sense.

PROP. 51.

To examine how far the pleasures and pains of the moral sense are agreeable to the foregoing theory.

THERE are certain tempers of mind, with the actions flowing from them, as of piety, humility, resignation, gratitude, &c. towards God; of benevolence, charity, generosity, compassion, humility, gratitude, &c. towards men; of temperance, patience, contentment, &c. in respect of a person's own private enjoyments or sufferings; which when he believes himself to be possessed of, and reflects upon, a pleasing consciousness and self-approbation rise up in his mind, exclusively of any direct explicit consideration of advantage likely to accrue to himself, from his possession of these good qualities. In like manner the view of them in others raises up a disinterested love and esteem for those others. And the opposite qualities of impiety, profaneness, uncharitableness, resentment, cruelty, envy, ingratitude, intemperance, lewdness, selfishness, &c. are attended with the condemnation both of ourselves and others. This is, in general, the state of the case; but there are many particular differences, according to the particular education, temper, profession, sex, &c. of each person.

Or, which is the same thing, the secondary ideas belonging to virtue and vice, duty and sin, innocence and guilt, merit and demerit, right and wrong, moral good and moral evil, just and unjust, fit and unfit, obligation and prohibition, *&c.* in one man, bear a great resemblance to those belonging to the same words in another, or to the corresponding words, if they have different languages; and yet do not exactly coincide, but differ more or less according to the difference in education, temper, *&c.*

Now both this general resemblance, and these particular differences in our ideas, and consequent approbation or disapprobation, seem to admit of an analysis and explanation from the following particulars.

First, children are, for the most part, instructed in the difference and opposition between virtue and vice, duty and sin, *&c.*; and have some general descriptions of the virtues and vices inculcated upon them. They are told, that the first are good, pleasant, beautiful, noble, fit, worthy of praise and reward, *&c.*; the last odious, painful, shameful, worthy of punishment, *&c.*; so that the pleasing and displeasing associations, previously annexed to these words in their minds, are by means of that confidence which they place in their superiors, transferred upon the virtues and vices respectively. And the mutual intercourses of life have the same effect in a less degree, with respect to adults, and those children who receive little or no instruction from their parents or superiors. Virtue is in general approved and set off by all the encomiums, and honourable appellations, that any other thing admits of, and vice loaded with censures and reproaches of all kinds, in all good conversation and books. And this happens oftener than the contrary, even in bad ones; so that as far as men are influenced in their judgments by those of others, ʻthe balance is, upon the whole, on the side of virtue.

Secondly,

Secondly, there are many immediate good consequences, which attend upon virtue, as many ill ones do upon vice, and that during our whole progress through life. Sensuality and intemperance subject men to diseases and pain, to shame, deformity, filthiness, terrors, and anxieties; whereas temperance is attended with ease of body, freedom of spirits, the capacity of being pleased with the objects of pleasure, the good opinion of others, the perfection of the senses, and of the faculties bodily and mental, long life, plenty, &c. anger, malice, envy, bring upon us the returns of anger, malice, envy, from others, with injuries, reproaches, fears, and perpetual disquietude; and in like manner good-will, generosity, compassion, are rewarded with returns of the same, with the pleasures of sociality and friendship, with good offices, and with the highest encomiums. And when a person becomes properly qualified by the previous love of his neighbour to love God, to hope and trust in him, and to worship him in any measure as he ought to do, this affords the sincerest joy and comfort; as, on the contrary, the neglect of God, or practical atheism, the murmuring against the course of providence, sceptical unsettledness, and fool-hardy impiety, are evidently attended with great anxieties, gloominess, and distraction, as long as there are any traces of morality or religion left upon mens minds. Now these pleasures and pains, by often recurring in various combinations, and by being variously transferred upon each other, from the great affinity between the several virtues and their rewards, with each other; also between the several vices, and their punishments, with each other; will at last beget in us a general, mixed, pleasing idea and consciousness, when we reflect upon our own virtuous affections or actions; a sense of guilt, and an anxiety, when we reflect on the contrary;

trary; and also raise in us the love and esteem of virtue, and the hatred of vice in others.

Thirdly, the many benefits which we receive immediately from, or which have some evident, though distant, connexion with the piety, benevolence, and temperance of others; also the contrary mischiefs from their vices; lead us first to the love and hatred of the persons themselves by association, as explained under the head of sympathy, and then by farther associations to the love and hatred of the virtues and vices, considered abstractedly, and without any regard to our own interest; and that whether we view them in ourselves or others. As our love and esteem for virtue in others is much increased by the pleasing consciousness, which our own practice of it affords to ourselves, so the pleasure of this consciousness is much increased by our love of virtue in others.

Fourthly, the great suitableness of all the virtues to each other, and to the beauty, order, and perfection of the world, animate and inanimate, impresses a very lovely character upon virtue; and the contrary self-contradiction, deformity, and mischievous tendency of vice, render it odious, and matter of abhorrence to all persons that reflect upon these things; and beget a language of this kind, which is borrowed, in great measure, from the pleasures and pains of imagination, and applied with a peculiar force and fitness to this subject from its great importance.

Fifthly, the hopes and fears which arise from the consideration of a future state, are themselves pleasures and pains of a high nature. When therefore a sufficient foundation has been laid by a practical belief of religion, natural and revealed, by the frequent view of, and meditation upon, death, by the loss of departed friends, by bodily pains, by worldly disappointments and afflictions, for forming strong associations of the pleasures of these hopes with duty, and the pains of these fears with sin, the reiterated

reiterated impreſſions of thoſe aſſociations will at laſt make duty itſelf a pleaſure, and convert ſin into a pain, giving a luſtre and deformity reſpectively to all their appellations; and that without any expreſs recollection of the hopes and fears of another world, juſt as in other caſes of aſſociation.

Sixthly, all meditations upon God, who is the inexhauſtible fountain, and infinite abyſs of all perfection, both natural and moral; alſo all the kinds of prayer, *i. e.* all the ways of expreſſing our love, hope, truſt, reſignation, gratitude, reverence, fear, deſire, *&c.* towards him; transfer, by aſſociation, all the perfection, greatneſs, and glorrouſneſs of his natural attributes upon his moral ones, *i. e.* upon moral rectitude. We ſhall by this means learn to be merciful, holy, and perfect, becauſe God is ſo; and to love mercy, holineſs, and perfection, wherever we ſee them.

And thus we may perceive, that all the pleaſures and pains of ſenſation, imagination, ambition, ſelf-intereſt, ſympathy, and theopathy, as far as they are conſiſtent with one another, with the frame of our natures, and with the courſe of the world, beget in us a moral ſenſe, and lead us to the love and approbation of virtue, and to the fear, hatred, and abhorrence of vice. This moral ſenſe therefore carries its own authority with it, inaſmuch as it is the ſum total of all the reſt, and the ultimate reſult from them; and employs the force and authority of the whole nature of man againſt any particular part of it, that rebels againſt the determinations and commands of the conſcience or moral judgment.

It appears alſo, that the moral ſenſe carries us perpetually to the pure love of God, as our higheſt and ultimate perfection, our end, centre, and only reſting place, to which yet we can never attain,

When the moral ſenſe is advanced to conſiderable perfection, a perſon may be made to love and hate, merely

merely becaufe he ought; *i. e.* the pleafures of moral beauty and rectitude, and the pains of moral deformity and unfitnefs, may be transferred, and made to coalefce almoft inftantaneoufly.

Scrupulofity may be confidered as a degeneration of the moral fenfe, refembling that by which the fear of God paffes into fuperftition; for it arifes, like this, from a confcioufnefs of guilt, explicit or implicit, from bodily indifpofition, and from an erroneous method of reafoning. It has alfo a moft intimate connexion with fuperftition (juft as moral rectitude has with the true love and fear of God); and, like fuperftition, it is, in many cafes, obferved to work its own cure by rectifying what is amifs; and fo by degrees removing both the explicit and implicit confcioufnefs of guilt. It feems alfo, that in this imperfect ftate men feldom arrive at any great degree of correctnefs in their actions without fome previous fcrupulofity, by which they may be led to eftimate the nature and confequences of affections and actions with care, impartiality and exactnefs.

The moral fenfe or judgment here fpoken of, is fometimes confidered as an inftinct, fometimes as determinations of the mind, grounded on the eternal reafons and relations of things. Thofe who maintain either of thefe opinions may, perhaps, explain them fo as to be confiftent with the foregoing analyfis of the moral fenfe from affociation. But if by inftinct be meant a difpofition communicated to the brain, and in confequence of this, to the mind, or to the mind alone, fo as to be quite independent of affociation; and by a moral inftinct, fuch a difpofition producing in us moral judgments concerning affections and actions; it will be neceffary, in order to fupport the opinion of a moral inftinct, to produce inftances, where moral judgments arife in us independently of prior affociations determining thereto.

In

In like manner, if by founding the morality of actions, and our judgment concerning this morality, on the eternal reasons and relations of things, be meant, that the reasons drawn from the relations of things, by which the morality or immorality of certain actions is commonly proved, and which, with the relations, are called eternal, from their appearing the same, or nearly the same, to the mind at all times, would determine the mind to form the corresponding moral judgment independently of prior associations, this ought also to be proved by the allegation of proper instances. To me it appears, that the instances are, as far as we can judge of them, of an opposite nature, and favour the deduction of all our moral judgments, approbations, and disapprobations, from association alone. However, some associations are formed so early, repeated so often, riveted so strong, and have so close a connexion with the common nature of man, and the events of life which happen to all, as, in a popular way of speaking, to claim the appellation of original and natural dispositions; and to appear like instincts, when compared with dispositions evidently factitious; also like axioms, and intuitive propositions, eternally true according to the usual phrase, when compared with moral reasonings of a compound kind. But I have endeavoured to shew in these papers that all reasoning, as well as affection, is the mere result of association.

CHAP.

CHAP. V.

A View of the Doctrine of PHILOSOPHICAL NECESSITY.

SECT. I.

General remarks on the mechanism of the human mind.

BESIDES the consequences flowing from the doctrine of association, which are delivered in the corollaries to the 14th proposition, there is another, which is thought by many to have a pernicious tendency in respect of morality and religion; and which therefore it will be proper that I should consider particularly.

The consequence I mean is that of the mechanism or necessity of human actions, in opposition to what is generally termed free-will. Here then I will,

First, state my notion of the mechanism or necessity of human actions.

Secondly, give such reasons as induce me to embrace the opinion of the mechanism of human actions.

Thirdly, consider the objections and difficulties attending this opinion.

And, lastly, alledge some presumptions in favour of it from its consequences.

By the mechanism of human actions I mean, that each action results from the previous circumstances of body and mind, in the same manner, and with the same certainty, as other effects do from their mechanical causes; so that a person cannot do indifferently either of the actions A, and its contrary a, while the previous circumstances are the same; but is under an absolute necessity of doing one of them, and that only. Agreeably to this I suppose, that by free-will is meant a power of doing either the action

A, or its contrary *a*; while the previous circumſtances remain the ſame.

If by free-will be meant a power of beginning motion, this will come to the ſame thing; ſince, according to the opinion of mechaniſm, as here explained, man has no ſuch power; but every action, or bodily motion, ariſes from previous circumſtances, or bodily motions, already exiſting in the brain, *i e.* from vibrations, which are either the immediate effect of impreſſions then made, or the remote compound effect of former impreſſions, or both.

But if by free-will be meant any thing different from theſe two definitions of it, it may not perhaps be inconſiſtent with the mechaniſm of the mind here laid down. Thus, if free-will be defined the power of doing what a perſon deſires or wills to do, of deliberating, ſuſpending, chooſing, *&c.* or of reſiſting the motives of ſenſuality, ambition, reſentment, *&c.* free-will, under certain limitations, is not only conſiſtent with the doctrine of mechaniſm, but even flows from it; ſince it appears from the foregoing theory, that voluntary and ſemivoluntary powers of calling up ideas, of exciting and reſtraining affections, and of performing and ſuſpending actions, ariſe from the mechaniſm of our natures. This may be called free-will in the popular and practical ſenſe, in contradiſtinction to that, which is oppoſed to mechaniſm, and which may be called free-will in the philoſophical ſenſe.

I proceed now to the arguments which favour the opinion of mechaniſm.

Firſt, then, it is evident to, and allowed by all, that the actions of mankind proceed, in many caſes, from motives, *i. e.* from the influence which the pleaſures and pains of ſenſation, imagination, ambition, ſelf-intereſt, ſympathy, theopathy, and the moral ſenſe, have over them. And theſe motives ſeem to act like all other cauſes. When the motive is ſtrong, the action is performed with vigour; when weak, feebly.

feebly. When a contrary motive intervenes, it checks or over-rules, in proportion to its relative strength, as far as one can judge. So that where the motives are the same, the actions cannot be different; where the motives are different, the actions cannot be the same. And it is matter of common observation, that this is the case in fact, in the principal actions of life, and such where the motives are of a magnitude sufficient to be evident. It is reasonable therefore to interpret the obscure cases by the evident ones; and to infer, that there are in all instances motives of a proper kind and degree, which generate each action; though they are sometimes not seen through their minuteness, or through the inattention or ignorance of the observer. Agreeably to which those persons who study the causes and motives of human actions, may decypher them much more completely, both in themselves, and those with whom they converse, than others can.

Suppose now a person able to decypher all his own actions in this way, so as to shew that they corresponded in kind and degree to the motives arising from the seven classes of pleasures and pains considered in this theory; also able to decypher the principal actions of others in the same way: this would be as good evidence, that motives were the mechanical causes of actions, as natural phænomena are for the mechanical operation of heat, diet, or medicines. Or if he could not proceed so far, but was able only to decypher most of his own actions, and many of the principal ones of others, still the evidence would scarce be diminished thereby, if the deficiency was no more than is reasonably to be expected from our ignorance and inattention, in respect of ourselves and others. Let the reader make the trial, especially upon himself, since such a self-examination cannot but be profitable, and may perhaps be pleasant; and that either according to the seven classes of pleasures and pains here laid down, or any other division,

vision, and judge as he thinks fit upon mature deliberation.

It may be of use in such an inquiry into a man's self, as I here propose, for him to consider in a short time after any material action is past, whether, if he was once more put into the same rigidly exact circumstances, he could possibly do otherwise than as he did. Here the power of imagination will intervene, and be apt to deceive the inquirer, unless he be cautious. For in this review other motives, besides those which did actually influence him, will start up; and that especially if the action be such as he wishes to have been performed with more vigour or less, or not to have been performed at all. But when these foreign motives are set aside, and the imagination confined to those which did in fact take place, it will appear impossible, as it seems to me, that the person should have done otherwise than the very thing which he did.

Secondly, according to the theory here laid down, all human actions proceed from vibrations in the nerves of the muscles, and these from others, which are either evidently of a mechanical nature, as in the automatic motions; or else have been shewn to be so in the account given of the voluntary motions.

And if the doctrine of vibrations be rejected, and sensation and muscular motion be supposed to be performed by some other kind of motion in the nervous parts, still it seems probable, that the same method of reasoning might be applied to this other kind of motion.

Lastly, to suppose that the action A, or its contrary a, can equally follow previous circumstances, that are exactly the same, appears to me the same thing, as affirming that one or both of them might start up into being without any cause; which, if admitted, appears to me to destroy the foundation of all general abstract reasoning; and particularly of that whereby the existence of the first cause is proved.

One of the principal objections to the opinion of mechanism is that deduced from the existence of the moral sense, whose history I have just given. But it appears from that history, that God has so formed the world, and perhaps (with reverence be it spoken) was obliged by his moral perfections so to form it, as that virtue must have amiable and pleasing ideas affixed to it; vice, odious ones. The moral sense is therefore generated necessarily and mechanically. And it remains to be inquired, whether the amiable and odious ideas above shewed to be necessarily affixed to virtue and vice respectively, though differently, according to the different events of each person's life, do not answer all the purposes of making us ultimately happy in the love of God, and of our neighbour; and whether they are not, *cæteris paribus*, the same intirely, or at least in all material respects, in those who believe mechanism, who believe free-will, and who have not entered into the discussion of the question at all; or if there be a difference, whether the associations arising from the opinion of necessity, do not tend more to accelerate us in our progress to the love of God, our only true happiness. It appears to me, that the difference is in general very small; also that this difference, whatever it be, is of such a nature as to be a presumption in favour of the doctrine of necessity, all things being duly considered.

When a person first changes his opinion from free-will to mechanism, or more properly first sees part of the mechanism of the mind, and believes the rest from analogy, he his just as much affected by his wonted pleasures and pains, hopes and fears, as before, by the moral and religious ones, as by others. And the being persuaded, that certain things have a necessary influence to change his mind for the better or the worse, *i.e.* so as to receive more sensible sympathetic, religious pleasures, or otherwise, will force him still more strongly upon the right method, *i. e.* put him upon inquiring after and pursuing this method.

If

If it be objected, that the moral sense supposes, that we refer actions to ourselves and others, whereas the opinion of mechanism annihilates all these associations, by which we refer actions to ourselves or others; I answer, that it does this just as the belief of the reality and infinite value of the things of another world annihilates all the regards to this world. Both have a tendency to these respective ends, which are indeed one and the same at the bottom; but both require time, in order to produce their full effects. When religion has made any one indifferent to this world, its pleasures and pains, then the kingdom of God, or pure unmixed happiness, comes in respect of him; so that he may then well refer all to God. However, a man may be thoroughly satisfied in a cool deliberate way, that honours, riches, &c. can afford no solid happiness; and yet desire them at certain times, eagerly perhaps, from former associations. But such a thorough general conviction, applied previously to the particular instances, is a great help in time of temptation, and will gradually destroy the wrong associations. In like manner, the opinion that God is the one only cause of all things, has a tendency to beget the most absolute resignation, and must be a great support in grievous trials and sufferings.

We may shew by a like method of reasoning, that the affections of gratitude and resentment, which are intimately connected with the moral sense, remain notwithstanding the doctrine of mechanism. For it appears from the account of resentment above delivered, that this, and by consequence gratitude, in their nascent state, are equally exerted towards all things, animate and inanimate, that are equally connected with pleasure and pain. By degrees all succeeding circumstances are left out, and our love and hatred confined to preceding ones, which we consider as the only causes. We then leave out inanimate objects intirely, brutes and children in most circumstances, and adults

adults in some. All which is chiefly done, because acknowledgments, rewards, threatenings, and punishments, with the other associated circumstances of gratitude and resentment, can have no use but with respect to living intelligent beings. By farther degrees we learn such a use of the words, cause and effect, as to call nothing a cause, whose cause, or preceding circumstance, we can see, denominating all such things mere effects, all others causes. And thus, because the secret springs of action in men are frequently concealed, both from the by-stander, and even from the agent himself, or not attended to, we consider men in certain circumstances as real causes; and intelligent beings, as the only ones that can be real causes; and thus confine our gratitude and resentment to them : whence it seems to follow, that as soon as we discover created intelligent beings not to be real causes, we should cease to make them the objects either of gratitude or resentment. But this is, in great measure, speculation ; for it will appear to every attentive person, that benevolence, compassion, &c. are amiable, and the objects of gratitude, envy and malice the contrary, from whatever causes they proceed, *i. e.* he will find his mind so formed already by association, that he cannot with-hold his gratitude or resentment: and it has been my business in the foregoing analysis of the affections, to point out the several methods by which this and such-like things are brought about. And for the same reasons, a person must ascribe merit and demerit, which are also intimately connected with the moral sense, to created intelligent beings, though he may have a full persuasion, that they are not real causes.

It does indeed appear, that this is owing to our present imperfect state, in which we begin with the idolatry of the creature, with the worship of every associated circumstance; and that as we advance in perfection, the associations relating to the one only ultimate, infinite cause, must at last overpower all the rest;

of the Human Mind. 341

rest; that we shall pay no regards but to God alone; and that all resentment, demerit, sin, and misery, will be utterly annihilated and absorbed by his infinite happiness and perfections. For our associations being in this, as in many other cases, inconsistent with each other, our first gross and transitory ones must yield to those which succeed and remain.

While any degree of resentment, or unpleasing affection is left, it may be shewn, that the same associations which keep it up, will turn it upon the creatures, and particularly upon ourselves. And, on the other hand, when the consideration of the ultimate cause seems ready to turn it from ourselves, it will also shew that it ought to be annihilated.

These may be considered as general remarks, tending to remove the difficulties arising from the consideration of the moral sense. I will now state the principal objections to the opinion of mechanism, in a direct, but short way, adding such hints as appear to me to afford a solution of them.

First, then, it may be said, that a man may prove his own free-will by internal feeling. This is true, if by free-will be meant the power of doing what a man wills or desires; or of resisting the motives of sensuality, ambition, &c. *i. e.* free-will in the popular and practical sense. Every person may easily recollect instances, where he has done these several things. But then these are intirely foreign to the present question. To prove that a man has free-will in the sense opposite to mechanism, he ought to feel, that he can do different things, while the motives remain precisely the same: and here I apprehend the internal feelings are intirely against free-will, where the motives are of a sufficient magnitude to be evident; where they are not, nothing can be proved.

Secondly, it may be said, that unless a man have free-will, he is not an agent. I answer, that this is true, if agency be so defined as to include free-will. But if agency have its sense determined, like other words,

words, from the associated appearances, the objection falls at once. A man may speak, handle, love, fear, &c, intirely by mechanism.

Thirdly, it may be said, that the denial of free-will in man is the denial of it in God also. But to this it may be answered, that one does not know how to put the question in respect of God, supposing free-will to mean the power of doing different things, the previous circumstances remaining the same, without gross anthropomorphitism. It does not at all follow, however, because man is subject to a necessity ordained by God, that God is subject to a prior necessity. On the contrary, according to the doctrine of mechanism, God is the cause of causes, the one only source of all power.

Fourthly, it may be said, that men are perpetually imposed upon, unless they have free-will, since they think they have. But here again free-will is put for the power of doing what a man wills or desires, &c.; for, in the sense opposite to mechanism, few persons have ever entered into the discussion of the point at all; and those who do with sufficient attention, cannot but determine against free-will, as it seems to me.

Fifthly, it may be said, that the doctrine of mechanism destroys the notion of a particular providence altering the course of nature so as to suit it to the actions of men. I answer, that laying down philosophical free-will, such an alteration in the course of nature may perhaps be necessary. But if man's actions, and the course of nature, be both fixed, they may be suited to each other in the best possible manner; which is all that can be required, in order to vindicate God's attributes, as well as all that man can desire.

Sixthly, it may be said, that all motives to good actions, and particularly to prayer, are taken away by denying free-will. I answer, that according to the mechanical system, prayer and good actions are the means for obtaining happiness; and that the belief

lief of this is the ftrongeft of motives to impel men to prayer and good works.

Seventhly, it may be faid, that the denial of free-will deftroys the diftinction between virtue and vice. I anfwer, that this is according as thefe words are defined. If free-will be included in the definition of virtue, then there can be no virtue without free-will. But if virtue be defined obedience to the will of God, a courfe of action proceeding from the love of God, or from benevolence, &c. free-will is not at all neceffary; fince thefe affections and actions may be brought about mechanically.

A folution analogous to this may be given to the objection taken from the notions of merit and demerit. Let the words be defined, and they will either include free-will, or, not including it, will not require it; fo that the propofition, *merit implies free-will*, will either be identical, or falfe.

Eighthly, it may be faid, that the doctrine of mechanifm makes God the author of fin. I anfwer, that till we arrive at felf-annihilation, fin always will, and ought to appear to arife from ourfelves; and that, when we are arrived thither, fin and evil of every kind vanifh. I anfwer alfo, that the doctrine of philofophical free-will does not remove our difficulties and perplexities, in refpect of the moral attributes of God, unlefs by transferring them upon the natural ones; *i. e.* by our fuppofing that fome prior neceffity compelled God to beftow free-will on his creatures. It feems equally difficult, in every way, to account for the origin of evil, natural or moral, confiftently with the infinity of the power, knowledge, and goodnefs of God. If we fuppofe, that all tends to happinefs ultimately, this removes the difficulty fo far as to produce acquiefcence in the will of God, and thankfulnefs to him; and that juft as much upon the fyftem of mechanifm as that of free-will. Moral evil has no difficulty in it, befides what arifes from the natural evil attending it.

Ninthly,

Ninthly, it may be said, that the exhortations of the scriptures presuppose free-will. I answer, that they are to be considered as motives impelling the will, and contributing, as far as they are attended to, to rectify it. A parent who believes the doctrine of mechanism may, consistently with it, or rather must necessarily, in consequence of this belief, exhort his child. Therefore God, who is pleased to call himself our heavenly father, may do the same. And if we embrace the opinion of universal restoration, then all the exhortations contained both in the word and works of God, will produce their genuine effect, and concur to work in us dispositions fit to receive happiness ultimately.

I come now to hint some consequences of the doctrine of mechanism, which seem to me to be strong presumptions in its favour.

First, then, it intirely removes the great difficulty of reconciling the prescience of God with the free-will of man. For it takes away philosophical free-will, and the practical is consistent with God's prescience.

Secondly, it has a tendency to beget the most profound humility and self annihilation; since, according to this, we are intirely destitute of all power and perfection in ourselves, and are what we are intirely by the grace and goodness of God.

Thirdly, it has a tendency to abate all resentment against men. Since all that they do against us is by the appointment of God, it is rebellion against Him to be offended with them.

Fourthly, it greatly favours the doctrine of universal restoration. Since all that is done is by the appointment of God, it cannot but end well at last.

Fifthly, it has a tendency to make us labour more earnestly with ourselves and others, particularly children, from the greater certainty attending all endeavours that operate in a mechanical way.

Lastly,

of the Human Mind.

Laftly, there are many well-known paffages of fcripture, which cannot be reconciled to the doctrine of philofophical free-will, without the greateft harfhnefs of interpretation.

It may alfo be objected to the whole foregoing theory, as well as to the doctrine of vibrations in particular, that it is unfavourable to the immateriality of the foul; and, by confequence, to its immortality. But to this I anfwer, that I am reduced to the neceffity of making a *poftulatum* at the entrance of my inquiries; which precludes all poffibility of proving the materiality of the foul from this theory afterwards. Thus I fuppofe, or poftulate, in my firft propofition, that fenfations arife in the foul from motions excited in the medullary fubftance of the brain. I do indeed bring fome arguments from phyfiology and pathology, to fhew this to be a reafonable *poftulatum*, when underftood in a general fenfe; for it is all one to the purpofe of the foregoing theory, whether the motions in the medullary fubftance be the phyfical caufe of the fenfations, according to the fyftem of the fchools; or the occafional caufe, according to *Malebranche*; or only an adjunct, according to *Leibnitz*. However, this is not fuppofing matter to be endued with fenfation, or any way explaining what the foul is; but only taking its exiftence, and connexion with the bodily organs in the moft fimple cafe, for granted, in order to make farther inquiries. Agreeably to which I immediately proceed to determine the fpecies of the motion, and by determining it, to caft light on fome important and obfcure points relating to the connexion between the body and the foul in complex cafes.

It does indeed follow from this theory, that matter, if it could be endued with the moft fimple kinds of fenfation, might alfo arrive at all that intelligence of which the human mind is poffeffed: whence this theory muft be allowed to overturn all the arguments which are ufually brought for the immateriality of the foul from the fubtlety of the internal fenfes,

and

and of the rational faculty. But I no-ways presume to determine whether matter can be endued with sensation or no. This is a point foreign to the purpose of my inquiries. It is sufficient for me, that there is a certain connexion, of one kind or other, between the sensations of the soul, and the motions excited in the medullary substance of the brain; which is what all physicians and philosophers allow.

I would not therefore be any-way interpreted so as to oppose the immateriality of the soul. On the contrary, I see clearly, and acknowledge readily, that matter and motion, however subtly divided, or reasoned upon, yield nothing more than matter and motion still. But then neither would I affirm, that this consideration affords a proof of the soul's immateriality. In like manner the unity of consciousness seems to me an inconclusive argument. For consciousness is a mental perception; and if perception be a monad, then every inseparable adjunct of it must be so too, *i. e*, vibrations, according to this theory, which is evidently false. Not to mention that it is difficult to know what is meant by the unity of consciousness.

But it is most worthy of notice, that the immateriality of the soul has little or no connexion with its immortality; and that we ought to depend upon Him who first breathed into man the breath of the present life, for our resurrection to a better. *All live unto Him.* And if we depend upon any thing else besides Him, for any blessing, we may be said so far to renounce our allegiance to Him, and to idolize that upon which we depend.

SECT.

SECT. II.

PROP. 1.

Religion presupposes free-will in the popular and practical sense; i. e. it presupposes a voluntary power over our affections and actions.

FOR religion being the regulation of our affections and actions according to the will of God, it presupposes, that after this will is made known to us, and we, in consequence thereof, become desirous of complying with it, a sufficient power of complying with it should be put into our hands. Thus, for instance, since religion commands us to love God and our neighbour, it presupposes that we have the power of generating these affections in ourselves, by introducing the proper generating causes, and making the proper associations, *i. e.* by meditation, religious conversation, reading practical books of religion, and prayer. Since religion requires of us to perform beneficent actions, and to abstain from injurious ones, also to abstain from all those self-indulgencies which would be hurtful to ourselves, it presupposes, either that we have a power of so doing, or at least a power of generating such dispositions of mind, as will enable us so to do. Farther, it presupposes that we have a power of making perpetual improvement in virtuous affections and actions, since this also is required of us by it. Still farther, since religion requires of a man this regulation of his affections and actions, and since the powers hitherto mentioned are all grounded upon a sufficient desire thus to regulate himself, it must presuppose a power of generating this sufficient desire, and so on till we come to something which the man is already possessed of, as part of his mental frame, either conferred in a supernatural way, or acquired in the usual course of nature. For religion, in requiring the powers above-mentioned, requires also whatever previous powers are neceffary to the actual exertion of thefe powers. But all thefe powers, of whatever order they are, the laft excepted, are thofe powers over our affections and actions, which I have, in the foregoing part of this work, endeavoured to derive from affociation, and fhewn to be the fame with thofe which are commonly called voluntary powers. It follows, therefore, that religion requires voluntary powers over our affections and actions, or free-will in the popular and practical fenfe.

This may be illuftrated by the confideration of the ftate of madmen, idiots, children, and brutes, in refpect of religion. For as they are all efteemed to be incapable of religion, and exempted from the obligation thereof, fo the reafon of this in all is evidently, that they are deftitute of the proper voluntary powers over their affections and actions; the affociations requifite thereto having never been formed in idiots, children, and brutes, and being confounded and deftroyed in madmen. For fuppofe the child to be grown up, and the madman to recover his fenfes, *i. e.* fuppofe the affociations requifite for the voluntary powers to be generated or reftored, and religion will claim them as its proper fubjects.

In like manner, it may be obferved, that when any action is commended or blamed, this is always done upon fuppofition, that the action under confideration was the effect of voluntary powers. Thus when a man commits an action otherwife blameable, through inattention, ignorance, or difeafe, he is excufed on account of its being involuntary; unlefs the inattention, ignorance, or difeafe, were themfelves voluntary, and then the blame remains. But commendation and blame are ideas that belong to religion: it appears therefore, that voluntary powers muft belong to it alfo.

I afferted above, that religion not only requires and prefuppofes the common voluntary powers, by which we *of* the Human Mind.

we perform and forbear actions, and new model our affections, but alſo whatever elſe, voluntary or involuntary, is neceſſary for the actual exertion of theſe powers. And the connexion between theſe points ſeems to be immediate and undeniable; to require any thing, muſt be to require all that is neceſſary for that thing. And yet ſince all men do not act up to the precepts of religion, it ſeems undeniable, on the other hand, that ſome want ſomething that is neceſſary, immediately or mediately, for the actual exertion of the proper voluntary powers over their affections and actions. Now I ſee no way of extricating ourſelves from this difficulty, but by ſuppoſing that thoſe who want this one neceſſary thing at preſent, will, however, obtain it hereafter, and that they who ſhall obtain it at any diſtant future time, may be ſaid to have obtained it already, in the eye of him to whom paſt, preſent, and future, are all preſent, *who quickeneth the dead, and calleth the things that be not as though they were.* For that the ſuppoſition of free-will, in the philoſophical ſenſe, cannot ſolve this difficulty, will appear, I think in the next propoſition.

COROLLARY. It may be reckoned ſome confirmation of religion, that the voluntary powers which it requires according to this propoſition, are an evident fact, and alſo that they are deducible from the frame of our natures, *i. e.* from our original faculties, and the law of aſſociation, taken together. For thus religion may be ſaid to harmonize with obſervation. and with the nature of man, its ſubject.

SECT.

SECT. III.

PROP. 2.

Religion does not prefuppofe free-will in the philofophical fenfe; i. e. *It does not prefuppofe a power of doing different things, the previous circumftances remaining the fame.*

FOR, firft, it has been fhewn, in the foregoing part of this work, that we do not, in fact, ever exert any fuch power in the important actions of our lives, or the ftrong workings of our affections, all thefe being evidently determinable by the previous circumftances. There are therefore no actions or affections left, except trifling and evanefcent ones, in which religion can prefuppofe philofophical free-will, or liberty; and even here the evidence for it is merely an *argumentum ab ignorantiâ*. But if religion requires philofophical liberty at all, it muft require it chiefly in the moft important actions and affections. It does not therefore require it at all. We cannot fuppofe religion to be at variance with common obfervation, and the frame of our natures.

Secondly, fome reafons have been given already, in the firft part of this work, and more will be added in the next propofition, to fhew that philofophical liberty cannot take place in man, but is an impoffibility. It is therefore impoffible, that religion fhould require it.

Thirdly, it appears from the courfe of reafoning ufed under the foregoing propofition, that all which religion does require and prefuppofe, is, firft, a fufficient defire, hope, fear, felf-intereft, or other fuch like motive, and then fufficient voluntary powers, whereby to regulate our affections and actions agreeably to the will of God. But philofophical liberty, or the power of doing different things, the previous circumftances remaining the fame, is fo far from being

ing required, in order to our obtaining any of thefe requifites, that it is inconfiftent with them. For the fufficient defire, &c. unlefs it be given by God in a fupernatural way, is of a factitious nature, and follows the previous circumftances with a rigorous exactnefs; in like manner the voluntary powers are all generated according to the law of affociation, which law operates in a mechanical, neceffary way, and admits of no variations, while the circumftances remain the fame; all which is, I prefume, fufficiently evident to thofe who have well confidered the foregoing part of this work. Thefe requifites are therefore inconfiftent with philofophical liberty, inafmuch as this implies, that though there be a defire fufficient to caufe the exertion of the will, this exertion may or may not follow; alfo, that though the voluntary powers depending on this exertion be completely generated by affociation, they may or may not follow it in fact. This fuppofition is indeed abfurd at firft fight; however, if it be admitted for a moment, in order to fee what would follow, it is manifeft, that the man will be rendered lefs able to comply with the will of God thereby, and that it will not add to, but take away from, the requifites propofed by religion. Philofophical liberty does not therefore help us to folve the difficulty mentioned under the laft propofition, but on the contrary increafes it.

If it fhould be faid that we are not to fuppofe the defire fufficient, and the voluntary powers complete, and then farther to fuppofe, that thefe may or may not take effect, but only to fuppofe defire in general, fufficient or infufficient, and voluntary powers in general complete or incomplete, and that thus it will not be unreafonable to fuppofe, that they may or may not take effect; whence the manifeft abfurdity mentioned in the laft paragraph will be removed; I anfwer, that this is to defert the hypothefis of philofophical liberty, the previous circumftances being
fup-

supposed different, that so their consequences may be different also. If any particular degree of desire or voluntary power be fixed upon, and all the other concurring circumstances of body and mind fixed likewise, *i. e.* if the previous circumstances be rigorously determinate, which is the supposition of philosophical liberty, this one fixed, determinate degree of desire, or voluntary power, cannot have the two opposite epithets of sufficient and insufficient, or of complete and incomplete, both predicated of it with truth, define sufficiency or completeness as you please. Philosophical liberty does not therefore allow us to suppose desire or voluntary power in general, in order that they either may or may not take effect.

Fourthly, it will appear, that religion does not presuppose philosophical liberty, if we enter upon the examination of those arguments which are commonly brought to shew that it does. These are, that unless philosophical liberty be admitted, there will be no foundation for commendation or blame, and consequently no difference between virtue and vice; that all punishment for actions usually called vicious, will be unjust; and that God will be the author of such actions, which it is impious to suppose; inasmuch as the notion of popular liberty is not sufficient to obviate these difficulties. Now, to this, I answer, that there are two different methods of speaking, and, as it were, two different languages, used upon these subjects; the one popular, and, when applied to God, anthropomorphitical; the other philosophical; and that the notion of popular liberty is sufficient to obviate these difficulties, while we keep to the popular language alone; also, that the philosophical language does of itself obviate these difficulties, while we keep to it alone; but that, if we mix these languages, then, and not till then, insuperable difficulties will arise, as might well be expected. Let us consider each of these positions particularly.

First then, I say that the supposition of popular liberty

liberty is sufficient to obviate the forementioned difficulties, whilst we keep to the popular language alone. For, in the popular language, a man is commended and blamed merely for the right or wrong use of his voluntary powers; the first is called virtue, the last vice; and rewards and punishments are said to be respectively due to them. Thus, when a man having an opportunity to do a beneficent action, exerts an act of will, and, in consequence thereof does it, he is commended for it; it is called a virtue, or a right use of his voluntary powers, and is said to deserve a reward; whereas, had he, in like circumstances, done a malevolent action, he would have been blamed for it; it would have been called a wrong use of his voluntary powers, or a vice; and a punishment inflicted upon him, in consequence hereof, would have been said to be just. This is a mere history of the fact, and a narration of the method in which the words here considered acquire their proper senses; and I appeal to the general tenor of writings and discourses for the support of what is here asserted. If no voluntary action be exerted, the words commendation, right use, virtue, reward, on one hand, also the words, blame, wrong use, vice, punishment, on the other, become intirely unapplicable. If there be, and the motive be good, suppose piety or benevolence the first set of words take place; if the motive be bad, the last. Men, in the common use of language, never consider whether the agent had it in his power to have done otherwise, the previous circumstances remaining the same; they only require that he should have done a beneficent action, from a benevolent intention. If they find this, they will apply the words, commendation, right use, &c. And the same holds in respect of injurious actions, and malevolent intentions. The agent will, in this case, be blamed, and said to be justly punished, without any farther inquiry. Sometimes, indeed, they do inquire farther, *viz.* into the

original

original of thefe intentions. But then this comes to the fame thing at laft; for if thefe intentions were generated voluntarily, it enhances the commendation or blame due to them; if, in great meafure, involuntarily, abates it. Popular liberty, or voluntary powers, do therefore afford fufficient foundation for commendation and blame, for the difference between virtue and vice, and for the juftice, of punifhing vice according to the popular language. Where it is to be remarked, that whatever will juftify punifhments inflicted by men, will juftify thofe inflicted by God in like circumftances, fince juftice is afcribed to God only in a popular and anthropomorphitical fenfe.

And as popular liberty fuffices for the forementioned purpofes, whilft we ufe the popular language, fo it vindicates God from the charge of being the author of fin, according to the fame language. For, according to this, all voluntary actions are afcribed to men, not to God; but fin, or vice, always prefuppofes an exertion of a voluntary power, according to the popular language; therefore fin muft be afcribed to man, and not to God, as long as we continue to fpeak the popular language.

Secondly, I fay, that if we keep to the philofophical language alone, it will obviate all difficulties, and enable us to talk confiftently and clearly upon thefe fubjects. For, according to this, virtue and vice are to actions, what fecondary qualities are to natural bodies; *i. e.* only ways of expreffing the relation which they bear to happinefs and mifery, juft as the fecondary qualities of bodies are only modifications of the primary ones. And the fame may be faid of all the other words belonging to the moral fenfe. Hence it follows, that, according to the philofophical language, we are to confider all the moral appellations of actions, as only denoting their relation to natural good and evil, and that moral good and evil are only compofitions and decompofitions

of

of natural. There is, however, a difference between moral good and moral evil, becaufe they are different and oppofite compofitions; they may alfo be attended with different and oppofite compofitions, from the frame of our natures, and circumftances of our lives, fuch as commendation and blame.

And as juftice in God is, by the fame language, exalted into benevolence, he may inflict punifhment, *i. e.* another fpecies of natural evil, juftly, provided it be confiftent with benevolence, *i. e.* with a balance of happinefs. Man may alfo inflict punifhment juftly, provided he does it according to fome definition of juftice amongft men, previoufly fettled and allowed, fuppofe compliance with the will of God, the laws of fociety, the greater good of the whole, &c.

Farther, fince all the actions of man proceed ultimately from God, the one univerfal caufe, we muft, according to this language, annihilate felf, and afcribe all to God. But then, fince vice, fin, &c. are only modifications and compofitions of natural evil, according to the fame language, this will only be to afcribe natural evil to him; and, if the balance of natural good be infinite, then even this natural evil will be abforbed and annihilated by it.

It may a little illuftrate what his here delivered, to remark, that as we fhould not fay of a fuperior being, whofe fight could penetrate to the ultimate conftitution of bodies, that he diftinguifhed colours, but rather, that he diftinguifhed thofe modifications of matter which produce the appearances of colours in us, fo we ought not to afcribe our fecondary ideas of virtue and vice to fuperior intelligences, and much lefs to the fupreme.

Thirdly, I fay, that if we mix thefe two languages, many difficulties and abfurdities muft enfue from this previous abfurdity. Thus, if, retaining the popular notions of moral good and evil, we fuppofe God, according

according to the philofophical language, to be benevolent only, *i. e.* to regard only natural good and evil, or to be the author of all actions, the confequence will be impious. If we adhere to the philofophical notions of virtue and vice, we muft not retain the popular notion of God's juftice, inafmuch as punifhment will then be unjuft ; as it will alfo be, if we join the popular notion of God's juftice with the philofophical one, of his being the author of all actions. Laftly, if we allow man to confider himfelf as the author of his own actions, he muft alfo confider virtue and vice according to the popular notions, and conceive of God as endued with the popular attribute of juftice, in order to be incited to virtue, and deterred from vice ; whereas, could man really annihilate himfelf, and refer all to God, perfect love would caft out fear, he would immediately become partaker of the divine nature, and, being one with God, would fee him to be pure benevolence and love, and all that he has made to be good.

The following remark may perhaps contribute to illuftrate this matter. Virtue and vice, merit and demerit, reward and punifhment, are applied to voluntary actions only, as before-mentioned. Hence they are efteemed unapplicable to involuntary ones. But involuntary actions are neceffary by a neceffity *ab extra*, which is generally feen ; and becaufe the neceffity *ab intra*, which caufes voluntary actions, is feldom feen, thefe are fuppofed not to be neceffary. Hence not neceffary and neceffary, are put for voluntary and involuntary, refpectively ; and moral appellations fuppofed peculiar to the firft, *i. e.* not neceffary ; inconfiftent with the laft, *i. e.* neceffary. Hence, when we come to difcover our miftake, and to find, that voluntary actions are neceffary, an inconfiftency arifes ; we apply moral appellations to them as voluntary from a primary affociation, deny thefe appellations of them on account of their new denomination

of

of neceffary, and a fecondary and tralatitious affociation. Here then, if we can either perfift in our miftake, and ftill fuppofe voluntary actions not to be neceffary, or, finding this miftake, can however perfift to apply moral appellations to fuch neceffary actions as are voluntary, from the primary affociation; or, laftly, not being able to withftand the force of the fecondary affociation, whereby moral appellations are denied of neceffary actions, voluntary as well as involuntary, can perceive that moral good and evil are only compofitions of natural, *i. e.* if we can either fee the whole truth, or fhut our eyes againft that part that offends us; no difficulty will arife.

Philofophical liberty is alfo fuppofed by fome neceffary, in order to folve the origin of evil, and to juftify the eternity of punifhment; and the obviating of thefe difficulties is brought as an argument in fupport of it. Now here I obferve,

Firft, that the origin of evil may be made confiftent with the benevolence of God, by fuppofing that every creature has a balance of happinefs; and, confequently, fince this is a fuppofition highly probable, there feems to be little need of philofophical liberty for this purpofe.

Secondly, that, fince this fuppofition is highly probable, the eternity of punifhment is highly improbable; and, confequently, that philofophical liberty may be needlefs here alfo.

Thirdly, that philofophical liberty will not folve the origin of evil. The method of reafoning ufed here is fome fuch as this. If man have not philofophical liberty, but always does the fame thing, where the previous circumftances are the fame, then all his actions are to be referred to God; confequently, if he have philofophical liberty, all his actions need not be referred to God; he is an independent creature in fome things, and is himfelf alone chargeable with fome of his actions. Let man act wrong in thefe in-

Of the Mechanism

dependent cases, and the evil which follows will be chargeable upon man, and not God; *i. e.* the origin of evil will be accounted for. But here it is to be observed, that there are some evils, or sufferings, which cannot be supposed to arise from the abuse of free-will in the creature that suffers, as in the pains which happen to children just born, and to brutes. These evils are not therefore chargeable upon *them.* If, therefore, they be chargeable upon free-will, it must be the free-will of some other creature. But this is as great a difficulty, as that which it is brought to solve; and cannot be solved but by supposing that God gives a balance of happiness to *A*, for what he suffers from *B*. Now this supposition, in its full extent, will solve the first difficulty, and make the hypothesis of free-will intirely unnecessary, as observed above. But, besides this, it is to be considered, that since free-will is thus the occasion of introducing evil into the world, the restless, selfish, objecting creature will ask why he has free-will, since it is not this, but happiness, which *he* desires, and hoped from the divine benevolence, the attribute now to be vindicated. He that produces any cause, does, in effect, produce the thing caused. To give a being a power of making itself miserable, if this being use that power, is just the same thing, in him who has infinite power and knowledge, as directly making him miserable; and appears to be no otherwise consistent with benevolence to that being, than upon supposition, that superior happiness is conferred upon him afterwards. Now this removes the difficulty in the case of necessity, as well as of free-will, in the eye of reason, of an infinite being; and clashes less and less without limits with the imagination, as we advance in intellect, disinterestedness, and absolute resignation to God.

If it be said, that God could not but bestow free-will upon his creatures, I answer, that this is *gratis dictum*,

dictum, there not being the least appearance of evidence for it; also, that it is making God subject to a necessity superior to himself, which would be to raise a greater difficulty than it solves. And, upon the whole, we may conclude, that the supposition of free-will, or liberty, in the philosophical sense, does not at all help us to account for the origin of evil.

Fourthly, since free-will cannot account for finite evil, much less can it account for infinite, *i.e.* for the eternity of punishment. And indeed many, who receive free-will, do, however, see its insufficiency for this purpose, and, in consequence thereof, believe that the punishments of a future state will not be eternal. It is true, indeed, that the arguments against the eternity of punishment are shorter, stronger, and clearer, upon the supposition of necessity, of God's being the real, ultimate author of all actions, than upon the supposition of free-will. But then this seems, if all things be duly considered, to be rather a presumption in favour of the doctrine of necessity, than otherwise.

The invention and application of the hypothesis of free-will, for the vindication of the divine benevolence, has probably arisen from the application of what passes in human affairs, in too strict a manner, to the relation between the creator and his creatures; *i. e.* to an anthropomorphitism of too gross a kind. Thus the actions of a son are free, in respect of his father; *i.e.* though the father can, and does influence the son in many things, yet the son's actions depend upon many circumstances, impressions, associations, *&c.* in which the father has no concern. It will therefore be a sufficient vindication of the father's benevolence to the son, if he has taken care, that the son suffers nothing from the things over which the father has power. What evils happen to the son, from quarters where the son is free in respect

spect of his father, *i. e.* uninfluenced by him, thefe are no-ways to be referred to the father. Now, it is very natural for humble and pious men, in confidering the fins and miferies of mankind, to fuppofe that we have fome fuch powers independent of God; and that all the evil, which happens to each perfon, is to be derived from thefe independent powers. But then this notion fhould not be haftily and blindly embraced and maintained, without an examination of the fact, and of the confiftency of fuch a notion with piety, in other refpects. The firft of thefe points I have already confidered in the foregoing part of this work; the laft I fhall now confider in the following propofition.

SECT.

SECT. IV.

PROP. 3.

The natural attributes of God, or his infinite power and knowledge, exclude the possibility of free-will in the philosophical sense.

FOR, to suppose that man has a power independent of God, is to suppose, that God's power does not extend to all things, *i. e.* is not infinite. If it be said, that the power itself depends upon God, but the exertion of it upon man, the same difficulty will recur; since the exertion does not depend upon God, there will be something produced in the world, which is not the effect of his power; *i. e.* his power will not extend to all things, consequently not be infinite. And the same thing holds, if we refine farther, and proceed to the exertion of the exertion, &c. If this depend upon man, God's power will be limited by man's; if upon God, we return to the hypothesis of necessity, and of God's being the author of all things. However, the simplest and clearest way is to suppose, that power, and the exertion of power, are one and the same thing; for power is never known but by its actual exertion, *i. e.* is no power till it be exerted. If, indeed, we say that man's actions depend both upon God and himself, this seems at first sight to solve the difficulty. Since they depend upon God, his power may be infinite; since they depend on man, they may be ascribed to *him*. But then the thing in man on which they depend, call it what you please, must either depend upon God or not; if it does, necessity returns; if not, God's infinite power is infringed. And the same thing will hold, as it appears to me, in any other way of stating this matter.

Again,

Again, to suppose that a man may do either the action *A*, or its opposite *a*, the previous circumstances remaining the same, is to suppose that one of them may arise without a cause; for the same previous circumstances cannot be the cause of the two opposite effects. Now, if any thing can arise without a cause, all things may, by parity of reason; which is contrary to the common foundation upon which writers have erected their arguments for the being and attributes of God. To say that free-will is the cause, is an identical proposition; since it is saying, that the power of doing different things, the previous circumstances remaining the same, is the cause that this may be done, *viz.* that either *A* or *a* may follow the same previous circumstances. Or, if we put for philosophical free-will the power of doing things without a cause, it will be a word of nearly the same import as chance. For chance is the ignorance or denial of a cause. It will therefore be as unfit to ascribe a real causality to free-will as to chance.

And as free-will is inconsistent with the infinite power of God, so it is with his infinite knowledge also. For infinite knowledge must include the knowledge of all future things, as well as of all past and present ones. Besides, past, present and future, are all present with respect to God, as has been observed before. Infinite knowledge must therefore include prescience. But free-will does not allow of prescience. Knowledge of all kinds presupposes the certainty of the thing known; *i. e.* presupposes that it is determined in respect of time, place, manner, *&c. i. e.* presupposes it to be necessary. Thus, if we consider any thing as known certainly, or certain simply, such as a mathematical truth, a past fact, *&c.* we shall find it to be necessary, and that it cannot be otherwise than it now is, or was formerly; which is the contrary to what is supposed of the actions of creatures

tures endued with free-will. Thefe actions, therefore, cannot be known, or foreknown, not being the objects of knowledge.

The maintainers of neceffity do indeed deny, that there is any fuch thing as uncertainty at all; unlefs as far as this is put relatively for the limitation of knowledge in any being, fo that the thing called uncertain may or may not be, for any thing that this being knows to the contrary. But if they do, for argument's fake, allow fuch a thing as abfolute uncertainty, *i. e.* that a thing either may or may not be, it is plain, that this abfolute uncertainty mult include the relative, *i. e.* exclude knowledge and foreknowledge. That action of *B* which either may or may not be, cannot be known certainly to be by *A*, becaufe it may not be; it cannot be known not to be, becaufe it may be. Suppofe *A* to make conjectures concerning any future action of *B*. Then this action may or may not be, for any thing *A* knows to the contrary; it alfo may or may not be in itfelf, provided there be any fuch thing as abfolute uncertainty. Suppofe *A*'s conjectures to pafs into a well-grounded probability of a high degree, that the action will happen, then both the relative and abfolute *may not*, are reduced to narrow limits. Suppofe *A*'s conjectures to arife to knowledge, or certainty, then both the relative and abfolute *may not*, vanifh. *A* cannot know, or be certain, that a thing will happen, at the fame time that it may or may not happen, for any thing that he knows to the contrary; nor can a thing be relatively certain, and abfolutely uncertain. *A*'s foreknowledge does therefore imply relative certainty; this requires abfolute certainty; and abfolute certainty is in exprefs terms oppofite to philofophical free-will. Foreknowledge is therefore inconfiftent with free-will; or rather free-will, if it were poffible, would exclude foreknowledge. It is not therefore poffible.

Nor

Nor does it alter the cafe here to alledge, that God's infinite knowledge muſt extend infinitely farther than man's, and, confequently, may extend to things uncertain in themfelves, fince the very terms *knowledge* and *uncertain* are inconfiſtent. To make them confiſtent, we muſt affix fome new and different fenfe to one of them, which would be to give up either the divine foreknowledge or free-will in reality, while we pretend in words to maintain them. If God's knowledge be fuppofed to differ fo much from man's in this fimple effential circumſtance, that the certainty of it does not imply the certainty of the thing known, we lofe all conception of it. And if the fame liberties were ufed with the divine power and benevolence, we fhould lofe all conception of the divine nature.

To which it may be added, that the reafoning in the laſt paragraph but one, concerning the knowledge of the being *A*, is not at all affeated or altered, by his rank, as to intelligence. Suppofe his intelleftual capacities to be greater and greater perpetually, ſtill all things remain precifely the fame without the leaſt variation. They will therefore, according to the analogy of ultimate ratio's, remain precifely the fame, though his knowledge be fuppofed infinite. It follows, therefore, that God's infinite and certain knowledge, or his fore-knowledge, is as inconfiſtent with philofophical free-will, as man's finite, but certain, knowledge or foreknowledge.

SECT. V.

On the practical Application of the Doctrine of Necessity.

THE doctrine of philosophical free-will is the cause and support of much pride and self-conceit; and this so much the more, as it is a doctrine not only allowed, but even insisted upon and required, and made essential to the distinction between virtue and vice. Hence men are commanded, as it were, to set a value upon their own actions, by esteeming them their own in the highest sense of the words, and taking the merit of them to themselves. For philosophical free-will supposes, that God has given to each man a sphere of action, in which he does not interpose; but leaves man to act intirely from himself, independently of his creator; and as, upon this foundation, the assertors of philosophical free-will ascribe all the demerit of actions to men, so they are obliged to allow men to take the merit of good actions to themselves, *i. e.* to be proud and self-conceited. This is the plain consequence of the doctrine of philosophical free-will. How far this objection against it overbalances the objections brought against the opposite doctrine of mechanism, I do not here consider. But it was necessary, in treating of the methods of attaining true humility, to shew in what relation the doctrine of free-will stood to this subject.

But we are not to suppose, that every Man, who maintains philosophical free-will, does also claim the merit of his good actions to himself. The scriptures are so full and explicit in ascribing all that is good to God, and the heart of a good man concurs so readily with them, that he will rather expofe himfelf to any perplexity of underftanding, than to the charge of fo great an impiety. Hence it is, that we fee, in the writings of many good men, philofophical free-will afferted, on one hand; and merit difclaimed, on the other; in both cafes, with a view to avoid confequences apparently impious; though it be impoffible to reconcile thefe doctrines to each other. However, this fubjection of the underftanding to the moral principle is a noble inftance of humility, and rectitude of heart.

As the affertors of philofophical free-will are not neceffarily proud, fo the affertors of the doctrine of mechanifm are much lefs neceffarily humble. For, however they may, in theory, afcribe all to God; yet the affociations of life beget the idea and opinion of *felf* again and again, refer actions to this felf, and connect a variety of applaufes and complacencies with thefe actions. Nay, men may be proud of thofe actions, which they directly and explicitly afcribe to God, *i. e.* proud, that they are inftruments in the hand of God for the performing fuch actions. Thus the pharifee, in our Saviour's parable, though he thanked God that he was no extortioner, &c. yet boafted of this, and made it a foundation for defpifing the publican. However, the frequent recollection, that all our actions proceed from God; that we have nothing which we did not receive from him; that there can be no reafon in ourfelves, why he fhould felect one, rather than another, for an inftrument of his glory in this world, &c. and the application of thefe important truths to the various real circumftances of our lives; muft greatly accelerate our progrefs to humility and felf-annihilation. And, when men are far advanced in this ftate, they may enjoy quiet and comfort, notwithftanding their paft fins and frailties; for they approach to the paradifiacal

radifiacal ſtate, in which our firſt parents, though naked, were not aſhamed. But the greateſt caution is requiſite here, leſt by a freſh diſobedience we come to know evil as well as good again, and, by deſiring to be God's, to be independent, make the return of ſhame, puniſhment, and myſtical death, neceſſary for our readmiſſion to the tree of life.

THE
CONCLUSION.

A Great part of this book having been printed while I was abroad, it unfortunately happened that my directions with respect to the *references* from one proposition to another were not observed; so that they are always to the numbers of the original, and not to those in this publication. However, to remedy this, I shall here insert a table of the corresponding numbers in both, that the reader may see, at one view, what they ought to have been.

In this Work.	In the Original.	In this Work.	In the Original.
1	1	20	58
2	2	21	59
3	3	22	60
4	8	23	61
5	10	24	66
6	12	25	67
7	14	26	69
8	15	27	70
9	21	28	73
10	22	29	77
11	31	30	78
12	32	31	79
13	33	32	80
14	34	33	81
15	42	34	82
16	44	35	83
17	45	36	84
18	51	37	85
19	52	38	86

The CONCLUSION.

In this Work.	In the Original.	In this Work.	In the Original.
39	87	46	94
40	88	47	95
41	89	48	96
42	90	49	97
43	91	50	98
44	92	51	99
45	93		

I would take this opportunity of obferving that by this attempt to make *Hartley's theory of the mind* more intelligible, and the ftudy of it more inviting, I did not expect to make this treatife fo very plain, as that any perfon altogether unacquainted with this kind of knowledge, fhould be able to read it with underftanding, and without difficulty. For this is abfolutely impoffible. I fuppofe my reader to be well acquainted with *Lock's Effay on the human underftanding*, and with the rudiments of logic and metaphyficks, as delivered in elementary treatifes. I muft alfo fuppofe him to know fo much of *anatomy* as not to be at a lofs for the meaning of the terms *brain, nerves, mufcles,* &c. and alfo that he is not deftitute of the rudiments of *mathematical knowledge*. But I have done all that the generality of perfons who have had a tolerably liberal education will want to facilitate the reading of my author. I have left out all thofe very difficult fpeculations, difperfed through the firft volume, which had not much connection with what is effential to the fyftem; fo that all that is moft valuable in the work may be read without interruption from unneceffary difficulties. If any trace of a reference to what is omitted

The CONCLUSION.

be ſtill retained, it is however ſo very immaterial, that the reader may very well neglect it, as not being neceſſary to the underſtanding of what is here ſelected.

After all that I have done, it muſt be ſuppoſed that the ſtudy of a work of this kind will require a conſiderable degree of attention, in ſome proportion to the great addition to the ſtock of valuable knowledge which it contains.

Treatiſes on ſubjects ſo novel and ſo important as theſe, cannot be expected to be made ſo eaſy, that the mind ſhall be entirely paſſive in the peruſal of them, as in the ordinary reading of hiſtory and romances. A vigorous exertion of the mental powers is neceſſary to make a man maſter of ſo capital a work as this; but then he will be amply rewarded for that exertion. Knowledge of this kind tends, in a very eminent degree, to enlarge the comprehenſion of the mind, to give a man a kind of ſuperiority to the world and to himſelf, ſo as to advance him in the ſcale of being, and conſequently to lay a foundation for equable and permanent happineſs.

Speculations of this kind have a more direct tendency to this great end of all ſcience, than thoſe branches of knowledge, for the advancement of which we are ſo much indebted to Bacon, to Newton, and to Boyle; and are inferior in their operation to nothing but the ſtudy of morals and theology. It is impoſſible to avoid reflecting here, how

abject

abject their minds must be, who are destitute of all these kinds of knowledge; who are wholly addicted to sensual enjoyments, or are lost in the tumult of a vain or bustling world. Even *philology*, or the *belles Lettres* rank far below any of the studies above mentioned, and are comparatively no more than the amusements of childhood.

I shall also take this opportunity of acquainting the reader that a *dissertation on the nature of judgement and reasoning*, &c. which was originally intended for this work, will be found prefixed to my *Examination of the doctrine of instinctive principles*, maintained by Dr. Reid, Dr. Beattie, and Dr. Oswald, with some additions to adapt it to the purpose for which it was there introduced.

I wish I could inform the reader of my having any certain intelligence that the subjects of this controversy were in the way of a free discussion by any of the writers on whom I have animadverted. I had indeed heard that Dr. Beattie (whose letter induced me to think that he would not decline this discussion) had written something with that view; but other reports say that his intentions have been overruled by the persuasion of some of his friends, of whom better things might have been expected. But all who are enemies of *free inquiry* are enemies of *truth*; and I hope that when Dr. Beattie shall have considered the nature and tendency of the advice that has been given him, his ingenuous temper will not suffer him to listen to it; but that he will

372 *The* CONCLUSION.

either frankly acknowledge the overfights with which I have charged him, or with the fame fpirit with which he wrote his book, ftand forth in its defence.

I will alfo frankly own, that I wifh to have an opportunity of explaining the origin of the metaphyfical fyftem which I have oppofed more fully than my acquaintance with the hiftory of it, at the time of my former publication, could admit; and particularly to explain the doctrine of *inftincts*, as it was firft propofed by Father Buffier the Jefuit, who wrote fo early as the year 1724; in whofe treatife *Des premieres Verités* the whole fyftem of *common fenfe*, as this writer himfelf terms it, is as fully, and as fpacioufly difplayed, as by any of the three Scotch writers.

A

BOOKS written by Dr. PRIESTLEY.

26. Letters to the Author of *Remarks on several late Publications relative to the Dissenters, in a Letter to Dr. Priestley*, 1s.

27. An APPEAL to the serious and candid Professors of Christianity, on the following Subjects, viz. 1. The Use of Reason in Matters of Religion. 2. The Power of Man to do the Will of God. 3. Original Sin. 4. Election and Reprobation. 5. The Divinity of Christ. And, 6. Atonement for Sin by the Death of Christ, the fifth Edition, 1d.

28. A FAMILIAR ILLUSTRATION of certain Passages of Scripture relating to the same Subject, 4d. or 3s. 6d. per Dozen.

29. The TRIUMPH of TRUTH; being an account of the Trial of Mr. Elwall, for Heresy and Blasphemy, at Stafford Assizes, before Judge Denton, &c. the second Edition, 1d.

30. CONSIDERATIONS for the Use of YOUNG MEN, and the Parents of YOUNG MEN, 2d.

Also published under the Direction of Dr. PRIESTLEY,
THE THEOLOGICAL REPOSITORY;
Consisting of original Essays, Hints, Queries, &c. calculated to promote religious Knowledge, in 3 Volumes, 8vo, Price 18s. in Boards.

Among other Articles, too many to be enumerated in an Advertisement, these three Volumes will be found to contain such original and truly valuable Observations on the Doctrine of the *Atonement*, the *Pre-existence of Christ*, and the *Inspiration of the Scriptures*, more especially respecting the *Harmony of the Evangelists*, and the Reasoning of the Apostle Paul, as cannot fail to recommend them to those Persons, who wish to make a truly free Enquiry into these important Subjects.

In the First Volume, which is now reprinted, several Articles are added, particularly Two Letters from Dr. THOMAS SHAW to Dr. BENSON, relating to the Passage of the Israelites through the Red Sea.

ERRATA.

In the Introductory Essays.

P. 22, l. 12, for *has*, read *have*.
— l. 21, for *after*, read *often*.
   30, l. 24, for *a*, read *the*.
— l. 25, for *action*, read *actions*.
   39, l. 19. for *where*, read *were*.

In the Work.

P. 35, l. 9, for *its*, read *it*.
   37, l. 2, for *dire* read *direct*.
   74, l. 7, for *altogether* read *all together*.
   107, l. 7, for *or*, read *are*.
   113, l. 19, for *painting*, read *pointing*.
— l. 32, for *cures*, read *curves*.
   134, l. 25, for *their*, read *the*.
   155, l. 4, for *affecting*, read *effecting*.
   174, l. 18, for *f*, read *if*.
   259, l. 1, for *vein*, read *vain*.
   266, l. 15, *light, poetry*, read *light. Poetry*.
   273, l. 28, for *waken*, read *weaken*.
   289, l. 20, for *and*, read *of*.
   325, l. 11, for *as*, read *as to*.
   338, l. 31. for *his*, read *is*.